Data Structures
Through C

Yashavant P. Kanetkar

WITHDRAWN

BPB PUBLICATIONS
B-14, CONNAUGHT PLACE, NEW DELHI-110001

FIRST EDITION 1999; Reprinted 2009

Distributors:

MICRO BOOK CENTRE
2, City Centre, CG Road,
Near Swastic Char Rasta,
AHMEDABAD-380009 Phone: 26421611

COMPUTER BOOK CENTRE
12, Shrungar Shopping Centre, M.G. Road,
BANGALORE-560001 Phone: 5587923, 5584641

MICRO BOOKS
Shanti Niketan Building, 8, Camac Street,
KOLKATTA-700017 Phone: 22826518, 22826519

BUSINESS PROMOTION BUREAU
8/1, Ritchie Street, Mount Road,
CHENNAI-600002 Phone: 28410796, 28550491

DECCAN AGENCIES
4-3-329, Bank Street,
HYDERABAD-500195
Phone: 24756400, 24756967

MICRO MEDIA
Shop No. 5, Mahendra Chambers,
150 D.N. Road, Next to Capital Cinema
V.T. (C.S.T.) Station,
MUMBAI-400001 Ph.: 22078296, 22078297

BPB PUBLICATIONS
B-14, Connaught Place, **NEW DELHI-110001**
Phone: 23325760, 23723393, 23737742

INFO TECH
G-2, Sidhartha Building, 96 Nehru Place,
NEW DELHI-110019
Phone: 26438245, 26415092, 26234208

INFO TECH
Shop No. 2, F-38, South Extension Part-1
NEW DELHI-110049
Phone: 24691288, 24641941

BPB BOOK CENTRE
376, Old Lajpat Rai Market,
DELHI-110006 PHONE: 23861747

NOTE: THE CD-ROM INCLUDED WITH THE BOOK HAS NO COMMERCIAL VALUE AND CANNOT BE SOLD SEPARATELY.

ISBN 81-7656-706-X

Published by Manish Jain for BPB Publications, B-14, Connaught Place, New Delhi-110 001 and Printed by Nikunj Print Process, Delhi,

Dedicated to

Prabhakar Kanetkar

About the Author

Yashavant Prabhakar Kanetkar obtained his B.E. from VJTI, Mumbai and his M. Tech. from IIT, Kanpur. He has programmed the PC since the days of a single floppy drive, 4.77 MHz microprocessor and 256 KB memory. Yashavant has a passion for writing and is an author of several books in C, C++, VC++, C#, DirectX and COM programming. He is a much sought after speaker on various technology subjects and is a regular columnist for Developer 2.0. His current affiliations include being a Director of KICIT, a training company and Lambent Technologies, a software development company.

Acknowledgments

Though what matters most in a book are its contents, it is the parts of the whole like cover, CD, layout, price etc. that make it an attractive proposition. I have been fortunate to get help and cooperation from many agencies involved in this book project.

Though the book cover bears only my name, it truly reflects the collective wisdom of numerous students to whom I taught "Data Structures" for several years. I have learnt a lot from them. Many thanks, wherever you are.

Writing and testing programs in a book is a monumental task calling for incredible patience. That Vineeta Prasad and Anil Gakhare had loads of it is chiefly responsible for getting the book in its current form. They also ensured that we chose the right algorithms while implementing the additional programs present in the CD.

"Experience data structures through animations"—that is the main theme of this book. Neeraj Srivastav took the responsibility of creating excellent animations while following stringent timelines. M.S. Prakash wrote instructions for installing and using the programs on the companion disk. Many thanks to both of you.

An author needs a lot of *instant* support from his publisher. Instant messaging is not for Manish Jain of BPB, because his emails itself are instantaneous. Bureaucracy and indifference are the words which do not figure in his dictionary.

And lastly many thanks to my wife Seema who cheered me in good times, encouraged me in bad times and understood me at all times. If I ever wear a hat, it would be off to her!!

Yashavant Kanetkar

Contents

Introduction

Technical book writing is a simple job. Pick up a technology that appeals you, spend some time understanding it, browse the net for some additional information and then keep writing till the time you do not reach the end. Easier said than done! In fact nothing can be farther from the truth. For one, choosing the technology is pretty confusing with so many computing technologies taking so big strides in the recent years. Secondly, none of them is so easy to master in a few months and thirdly presenting what you have understood in a simple manner is not everybody's cup of tea.

I have realized all these facts more emphatically while writing this book, because I have been writing this book for last 10 years!! It all began with attempting to write articles that would explain quick sort algorithm and threaded binary trees. Once I had a critical mass of written material I thought of compiling it in the form of a book. I however wanted the book to be a *different* data structures book. Different in the sense that it should go beyond merely explaining how stacks, queues and linked lists work. I wanted the readers to *experience* sorting of an array, traversing of a doubly linked list, construction of a binary tree, etc. I had a hell of a time imagining, understanding and programming these complicated data structures. I wanted that the readers of this book should not be required to undergo that agony. And today I am satisfied that I have been able to achieve this through the CD that comes with this book. It lets the reader experience the working of different data structures through carefully prepared animations. I have pinned my hopes that the readers would appreciate this approach.

I have tried to make this book different in one more way. Instead of merely learning how to perform different operations on a linked list, I think one can appreciate it better if one comes to know that all floppies and hard disks make use of File Allocation Table (FAT) which is nothing but a linked list. There are numerous such examples and I have also tried to provide animations for most of them on the accompanying CD.

Apart from this I have tried to explain all data structures with examples and figures. I have also provided exercises at the end of each chapter to hone your skills. If you need some more, keep looking at www.funducode.com, or better still, add it to your *favourites* folder.

I don't know when I would sit down to write the next edition of this book. If I do, I would try to realize one of my dreams—create an animated cover for it. After all, isn't dreaming man's biggest ability? Ask Harry Potter!!

CHAPTER
ONE

Analysis Of Algorithms
Justifying The Means

ot every time is the dictum "ends justify the means" correct, more so in Computer Science. Just because we got the right answer (end) does not mean that the method (means) that we employed to obtain it is correct. In fact the efficiency of obtaining the correct answer is largely dependent on the method employed to obtain it. And at times getting a correct solution late is as bad as getting a wrong solution.

The method of solving a problem is known as an algorithm. More precisely, an algorithm is a sequence of instructions that act on some input data to produce some output in a finite number of steps. An algorithm must have the following properties:

(a) Input – An algorithm must receive some input data supplied externally.

(b) Output – An algorithm must produce at least one output as the result.

(c) Finiteness – No matter what is the input, the algorithm must terminate after a finite number of steps. For example, a procedure which goes on performing a series of steps infinitely is not an algorithm.

(d) Definiteness – The steps to be performed in the algorithm must be clear and unambiguous.

(e) Effectiveness – One must be able to perform the steps in the algorithm without applying any intelligence. For example, the step—Select three numbers which form a Pythogorian triplet—is not effective.

All algorithms basically fall under two broad categories—Iterative (repetitive) algorithms and Recursive algorithms. Iterative algorithms typically use loops and conditional statements. As against this, the Recursive algorithms use a 'divide and conquer' strategy. As per this strategy the Recursive algorithm breaks down a large problem into small pieces and then applies the algorithm to each of these small pieces. This often makes the recursive algorithm small, straightforward, and simple to understand.

Why Analyze Algorithms

An algorithm must not only be able to solve the problem at hand, it must be able to do so in as efficient a manner as possible. There might be different ways (algorithms) in which we can solve a given problem. The characteristics of each algorithm will determine how efficiently each will operate. Determining which algorithm is efficient than the other involves analysis of algorithms.

While analyzing an algorithm *time* required to execute it is determined. This time is not in terms of number of seconds or any such time unit. Instead it represents the number of operations that are carried out while executing the algorithm. Time units are not useful since while analyzing algorithms our main concern is the relative efficiency of the different algorithms. Do also note that an algorithm cannot be termed as better because it takes less time units or worse because it takes more time units to execute. A worse algorithm may take less time units to execute if we move it to a faster computer, or use a more efficient language. Hence while comparing two algorithms it is assumed that all other things like speed of the computer and the language used are same for both the algorithms.

Note that while analyzing the algorithm we would not be interested in the actual number of operations done for some specific size of input data. Instead, we would try to build an equation that relates the number of operations that a particular algorithm does to the size of the input. Once the equations for two algorithms are formed we can then compare the two algorithms by comparing that rate at which their equations grow. This growth rate is critical since there are situations where one algorithm needs fewer operations than the other when the input size is small, but many more when the input size gets large.

While analyzing iterative algorithms we need to determine how many times the loop is executed. To analyze a recursive algorithm one needs to determine amount of work done for three things— breaking down the large problem to smaller pieces, getting solution for each piece and combining the individual solutions to get the solution to the whole problem. Combining this information and the number of the smaller pieces and their sizes we then need to create a recurrence relation for the algorithm. This recurrence relation can then be converted into a closed form that can be compared with other equations.

What Is Analysis

The analysis of an algorithm provides information that gives us a general idea of how long an algorithm will take for solving a problem. For comparing the performance of two algorithms we have to estimate the time taken to solve a problem using each algorithm for a set of N input values. For example, we might determine the number of comparisons a searching algorithm does to search a value in a list of N values, or we might determine the number of arithmetic operations it performs to add two matrices of size N*N.

As said earlier, a number of algorithms might be able to solve a problem successfully. Analysis of algorithms gives us the scientific reason to determine which algorithm should be chosen to solve the problem. For example, consider the following two algorithms to find the biggest of four values:

Algorithm One:

```
big = a
if ( b > big )
     big = b
endif
if ( c > big )
     big = c
endif
if ( d > big )
     big = d
endif
return big
```

Algorithm Two:

```
if ( a > b )
    if ( a > c )
        if ( a > d )
            return a
        else
            return d
        endif
    else
        if ( c > d )
            return c
        else
            return d
        endif
    endif
else
    if ( b > c )
        if ( b > d )
            return b
        else
            return d
        endif
    else
        if ( c > d )
            return c
        else
            return d
        endif
    endif
endif
```

On careful examination of the two algorithms, you can observe that each does exactly three comparisons to find the biggest number. Even though the first is easier for us to read and understand, they are both of the same level of complexity for a computer to execute. In terms of time, these two algorithms are the same, but in terms of space, the first needs more because of the temporary variable called **big**. This extra space is not significant if we are comparing numbers or characters, but it may be with other types of data, like say record of an employee. A record may typically contain 15-20 fields and the criterion for determining the larger of the two records might be complex, like say, assigning weights to values in different fields. The purpose of determining the number of comparisons is to then use them to figure out which of the algorithms under consideration can solve the problem more efficiently.

What Analysis Doesn't Do

The analysis of algorithms does not give a formula that helps us determine how many seconds or computer cycles a particular algorithm will take to solve a problem. This is not useful information to choose the right algorithm because it involves lots of variables like:

– Type of computer
– Instruction set used by the Microprocessor
– What optimization compiler performs on the executable code, etc.

No doubt that all these factors have a direct bearing on how fast a program for an algorithm will run. However, if decide to take them into consideration we might end up with a situation where by moving a program to a faster computer, the algorithm would become better because it now completes its job faster. That paints a wrong picture. Hence the analysis of algorithms should be done regardless of the computer on which the program that implements the algorithm is going to get executed.

What To Count And Consider

An algorithm may consist of several operations and it may not be possible to count every one of them as a function of N, the number of inputs. The difference between an algorithm that does N+5 operations and one that does N+250 operations becomes meaningless as N gets very large.

For example, suppose we have an algorithm that counts the number of characters in a file. An algorithm for that might look like the following:

```
Count = 0
While there are more characters in the file do
     Increment Count by 1
     Get the next character
End while
Print Count
```

If there are 500 characters present in the file we need to initialize Count once, check the condition 500 + 1 times (the +1 is for the last check when the file is empty), and increment the counter 500 times. The total number of operations is:

Initializations – 1
Increments – 500
Conditional checks – 500 + 1
Printing – 1

As can be seen from the above numbers the number of increments and conditional checks are far too many as compared to number of initialization and printing operations. The number of initialization and printing operations would remain same for a file of any size and they become a much smaller percentage of the total as the file size increases. For a large file the number of initialization and printing operations would be insignificant as compared to the number of increments and conditional checks. Thus, while doing analysis of this algorithm the cost of the initialization becomes meaningless as the number of input values increases.

It is very important to decide what to count while analyzing an algorithm. We must first identify which is the significant operation or operations in the algorithm. Once that is decided, we should determine which of these operations are integral to the algorithm and which merely contribute to the overheads. There are two classes of operations that are typically chosen for the significant operation—comparison or arithmetic.

For example, in Searching and Sorting algorithms the important task being done is the comparison of two values. While searching the comparison is done to check if the value is the one we are looking for, whereas in sorting the comparison is done to see whether values being compared are out of order. Comparison operations include equal, not equal, less than, greater than, less than or equal and greater than or equal.

The arithmetic operations fall under two groups—additive and multiplicative. Additive operators include addition, subtraction, increment, and decrement. Multiplicative operators include multiplication, division, and modulus. These two groups are counted separately because multiplication operations take longer time to execute than additions.

Cases To Consider During Analysis

Choosing the input to consider when analyzing an algorithm can have a significant impact on how an algorithm will perform. For example, if the input list is already sorted, some sorting algorithms will perform very well, but other sorting algorithms may perform very poorly. The opposite may be true if the list is randomly arranged instead of sorted. Hence multiple input sets must be considered while analyzing an algorithm. These include the following:

(a) Best Case Input – This represents the input set that allows an algorithm to perform most quickly. With this input the algorithm takes shortest time to execute, as it causes the algorithms to do the least amount of work. For example, for a searching algorithm the best case would be if the value we are searching for is found in the first location that the search algorithm checks. As a result, this algorithm would need only one comparison irrespective of the complexity of the algorithm. No matter how large is the input, searching in a best case will result in a constant time of 1. Since the best case for an algorithm would usually be very small and frequently constant value, a best case analysis is often not done.

(b) Worst Case Input – This represents the input set that allows an algorithm to perform most slowly. Worst case is an important analysis because it gives us an idea of the most time an algorithm will ever take. Worst case analysis requires that we identify the input values that cause an algorithm to do the most work. For example, for a searching algorithm, the worst case is one where the value is in the last place we check or is not in the list. This could involve comparing the key to each list value for a total of N comparisons.

(c) Average Case Input – This represents the input set that allows an algorithm to deliver an average performance. Doing Average-case analysis is a four-step process. These steps are as under:

   (i) Determine the number of different groups into which all possible input sets can be divided.

   (ii) Determine the probability that the input will come from each of these groups.

(iii) Determine how long the algorithm will run for each of these groups. All of the input in each group should take the same amount of time, and if they do not, the group must be split into two separate groups.

Calculate average case time using the formula:

$$A(n) = \sum_{i=1}^{m} p_i * t_i$$

where,

n = Size of input
m = Number of groups
p_i = Probability that the input will be from group i
t_i = Time that the algorithm takes for input from group i.

Rates Of Growth

While doing analysis of algorithms more than the exact number of operations performed by the algorithm, it is the rate of increase in operations as the size of the problem increases that is of more importance. This is often called the rate of growth of the algorithm.--What happens with small sets of input data is not as interesting as what happens when the data set gets large.

Table 1-1 shows rate of growth for some of the common classes of algorithms for a wide range of input sizes. You can observe that there isn't a significant difference in values when the input is small, but once the input value gets large, there are big differences. Hence while doing analysis of algorithm we must consider what happens when the size of the input is large, because small input sets can hide rather dramatic differences.

n	log n	n log n	n^2	n^3	2^n
1	0.0	0.0	1.0	1.0	2.0
2	1.0	2.0	4.0	8.0	4.0
5	2.3	11.6	25.0	125.0	32.0
10	3.3	33.2	100.0	1000.0	1024.0
15	3.9	58.6	225.0	3375.0	32768.0
20	4.3	86.4	400.0	8000.0	1048576.0
30	4.9	147.2	900.0	27000.0	1073741824.0
40	5.3	212.9	1600.0	64000.0	1099511627776.0
50	5.6	282.2	2500.0	125000.0	1125899906842620.0

Table 1-1. *Rate of increase in common algorithm classes.*

The data in Table 1-1 also illustrate that the faster growing functions increase at such a rate that they quickly dominate the slower-growing functions. Thus, if the algorithm's complexity is a combination of a two of these classes, we can safely ignore the slower growing terms. On discarding these terms we are left with what we call the order of the function or related algorithm. Based on their order algorithms can be grouped into three categories:

(a)   Algorithms that grow at least as fast as some function

(b)   Algorithms that grow at the same rate

(c)   Algorithms that grow no faster

The categories (a), (b), (c) mentioned above are commonly known as Big Omega $\Omega(f)$, Big Oh $O (f)$ and Big Theta $\theta (f)$, respectively.

Of these, the Big Omega category of functions is not of much interest to us since for all values of **n** greater than some threshold value n_0 all the functions in $\Omega(f)$ have values that are at least as large as **f**. That is, all functions in this category grow as fast as **f** or even faster.

While analyzing algorithms we are on the lookout for an algorithm that does better than the one that we are considering. Since big theta category represents a class of functions that grow at the same rate as the function **f** this category too is not of interest to us.

Big Oh **O(f)** category represents the class of functions that grow no faster than **f**. This means that for all values of **n** greater than some threshold n_0, all the functions in $O(f)$ have values that are no greater than **f**. Thus the class $O(f)$ has **f** as an upper bound, so none of the functions in this class grow faster than **f**. This means that if **g(x) ε O(f)**, **g(n) < cf(n)** for all **n** > n_0 (where **c** is a positive constant).

The Big Oh class of functions would be of interest to us. While considering two algorithms, we will want to know if the function categorizing the behavior of the first is in big oh of the second. If so, we know that the second algorithm does no better than the first in solving the problem.

Analysis of Sequential Search Algorithm

The Sequential Search Algorithm is the simplest searching algorithm. We will see that this algorithm is not very efficient but will successfully search in any list.

In any searching algorithm the aim is to look through a list to find a particular element. Although not required, while doing a sequential search the list is considered to be unsorted.

Sequential search looks at elements, one at a time, from the first in the list until a match is found. It returns the index of where the value being searched is found. If the value is not found the algorithm returns an index value that is outside the range of the list of elements. Assuming that the elements of the list are located in positions 0 to N-1 in the list, we can return a value -1 if the element being searched is not in the list. The complete algorithm for sequential search in pseudo code form is given below. For the sake of simplicity, we have assumed that there is no repetition of values in the list.

Sequentialsearch (list, value, N)
List   the elements to be searched
value   the value being searched for
N   the number of elements in the list

For i = 1 to N do
    If (value = list[i])
        Return i
    End if
End for
Return 0

Let us now analyze this algorithm.

Worst Case Analysis

There are two worst cases for the sequential search algorithm:

- The value being searched matches the last element in the list
- The value being searched is not present in the list.

For both these cases we need to find out how many comparisons are done. Since we have assumed all the elements in the list are unique in both the cases N comparisons would be made.

Average Case Analysis

There are two average-case analyses that can be done for a search algorithm. The first assumes that the search is always successful and the other assumes that the value being searched will sometimes not be found.

If the value begin searched is present in the list, it can be present at any one of the N places. Since all these possibilities are equally likely, there is a probability of 1/N for each potential location.

The number of comparisons made if the value being searched is found at first, second, third location, etc. would be 1, 2, 3 and so on. This means that the number of comparisons made is the same as the location where the match occurs. This gives the following equation for this average case:

$$A(N) = \frac{1}{N} \sum_{i=1}^{N} i$$

$$A(N) = \frac{1}{N} * \frac{N(N+1)}{2}$$

$$A(N) = \frac{N+1}{2}$$

Let us now consider the possibility that the value being searched is not present in the list. Now there are N+1 possibilities. For the case where the value being searched is not in the list there will be N comparisons. If we assume that all N+1 possibilities are equally likely, we get the following equation for this average case:

$$A(N) = \left(\frac{1}{N+1}\right) * \left[\left(\sum_{i=1}^{N} i\right) + N\right]$$

$$A(N) = \left(\frac{1}{N+1}\sum_{i=1}^{N} i\right) + \left(\frac{1}{N+1} * N\right)$$

$$A(N) = \left(\frac{1}{N+1} * \frac{N(N+1)}{2}\right) + \frac{N}{N+1}$$

$$A(N) = \frac{N}{2} + \frac{N}{N+1} = \frac{N}{2} + 1 - \frac{1}{N+1}$$

$$A(N) \approx \frac{N+2}{2} \quad \text{(As N gets very large, } \frac{1}{N+1} \text{ becomes almost 0)}$$

We can observe that by including the possibility of the target not being in the list only increases the average case by ½. When we consider this amount relative to the size of the list, which could be very large, this ½ is not significant.

Exercise

[1]   Two different procedures are written for a given problem. One has a computing time given by 2^n and that for the other is n^3. Specify the range of n for which each would be suitable.

[2]   Determine the time complexity of the following algorithm.

```
old = 1
```

```
new = 1
print old, new
n = 20
for i = 1 to n
  a = old + new
  print a
  old = new
  new = a
end for
```

[3] Determine the frequency counts for all statements in the following two program segments:

```
1  for i := 1 to n do        1  i := 1
2    for j := 1 to i do      2  while i <= n do
3      for k := 1 to j do    3  begin
4        x := x + 1 ;         4    x := x + 1 ;
                              5    i := i + 1 ;
                              6  end
```

[4] Compare the two functions n^2 and $2^n / 4$ for various values for **n**. Determine when the second becomes larger than the first.

[5] Which function grows faster?

i. $\sqrt{n}$ or $\log n$?
ii. $n^{\log n}$ or $\log n^n$?

Prove your claim.

[6] List the following functions from highest to lowest order. If any are of the same order, circle them on your list

2^n $\log \log n$ $n^3 + \log n$

$\log n$	$n - n^2 + 5n^3$	2^{n-1}
n^2	n^3	$n \log n$
$(\log n)^2$	$\sqrt{n}$	6
$n!$	n	$(3/2)^n$

[7] For each of the following pairs of functions $f(n)$ and $g(n)$, either $f(n) = O[g(n)]$ or $g(n) = O[f(n)]$, but not both. Determine which is the case.

(a) $f(n) = (n^2 - n)/2$, $g(n) = 6n$

(b) $f(n) = n + 2\sqrt{n}$, $g(n) = n^2$

(c) $f(n) = n + n \log n$, $g(n) = n\sqrt{n}$

(d) $f(n) = n^2 + 3n + 4$, $g(n) = n^3$

(e) $f(n) = n \log n$, $g(n) = n\sqrt{n}/2$

(f) $f(n) = n + \log n$, $g(n) = \sqrt{n}$

(g) $f(n) = 2(\log n)^2$, $g(n) = \log n + 1$

(h) $f(n) = 4n \log n + n$, $g(n) = (n^2 - n)/2$

CHAPTER
TWO

Arrays
Friends Are Friends

A rray is one data structure that has been used (as well as abused) more than any other. Arrays are simple yet reliable and are used in more situations than you can count. Yet they have problems that are typical to them, which at times lead to serious performance issues. They are like old friends. You accept and live with their qualities—good as well as bad.

Data structures are classified into two categories—linear and nonlinear. A data structure is said to be linear if its elements form a sequence. Elements in a nonlinear data structure do not form a sequence. There are two ways of representing linear data structures in memory. One way is to have the linear relationship between the elements by means of sequential memory locations. Such linear structures are called **arrays**.

The other way is to have the linear relationship between the elements represented by means of pointers or links. Such linear structures are called **linked lists**. In a linked list each node contains the data and the address of the next node. Figure 2-1(a) and Figure 2-1(b) shows the representation of an array and a linked list.

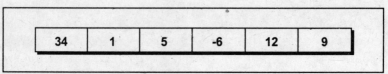

Figure 2-1(a). *An array of 6 integers.*

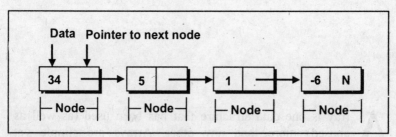

Figure 2-1(b). *A linked list containing 4 integers.*

Arrays are useful when the number of elements to be stored is fixed. They are easy to traverse, search and sort. On the other hand linked lists are useful when the number of data items in the collection are likely to vary. Linked lists are difficult to maintain as compared to an array. We would discuss linked lists in more detail in Chapter 4.

What Are Arrays?

An Array is a finite collection of similar elements stored in adjacent memory locations. By 'finite' we mean that there are specific number of elements in an array and by 'similar' we mean that all the elements in an array are of the same type. For example, an array may contain all integers or all characters but not both. However, there can be array of structures, where each structure may contain an integer and a character.

An array containing **n** number of elements is referenced using an index that varies from **0** to **n - 1**. For example, the elements of an array **arr[n]** containing **n** elements are denoted by **arr[0], arr[1], arr[2], ..., arr[n-1]**, where **0** is the lower bound and **n - 1** is the upper bound of the array. In general, the lowest index of an array is called its **lower bound** and the highest index is called its **upper bound**. The number of elements in the array is called its **range**. No matter how big an array is, its elements are always stored in contiguous memory locations.

Intuitively, an array is a set of pairs of an index and a value. For each index there is a value associated with it. This arrangement of array elements is hown in Figure 2-2.

a[0]	a[1]	a[2]	a[3]	a[4]	a[5]
34	1	5	-6	12	9

Figure 2-2. *Elements in an array with their indices.*

An array is further categorized as a one-dimensional array and a multi-dimensional array. A multi-dimensional array can be a 2-D array, 3-D array, 4-D array, etc. Whether an array is a 1-D array or a 2-D can be judged by the syntax used to declare the array. The following examples show how to declare one-dimensional as well as multi-dimensional arrays.

arr1[5]   A 1-D array holding 5 elements.

arr2[2][5]   A 2-D array with 2 rows and 5 columns holding 10 elements.

arr3[2][5][3] A 3-D array with two 2-D arrays each of which is having 5 rows and 3 columns, thus holding totally 30 elements.

Array Operations

There are several operations that can be performed on an array. These operations are listed in Table 2-1.

Operation	Description
Traversal	Processing each element in the array
Search	Finding the location of an element with a given value
Insertion	Adding a new element to an array
Deletion	Removing an element from an array
Sorting	Organizing the elements in some order
Merging	Combining two arrays into a single array
Reversing	Reversing the elements of an array

Table 2-1. *Operations performed on arrays.*

Let us now see a program that shows how to perform these operations on an array.

```c
#include <stdio.h>
#include <conio.h>

#define MAX 5

void insert ( int *, int pos, int num ) ;
void del ( int *, int pos ) ;
void reverse ( int * ) ;
void display ( int * ) ;
void search ( int *, int num ) ;

void main( )
{
    int arr[5] ;

    clrscr( ) ;

    insert ( arr, 1, 11 ) ;
    insert ( arr, 2, 12 ) ;
    insert ( arr, 3, 13 ) ;
    insert ( arr, 4, 14 ) ;
    insert ( arr, 5, 15 ) ;

    printf ( "\nElements of Array: " ) ;
    display ( arr ) ;

    del ( arr, 5 ) ;
    del ( arr, 2 ) ;
    printf ( "\n\nAfter deletion: " ) ;
    display ( arr ) ;

    insert ( arr, 2, 222 ) ;
    insert ( arr, 5, 555 ) ;
    printf ( "\n\nAfter insertion: " ) ;
```

```
        display ( arr ) ;
        reverse ( arr ) ;
        printf ( "\n\nAfter reversing: " ) ;
        display ( arr ) ;
        search ( arr, 222 ) ;
        search ( arr, 666 ) ;

        getch( ) ;
}

/* inserts an element num at given position pos */
void insert ( int *arr, int pos, int num )
{
        /* shift elements to right */
        int i ;
        for ( i = MAX - 1 ; i >= pos ; i-- )
            arr[i] = arr[i - 1] ;
        arr[i] = num ;
}

/* deletes an element from the given position pos */
void del ( int *arr, int pos )
{
        /* skip to the desired position */
        int i ;
        for ( i = pos ; i < MAX ; i++ )
            arr[i - 1] = arr[i] ;
        arr[i - 1] = 0 ;
}

/* reverses the entire array */
void reverse ( int *arr )
{
        int i ;
        for ( i = 0 ; i < MAX / 2 ; i++ )
        {
            int temp = arr[i] ;
            arr[i] = arr[MAX - 1 - i] ;
```

```
            arr[MAX - 1 - i] = temp ;
    }
}

/* searches array for a given element num */
void search ( int *arr, int num )
{
    /* Traverse the array */
    int i ;
    for ( i = 0 ; i < MAX ; i++ )
    {
        if ( arr[i] == num )
        {
            printf ( "\n\nThe element %d is present at %dth position.", num,
                                i + 1 ) ;
            return ;
        }
    }

    if ( i == MAX )
        printf ( "\n\nThe element %d is not present in the array.", num ) ;
}

/* displays the contents of a array */
void display ( int *arr )
{
    /* traverse the entire array */
    int i ;
    printf ( "\n" ) ;
    for ( i = 0 ; i < MAX ; i++ )
        printf ( "%d\t", arr[i] ) ;
}
```

Output:

Elements of Array:
11   12   13   14   15

After deletion:
11   13   14   0   0

After insertion:
11   222   13   14   555

After reversing:
555   14   13   222   11

The element 222 is present at 4th position.

The element 666 is not present in the array.

In this program we created an array **arr** which contains 5 **int**s. Then the base address of this array is passed to functions like **insert( )**, **del( )**, **display( )**, **reverse( )** and **search( )** to perform different operation on the array.

The **insert( )** function takes two arguments, the position **pos** at which the new number has to be inserted and the number **num** that has to be inserted. In this function, first through a loop, we have shifted the numbers, from the specified position, one place to the right of their existing position. Then we have placed the number **num** at the vacant place. The insertion of an element has been illustrated in Figure 2-3.

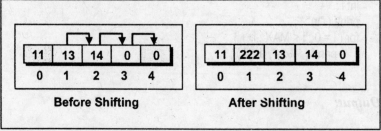

Figure 2-3. *Shifting of elements to the right while inserting an element at 1ˢᵗ position.*

The **del( )** function deletes the element present at the given position **pos**. While doing so, we have shifted the numbers placed after the position from where the number is to be deleted, one place to the left of their existing positions. The place that is vacant after deletion of an element is filled with 0. The deletion of an element has been illustrated in Figure 2-4.

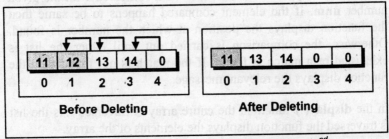

Figure 2-4. *Shifting of elements to the left while deleting 2nd element of an array.*

In **reverse( )** function, we have reversed the entire array by swapping the elements, like **arr[0]** with **arr[4]**, **arr[1]** with **arr[3]** and so on. The process of reversing is illustrated in Figure 2-5.

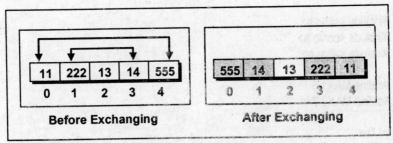

Figure 2-5. *Swapping of elements while reversing an array.*

Note that swapping should continue for **MAX / 2** times only, irrespective of whether **MAX** is even or odd. However, if by mistake the swapping of elements is done for **MAX** times the array would get reversed twice. As a result, the elements would occupy the same place at which they were placed before swapping. In other words the array would not change.

The **search( )** function searches the array for the specified number. In this function, the 0th element has been compared with the given number **num**. If the element compared happens to be same then the function displays the position at which the number is found. Otherwise, the comparison is carried out until either the list is exhausted or a match is found. If the match is not found then the function displays the relevant message.

In the **display( )** function, the entire array is traversed. As the list is traversed the function displays the elements of the array.

Merging Of Two Arrays

Merging of arrays involves two steps–sorting the arrays that are to be merged, and adding the sorted elements of both the arrays to a new array in a sorted order. Let us now see a program that demonstrates merging of two arrays into a third array.

```
#include <stdio.h>
#include <conio.h>
#include <alloc.h>

#define MAX1 5
#define MAX2 7

int *arr ;

int* create ( int ) ;
void sort ( int *, int ) ;
void display ( int *, int ) ;
int* merge ( int *, int * ) ;
```

```
void main( )
{
    int *a, *b, *c ;

    clrscr( ) ;

    printf ( "\nEnter elements for first array: \n\n" ) ;
    a = create ( MAX1 ) ;

    printf ( "\nEnter elements for second array: \n\n" ) ;
    b = create ( MAX2 ) ;

    sort ( a, MAX1 ) ;
    sort ( b, MAX2 ) ;

    printf ( "\nFirst array: \n" ) ;
    display ( a, MAX1 ) ;
    printf ( "\n\nSecond array: \n" ) ;
    display ( b, MAX2 ) ;
    printf ( "\n\nAfter Merging: \n" ) ;

    c = merge ( a, b ) ;
    display ( c, MAX1 + MAX2 ) ;

    getch( ) ;
}

/* creates array of given size, dynamically */
int* create ( int size )
{
    int *arr, i ;
    arr = ( int * ) malloc ( sizeof ( int ) * size ) ;

    for ( i = 0 ; i < size ; i++ )
    {
        printf ( "Enter the element no. %d: ", i + 1 ) ;
        scanf ( "%d", &arr[i] ) ;
    }
```

```
        return arr ;
}

/* sorts array in ascending order */
void sort ( int *arr, int size )
{
    int i, temp, j ;
    for ( i = 0 ; i < size ; i++ )
    {
        for ( j = i + 1 ; j < size ; j++ )
        {
            if ( arr[i] > arr[j] )
            {
                temp = arr[i] ;
                arr[i] = arr[j] ;
                arr[j] = temp ;
            }
        }
    }
}

/* displays the contents of array */
void display ( int *arr, int size )
{
    int i ;
    for ( i = 0 ; i < size ; i++)
        printf ( "%d\t", arr[i] ) ;
}

/* merges two arrays of different size */
int* merge ( int *a, int *b )
{
    int *arr ;
    int i, k, j ;
    int size = MAX1 + MAX2 ;
    arr = ( int * ) malloc( sizeof ( int ) * ( size ) ) ;

    for ( k = 0, j = 0, i = 0 ; i <= size ; i++ )
```

```
{
    if ( a[k] < b[j] )
    {
        arr[i] = a[k] ;
        k++ ;
        if ( k >= MAX1 )
        {
            for ( i++ ; j < MAX2 ; j++, i++ )
                arr[i] = b[j] ;
        }
    }
    else
    {
        arr[i] = b[j] ;
        j++ ;
        if ( j >= MAX2 )
        {
            for ( i++ ; k < MAX1 ; k++, i++ )
                arr[i] = a[k] ;
        }
    }
}

return arr ;
}
```

Output:

Enter elements for first array:

Enter the element no. 1: 67
Enter the element no. 2: 12
Enter the element no. 3: -4
Enter the element no. 4: 43
Enter the element no. 5: 2

Enter elements for second array:

Enter the element no. 1: 8
Enter the element no. 2: 10
Enter the element no. 3: -2
Enter the element no. 4: 39
Enter the element no. 5: 6
Enter the element no. 6: 7
Enter the element no. 7: 19

First array:
-4   2   12   43   67

Second array:
-2   6   7   8   10   19   39

After Merging:
-4   -2   2   6   7   8   10   12   19   39
43   67

In this program we have defined some functions that are used to perform different types of operations on arrays. The function **create( )** is used to create an array of **int**s, function **sort( )** is used to sort the elements of an array in ascending order, function **merge( )** is used to add elements of two arrays to the new array and lastly function **display( )** is used to display the contents of an array.

All the arrays used here are created dynamically because the size of the each array is different from the other. When the size of the array is not known while declaring it, then initially we declare a pointer. To actually create the array of desired size we have passed either **MAX1** or **MAX2** to the **create( )** function. The array is then created dynamically using the function **malloc( )**. Finally, the base address of the array is stored in the pointer.

Inside the function **merge( )**, a **for** loop is executed for **size** number of times. Here, **size** is the sum of the number of elements present in the arrays that are pointed by **a** and **b** respectively.

Before placing the element in the new array **arr** that is pointed by we have sequentially compared the elements of two arrays which are pointed by **a** and **b** respectively. The element that is found to be smaller is added first to the array that is pointed by **arr**. Thus, for example, if **a[k]** is smaller than **b[j]** then **a[k]** would get copied to **arr[i]** and **k** would get incremented by 1. The element **b[j]** would then get compared with the new element **a[k]**. While comparing if any of the two arrays gets exhausted, then the remaining elements of the other array would get copied to the array that is pointed by **arr**.

On execution, the program would ask to enter 5 integers for the array pointed by **a** and 7 integers for the array pointed by **b**.

Two-Dimensional Arrays

A 2-dimensional array is a collection of elements placed in **m** rows and **n** columns. The syntax used to declare a 2-D array includes two subscripts, of which one specifies the number of rows and the other specifies the number of columns of an array. These two subscripts are used to reference an element in an array. For example, **arr[3][4]** is a 2-D array containing 3 rows and 4 columns and **arr[0][2]** is an element placed at 0th row and 2nd column in the array. The two-dimensional array is also called a **matrix**. The pictorial representation of a matrix is shown in Figure 2-6.

	COLUMN			
	0	**1**	**2**	**3**
0	12	1	-9	23
1	14	7	11	121
2	6	78	15	34

ROW

Figure 2-6. *Representation of a 2-D array.*

Row Major And Column Major Arrangement

Rows and columns of a matrix are only a matter of imagination. When a matrix gets stored in memory all elements of it are stored linearly since computer's memory can only be viewed as consecutive units of memory. This leads to two possible arrangements of elements in memory–Row Major arrangement and Column Major arrangement. Figure 2-7 illustrates these two possible arrangements for a 2-D array.

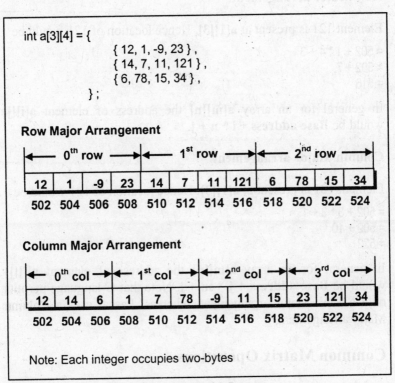

```
int a[3][4] = {
                { 12, 1, -9, 23 },
                { 14, 7, 11, 121 },
                { 6, 78, 15, 34 },
            };
```

Row Major Arrangement

| ← 0th row → | 1st row → | 2nd row → |

| 12 | 1 | -9 | 23 | 14 | 7 | 11 | 121 | 6 | 78 | 15 | 34 |

502 504 506 508 510 512 514 516 518 520 522 524

Column Major Arrangement

| ← 0th col → | 1st col → | 2nd col → | 3rd col → |

| 12 | 14 | 6 | 1 | 7 | 78 | -9 | 11 | 15 | 23 | 121 | 34 |

502 504 506 508 510 512 514 516 518 520 522 524

Note: Each integer occupies two-bytes

Figure 2-7. *Possible arrangements of 2-D array.*

Since the array elements are stored in adjacent memory locations we can access any element of the array once we know the base address (starting address) of the array and number of rows and columns present in the array.

For example, if the base address of the array shown in Figure 2-7 is 502 and we wish to refer the element 121, then the calculation involved would be as follows:

Row Major arrangement:

Element 121 is present at **a[1][3]**. Hence location of 121 would be

= 502 + 1 * 4 + 3

= 502 + 7

= 516

In general for an array **a[m][n]** the address of element **a[i][j]** would be **Base address + i * n + j.**

Column Major arrangement:

Element 121 is present at **a[1][3]**. Hence location of 121 would be

= 502 + 3 * 3 + 1

= 502 + 10

= 522

In general for an array **a[m][n]** the address of element **a[i][j]** would be **Base address + j * m + i.** Note that C language permits only a Row Major arrangement, whereas, Pascal uses a Column Major arrangement.

Common Matrix Operations

Common matrix operations are addition, multiplication, transposition, evaluation of the determinant of a square matrix, etc. The following program demonstrates these different matrix operations.

```
#include <stdio.h>
#include <conio.h>

#define MAX 3

void create ( int [3][3] ) ;
void display ( int [3][3] ) ;
```

```
void matadd ( int [3][3], int [3][3], int [3][3] ) ;
void matmul ( int [3][3], int [3][3], int [3][3] ) ;
void transpose ( int [3][3], int [3][3] ) ;

void main( )
{
    int mat1[3][3], mat2[3][3], mat3[3][3], mat4[3][3], mat5[3][3] ;

    clrscr( ) ;

    printf ( "\nEnter elements for first array: \n\n" ) ;
    create ( mat1 ) ;

    printf ( "\nEnter elements for second array: \n\n" ) ;
    create ( mat2 ) ;

    printf ( "\nFirst Array: \n" ) ;
    display ( mat1 ) ;
    printf ( "\nSecond Array:\n" ) ;
    display ( mat2 ) ;

    matadd ( mat1, mat2, mat3 ) ;
    printf ( "\nAfter Addition: \n" ) ;
    display ( mat3 ) ;

    matmul ( mat1, mat2, mat4 ) ;
    printf ( "\nAfter Multiplication: \n" ) ;
    display ( mat4 ) ;

    transpose ( mat1, mat5 ) ;
    printf ( "\nTranspose of first matrix: \n" ) ;
    display ( mat5 ) ;

    getch( ) ;
}

/* creates matrix mat */
void create ( int mat[3][3] )
```

```
{
    int i, j ;

    for ( i = 0 ; i < MAX ; i++ )
    {
        for ( j = 0 ; j < MAX ; j++ )
        {
            printf ( "Enter the element: " ) ;
            scanf ( "%d", &mat[i][j] ) ;
        }
    }
}

/* displays the contents of matrix */
void display ( int mat[3][3] )
{
    int i, j ;

    for ( i = 0 ; i < MAX ; i++ )
    {
        for ( j = 0 ; j < MAX ; j++ )
            printf ( "%d\t", mat[i][j] ) ;
        printf ( "\n" ) ;
    }
}

/* adds two matrices m1 and m2 */
void matadd ( int m1[3][3], int m2[3][3], int m3[3][3] )
{
    int i, j ;

    for ( i = 0 ; i < MAX ; i++ )
    {
        for ( j = 0 ; j < MAX ; j++ )
            m3[i][j] = m1[i][j] + m2[i][j] ;
    }
}
```

```
/* multiplies two matrices m1 and m2 */
void matmul ( int m1[3][3], int m2[3][3], int m3[3][3] )
{
    int i, j, k ;
    for ( k = 0 ; k < MAX ; k++ )
    {
        for ( i = 0 ; i < MAX ; i++ )
        {
            m3[k][i] = 0 ;
            for ( j = 0 ; j < MAX ; j++ )
                m3[k][i] += m1[k][j] * m2[j][i] ;
        }
    }
}

/* obtains transpose of matrix m1 */
void transpose ( int m1[3][3], int m2[3][3] )
{
    int i, j ;

    for ( i = 0 ; i < MAX ; i++ )
    {
        for ( j = 0 ; j < MAX ; j++ )
            m2[i][j] = m1[j][i] ;
    }
}
```

Output:

Enter elements for first array:

Enter the element: 1
Enter the element: 2
Enter the element: 3
Enter the element: 2
Enter the element: 1
Enter the element: 4

Enter the element: 4
Enter the element: 3
Enter the element: 2

Enter elements for second array:

Enter the element: 3
Enter the element: 2
Enter the element: 3
Enter the element: 4
Enter the element: 3
Enter the element: 2
Enter the element: 1
Enter the element: 3
Enter the element: 1

First Array:
1   2   3
2   1   4
4   3   2

Second Array:
3   2   3
4   3   2
1   3   1

After Addition:
4   4   6
6   4   6
5   6   3

After Multiplication:
14   17   10
14   19   12
26   23   20

Transpose of first matrix:
1   2   4

```
2    1    3
3    4    2
```

In this program we have defined some functions that perform different matrix operations like addition, multiplication, transposition, etc. The function **create( )** is used to create an array of **ints**. The **display( )** function displays the elements of the matrix.

The function **matadd( )** adds the elements of two matrices **mat1** and **mat2** and stores the result in the third matrix **mat3**. Similarly, the function **matmul( )** multiplies the elements of matrix **mat1** with the elements of matrix **mat2** and stores the result in **mat4**.

The function **transpose( )**, transposes a matrix. A transpose of a matrix is obtained by interchanging the rows with corresponding columns of a given matrix. The transposed matrix is stored in **mat5**.

More Matrix Operations

In addition to matrix operations that we discussed in previous program there are some more operations that can be performed on a matrix. These operations include calculating the determinant value for a given matrix, checking whether a matrix is a singular matrix or an orthogonal matrix, etc. Let us see a program in which we have implemented these operations, for a 3 x 3 matrix.

```
#include <stdio.h>
#include <conio.h>
#include <math.h>

#define MAX 3

void matrix ( int [3][3] ) ;
void create ( int [3][3] ) ;
```

```
void display ( int [3][3] ) ;
void matmul ( int [3][3], int [3][3], int [3][3] ) ;
void transpose ( int [3][3], int [3][3] ) ;
int determinant ( int [3][3] ) ;
int isortho ( int [3][3] ) ;

void main( )
{
    int mat [3][3], d ;

    clrscr( ) ;

    printf ( "\nEnter elements for array: \n\n" ) ;
    create ( mat ) ;

    printf ( "\nThe Matrix: \n" ) ;
    display ( mat ) ;

    d = determinant ( mat ) ;
    printf ( "\nThe determinant for given matrix: %d.\n", d ) ;

    if ( d == 0 )
        printf ( "\nMatrix is singular.\n" ) ;
    else
        printf ( "\nMatrix  is not singular.\n" ) ;

    d = isortho ( mat ) ;

    if ( d != 0 )
        printf ( "\nMatrix is orthogonal.\n" ) ;
    else
        printf ( "\nMatrix is not orthogonal.\n" ) ;

    getch( ) ;
}

/* initializes the matrix mat with 0 */
void matrix ( int mat[3][3] )
```

```
{
    int i, j ;
    for ( i = 0 ; i < MAX ; i++ )
    {
        for ( j = 0 ; j < MAX ; j++ )
            mat[i][j] = 0 ;
    }
}

/* creates matrix mat */
void create ( int mat[3][3] )
{
    int n, i, j ;
    for ( i = 0 ; i < MAX ; i++ )
    {
        for ( j = 0 ; j < MAX ; j++ )
        {
            printf ( "Enter the element: " ) ;
            scanf ( "%d", &n ) ;
            mat[i][j] = n ;
        }
    }
}

/* displays the contents of matrix */
void display ( int mat[3][3] )
{
    int i, j ;
    for ( i = 0 ; i < MAX ; i++ )
    {
        for ( j = 0 ; j < MAX ; j++ )
            printf ( "%d\t", mat[i][j] ) ;
        printf ( "\n" ) ;
    }
}

/* multiplies two matrices */
void matmul ( int mat1[3][3], int mat2[3][3], int mat3[3][3] )
```

```
{
    int i, j, k ;
    for ( k = 0 ; k < MAX ; k++ )
    {
        for ( i = 0 ; i < MAX ; i++ )
        {
            mat3[k][i] = 0 ;
            for ( j = 0 ; j < MAX ; j++ )
                mat3[k][i] += mat1[k][j] * mat2[j][i] ;
        }
    }
}

/* obtains transpose of matrix m1 */
void transpose ( int mat[3][3], int m[3][3] )
{
    int i, j ;
    for ( i = 0 ; i < MAX ; i++ )
    {
        for ( j = 0 ; j < MAX ; j++ )
            m[i][j] = mat[j][i] ;
    }
}

/* finds the determinant value for given matrix */
int determinant( int mat[3][3] )
{
    int sum, i, j, k, p ;
    sum = 0 ; j = 1 ; k = MAX - 1 ;

    for ( i = 0 ; i < MAX ; i++ )
    {
        p = pow ( -1, i ) ;

        if ( i == MAX - 1 )
            k = 1 ;
        sum = sum + ( mat[0][i] * ( mat[1][j] *
                            mat[2][k] - mat[2][j] *
```

```
                                mat[1][k] ) ) * p ;
        j = 0 ;
    }

    return sum ;
}

/* checks if given matrix is an orthogonal matrix */
int isortho ( int mat[3][3] )
{
    /* transpose the matrix */
    int m1[3][3], m2[3][3], i
    transpose ( mat, m1 ) ;

    /* multiply the matrix with its transpose */
    matmul ( mat, m1, m2 ) ;

    /* check for the identity matrix */
    for ( i = 0  ; i < MAX ; i++ )
    {
        if ( m2[i][i] == 1 )
            continue ;
        else
            break ;
    }
    if ( i == MAX )
        return 1 ;
    else
        return 0 ;
}
```

Output:

Enter elements for array:

Enter the element: 1
Enter the element: 0

Enter the element: 0
Enter the element: 0
Enter the element: 1
Enter the element: 0
Enter the element: 0
Enter the element: 0
Enter the element: 1

The Matrix:
1   0   0
0   1   0
0   0   1

The determinant for given matrix: 1

Matrix is not singular.

Matrix is orthogonal.

In this program, in addition to functions **create( )**, **display( )**, **matmul( )**, and **transpose( )** (which we discussed in previous program), there are two more functions **determinant( )** and **isortho( )**.

The **determinant( )** function calculates the determinant value for a given matrix. Here, the matrix for which the determinant value has to be calculated is a square matrix. A square matrix is the one in which the number of rows is equal to the number of columns. We have calculated the determinant value through a loop as shown below:

In 1st iteration when i = 0:

```
p = pow ( -1, 0 ) ;
sum = sum + ( mat[0][0] * ( mat[1][1] * mat[2][2] –
          mat[2][1] * mat[1][2] ) ) * p ;
    = 0 + ( 1 * ( 1 * 1 - 0 * 0 ) ) * 1 ;
```

= 1

In 2nd iteration when i = 1:

p = pow (-1, 1) ;
sum = sum + (mat[0][1] * (mat[1][0] * mat[2][2] –
　　　　mat[2][0] * mat[1][2])) * p ;
　 = 1 + (0 * (0 * 1 - 0 * 0)) * -1 ;
　 = 1

In 3rd iteration when i = 2:

p = pow (-1, 2) ;
sum = sum + (mat[0][2] * (mat[1][0] * mat[2][1] –
　　　　mat[[2][0] * mat[1][1])) * p ;
　 = 1 + (0 * (0 * 0 - 0 * 1)) * 1 ;
　 = 1

A matrix is called **singular** if the determinant value of a matrix is 0. The determinant value for the matrix that we have keyed in is 1 hence it is not a singular matrix.

The **isortho( )** function checks whether or not a given matrix is orthogonal. A square matrix is said to be **orthogonal**, if the matrix obtained by multiplying the matrix with its transpose is an identity matrix. In other words, if A is a matrix and T is its transpose, then matrix B obtained by multiplying A with T is called orthogonal if it is an identity matrix. An identity matrix is a square matrix in which the elements in the leading diagonal are 1.

Hence in **isortho( )** function, first we have called **transpose( )** function which stores the transpose of the given matrix, in **m1**. Then we have called **matmul( )** function to obtain the product of the matrix and its transpose. The resultant matrix is stored in **m2**. Then through a loop we have checked if the matrix **m2** is an identity matrix or not and returned a suitable value.

Array Of Pointers

The way there can be an array of **ints** or an array of **floats**, we can also have an array of pointers. Since a pointer variable always contains an address, an array of pointers would be nothing but a collection of addresses. The addresses present in an array of pointers can be addresses of isolated variables or even the addresses of other array elements. The rules that apply to an ordinary array, also apply to an array of pointers as well. Figure 2-8(a) and 2-8(b) shows the memory representation of an array of integers and an array of pointers respectively.

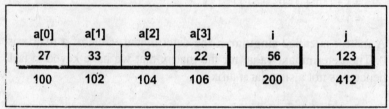

Figure 2-8(a). *Memory representation of an array of integers and integer variables i and j.*

b[0]	b[1]	b[2]	b[3]	b[4]	b[5]
100	102	104	106	200	412
8112	8114	8116	8118	8120	8122

Figure 2.8(b). *Memory representation of an array of pointers.*

Multidimensional Arrays

A 3-dimensional array can be thought of as an array of arrays of arrays. Figure 2-9 shows a 3-D array, which is a collection of three 2-D arrays each containing 4 rows and 2 columns.

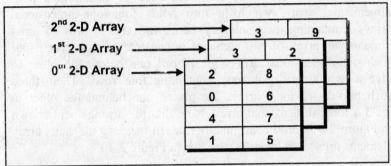

Figure 2-9. *Representation of a 3-D array.*

This array can be defined as:

```
int a[3][4][2] = {
                {
                        { 2, 8 },
                        { 0, 6 },
                        { 4, 7 },
                        { 1, 5 }
                },
                {
                        { 3, 2 },
                        { 8, 6 },
                        { 1, 6 },
                        { 4, 5 },
                },
                {
                        { 3, 9 },
                        { 1, 8 },
                        { 6, 5 },
                        { 4, 0 }
                }
```

The outer array has three elements, each of which is a two-dimensional array, which in turn holds four one-dimensional arrays containing two integers each. In other words, a one-dimensional array of two elements is constructed first. Then four such one-dimensional arrays are placed one below the other to give a two-dimensional array containing four rows. Then, three such two-dimensional arrays are placed one behind the other to yield a three-dimensional array. Note that the arrangement shown in Figure 2-9 is only conceptually true. In memory the same array elements are stored linearly as shown in Figure 2-10.

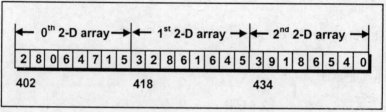

Figure 2-10. *Memory representation of a 3-D array.*

As said earlier, C permits only a Row Major arrangement for multi-dimensional arrays. So the element 9 in the array shown in Figure 2-10 can be accessed as follows:

The array **a** can be defined as **int a[3][4][2]**. Element 9 is present at **a[2][0][1]** indicating that it is present in 0th row, 1st column of 2nd 2-D array. Hence address of 9 can be obtained as:

$$402 + 2 * 4 * 2 + 0 * 2 + 1 = 402 + 17$$
$$= 436$$

For any 3-D array **a[x][y][z]** the element **a[i][j][k]** can be accessed as **Base address + i * y * z + j * z + k**.

Arrays And Polynomials

Polynomials like $5X^4 + 2X^3 + 7X^2 + 10X - 8$ can be maintained using an array. Arithmetic operations like addition and multiplication of polynomials are common and often we need to write a program involving these operations. If we want to write a program that lets us perform these operations then we need a way to represent the polynomial. The simplest way to represent a polynomial of degree "n" is to store the coefficient of (n + 1) terms of a polynomial in an array. To achieve this, each element of the array should consist of two values, namely coefficient and exponent. While maintaining the polynomial it is assumed that the exponent of each successive term is less than that of the previous term. Once we build an array to represent a polynomial, we can use such an array to perform common polynomial operations like addition and multiplication. The following program demonstrates how we can store polynomials and add them.

```
#include <stdio.h>
#include <conio.h>

#define MAX 10

struct term
{
    int coeff ;
    int exp ;
} ;

struct poly
{
    struct term t [10] ;
    int noofterms ;
} ;
```

```
void initpoly ( struct poly * ) ;
void polyappend ( struct poly *, int c, int e ) ;
struct poly polyadd ( struct poly, struct poly ) ;
void display ( struct poly ) ;

void main( )
{
    struct poly p1, p2, p3 ;

    clrscr( ) ;

    initpoly ( &p1 ) ;
    initpoly ( &p2 ) ;
    initpoly ( &p3 ) ;

    polyappend ( &p1, 1, 7 ) ;
    polyappend ( &p1, 2, 6 ) ;
    polyappend ( &p1, 3, 5 ) ;
    polyappend ( &p1, 4, 4 ) ;
    polyappend ( &p1, 5, 2 ) ;

    polyappend ( &p2, 1, 4 ) ;
    polyappend ( &p2, 1, 3 ) ;
    polyappend ( &p2, 1, 2 ) ;
    polyappend ( &p2, 1, 1 ) ;
    polyappend ( &p2, 2, 0 ) ;

    p3 = polyadd ( p1, p2 ) ;

    printf ( "\nFirst polynomial:\n" ) ;
    display ( p1 ) ;

    printf ( "\n\nSecond polynomial:\n" ) ;
    display ( p2 ) ;

    printf ( "\n\nResultant polynomial:\n" ) ;
    display ( p3 ) ;
```

```
        getch( ) ;
}

/* initializes elements of struct poly */
void initpoly ( struct poly *p )
{
    int i ;
    p -> noofterms = 0 ;
    for ( i = 0 ; i < MAX ; i++ )
    {
        p -> t[i].coeff = 0 ;
        p -> t[i].exp = 0 ;
    }
}

/* adds the term of polynomial to the array t */
void polyappend ( struct poly *p, int c, int e )
{
    p -> t[p -> noofterms].coeff = c ;
    p -> t[p -> noofterms].exp = e ;
    ( p -> noofterms ) ++ ;
}

/* displays the polynomial equation */
void display ( struct poly p )
{
    int flag = 0, i ;
    for ( i = 0 ; i < p.noofterms ; i++ )
    {
        if ( p.t[i].exp != 0 )
            printf ( "%d x^%d + ", p.t[i].coeff, p.t[i].exp ) ;
        else
        {
            printf ( "%d", p.t[i].coeff ) ;
            flag = 1 ;
        }
    }
    if ( !flag )
```

```
        printf ( "\b\b  " ) ;

}

/* adds two polynomials p1 and p2 */
struct poly polyadd ( struct poly p1, struct poly p2 )
{
    int i, j, c ;
    struct poly p3 ;
    initpoly ( &p3 ) ;

    if ( p1.noofterms > p2.noofterms )
        c = p1.noofterms ;
    else
        c = p2.noofterms ;

    for ( i = 0, j = 0 ; i <= c ; p3.noofterms++ )
    {
        if ( p1.t[i].coeff == 0 && p2.t[j].coeff == 0 )
            break ;
        if ( p1.t[i].exp >= p2.t[j].exp )
        {
            if ( p1.t[i].exp == p2.t[j].exp )
            {
                p3.t[p3.noofterms].coeff = p1.t[i].coeff + p2.t[j].coeff ;
                p3.t[p3.noofterms].exp = p1.t[i].exp ;
                i++ ;
                j++ ;
            }
            else
            {
                p3.t[p3.noofterms].coeff = p1.t[i].coeff ;
                p3.t[p3.noofterms].exp = p1.t[i].exp ;
                i++ ;
            }
        }
        else
        {
```

```
        p3.t[p3.noofterms].coeff = p2.t[j].coeff ;
        p3.t[p3.noofterms].exp = p2.t[j].exp ;
        j++ ;
     }
  }
  return p3 ;
}
```

Output:

First polynomial:
1 x^7 + 2 x^6 + 3 x^5 + 4 x^4 + 5 x^2

Second polynomial:
1 x^4 + 1 x^3 + 1 x^2 + 1 x^1 + 2

Resultant polynomial:
1 x^7 + 2 x^6 + 3 x^5 + 5 x^4 + 1 x^3 + 6 x^2 + 1 x^1 + 2

In this program, the structure **poly** contains another structure element of the type **struct term**. This structure stores the coefficient and exponent of the term of a polynomial. The element **noofterms** stores the total number of terms that a variable of the type **struct poly** is supposed to hold. The function **polyappend( )** adds the term of a polynomial to the array **t**. The function **polyadd( )** adds the polynomials represented by the two variables **p1** and **p2**. The function **display( )** displays the polynomial.

In **main( )**, we have called the function **polyappend( )** several times to build the two polynomials which are represented by the variables **p1** and **p2**. Next, the function **polyadd( )** is called by passing three arguments **p1** and **p2** which returns the addition of polynomials **p1** and **p2** which we are collecting in **p3**. In this function, arrays representing the two polynomials are traversed. While traversing, the polynomials are compared on a term-by-term basis. If the exponents of the two terms being compared are equal then their coefficients are added and the result is stored in the third polynomial. If the exponents of two terms are not equal then the term with the bigger exponent is added to the third polynomial. If the term with an exponent is present in only one of the two polynomials then that term is added as it is to the third polynomial.

Lastly, the terms of the resulting polynomial are displayed using the function **display( )**.

Multiplication Of Polynomials

Let us now see a program that carries out multiplication of two polynomials.

```c
/#include <stdio.h>
#include <conio.h>

#define MAX 10

struct term
{
    int coeff ;
    int exp ;
} ;

struct poly
{
    struct term t [10] ;
    int noofterms ;
} ;

void initpoly ( struct poly *) ;
void polyappend ( struct poly *, int, int ) ;
struct poly polyadd ( struct poly, struct poly ) ;
struct poly polymul ( struct poly, struct poly ) ;
void display ( struct poly ) ;
```

```
void main( )
{
    struct poly p1, p2, p3 ;

    clrscr( ) ;

    initpoly ( &p1 ) ;
    initpoly ( &p2 ) ;
    initpoly ( &p3 ) ;

    polyappend ( &p1, 1, 4 ) ;
    polyappend ( &p1, 2, 3 ) ;
    polyappend ( &p1, 2, 2 ) ;
    polyappend ( &p1, 2, 1 ) ;

    polyappend ( &p2, 2, 3 ) ;
    polyappend ( &p2, 3, 2 ) ;
    polyappend ( &p2, 4, 1 ) ;

    p3 = polymul ( p1, p2 ) ;

    printf ( "\nFirst polynomial:\n" ) ;
    display ( p1 ) ;

    printf ( "\n\nSecond polynomial:\n" ) ;
    display ( p2 ) ;

    printf ( "\n\nResultant polynomial:\n" ) ;
    display ( p3 ) ;

    getch( ) ;
}

/* initializes elements of struct poly */
void initpoly ( struct poly *p )
{
    int i ;
    p -> noofterms = 0 ;
```

```
    for ( i = 0 , i < MAX ; i++ )
    {
        p -> t[i].coeff = 0 ;
        p -> t[i].exp = 0 ;
    }
}

/* adds the term of polynomial to the array t */
void polyappend ( struct poly *p, int c, int e )
{
    p -> t[p -> nooterms].coeff = c ;
    p -> t[p -> nooterms].exp = e ;
    ( p -> nooterms ) ++ ;
}

/* displays the polynomial equation */
void display ( struct poly p )
{
    int flag = 0, i ;
    for ( i = 0 ; i < p.noofterms ; i++ )
    {
        if ( p.t[i].exp != 0 )
            printf ( "%d x^%d + ", p.t[i].coeff, p.t[i].exp ) ;
        else
        {
            printf ( "%d", p.t[i].coeff ) ;
            flag = 1 ;
        }
    }
    if ( !flag )
        printf ( "\b\b " ) ;

}
/* adds two polynomials p1 and p2 */
struct poly polyadd ( struct poly p1, struct poly p2 )
{
    int i, j, c ;
    struct poly p3 ;
```

```
    initpoly ( &p3 ) ;

    if ( p1.noofterms > p2.noofterms )
        c = p1.noofterms ;
    else
        c = p2.noofterms ;

    for ( i = 0, j = 0 ; i <= c ; p3.noofterms++ )
    {
        if ( p1.t[i].coeff == 0 && p2.t[j].coeff == 0 )
            break ;
        if ( p1.t[i].exp >= p2.t[j].exp )
        {
            if ( p1.t[i].exp == p2.t[j].exp )
            {
                p3.t[p3.noofterms].coeff = p1.t[i].coeff + p2.t[j].coeff ;
                p3.t[p3.noofterms].exp = p1.t[i].exp ;
                i++ ;
                j++ ;
            }
            else
            {
                p3.t[p3.noofterms].coeff = p1.t[i].coeff ;
                p3.t[p3.noofterms].exp = p1.t[i].exp ;
                i++ ;
            }
        }
        else
        {
            p3.t[p3.noofterms].coeff = p2.t[j].coeff ;
            p3.t[p3.noofterms].exp = p2.t[j].exp ;
            j++ ;
        }
    }
    return p3 ;
}

/* multiplies two polynomials p1 and p2 */
```

```
struct poly polymul ( struct poly p1, struct poly p2 )
{
    int coeff, exp ;
    struct poly temp, p3 ;

    initpoly ( &temp ) ;
    initpoly ( &p3 ) ;

    if ( p1.noofterms != 0 && p2.noofterms != 0 )
    {
        int i ;
        for ( i = 0 ; i < p1.noofterms ; i++ )
        {
            int j ;

            struct poly p ;
            initpoly ( &p ) ;

            for ( j = 0 ; j < p2.noofterms ; j++ )
            {
                coeff = p1.t[i].coeff * p2.t[j].coeff ;
                exp = p1.t[i].exp + p2.t[j].exp ;
                polyappend ( &p, coeff, exp ) ;
            }

            if ( i != 0 )
            {
                p3 = polyadd ( temp, p ) ;
                temp = p3 ;
            }
            else
                temp = p ;
        }
    }
    return p3 ;
}
```

Output:

First polynomial:
1 x^4 + 2 x^3 + 2 x^2 + 2 x^1

Second polynomial:
2 x^3 + 3 x^2 + 4 x^1

Resultant polynomial:
2 x^7 + 7 x^6 + 14 x^5 + 18 x^4 + 14 x^3 + 8 x^2

To carry out multiplication of two given polynomial equations, the function **polymul( )** is used. As done in previous program, here too we have called **polyappend( )** function several times to build the two polynomials which are represented by the variables **p1** and **p2**. Next the function **polymul( )** is called by passing two arguments **p1** and **p2** which returns the multiplication of polynomials **p1** and **p2** and returns the resultant polynomial which we are collecting in the third polynomial **p3**.

In **polymul( )** function, first we have checked that whether the two polynomials **p1** and **p2** are non-empty. If they are not then the control goes in a pair of **for** loop. Here each term of first polynomial contained in **p1** is multiplied with every term of second polynomial contained in **p2**. While doing so we have called **polyappend( )** to add the terms to **p**. The first resultant polynomial equation is stored in temporary variable **temp** of the type **struct poly**. There onwards the function **polyadd( )** is called to add the resulting polynomial equations.

Lastly, the terms of the resulting polynomial are displayed using the function **display( )**.

Exercise

[A] Fill in the blanks:

(a) A data structure is said to be _____ if its elements form a sequence.

(b) An Array is a collection of _____ elements stored in _____ memory locations.

(c) Index of an array containing **n** elements varies from _____ to _____.

(d) A 2-D array is also called _____.

[B] Pick up the correct alternative for each of the following questions:

(a) To traverse an array means
    (1) To process each element in an array
    (2) To delete an element from an array
    (3) To insert an element into an array
    (4) To combine two arrays into a single array

(b) Merging refers to
    (1) Inserting elements into an array
    (2) Processing elements of an array
    (3) Combining two arrays into a single array
    (4) Deleting elements from an array

(c) Sorting of an array refers to
    (1) Processing elements of an array
    (2) Deleting elements from an array
    (3) Both (1) and (2)
    (4) Organizing elements in an array in some order

[C] Write programs for the following:

(a) Write a program to find out the maximum and the second maximum number from an array of integers.

(b) Write a program that accepts a number as input in English language format such as One Twenty Three (for 123) and prints the decimal form of it.

(c) The Mode of an array of numbers is the number **m** in the array that is repeated most frequently. If more than one number is repeated with equal maximal frequencies, there is no mode. Write a program that accepts an array of numbers and returns the mode or an indication that the mode does not exist.

(d) Write a program to delete duplicate elements from an array of 20 integers.

(e) A square matrix is called symmetric if for all values of **i** and **j** **a[i][j]** = **a[j][i]**. Write a program, which verifies whether a given 5 x 5 matrix is symmetric, or not.

(f) Build an array called **chess** to represent a chessboard and write a function that would be capable of displaying position of each coin on the chessboard.

(g) There are two arrays **A** and **B**. **A** contains 25 elements, whereas, **B** contains 30 elements. Write a function to create an array **C** that contains only those elements that are common to **A** and **B**.

(h) A magic square of 5 rows x 5 columns contains different elements. Write a function to verify whether the sum of each individual column elements, sum of each individual row elements and sum of diagonal elements is equal or not.

(i) Usually a polynomial is stored in an array with exponents of each term in decreasing order. Write a procedure to reverse this order, so that now the terms are arranged in increasing order.

[D] Answer the following:

(a) Find the location of the element **a[1][2][2][1]** from a 4-D integer array **a[4][3][4][3]** if the base address of the array is **1002**.

(b) Design a data structure for a banking system where the maximum number of clients is 150. Information to be stored about clients—name, address, account no., balance, status as Low/Medium/High depending on balance.

(c) Design a data structure for Income Tax department to hold information for maximum 200 persons. Information to be stored about persons—Income Tax no., tax amount, name, address, whether tax paid or not for previous year, group as High/Low depending on amount of tax to be paid and category which would vary from 1 to 10.

CHAPTER
THREE

Strings
Appearances Are Misleading

S trings are perhaps as old as programming languages themselves. They have been around for so long that they are almost taken for granted. They appear similar to arrays, their close cousins. But beyond their external grab they have some major challenges to offer. Take the multiple ways to represent them, for example. They can be represented—either as a linked list or as arrays, length-preceded or null-terminated, etc. As if, this is not enough there are issues like **ASCII** strings and Unicode strings. Read this chapter to gain an insight into these vital issues...

What Are Strings?

The way a group of integers can be stored in an integer array, a group of characters can also be stored in a character array. An array of characters is often called a string. Character arrays are used by programming languages to manipulate text such as words and sentences.

A string constant is a one-dimensional array of characters terminated by a null ('\0') character. The terminating null ('\0') is important, because it is the only way the function that works with string can know where a string ends. In fact, a string not terminated by a '\0' is not really a string, but merely a collection of characters.

Representation of Strings

A string can be represented using an array or a linked list. A string of characters having length **n** can be implemented by a one-dimensional array of **n** elements where the ith element of the array stores the ith character of the string. The advantage of such a representation is that the array elements can be directly accessed and this could speed up several operations on strings. Array representation of string in memory is shown in Figure 3-1.

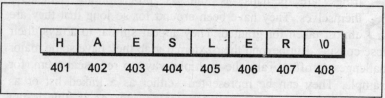

Figure 3-1. *Array representation of characters.*

An alternative representation of strings can be done using a linked list. A pointer to the linked list identifies a string represented by a linked list. Each node in the list contains a character and a pointer to the next character in the string. The pointer of the node containing the last character in the string is set to **NULL**. The representation of string as a linked list is shown in Figure 3-2.

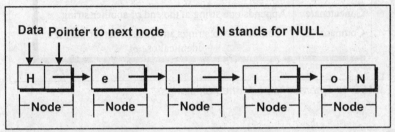

Figure 3-2. *Representation of a string as a linked list.*

Operations On Strings

While working with strings, we are often required to alter the characters present in a string. Table 3-1 gives a list of operations that can be performed to manipulate a string.

The number of characters in a string is called its length. The string with zero character is called an **empty string** or the **null string.**

Operation	Description
Length	Finds the length of the string
Copy	Copies the contents of one string to another string
Concatenate	Appends one string at the end of another string
Compare	Compares two strings and finds whether they are identical or not

Table 3-1. *Operations performed on strings.*

The following program shows how to implement operations shown in Table 3-1.

```
#include <stdio.h>
#include <conio.h>
#include <string.h>

int xstrlen ( char * ) ;
void xstrcpy ( char *, char * ) ;
void xstrcat ( char *, char * ) ;
int xstrcmp ( char *, char * ) ;
void show ( char * ) ;

void main( )
{
    char s1[ ] = "kicit" ;
    char s2[ ] = "Nagpur" ;
    char s3[20] ;
    int len ;

    clrscr( ) ;
```

```
    printf ( "\nString s1: %s", s1 ) ;
    len = xstrlen ( s1 ) ;
    printf ( "\nlength of the string s1: %d", len ) ;

    printf ( "\nString s2: %s", s2 ) ;

    xstrcpy ( s3, s1 ) ;
    printf ( "\nString s3 after copying s1 to it: %s", s3 ) ;

    xstrcat ( s3, s2 ) ;
    printf ( "\nString s3 after concatenation: %s", s3 ) ;

    if ( xstrcmp ( s1, s2 ) == 0 )
        printf ( "\nThe strings s1 and s2 are similar" ) ;
    else
        printf ( "\nThe strings s1 and s2 are not similar" ) ;

    getch( ) ;
}

/* finds the length of the string */
int xstrlen ( char *s )
{
    int l = 0 ;
    while ( *s )
    {
        l++ ;
        s++ ;
    }
    return l ;
}

/* copies source string s to the target string t */
void xstrcpy ( char *t, char *s )
{
    while ( *s )
    {
        *t = *s ;
```

```
            t++ ;
            s++ ;
        }
        *t = '\0' ;
}

/* concatenates the two strings */
void xstrcat ( char *t, char *s )
{
    while ( *t )
        t++ ;
    while ( *s )
        *t++ = *s++ ;
    *t = '\0' ;
}

/* compares two strings s and t for equality */
int xstrcmp ( char *s, char *t )
{
    while ( *s == *t )
    {
        if ( ! ( *s ) )
            return 0 ;
        s++ ;
        t++ ;
    }
    return ( *s - *t ) ;
}
```

Output:

String s1: kicit
length of the string s1: 5
String s2: Nagpur
String s3 after copying s1 to it: kicit
String s3 after concatenation: kicitNagpur
The strings s1 and s2 are not similar

In this program we have created three arrays of characters, **s1**, **s2** and **s3**.

The function **xstrlen( )** is fairly simple. It receives only one parameter as the base address of a character array. All that it does is it keeps counting the characters till the end of string is not met. Or in other words it keeps counting characters till the pointer **s** doesn't point to '\0'.

The function **xstrcpy( )** receives two parameters. Both the parameters are the base addresses to the target and source strings respectively. This function copies the source string whose base address is received in pointer **s**, to the target string whose base address is stored in the pointer **t**. The function goes on copying the source string into the target string till it doesn't encounter the end of source string. It is our responsibility to see to it that target string's dimension is big enough to hold the string being copied into it.

The function **xstrcat( )** also receives two parameters. Here also the parameters are the pointers to the base addresses of the target and source strings respectively. This function adds the source string whose base address is stored in pointer **s** at the end of target string whose base address is stored in pointer **t**. In the first **while** loop we have made the pointer **t** to point to the end of the string. In the second **while** loop the contents of source string pointed to by **s** are added character by character to the target string pointed to by **t**. Lastly, we have added a null terminating character '\0' at the end of the target string pointed to by **t**.

Another useful string function is **xstrcmp( )** which compares two strings to find out whether they are same or different. The two strings **s1** and **s2** pointed to by **s** and **t** respectively, are compared character by character until there is a mismatch or end of one of the string is reached, whichever occurs first. If the two strings are identical, **xstrcmp( )** function returns a 0. Otherwise, it returns the numeric difference between the **ASCII** values of the first non-matching pair of characters.

Pointers And Strings

Suppose we wish to store "Hello". We may either store it in a string or we may ask the compiler to store it at some location in memory and assign the address of the string to a **char** pointer. This is shown below:

```
char str[ ] = "Hello" ;
char *p = "Hello" ;
```

There is a subtle difference in usage of these two forms. For example, we cannot assign a string to another, whereas, we can assign a **char** pointer to another **char** pointer. This is shown in the following program:

```
void main( )
{
    char str1[ ] = "Hello" ;
    char str2[10] ;

    char *s = "Good Morning" ;
    char *q ;

    str2 = str1 ;  /* error */
    q = s ;  /* works */
}
```

Also, once a string has been defined it cannot be initialised to another set of characters. Unlike strings, such an operation is perfectly valid with **char** pointers. This is shown in the following program:

```
void main( )
{
    char str1[ ] = "Hello" ;
    char *p = "Hello" ;
    str1 = "Bye" ;  /* error */
    p = "Bye" ;  /* works */
}
```

A Two-Dimensional Array of Strings

In the previous chapter we saw how to create and maintain 2-D numeric arrays. Let's now look at a similar phenomenon, but one dealing with characters. The best way to understand this concept is through a program. Our example program asks you to type your name. When you do so, it checks your name against a master list to see if you are worthy of entry to the palace. Here's the program...

```
#include <stdio.h>
#include <conio.h>
#include <string.h>

#define MAX1 6
#define MAX2 10

char masterlist[MAX1][MAX2] ;
int count ;

int add ( char *s ) ;
int find ( char *s ) ;

void main( )
{
    char yourname[MAX2] ;
    int flag ;

    clrscr( ) ;
```

```
        flag = add ( "akshay" ) ;
        if ( flag == 0 )
            printf ( "\nUnable to add string" ) ;

        flag = add ( "parag" ) ;
        if ( flag == 0 )
            printf ( "\nUnable to add string" ) ;

        flag = add ( "raman" ) ;
        if ( flag == 0 )
            printf ( "\nUnable to add string" ) ;

        flag = add ( "srinivas" ) ;
        if ( flag == 0 )
            printf ( "\nUnable to add string" ) ;

        flag = add ( "gopal" ) ;
        if ( flag == 0 )
            printf ( "\nUnable to add string" ) ;

        flag = add ( "rajesh" ) ;
        if ( flag == 0 )
            printf ( "Unable to add string" ) ;

        printf ( "Enter your name: " ) ;
        gets ( yourname ) ;
        flag = find ( yourname ) ;
        if ( flag == 1 )
            printf ( "Welcome, you can enter the palace\n" ) ;
        else
            printf ( "Sorry, you are a trespasser" ) ;

        getch( ) ;
}

/* adds string to the array */
int add ( char *s )
{
```

```
    if ( count < MAX1 )
    {
        if ( strlen ( s ) < MAX2 )
        {
            strcpy ( &masterlist[count][0], s ) ;
            count++ ;
            return 1 ;
        }
    }

    return 0 ;
}

/* finds the given string */
int find ( char *s )
{
    int flag = 0, i ;

    for ( i = 0 ; i < count ; i++ )
    {
        if ( strcmp ( &masterlist[i][0], s ) == 0 )
        {
            flag = 1 ;
            break ;
        }
    }

    return flag ;
}
```

Output:

Enter your name: sanjay
Sorry, you are a trespasser

Enter your name: akshay
Welcome, you can enter the palace

Here we have used two global variables—a 2-D array of characters called **masterlist** and an integer called **count,** which counts the number of strings·that would get added to the **masterlist** array. The order of subscripts in the array declaration is important. The first subscript **MAX1** gives the number of items in the array, while the second subscript **MAX2** gives the length of each item in·the array.

Notice how the two-dimensional character array has been initialised. We have called **add( )** function to add new string to the 2-D array. The **add( )** function allows addition of a string to the array if following two conditions are satisfied.

(a) The number of strings to be added to the array is less than MAX1.

(b) The length of string to be added is less than MAX2.

Instead of initializing names, we could have supplied these names from the keyboard using the **scanf( )** function. In such a case the **add( )** function would have then looked like this...

```
int add( )
{
    if ( count < MAX1 )
    {
        char s[MAX2] ;

        printf ( "\nEnter string: " ) ;
        scanf ( "%s", s ) ;

        if ( strlen ( s ) < MAX2 )
        {
            strcpy ( &masterlist[count][0], s ) ;
            count++ ;
            return 1 ;
        }
        else
```

```
                printf ( "\nString length should not be more than %d ",
                        MAX2 - 1 ) ;
        }

    return 0 ;
}
```

The function **find( )** checks if the given name is present in the **masterlist** array. While comparing the strings through **strcmp( )**, note that the addresses of the two strings are being passed to **strcmp( )**. If the two strings match, **strcmp( )** would return a value 0, otherwise it would return a non-zero value.

The variable **flag** is used to keep a record whether the control did reach inside **if** or not. To begin with we have set this flag to 0. Later through the loop if the names match the **flag** is set to 1. When the control reaches beyond the **for** loop, if **flag** is still set to 0 it means that none of the names in the **masterlist** matched with the one supplied from the keyboard.

The names would be stored in memory as shown in Figure 3-3. Note that each string ends with a '\0'. The arrangement as you can appreciate is similar to that of a two-dimensional numeric array.

akshay\0	parag\0	raman\0	srinivas\0	gopal\0	rajesh\0
1001	1011	1021	1031	1041	1051

Figure 3-3. *Memory representation of 2-D array of characters.*

Here, 1001, 1011, 1021, etc. are the base addresses of successive names. As seen from the above figure, some of the names do not occupy all the bytes reserved for them. For example, even though

10 bytes are reserved for storing the name "akshay", it occupies only 7 bytes. Thus, 3 bytes go waste. In fact more the number of names, more would be the wastage. Can this not be avoided? Yes, it can be... by using a data type called an array of pointers to strings, which is our next topic of discussion.

Array of Pointers To Strings

As we know, a pointer variable always contains an address. Therefore, if we construct an array of pointers it would contain a number of addresses. Let us see how the names in the earlier example can be stored in an array of pointers.

```
char *names[ ] = {
                "akshay",
                "parag",
                "raman",
                "srinivas",
                "gopal",
                "rajesh"
            };
```

In this declaration **names** is an array of pointers. It contains base addresses of respective names. That is, base address of "akshay" is stored in **names[0]**, base address of "parag" is stored in **names[1]** and so on. This is depicted in Figure 3-4.

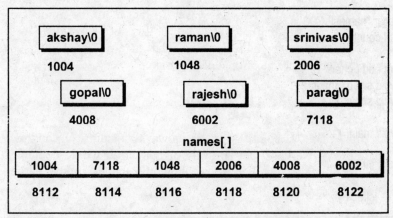

Figure 3-4. *Memory representation of array of pointers.*

In the two-dimensional array of characters, the strings were occupying a total of 60 bytes. As against this, by using the array of pointers to strings the same strings can now be stored using only 53 bytes, 41 bytes for the actual strings and 12 for the array of pointers. A substantial saving that goes on increasing with the number of names being stored.

Thus, one reason to store strings in an array of pointers is to make more efficient use of available memory.

Another reason to use array of pointers to store strings is to obtain greater ease in the manipulation of the strings. The following program shows this. The purpose of the program is very simple. We want to exchange the positions of the names "raman" and "srinivas".

```
#include <stdio.h>
#include <conio.h>
#include <string.h>
```

```
#define MAX 6

char *names[MAX] ;
int count ;

int add ( char * ) ;
void swap ( int, int ) ;
void show( ) ;

void main( )
{
    int flag ;

    clrscr( ) ;

    flag = add ( "akshay" ) ;
    if ( flag == 0 )
        printf ( "Unable to add string" ) ;

    flag = add ( "parag" ) ;
    if ( flag == 0 )
        printf ( "Unable to add string" ) ;

    flag = add ( "raman" ) ;
    if ( flag == 0 )
        printf ( "Unable to add string" ) ;

    flag = add ( "srinivas" ) ;
    if ( flag == 0 )
        printf ( "Unable to add string" ) ;

    flag = add ( "gopal" ) ;
    if ( flag == 0 )
        printf ( "Unable to add string" ) ;

    flag = add ( "rajesh" ) ;
    if ( flag == 0 )
        printf ( "Unable to add string" ) ;
```

```
    printf ( "\nNames before swapping:\n" ) ;
    show ( ) ;

    swap ( 2, 3 ) ;
    printf ( "\nNames after swapping:\n" ) ;
    show ( ) ;

    getch( ) ;
}

/* adds given string */
int add ( char *s )
{
    if ( count < MAX )
    {
        names[count] = s ;
        count++ ;
        return 1 ;
    }
    else
        return 0 ;
}

/* swaps the names at given two positions */
void swap ( int i, int j )
{
    char *temp ;
    temp = names[i] ;
    names[i] = names[j] ;
    names[j] = temp ;
}

/* displays the elements */
void show ( )
{
    int i ;
    for ( i = 0 ; i < count ; i++ )
        puts ( names[i] ) ;
```

}

Output:

Names before swapping:
akshay
parag
raman
srinivas
gopal
rajesh

Names after swapping:
akshay
parag
srinivas
raman
gopal
rajesh

In this program all that we are required to do is exchange the addresses of the names stored in the array of pointers, rather than the names themselves. Thus, by effecting just one change we are able to interchange names. This makes managing strings very convenient.

Thus, from the point of view of efficient memory usage and ease of programming, an array of pointers to strings definitely scores over a two-dimensional character array. That is why even though in principle strings can be stored and handled through a two-dimensional array of characters, in actual practice it is the array of pointers to strings, which is more commonly used.

Limitation Of Array Of Pointers To Strings

When we are using a two-dimensional array of characters we are at liberty to either initialize the strings where we are declaring the array, or receive the strings using **scanf( )** function. However, when we are using an array of pointers to strings we can initialize the strings at the place where we are declaring the array, but we cannot receive the strings from keyboard using **scanf( )**. Thus, the following program would never work out.

```c
void main( )
{
    char *names[6] ;
    int i ;

    for ( i = 0 ; i <= 5 ; i++ )
    {
        printf ( "\nEnter name: " ) ;
        scanf ( "%s", names[i] ) ;
    }
}
```

The program doesn't work because when we are declaring the array it is containing garbage values. It would be definitely wrong to send these garbage values to **scanf( )** as the addresses where it should keep the strings received from the keyboard.

As a compromise solution we may first allocate space for each name using **malloc( )** and then store the address returned by **malloc( )** in the array of pointers to strings. This is shown in the following program:

```c
#include <stdio.h>
#include <conio.h>
#include <alloc.h>
```

```c
#include <string.h>

void main( )
{
    char *name[5] ;
    char str[20] ;
    int i ;

    clrscr( ) ;

    for ( i = 0 ; i < 5 ; i++ )
    {
        printf ( "Enter a String: " ) ;
        gets ( str ) ;
        name[i] = ( char * ) malloc ( strlen ( str ) + 1 ) ;
        strcpy ( name[i], str ) ;
    }

    printf ( "\nThe strings are:" ) ;

    for ( i = 0 ; i < 5 ; i++ )
        printf ( "\n%s", name[i] ) ;

    for ( i = 0 ; i < 5 ; i++ )
        free ( name[i] ) ;

    getch( ) ;
}
```

Output:

Enter a String: akshay
Enter a String: parag
Enter a String: srinivas
Enter a String: raman
Enter a String: gopal

The strings are:

akshay
parag
srinivas
raman
gopal

Pattern Matching

Today word processing is no longer restricted to simply creating a textual file and getting it printed out. Word processing applications that are used today perform a wide variety of jobs, the most challenging of them is to search for a given sequence of characters or a word. Finding the position where a string (usually called pattern string) first appears in the given string is called **Pattern Matching**.

In pattern matching we check whether or not a given pattern string **p** appears in a text string **s**. The easiest way to approach this problem is to construct an algorithm, which would take two parameters, a pattern string **p** and a search string **s** and return the position at which a match is found.

Many string-searching algorithms have been developed till date. However, the performance of these algorithms depends on the nature of the string and the pattern to be searched. We shall discuss an algorithm called Brute-Force algorithm in this chapter. The other algorithms like Knuth-Morris-Pratt algorithm, Boyer Moore or Rabin Karp algorithm are beyond the scope of this book.

Brute Force Algorithm

This is the simplest of all the algorithms used for pattern matching. According to this algorithm the string **s** in which the pattern string is to be searched is scanned character by character. Beginning from the 0th character of the string **s**, each character is compared with each and every character of the pattern string **p**. This process continues till either there is no mismatch or the pattern string **p** is not exhausted. If a match is found then the index of the character of **s** from which the comparison began is returned as the position where the pattern string **p** is found. However, if there is a mismatch then next character of the string **s** is considered and there onwards again it is compared with the characters of the pattern string **p**. How long would this process continue? The process ends either when a match is found or when the number of characters in the string **s** that remain to be scanned is less than the total number of characters in the pattern string **p**.

Let us now see a program that implements this algorithm.

```
#include <stdio.h>
#include <conio.h>
#include <string.h>

int xstrsearch ( char *, char * ) ;
void show( ) ;

void main( )
{
    char s1[ ] = "NagpurKicit" ;
    char s2[ ] = "Kicit" ;
    int pos ;

    clrscr( ) ;

    printf ( "String s1: %s\n", s1 ) ;

    printf ( "String s2: %s\n", s2 ) ;

    /* search if s2 is present in s1 */
    pos = xstrsearch ( s1, s2 ) ;
    printf ( "\nThe pattern string is found at position: %d\n", pos ) ;
```

```
    getch( ) ;
}

/* searches for the given pattern s2 into the string s1 */
int xstrsearch ( char * s1, char * s2 )
{
    int i, j, k ;
    int l1 = strlen ( s1 ) ;
    int l2 = strlen ( s2 ) ;

    for ( i = 0 ; i <= l1 - l2 ; i++ )
    {
        j = 0 ;
        k = i ;
        while ( ( s1[k] == s2[j] ) && ( j < l2 ) )
        {
            k++ ;
            j++ ;
        }
        if ( j == l2 )
            return i ;
    }
    return -1 ;
}
```

Output:

String s1: NagpurKicit
String s2: Kicit

The pattern string is found at position: 6

In this program, the function **xstrsearch( )** implements the logic of the Brute-Force algorithm.

The function **xstrsearch( )** receives two parameters. The first is the base address of the search string **s1** and the second is the address of the pattern string **s2**. Then we have obtained the length **l1** of the search string and length **l2** of the pattern string. The process of searching begins through a **for** loop. This loop gets terminated if a matching pattern is found or if the number of characters that remain to be scanned is less than the number of characters present in the pattern string **s2**. In other words the loop runs till the value of loop counter **i** (of **for** loop) is less than l1 – l2.

Through the **while** loop l2 number of characters of search string **s1** are compared with all characters of pattern string **s2**. The loop terminates if there is a mismatch or the pattern string is exhausted. If a match were found then at this stage the value of **j** would be equal to **l2**. Hence the index **i** would be returned as the position at which the pattern string is found. However, if string **s1** does not contain any matching string then –1 is returned.

In the program given above (l1 – l2 + 1) * l2 (i.e. 35) comparisons would be required to find a mismatch. Still, due to simplicity of algorithm, this algorithm is implemented very often for string searching applications.

Few More String Functions

Having gained knowledge about how strings are managed in C, let us now see a program that defines and uses a variety of elegant functions that work on strings.

```
#include <stdio.h>
#include <conio.h>
#include <string.h>
#include <alloc.h>

int search ( char *, char ) ;
int isequals ( char *, char * ) ;
int issmaller ( char *, char * ) ;
int isgreater ( char *, char * ) ;
char * getsub ( char *, int, int ) ;
```

```c
char * leftsub ( char *, int n ) ;
char * rightsub ( char *, int n ) ;
void upper ( char * ) ;
void lower ( char * ) ;
void reverse ( char * ) ;
int replace ( char *, char, char ) ;
int setat ( char *, char, int ) :

void main( )
{
    char s1[ ] = "Hello" ;
    char s2[ ] = "Hello World" ;
    char s3[ ] = "Four hundred thirty two" ;
    char ch, *s ;
    int i ;

    clrscr( ) ;

    printf ( "\nString s1: %s", s1 ) ;

    /* check for the first occurrence of a character */
    printf ( "\nEnter character to search: " ) ;
    scanf ( "%c", &ch ) ;
    i = search ( s1, ch ) ;
    if ( i != -1 )
        printf ( "The first occurrence of character %c is found at index no.
                %d\n", ch, i ) ;
    else
        printf ( "Character %c is not present in the list.\n", ch ) ;

    printf ( "\nString s2: %s", s2 ) ;

    /* compares two strings s1 and s2 */
    i = isequals ( s1, s2 ) ;
    if ( i == 1 )
        printf ( "\nStrings s1 and s2 are identical" ) ;
    else
        printf ( "\nStrings s1 and s2 are not identical") ;
```

```
i = issmaller ( s1, s2 ) ;
if ( i == 1 )
    printf ( "\nString s1 is smaller than string s2" ) ;
else
    printf ( "\nString s1 is not smaller than string s2" ) ;

i = isgreater ( s1, s2 ) ;
if ( i == 1 )
    printf ( "\nString s1 is greater than string s2\n" ) ;
else
    printf ( "\nString s1 is not greater than string s2\n" ) ;

/* extract characters at given position */
printf ( "\nString s3: %s", s3 ) ;
s = getsub ( s3, 5, 7 ) ;
printf ( "\nSub string: %s", s ) ;
free ( s ) ;

/* extract leftmost n characters */
s = leftsub ( s3, 4 ) ;
printf ( "\nLeft sub string: %s", s ) ;
free ( s ) ;

/* extract rightmost n characters */
s = rightsub ( s3, 3 ) ;
printf ( "\nRight sub string: %s", s ) ;
free ( s ) ;

/* convert string to uppercase */
upper ( s3 ) ;
printf ( "\nString in upper case: %s", s3 ) ;

/* convert string to lowercase */
lower ( s3 ) ;
printf ( "\nString in lower case: %s", s3 ) ;

/* reverse the given string */
reverse ( s3 ) ;
```

```
        printf ( "\nReversed string: %s", s3 ) ;

        /* replace first occurrence of one char with new one */
        replace ( s1, 'H' , 'M' ) ;
        printf ( "\nString s1: %s", s1 ) ;

        /* sets a char at a given position */
        i = setat ( s1, 'M', 3 ) ;
        if ( i )
            printf ( "\nString s1: %s", s1 ) ;
        else
            printf ( "\nInvalid position." ) ;

        getch( ) ;
}

/* check for the first occurrence of a character */
int search ( char *str, char ch )
{
    int i = 0 ;

    while ( *str )
    {
        if ( *str == ch )
            return i ;
        str++ ;
        i++ ;
    }
    return -1 ;
}

/* checks whether two strings are equal */
int isequals ( char *s, char *t )
{
    while ( *s || *t )
    {
        if ( *s != *t )
            return 0 ;
```

```
        s++ ;
        t++ ;
    }
    return 1 ;
}

/* checks whether first string is less than second */
int issmaller ( char *s, char *t )
{
    while ( *t )
    {
        if ( *s != *t )
        {
            if ( *s < *t )
                return 1 ;
            else
                return 0 ;
        }
        t++ ;
        s++ ;
    }
    return 0 ;
}

/* checks whether first string is greater than second */
int isgreater ( char *s, char *t )
{
    while ( *s )
    {
        if ( *s != *t )
        {
            if ( *s > *t )
                return 1 ;
            else
                return 0 ;
        }
        s++ ;
        t++ ;
```

```
    }
    return 0 ;
}

/* extracts the character at given position */
char * getsub ( char *str, int spos, int n )
{
    char *s = str + spos ;
    char *t = ( char * ) malloc ( n + 1 ) ;
    int i = 0 ;

    while ( i < n )
    {
        t[i] = *s ;
        s++ ;
        i++ ;
    }
    t[i] = '\0' ;

    return t ;
}

/* extracts leftmost n characters from the string */
char * leftsub ( char *s, int n )
{
    char *t = ( char * ) malloc ( n + 1 ) ;
    int i = 0 ;

    while ( i < n )
    {
        t[i] = *s ;
        s++ ;
        i++ ;
    }
    t[i] = '\0' ;

    return t ;
}
```

```
/* extracts rightmost n characters from the string */
char * rightsub ( char *str, int n )
{
    char *t = ( char * ) malloc ( n + 1 ) ;
    int l = strlen ( str ) ;
    char *s = str + ( l - n ) ;
    int i = 0 ;

    while ( i < n )
    {
        t[i] = *s ;
        s++ ;
        i++ ;
    }
    t[i] = '\0' ;

    return t ;
}

/* converts string to uppercase */
void upper ( char *s )
{
    while ( *s )
    {
        if ( *s >= 97 && *s <= 123 )
            *s -= 32 ;
        s++ ;
    }
}

/* converts string to lowercase */
void lower ( char *s )
{
    while ( *s )
    {
        if ( *s >= 65 && *s <= 91 )
            *s += 32 ;
        s++ ;
```

```
        }
}

/* reverses a string */
void reverse ( char *str )
{
        int l = strlen ( str ) ;
        char ch, *t = ( str + l - 1 ) ;
        int i = 0 ;

        while ( i < l / 2 )
        {
                ch = *str ;
                *str = *t ;
                *t = ch ;

                str++ ;
                t-- ;
                i++ ;
        }
}

/* replaces the first occurrence of char with new char */
int replace ( char *str, char oldch, char newch )
{
        while ( *str )
        {
                if ( *str == oldch )
                {
                        *str = newch ;
                        return 1 ;
                }
                str++ ;
        }
        return 0 ;
}

/* sets a char at a given position */
```

```
int setat ( char *str, char ch, int i )
{
    if ( i < 0 || strlen ( str ) < i )
        return 0 ;
    * ( str + i ) = ch ;
    return 1 ;
}
```

Output:

```
String s1: Hello
Enter character to search: i
The first occurrence of character I is found at index no. 2

String s2: Hello World
Strings s1 and s2 are not identical
String s1 is smaller than string s2
String s1 is not greater than string s2

String s3: Four hundred thirty two
Sub string: hundred
Left sub string: Four
Right sub string: two
String in upper case: FOUR HUNDRED THIRTY TWO
String in lower case: four hundred thirty two
Reversed string: owt ytriht derdnuh ruof
String s1: Mello
String s1: MelMo
```

In this program several functions are called from **main( )** that are used to perform different types of operations on the string.

The function **search( )** searches for the first occurrence of a character in the string. It receives two parameters as the base address of the string and the character to be search in the string. It returns the index position of the character where it was first found. If the character is not present in the string then it returns −1.

The functions **isequals( )**, **issmaller( )** and **isgreater( )** checks whether the first string is equal to, smaller than or greater than the second string respectively. Each of these functions receives as parameters the addresses of the first and the second string. In each of these functions a **while** loop is executed that compares two strings. The function **isequals( )** returns 1 if the two strings are identical, otherwise it returns 0. The other two functions also work on similar lines.

The functions **getsub( )**, **leftsub( )** and **rightsub( )** are used to extract specified number of characters from a specified position in a string. They differ only in the starting position from which the characters are to be extracted. The function **getsub( )** receives three parameters. The first is the base address of the string from which the characters are to be extracted. The second is the starting position of the string from where the extraction should begin and the third is the number of characters to be extracted. Both the functions **leftsub( )** and **rightsub( )** receive two parameters that represents the base address of the string and the number of characters to be extracted from the left side or right side of the string respectively. Note that none of these three functions make any changes to the contents of the string from which characters are being extracted. Instead they create a new string **t** by allocating new memory of sufficient size and returns **t** as a final result of the extraction operation.

The functions **upper( )** and **lower( )** are the conversion functions which convert the given string into upper case and lower case respectively. Both the functions receive one parameter—the base address of the string that is to be converted. In case of **upper( )** function all small case characters present in a string are converted to upper case by subtracting 32 from the **ASCII** value of the character. Similar steps are carried out in **lower( )** function, except that instead of subtracting 32 we have added 32 to the **ASCII** value of the character found in upper case.

The function **reverse( )** reverses the string. Here we have made **char** pointer **t** to point to the end of the string **str**. Then a **while** loop is executed exactly half number of times as the length of the string. In the first iteration of **while** loop the element of the starting position is swapped with the element in the last position. In the second iteration of the **while** loop the second element is swapped with the second last element, and so on.

The function **replace( )** replaces the first occurrence of a given character present in the string with the new character. This function receives three parameters. The first parameter is the base address of the string, the second is the old character **oldch** that is to be replaced and the third is the new character **newch** that is to be placed in the string. In the function a **while** loop is executed which searches for the first occurrence of the **oldch**, and if it is found then it copies the contents of **newch** in place of **oldch**.

The function **setat( )** sets a given character at a particular position. It receives three parameters—first is the base address of the string, second is the character that is to be set and the third is the position at which the character is to be set. The function returns 1 if the value is successfully set, otherwise its returns 0.

Exercise

[A] Fill in the blanks:

(a) A _____ is nothing but an array of characters.

(b) A string is terminated by a _____ character, which is written as _____.

(c) An array of pointers to strings stores _____ of the strings.

(d) The _____ function compares two strings to know if the two given strings are identical.

[B] Choose the correct alternative for the following:

(a) Pattern matching is the process to
   (1) To check if one string is present in the other string
   (2) To check if two strings are of same length
   (3) To check if two strings are identical
   (4) To compares two strings to know the count of similar characters.

(b) The length of a string
   (1) Is the total number of characters of the string excluding blank space
   (2) Is the total number of characters in the string
   (3) Is the total number of characters which are repeated in the string
   (4) None of the above

(c) To copy one string into another means
   (1) To add one string at the end of another string
   (2) To create new string
   (3) To copy the target string to the source string
   (4) To copy source string to the target string

(d) To concatenate a string means
   (1) To copy one string to another
   (2) To add one string at the end of the other
   (3) To add one string at the beginning of the other
   (4) To form a new string containing unique characters from both the strings

(e) The '\0' character indicates
   (1) Where the string begins
   (2) Where the string ends
   (3) The string is empty
   (4) The length of a string

[C] Answer the following:

(a) How many bytes would be occupied by the following array of pointers to strings? How many bytes would be required to store the same strings, if they are stored in a two-dimensional character array?

```
char *s[ ] = {
                "Hammer and tongue",
                "Tooth and nail",
                "Spit and polish"
                "You and C"
        };
```

(b) Can an array of pointers to strings be used to collect strings from the keyboard? If not, why not?

[D] Write programs for the following:

(a) Write a program using Brute-Force algorithm to search for a pattern string in a text where the text is scanned from right to left.

(b) Write a program to delete a sub-string of given string. For example if the string is 'What is life' and the sub-string to be deleted is 'life' then first check if sub-string 'life' is present in the string and if present then delete it.

(c) Write a program, which deletes all the blank spaces except a single space between two words. For example, if a string is "No   pains, No   gains", then the program should return a string as "No pains, No gains"

(d) Write a program, which counts number of words, lines and characters in a given text.

(e) Write a program to implement find and replace utility. The program should ask the user to enter two words, one to be searched and the other to replace the searched word.

(f) Write a program to count the occurrences of character 'e' in the following array of pointers to strings.

```
char *s[ ] = {
                "We will teach you how to... ",
                "Move a mountain",
                "Level a building",
                "Erase the past",
                "Make a million",
                "...all through C"
            };
```

CHAPTER
FOUR

Linked Lists
Stay Connected

U nited we stand, divided we fall! This has been proved
umpteen numbers of times. More united and connected we
are, more is the flexibility and scalability. Same is true with
linked lists. This is perhaps one data structure that has been used at
more number of places in computing than you can count. But,
beware, they are not simple. But the flexibility and performance
they offer is worth the pain of learning them.

For storing similar data in memory we can use either an array or a linked list. Arrays are simple to understand and elements of an array are easily accessible. But arrays suffer from the following limitations:

- Arrays have a fixed dimension. Once the size of an array is decided it cannot be increased or decreased during execution. For example, if we construct an array of **100** elements and then try to stuff more than **100** elements in it, our program may crash. On the other hand, if we use only **10** elements then the space for balance **90** elements goes waste.

- Array elements are always stored in contiguous memory locations. At times it might so happen that enough contiguous locations might not be available for the array that we are trying to create. Even though the total space requirement of the array can be met through a combination of non-contiguous blocks of memory, we would still not be allowed to create the array.

- Operations like insertion of a new element in an array or deletion of an existing element from the array are pretty tedious. This is because during insertion or deletion each element after the specified position has to be shifted one position to the right (in case of insertion) or one position to the left (in case of deletion). Refer Chapter 2 for more details.

Linked list overcomes all these disadvantages. A linked list can grow and shrink in size during its lifetime. In other words, there is no maximum size of a linked list. The second advantage of linked lists is that, as nodes (elements) are stored at different memory locations it hardly happens that we fall short of memory when required. The third advantage is that, unlike arrays, while inserting or deleting the nodes of the linked list, shifting of nodes is not required.

What Is A Linked List

Linked list is a very common data structure often used to store similar data in memory. While the elements of an array occupy contiguous memory locations, those of a linked list are not constrained to be stored in adjacent locations. The individual elements are stored "somewhere" in memory, rather like a family dispersed, but still bound together. The order of the elements is maintained by explicit links between them. For instance, the marks obtained by different students can be stored in a linked list as shown in Figure 4-1.

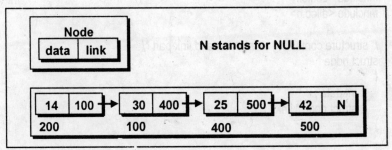

Figure 4-1. *Linked list.*

Observe that the linked list is a collection of elements called nodes, each of which stores two items of information—an element of the list and a link. A link is a pointer or an address that indicates explicitly the location of the node containing the successor of the list element. In Figure 4-1, the arrows represent the links. The **data** part of each node consists of the marks obtained by a student and the **link** part is a pointer to the next node. The **NULL** in the last node indicates that this is the last node in the list.

Operations On Linked List

There are several operations that we can think of performing on linked lists. The following program shows how to build a linked list by adding new nodes at the beginning, at the end or in the middle of the linked list. It also contains a function **display( )** which displays all the nodes present in the linked list and a function **delete( )** which can delete any node in the linked list. Go through the program carefully, a step at a time.

```
#include <stdio.h>
#include <conio.h>
#include <alloc.h>

/* structure containing a data part and link part */
struct node
{
    int data ;
    struct node * link ;
} ;

void append ( struct node **, int ) ;
void addatbeg ( struct node **, int ) ;
void addafter ( struct node *, int, int ) ;
void display ( struct node * ) ;
int count ( struct node * ) ;
void delete ( struct node **, int ) ;

void main( )
{
    struct node *p ;
    p = NULL ; /* empty linked list */

    printf ( "\nNo. of elements in the Linked List = %d", count ( p ) ) ;
    append ( &p, 14 ) ;
    append ( &p, 30 ) ;
    append ( &p, 25 ) ;
```

```
        append ( &p, 42 ) ;
        append ( &p, 17 ) ;
        clrscr( ) ;
        display ( p ) ;

        addatbeg ( &p, 999 ) ;
        addatbeg ( &p, 888 ) ;
        addatbeg ( &p, 777 ) ;

        display ( p ) ;

        addafter ( p, 7, 0 ) ;
        addafter ( p, 2, 1 ) ;
        addafter ( p, 5, 99 ) ;

        display ( p ) ;
        printf ( "\nNo. of elements in the Linked List = %d", count ( p ) ) ;

        delete ( &p, 99 ) ;
        delete ( &p, 1 ) ;
        delete ( &p, 10 ) ;

        display ( p ) ;
        printf ( "\nNo. of elements in the linked list = %d", count ( p ) ) ;
}

/* adds a node at the end of a linked list */
void append ( struct node **q, int num )
{
        struct node *temp, *r ;

        if ( *q == NULL )  /* if the list is empty, create first node */
        {
                temp = malloc ( sizeof ( struct node ) ) ;
                temp -> data = num ;
                temp -> link = NULL ;
                *q = temp ;
        }
```

```
    else
    {
        temp = *q ;

        /* go to last node */
        while ( temp -> link != NULL )
            temp = temp -> link ;

        /* add node at the end */
        r = malloc ( sizeof ( struct node ) ) ;
        r -> data = num ;
        r -> link = NULL ;
        temp -> link = r ;
    }
}

/* adds a new node at the beginning of the linked list */
void addatbeg ( struct node **q, int num )
{
    struct node *temp ;

    /* add new node */
    temp = malloc ( sizeof ( struct node ) ) ;

    temp -> data = num ;
    temp -> link = *q ;
    *q = temp ;
}

/* adds a new node after the specified number of nodes */
void addafter ( struct node *q, int loc, int num )
{
    struct node *temp, *r ;
    int i ;

    temp = q ;
    /* skip to desired portion */
    for ( i = 0 ; i < loc ; i++ )
```

```
        {
            temp = temp -> link ;

            /* if end of linked list is encountered */
            if ( temp == NULL )
            {
                printf ( "\nThere are less than %d elements in list", loc ) ;
                return ;
            }
        }

        /* insert new node */
        r = malloc ( sizeof ( struct node ) ) ;
        r -> data = num ;
        r -> link = temp -> link ;
        temp -> link = r ;
}

/* displays the contents of the linked list */
void display ( struct node *q )
{
    printf ( "\n" ) ;

    /* traverse the entire linked list */
    while ( q != NULL )
    {
        printf ( "%d ", q -> data ) ;
        q = q -> link ;
    }
}

/* counts the number of nodes present in the linked list */
int count ( struct node * q )
{
    int c = 0 ;

    /* traverse the entire linked list */
    while ( q != NULL )
```

```
        {
                q = q -> link ;
                c++ ;
        }

        return c ;
}

/* deletes the specified node from the linked list */
void delete ( struct node **q, int num )
{
        struct node *old, *temp ;

        temp = *q ;

        while ( temp != NULL )
        {
                if ( temp -> data == num )
                {
                        /* if node to be deleted is the first node in the linked list */
                        if ( temp == *q )
                                *q = temp > link ;

                        /* deletes the intermediate nodes in the linked list */
                        else
                                old -> link = temp -> link ;

                        /* free the memory occupied by the node */
                        free ( temp ) ;
                        return ;
                }

                /* traverse the linked list till the last node is reached */
                else
                {
                        old = temp ;  /* old points to the previous node */
                        temp = temp -> link ;  /* go to the next node */
                }
```

```
    }

    printf ( "\nElement %d not found", num ) ;
}
```

Output:

```
14 30 25 42 17
777 888 999 14 30 25 42 17
777 888 999 1 14 30 99 25 42 17 0
No. of elements in the Linked List = 11
Element 10 not found
777 888 999 14 30 25 42 17 0
No. of elements in the linked list = 9
```

To begin with we have defined a structure for a node. It contains a data part and a link part. The variable **p** has been declared as pointer to a node. We have used this pointer as pointer to the first node in the linked list. No matter how many nodes get added to the linked list, **p** would continue to pointer to the first node in the list. When no node has been added to the list, **p** has been set to **NULL** to indicate that the list is empty.

The **append( )** function has to deal with two situations:

(a) The node is being added to an empty list.

(b) The node is being added at the end of an existing list.

In the first case, the condition

```
if ( *q == NULL )
```

gets satisfied. Hence, space is allocated for the node using **malloc( )**. Data and the link part of this node are set up using the statements

```
temp -> data = num ;
```

temp -> link = NULL ;

Lastly, **p** is made to point to this node, since the first node has been added to the list and **p** must always point to the first node. Note that ***q** is nothing but equal to **p**.

In the other case, when the linked list is not empty, the condition

if (***q** == NULL)

would fail, since ***q** (i.e. **p** is non-**NULL**). Now **temp** is made to point to the first node in the list through the statement

temp = *q ;

Then using **temp** we have traversed through the entire linked list using the statements

while (temp -> link != NULL)
   temp = temp -> link ;

The position of the pointers before and after traversing the linked list is shown in Figure 4-2.

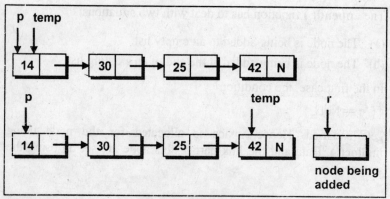

Figure 4-2. Working of **append( )** function.

Each time through the loop the statement **temp = temp -> link** makes **temp** point to the next node in the list. When **temp** reaches the last node the condition **temp -> link != NULL** would fail. Once outside the loop we allocate space for the new node through the statement

r = malloc (sizeof (struct node)) ;

Once the space has been allocated for the new node its **data** part is stuffed with **num** and the **link** part with **NULL**. Note that this node is now going to be the last Node in the list.

All that now remains to be done is connecting the previous last node with the new last node. The previous last node is being pointed to by **temp** and the new last node is being pointed to by **r**. They are connected through the statement

temp -> link = r ;

this link gets established.

There is often a confusion as to how the statement **temp = temp -> link** makes **temp** point to the next node in the list. Let us understand this with the help of an example. Suppose in a linked list containing 4 nodes, **temp** is pointing at the first node. This is shown in Figure 4-3.

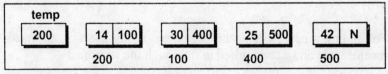

Figure 4-3. *Connection of nodes.*

Instead of showing the links to the next node we have shown the addresses of the next node in the link part of each node.

When we execute the statement

temp = temp -> link ;

the right hand side yields **100**. This address is now stored in **temp**. As a result, **temp** starts pointing to the node present at address **100**. In effect the statement has shifted **temp** so that it has started pointing to the next node in the list.

Let us now understand the **addatbeg( )** function. Suppose there are already 5 nodes in the list and we wish to add a new node at the beginning of this existing linked list. This situation is shown in Figure 4-4.

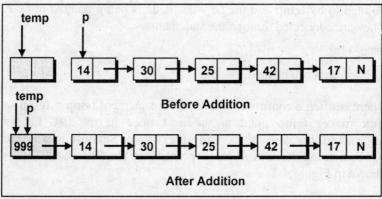

Figure 4-4. *Working of **addatbeg( )** function.*

For adding a new node at the beginning, firstly space is allocated for this node and data is stored in it through the statement

temp -> data = num ;

Now we need to make the **link** part of this node point to the existing first node. This has been achieved through the statement

temp -> link = *q ;

Lastly, this new node must be made the first node in the list. This has been attained through the statement

`*q = temp ;`

The **addafter( )** function permits us to add a new node after a specified number of node in the linked list.

To begin with, through a loop we skip the desired number of nodes after which a new node is to be added. Suppose we wish to add a new node containing data as **99** after the 3rd node in the list. The position of pointers once the control reaches outside the **for** loop is shown in Figure 4-5(a). Now space is allocated for the node to be inserted and **99** is stored in the data part of it.

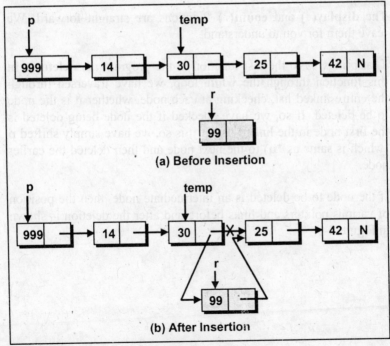

(a) Before Insertion

(b) After Insertion

Figure 4-5. Working of **addafter( )** function.

All that remains to be done is readjustment of links such that **99** goes in between **30** and **25**. This is achieved through the statements

```
r -> link = temp -> link ;
temp -> link = r ;
```

The first statement makes link part of node containing **99** to point to the node containing **25**. The second statement ensures that the link part of node containing **30** points to the node containing **99**. On execution of the second statement the earlier link between **30** and **25** is severed. So now **30** no longer points to **25**, it points to **99**.

The **display( )** and **count( )** functions are straight forward. We leave them for you to understand.

That brings us to the last function in the program i.e. **delete( )**. In this function through the **while** loop, we have traversed through the entire linked list, checking at each node, whether it is the node to be deleted. If so, we have checked if the node being deleted is the first node in the linked list. If it is so, we have simply shifted **p** (which is same as ***q**) to the next node and then deleted the earlier node.

If the node to be deleted is an intermediate node, then the position of various pointers and links before and after the deletion is shown in Figure 4-6.

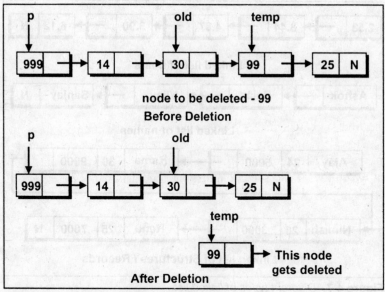

Figure 4-6. *Working of delete( ) function.*

A common and a wrong impression that beginners carry is that a linked list is used only for storing integers. However, a linked list can virtually be used for storing any similar data. For example, there can exist a linked list of **float**s, a linked list of names, or even a linked list of records, where each record contains name, age and salary of an employee. These linked lists are shown in Figure 4-7.

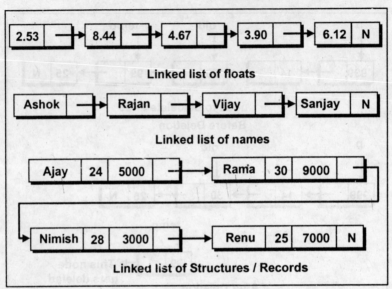

Figure 4-7. *Different types of linked list.*

Ascending Order Linked List

Now that we have understood how a linked list can be maintained how about ensuring that every element added to the linked list gets inserted at such a place that the linked list is always maintained in ascending order? Here it is...

```
#include <stdio.h>
#include <conio.h>
#include <alloc.h>

/* structure containing a data part and link part */
struct node
{
    int data ;
```

```
        struct node *link ;
} ;

void add ( struct node **, int ) ;
void display ( struct node * ) ;
int count ( struct node * ) ;

void main( )
{
        struct node *p ;
        p = NULL ; /* empty linked list */

        add ( &p, 5 ) ;
        add ( &p, 1 ) ;
        add ( &p, 6 ) ;
        add ( &p, 4 ) ;
        add ( &p, 7 ) ;

        display ( p ) ;
        printf ( "\nNo. of elements in Linked List = %d", count ( p ) ) ;
}

/* adds node to an ascending order linked list */
void add ( struct node **q, int num )
{
        struct node *r, *temp = *q ;

        r = malloc ( sizeof ( struct node ) ) ;
        r -> data = num ;

        /* if list is empty or if new node is to be inserted before the first node */
        if ( *q == NULL || ( *q ) -> data > num )
        {
                *q = r ;
                ( *q ) -> link = temp ;
        }
        else
        {
```

```
        /* traverse the entire linked list to search the position to insert the
            new node */
        while ( temp != NULL )
        {
            if ( temp -> data <= num && ( temp -> link -> data > num ||
                                        temp -> link == NULL ))
            {
                r -> link = temp -> link ;
                temp -> link = r ;
                return ;
            }
            temp = temp -> link ;   /* go to the next node */
        }
    }
}

/* displays the contents of the linked list */
void display ( struct node *q )
{
    printf ( "\n" ) ;

    /* traverse the entire linked list */
    while ( q != NULL )
    {
        printf ( "%d ", q -> data ) ;
        q = q -> link ;
    }
}

/* counts the number of nodes present in the linked list */
int count ( struct node *q )
{
    int c = 0 ;

    /* traverse the entire linked list */
    while ( q != NULL )
    {
        q = q -> link ;
```

```
        c++ ;
    }

    return c ;
}
```

Output:

```
1 4 5 6 7
No. of elements in Linked List = 5
```

Let us now try to understand the function **add( )** that is responsible for maintaining the linked list in ascending order. It takes two parameters. The first parameter **q** is of the type **struct node **** which collects the address of the pointer **p**. The pointer **p** holds either the address of the first node of the linked list, or a **NULL** value in case of empty linked list. The other parameter **num** holds the data that is to be inserted in the list.

Initially memory is allocated for the new node, its address is stored in pointer **r** and using **r** the value of **num** is stored in its **data** part.

Now we need to establish the links. There are four different places in the list where the new node can be added depending upon which value it contains, they are as follows:

(a) To the empty list
(b) Before the first node in the list
(c) At the end of an existing list
(d) In the middle of the list

All these four cases are discussed below.

Case (a) and (b):

A condition is checked through the statement

if (*q == NULL || (*q) -> data > num)

this is done to check whether the list is empty or whether the new node to be added is the first node. In either case using **q** the pointer **p** is made to point to the new node (as **q** holds the address of **p**). This is done through the statement

*q = r ;

The value of **temp** is stored in the **link** part of the new node. Pointer **temp** holds a value **NULL** if the list is empty and holds the address of the first node if the new node that is to be added is added before the first node.

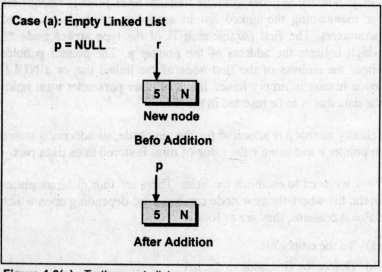

Figure 4-8(a). *To the empty list.*

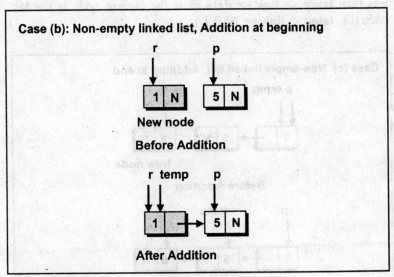

Figure 4-8(b). *Before the first node in the list.*

Case (c) and (d):

If both the conditions are false then we need to search the position where the new node must be inserted such that the list is maintained in the ascending order. For this, we need to traverse the list and this is done through a **while** loop.

Initially the pointer **temp** points to the first node and each time through the **while** loop it is made to point to the next node in the list. This is done through the statement

temp = temp -> link ;

Inside the **while** loop, **num** is compared with the **data** part of the current node (node pointed to by **temp**) and the **data** part of the next node (node pointed to by **temp -> link**). The new node should be inserted if **temp -> data** is smaller than or equal to the **num** and less than **temp -> link -> data** or if the current node is the last node (i.e. **temp -> link == NULL**).

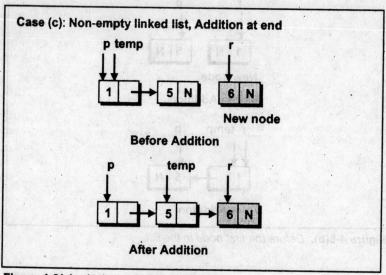

Figure 4-8(c). *At the end of an existing list.*

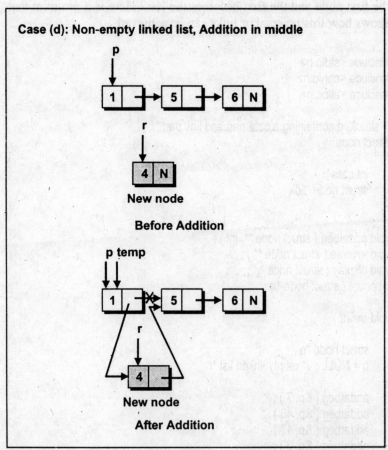

Figure 4-8(d). *In the middle of the list.*

Reversing The Links

Having had a feel of linked list let us explore what further operations can be performed on a linked list. How about reversing the links in the existing linked list such that the last node becomes the first node and the first becomes the last? Here is a program that shows how this reversal of links can be achieved.

```c
#include <stdio.h>
#include <conio.h>
#include <alloc.h>

/* structure containing a data part and link part */
struct node
{
    int data ;
    struct node *link ;
} ;

void addatbeg ( struct node **, int ) ;
void reverse ( struct node ** ) ;
void display ( struct node * ) ;
int count ( struct node * ) ;

void main( )
{
    struct node *p ;
    p = NULL ; /* empty linked list */

    addatbeg ( &p, 7 ) ;
    addatbeg ( &p, 43 ) ;
    addatbeg ( &p, 17 ) ;
    addatbeg ( &p, 3 ) ;
    addatbeg ( &p, 23 ) ;
    addatbeg ( &p, 5 ) ;

    clrscr( ) ;
    display ( p ) ;
    printf ( "\nNo. of elements in the linked list = %d", count ( p ) ) ;

    reverse ( &p ) ;
    display ( p ) ;
```

```
        printf ( "\nNo. of elements in the linked list = %d", count ( p ) ) ;
}

/* adds a new node at the beginning of the linked list */
void addatbeg ( struct node **q, int num )
{
        struct node *temp ;

        /* add new node */
        temp = malloc ( sizeof ( struct node ) ) ;
        temp -> data = num ;
        temp -> link = *q ;
        *q = temp ;
}

void reverse ( struct node **x )
{
        struct node *q, *r, *s ;

        q = *x ;
        r = NULL ;

        /* traverse the entire linked list */
        while ( q != NULL )
        {
            s = r ;
            r = q ;
            q = q -> link ;
            r -> link = s ;
        }

        *x = r ;
}

/* displays the contents of the linked list */
void display ( struct node *q )
{
        printf ( "\n" ) ;
```

```
        /* traverse the entire linked list */
        while ( q != NULL )
        {
            printf ( "%d ", q -> data )
            q = q -> link ;
        }
    }

/* counts the number of nodes present in the linked list */
int count ( struct node * q )
{
    int c = 0 ;

    /* traverse the entire linked list */
    while ( q != NULL )
    {
        q = q -> link ;
        c++ ;
    }

    return c .
}
```

Output:

```
5 23 3 17 43 7
No. of elements in the linked list = 6
7 43 17 3 23 5
No. of elements in the linked list = 6
```

The function **reverse( )** receives the parameter **struct node ** x**, which is the address of the pointer to the first node of the linked list. To traverse the linked list a variable **q** of the type **struct node * ** is required. We have initialized **q** with the value of **x**. So **q** also starts pointing to the first node.

To begin with, we need to store the **NULL** value in the **link** part of the first node, which is done through the statements

```
s = r ;
r = q ;
r -> link = s ;
```

r which is of the type **struct node *** is initialized to a **NULL** value. Since **r** contains **NULL**, **s** would also contain **NULL**. Now **r** is assigned **q** so that **r** also starts pointing to the first node. Finally **r -> link** is assigned **s** so that **r -> link** becomes **NULL**, which is nothing but the **link** part of the first node.

But if we store a **NULL** value in the link part of the first node then the address of the second node is lost. Hence before storing a **NULL** value in the **link** part of the first node, **q** is made to point to the second node through the statement

```
q = q -> link ;
```

During the second iteration of the **while** loop, **r** points to the first node and **q** points to the second node. Now the **link** part of the second node should point to the first node, which is done through the same statements

```
s = r ;
r = q ;
r -> link = s ;
```

Since **r** points to the first node, **s** would also point to the first node. Now **r** is assigned the value of **q** so that **r** now starts pointing to the second node. Finally **r -> link** is assigned with **s** so that **r -> link** starts pointing to the first node. But if we store the value of **s** in the **link** part of second node, then the address of the third node would be lost. Hence before storing the value of **s** in **r -> link**, **q** is made to point to the third node through the statement q = q -> link ;

While traversing the nodes through the **while** loop each time **q** starts pointing to the next node in the list and **r** starts pointing to the previous node. As a result, when the **while** loop ends all the links has been adjusted properly such that last node becomes the first node and first node becomes the last node.

Finally outside the **while** loop the statement $*x = r$, is executed. This ensures that the pointer **p** now starts pointing to the node, which is the last node of the original list. This is shown in Figure 4-9.

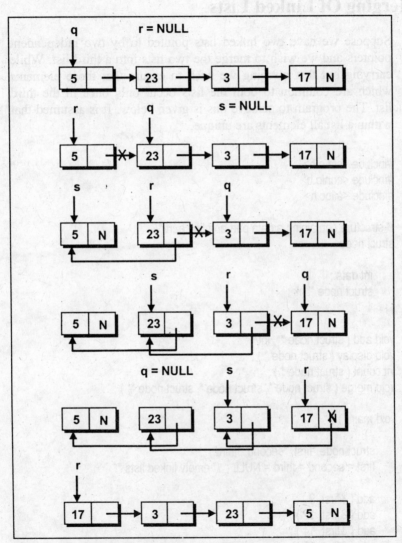

Figure 4-9. *Reversing the links.*

Merging Of Linked Lists

Suppose we have two linked lists pointed to by two independent pointers and we wish to merge the two lists into a third list. While carrying out this merging we wish to ensure that those elements which are common to both the lists occur only once in the third list. The program to achieve this is given below. It is assumed that within a list all elements are unique.

```c
#include <stdio.h>
#include <conio.h>
#include <alloc.h>

/* structure containing a data part and link part */
struct node
{
    int data ;
    struct node *link ;
} ;

void add ( struct node **, int ) ;
void display ( struct node * ) ;
int count ( struct node * ) ;
void merge ( struct node *, struct node *, struct node ** ) ;

void main( )
{
    struct node *first, *second, *third ;
    first = second = third = NULL ;  /* empty linked lists */

    add ( &first, 9 ) ;
    add ( &first, 12 ) ;
    add ( &first, 14 ) ;
    add ( &first, 17 ) ;
    add ( &first, 35 ) ;
    add ( &first, 61 ) ;
    add ( &first, 78 ) ;
```

```
        clrscr( ) ;
        printf ( "First linked list: " ) ;
        display ( first ) ;
        printf ( "\nNo. of elements in Linked List: %d", count ( first ) ) ;

        add ( &second, 12 ) ;
        add ( &second, 17 ) ;
        add ( &second, 24 ) ;
        add ( &second, 36 ) ;
        add ( &second, 59 ) ;
        add ( &second, 64 ) ;
        add ( &second, 87 ) ;

        printf ( "\n\nSecond linked list: " ) ;
        display ( second ) ;
        printf ( "\nNo. of elements in Linked List: %d", count ( second ) ) ;

        merge ( first, second, &third ) ;

        printf ( "\n\nThe merged list: " ) ;
        display ( third ) ;
        printf ( "\nNo. of elements in Linked List: %d", count ( third ) ) ;
}

/* adds node to an ascending order linked list */
void add ( struct node **q, int num )
{
        struct node *r, *temp = *q ;

        r = malloc ( sizeof ( struct node ) ) ;
        r -> data = num ;

        /* if list is empty or if new node is to be inserted before the first node */
        if ( *q == NULL || ( *q ) -> data > num )
        {
                *q = r ;
                ( *q ) -> link = temp ;
        }
```

```c
else
{
    /* traverse the entire linked list to search the position to insert the
       new node */
    while ( temp != NULL )
    {
        if ( temp -> data < num && ( temp -> link -> data > num ||
                                     temp -> link == NULL ))
        {
            r -> link = temp -> link ;
            temp -> link = r ;
            return ;
        }
        temp = temp -> link ;  /*go to next node */
    }

    r -> link = NULL ;
    temp -> link = r ;
}
}

/* displays the contents of the linked list */
void display ( struct node *q )
{
    printf ( "\n" ) ;

    /* traverse the entire linked list */
    while ( q != NULL )
    {
        printf ( "%d ", q -> data ) ;
        q = q -> link ;
    }
}

/* counts the number of nodes present in the linked list */
int count ( struct node * q )
{
    int c = 0 ;
```

```
    /* traverse the entire linked list */
    while ( q != NULL )
    {
        q = q -> link ;
        c++ ;
    }

    return c ;
}

/* merges the two linked lists, restricting the common elements to occur only
   once in the final list */
void merge ( struct node *p, struct node *q, struct node **s )
{
    struct node *z ;

    z = NULL ;

    /* if both lists are empty */
    if ( p == NULL && q == NULL )
        return ;

    /* traverse both linked lists till the end. If end of any one list is reached
       loop is terminated */
    while ( p != NULL && q != NULL )
    {
        /* if node being added in the first node */
        if ( *s == NULL )
        {
            *s = malloc ( sizeof ( struct node ) ) ;
            z = *s ;
        }
        else
        {
            z -> link = malloc ( sizeof ( struct node ) ) ;
            z = z -> link ;
        }
```

```
        if ( p -> data < q -> data )
        {
            z -> data = p -> data ;
            p = p -> link ;
        }
        else
        {
            if ( q -> data < p -> data )
            {
                z -> data = q -> data ;
                q = q -> link ;
            }
            else
            {
                if ( p -> data == q -> data )
                {
                    z -> data = q -> data ;
                    p = p -> link ;
                    q = q -> link ;
                }
            }
        }
    }

    /* if end of first list has not been reached */
    while ( p != NULL )
    {
        z -> link = malloc ( sizeof ( struct node ) ) ;
        z = z -> link ;
        z -> data = p -> data ;
        p = p -> link ;
    }

    /* if end of second list has not been reached */
    while ( q != NULL )
    {
        z -> link = malloc ( sizeof ( struct node ) ) ;
        z = z -> link ;
```

```
        z -> data = q -> data ;
        q = q -> link ;
    }

    z -> link = NULL ;
}
```

Output:

First linked list:
9 12 14 17 35 61 79
No. of elements in Linked List: 7

Second linked list:
12 17 24 36 59 64 87
No. of elements in Linked List: 7

The merged list:
9 12 14 17 24 35 36 59 61 64 79 87
No. of elements in Linked List: 12

In this program, as usual, we begin by building a structure to accommodate the data and link, which together represent a node. We nave used pointers **first**, **second** and **third** to point to the three linked lists. Since to begin with all the three linked lists are empty, these pointers contain **NULL**. Next, by calling the function **add( )** repeatedly two linked lists are built, one being pointed to by **first** and other by the pointer **second**. Finally, the **merge( )** function is called to merge the two lists into one. This merged list is pointed to by the pointer **third**.

While merging the two lists it is assumed that the lists themselves are in ascending order. While building the two lists the **add( )** function makes sure that when a node is added the elements in the lists are maintained in ascending order.

The function **merge( )** receives three parameters. The first two parameters **p** and **q** are of the type **struct node *** which point to the two lists that are to be merged. The third parameter **s** is of the type **struct node **** which holds the address of pointer **third** which is a pointer to the resultant merged list. Before calling **merge( ) third** contains a **NULL** value.

First of all we check if both the lists that are to be merged, are empty or not. If the lists are empty then the control simply returns from the function. Otherwise, a loop is executed to traverse the lists, that are pointed to by **p** and **q**. If end of any of the list is reached then the loop is terminated.

To begin with, a **NULL** value is stored in **z**, which is going to point to the resultant merged list. Inside the **while** loop, we check the special case of adding the first node to the merged list pointed to by **z**. If the node being added is the first node then **z** is made to point to the first node of the merged list through the statement

z = *s

Next, the data from both the lists are compared and whichever is found to be smaller is stored in the **data** part of the first node of the merged list. The pointers that point to the merged list and to the list from where we copied the data are incremented appropriately.

During the next iteration of the **while** loop the **if** condition for first node fails and we reach the **else** block. Here we allocate the memory for the new node and its address is stored in **z -> link**. Then **z** is made to point to this node, through the statement

z = z -> link ;

While comparing the data, if we find that the data of both the lists are equal then the data is added only once to the merged list and pointers of all the three lists are incremented, this is done through the statements

```
if ( p -> data == q -> data )
{
    z -> data = q -> data ;
    p = p -> link ;
    q = q -> link ;
}
```

The procedure of comparing, adding the data to the merged list and incrementing the pointer of the merged list and the list from where the data is added is repeated till any of the list ends.

If we reach end of first and/or second list the **while** loop terminates. If we have reached end only one list then the remaining elements of the other list are simply dumped in the merged list as they are already in the ascending order. The working of the merge function is shown in Figure 4-10.

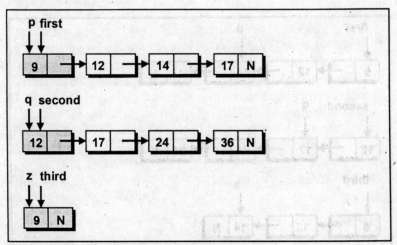

Figure 4-10. *Merging of two linked lists.*

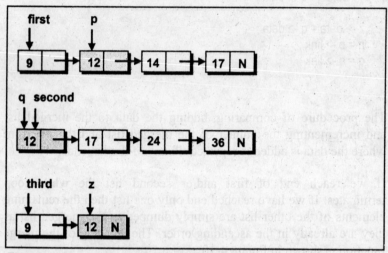

Figure 4-10. *Merging two linked lists (Contd.).*

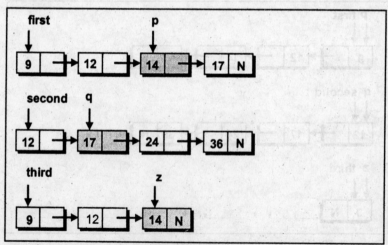

Figure 4-10. *Merging two linked lists (Contd.).*

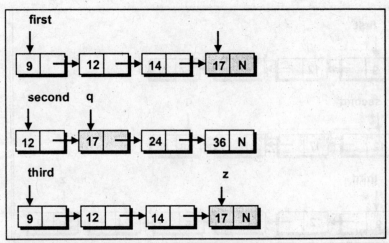

Figure 4-10. *Merging two linked lists (Contd.).*

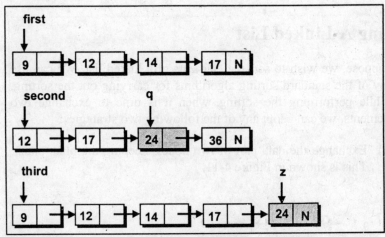

Figure 4-10. *Merging two linked lists (Contd.).*

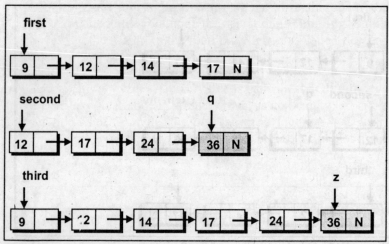

Figure 4-10. *Merging two lists (Contd.).*

Sorting A Linked List

Suppose, we wish to sort the elements of a linked list. We can use any of the standard sorting algorithms for carrying out the sorting. While performing the sorting, when it is time to exchange two elements, we can adopt any of the following two strategies:

(a) Exchange the data part of two nodes, keeping the links intact. This is shown in Figure 4-11.

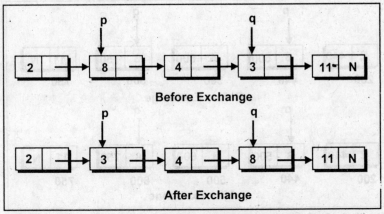

Figure 4-11. *Sorting the list by exchanging the data part of the node.*

Suppose the elements **8** and **3** are to be exchanged. While carrying out the exchange only **8** gets exchanged with **3**. The link part of node being pointed to by **p** and the link part of node being pointed to by **q** remains unchanged. To make this absolutely clear take a look at Figure 4-12. In this instead of showing links we have shown the actual addresses of nodes. Referring to Figure 4-12, you can observe that after the exchange of **8** and **3** the addresses stored in nodes pointed to by **p** and **q** (i.e. addresses **500** and **750**) have remained intact.

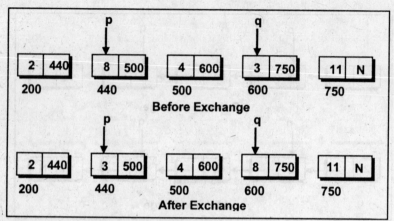

Figure 4-12. *Sorting by keeping the links intact.*

(b) Keep the data in the nodes intact. Simply readjust the links such that effectively the order of the nodes changes. This is shown in Figure 4-13.

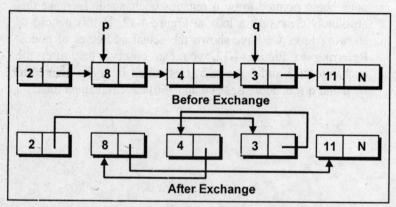

Figure 4-13. *Adjustment of links for sorting the list.*

Instead of links if you look at actual physical addresses stored in the link part you may get a clearer idea about how the links are being readjusted. This is shown in Figure 4-14.

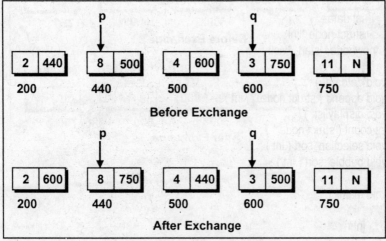

Figure 4-14. *Adjustment of links for sorting the list.*

Of the two methods suggested above, the first one is easier to implement, but the second one is likely to be more efficient. This is because if the data part contains an employee record (containing name, age, salary etc.) then to carry out exchange of this record would be inefficient time wise as well as space wise. Instead if we adopt second method, since we are readjusting only the links this would involve only pointers and not the bulky structures representing records.

In this chapter we would implement both the methods to sort a linked list. Here is a program for the first one.

```
#include <stdio.h>
#include <conio.h>
```

```
#include <alloc.h>

/* structure containing a data part and link part */
struct node
{
    int data ;
    struct node *link ;
} *newnode, *start, *visit ;

void getdata( ) ;
void append ( struct node **, int ) ;
void displaylist( ) ;
int count ( struct node * ) ;
void selection_sort ( int ) ;
void bubble_sort ( int ) ;

void main( )
{
    int n ;

    getdata( ) ;

    printf ( "\n\nLinked list Before Sorting: " ) ;
    displaylist( ) ;

    n = count ( start ) ;

    selection_sort ( n ) ;
    printf ( "\nLinked list After Selection Sorting: " ) ;
    displaylist( ) ;
    getch( ) ;

    getdata( ) ;
    printf ( "\n\nLinked list Before Sorting: " ) ;
    displaylist( ) ;

    n = count ( start ) ;
```

```
        bubble_sort ( n ) ;
        printf ( "\nLinked list After Bubble Sorting: " ) ;
        displaylist( ) ;
        getch( ) ;
}

void getdata( )
{
        int val, n ;
        char ch ;
        struct node *new ;

        clrscr( ) ;

        new = NULL ;
        do
        {
                printf ( "\nEnter a value: " ) ;
                scanf ( "%d", &val ) ;

                append ( &new, val ) ;

                printf ( "Any More Nodes (Y/N): " ) ;
                ch = getche( ) ;
        } while ( ch == 'y' || ch == 'Y' ) ;

        start = new ;
}

/* adds a node at the end of a linked list */
void append ( struct node **q, int num )
{
        struct node *temp ;
        temp = *q ;

        if ( *q == NULL )  /* if the list is empty, create first node */
        {
                *q = malloc ( sizeof ( struct node ) ) ;
```

```
            temp = *q ;
        }
        else
        {
            /* go to last node */
            while ( temp -> link != NULL )
                temp = temp -> link ;

            /* add node at the end */
            temp -> link = malloc ( sizeof ( struct node ) ) ;
            temp = temp -> link ;
        }

        /* assign data to the last node */
        temp -> data = num ;
        temp -> link = NULL ;
}

/* displays the contents of the linked list */
void displaylist( )
{
    visit = start ;

    /* traverse the entire linked list */
    while ( visit != NULL )
    {
        printf ( "%d ", visit -> data ) ;
        visit = visit -> link ;
    }
}

/* counts the number of nodes present in the linked list */
int count ( struct node * q )
{
    int c = 0 ;

    /* traverse the entire linked list */
    while ( q != NULL )
```

```
    {
        q = q -> link ;
        c++ ;
    }

    return c ;
}

void selection_sort ( int n )
{
    int i, j, k, temp ;
    struct node *p, *q ;

    p = start ;
    for ( i = 0 ; i < n - 1 ; i++ )
    {
        q = p -> link ;

        for ( j = i + 1 ; j < n ; j++ )
        {
            if ( p -> data > q -> data )
            {
                temp = p -> data ;
                p -> data = q -> data ;
                q -> data = temp ;
            }
            q = q > link ;
        }
        p = p -> link ;
    }
}

void bubble_sort ( int n )
{
    int i, j, k, temp ;
    struct node *p, *q ;

    k = n ;
```

```
for ( i = 0 ; i < n - 1 ; i++, k-- )
{
    p = start ;
    q = p -> link ;

    for ( j = 1 ; j < k ; j++ )
    {
        if ( p -> data > q -> data )
        {
            temp = p -> data ;
            p -> data = q -> data ;
            q -> data = temp ;
        }
        p = p -> link ;
        q = q -> link ;
    }
}
}
```

Output:

```
Enter a value: 29
Any More Nodes (Y/N): Y
Enter a value: 7
Any More Nodes (Y/N): Y
Enter a value: 99
Any More Nodes (Y/N): Y
Enter a value: 3
Any More Nodes (Y/N): N

Linked List Before Sorting: 29 7 99 3
Linked List After Selection Sorting: 3 7 29 99

Enter a value: 37
Any More Nodes (Y/N): Y
Enter a value: 49
Any More Nodes (Y/N): Y
```

Enter a value: 13
Any More Nodes (Y/N): Y
Enter a value: 2
Any More Nodes (Y/N): N

Linked List Before Sorting: 37 49 13 2
Linked List After Bubble Sorting: 2 13 37 49

In the above program, we have added nodes to the linked list using **getdata( )**, which in turn calls **append( )**. After accepting the data, we have sorted the linked list using **selection_sort( )** function. The same procedure of receiving data, building a linked list and sorting is repeated again; the only difference being, this time we have used the **bubble_sort( )** function to carry out the sorting.

In the bubble sort logic each node's value is compared with other nodes in turn. On comparison if the pair of numbers being compared are not found to be in order then the contents of the two nodes being compared are exchanged.

In the selection sort logic instead of comparing a node's value with the values of all other nodes, the values of successive pairs of nodes are compared. Once again if the pair of numbers being compared are not found in order then the numbers are exchanged.

Both the functions suffer from the limitation that they swap the data part of the node. Consider a case where we have to sort records. In this case, to perform one exchange of records, we need to copy the entire record thrice using the following statements:

```
struct emp
{
    char name ;
    int age ;
    float salary ;
} temp ;
```

```
struct empl
{
    char name ;
    int age ;
    float salary ;
    struct empl *link ;
} *p, *q ;

strcpy ( temp.name, p -> name ) ;
strcpy ( p -> name, q -> name ) ;
strcpy ( q -> name, temp.name )

temp.age = p -> age ;
p -> age = q -> age ;
q -> age = temp.age ;

temp.sal = p -> sal ;
p -> sal = q -> sal ;
q -> sal = temp.sal ;
```

Thus a great deal of time would be lost in swapping the records.

This limitation can be overcome if we readjust links instead of exchanging data. This has been achieved through the following program.

```
#include <stdio.h>
#include <conio.h>
#include <alloc.h>

/* structure containing a data part and link part */
struct node
{
    int data ;
    struct node *link ;
} *start, *visit ;
```

```
void getdata( ) ;
void append ( struct node **q, int num ) ;
vcid displaylist( ) ;
void selection_sort( ) ;
void bubble_sort( ) ;

void main( )
{
    getdata( ) ;
    printf ( "\n\nLinked List Before Sorting:\n" ) ;
    displaylist( ) ;

    selection_sort( ) ;
    printf ( "\nLinked List After Selection Sorting:\n" ) ;
    displaylist( ) ;
    getch( ) ;

    getdata( ) ;
    printf ( "\n\nLinked List Before Sorting:\n" ) ;
    displaylist( ) ;

    bubble_sort( ) ;
    printf ( "\nLinked List After Bubble Sorting:\n" ) ;
    displaylist( ) ;
    getch( ) ;
}

void getdata( )
{
    int val, n ;
    char ch ;
    struct node *newnode;

    newnode = NULL ;
    do
    {
        printf ( "\nEnter a value: " ) ,
        scanf ( "%d", &val ) ;
```

```
            append ( &newnode, val ) ;

            printf ( "Any More Nodes (Y/N): " ) ;
            ch = getche( ) ;
        } while ( ch == 'y' || ch == 'Y' ) ;

        start = newnode ;
}

/* adds a node at the end of a linked list */
void append ( struct node **q, int num )
{
    struct node *temp ;
    temp = *q ;

    if ( *q == NULL )  /* if the list is empty, create first node */
    {
        *q = malloc ( sizeof ( struct node ) ) ;
        temp = *q ;
    }
    else
    {
        /* go to last node */
        while ( temp -> link != NULL )
        temp = temp -> link ;

        /* add node at the end */
        temp -> link = malloc ( sizeof ( struct node ) ) ;
        temp = temp -> link ;
    }

    /* assign data to the last node */
    temp -> data = num ;
    temp -> link = NULL ;
}

/* displays the contents of the linked list */
void displaylist( )
```

```
{
    visit = start ;

    /* traverse the entire linked list */
    while ( visit != NULL )
    {
        printf ( "%d ", visit -> data ) ;
        visit = visit -> link ;
    }
}

void selection_sort( )
{
    struct node *p, *q, *r, *s, *temp ;

    p = r = start ;
    while ( p -> link != NULL )
    {
        s = q = p -> link ;
        while ( q != NULL )
        {
            if ( p -> data > q -> data )
            {
                if ( p -> link == q )  /* Adjacent Nodes */
                {
                    if ( p == start )
                    {
                        p -> link = q -> link ;
                        q -> link = p ;

                        temp = p ;
                        p = q ;
                        q = temp ;

                        start = p ;
                        r = p ;
                        s = q ;
                        q = q -> link ;
```

```
        }
        else
        {
                p -> link = q -> link ;
                q -> link = p ;
                r -> link = q ;

                temp = p ;
                p = q ;
                q = temp ;

                s = q ;
                q = q -> link ;
        }
}
else
{
        if ( p == start )
        {
                temp = q -> link ;
                q -> link = p -> link ;
                p -> link = temp ;

                s -> link = p ;

                temp = p ;
                p = q ;
                q = temp ;

                s = q ;
                q = q -> link ;
                start = p ;
        }
        else
        {
                temp = q -> link ;
                q -> link = p -> link ;
                p -> link = temp ;
```

```
                    r -> link = q ;
                    s -> link = p ;

                    temp = p ;
                    p = q ;
                    q = temp ;

                    s = q ;
                    q = q -> link ;
                }
            }
        }
        else
        {
            s = q ;
            q = q -> link ;
        }
    }
    r = p ;
    p = p -> link ;
    }
}

void bubble_sort( )
{
    struct node *p, *q, *r, *s, *temp ;
    s = NULL ;

    /* r precedes p and s points to the node up to which comparisons are to
       be made */
    while ( s != start -> link )
    {
        r = p = start ;
        q = p -> link ;

        while ( p != s )
        {
            if ( p -> data > q -> data )
```

```
            {
                if ( p == start )
                {
                        temp = q -> link ;
                        q -> link = p ;
                        p -> link = temp ;

                        start = q ;
                        r = q ;
                }
                else
                {
                        temp = q -> link ;
                        q -> link = p ;
                        p -> link = temp ;

                        r -> link = q ;
                        r = q ;
                }
            }
            else
            {
                r = p ;
                p = p -> link ;
            }
            q = p -> link ;
            if ( q == s )
                s = p ;
        }
    }
}
```

Output:

Enter a value: 29
Any More Nodes (Y/N): Y
Enter a value: 7

Any More Nodes (Y/N): Y
Enter a value: 99
Any More Nodes (Y/N): Y
Enter a value: 3
Any More Nodes (Y/N): N

Linked List Before Sorting: 29 7 99 3
Linked List After Selection Sorting: 3 7 29 99

Enter a value: 37
Any More Nodes (Y/N): Y
Enter a value: 49
Any More Nodes (Y/N): Y
Enter a value: 13
Any More Nodes (Y/N): Y
Enter a value: 2
Any More Nodes (Y/N): N

Linked List Before Sorting: 37 49 13 2
Linked List After Bubble Sorting: 2 13 37 49

Unlike the previous program we have omitted the **count( )** function. Instead we have traversed the entire linked list while carrying out the sorting.

Let us understand the **selection_sort( )** and the **bubble_sort( )** functions one by one. In **selection_sort( )**, pointers **p** and **q** point to the nodes being compared and the pointers **r** and **s** point to the node prior to **p** and **q** respectively. Initially, **p** and **r** are set to **start**, where **start** is a pointer to the first node in the list. Also, to begin with **q** and **s** are set to **p -> link**. The outer loop is controlled by the condition **p -> link != NULL** and the inner loop is controlled by the condition **q != NULL**.

While adjusting the links of the nodes being compared, we would encounter one of the following four cases:

(a) Nodes being compared are adjacent to one another and **p** is pointing to the first node in the list.

(b) Nodes being compared are adjacent to one another and **p** is not pointing to the first node.

(c) Nodes being compared are not adjacent to one another and **p** is pointing to the first node.

(d) Nodes being compared are not adjacent to one another and **p** is not pointing to the first node.

Let us now understand these cases one by one.

Case (a):

When the nodes being compared are adjacent and **p** is pointing to the first node, the following operations are performed:

```
p -> link = q -> link ;
q -> link = p ;

temp = p ;
p = q ;
q = temp

start = p ;
r = p ;
s = q ;
q = q -> link ;
```

You can trace these operations with the help of following Figure 4-15.

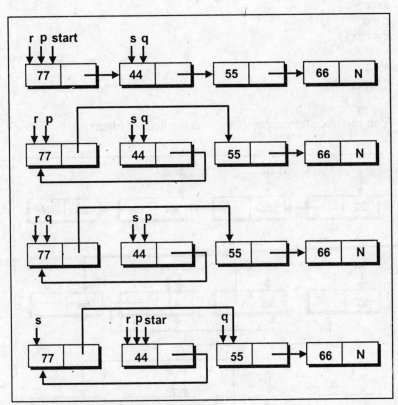

Figure 4-15. *Selection sort: case (a)*.

Case (b):

When the nodes being compared are adjacent and **p** is not pointing to the first node, the following operations are performed:

```
p -> link = q -> link ;
q -> link = p ;
r -> link = q ;
```

```
temp = p ;
p = q ;
q = temp ;

s = q ;
q = q -> link ;
```

You can trace these operations with the help of Figure 4-16.

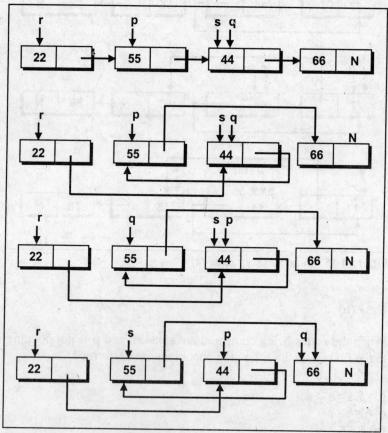

Figure 4-16. *Selection sort:* ***case (b)***.

Case (c):

When the nodes being compared are not adjacent and **p** is pointing to the first node, the following operations are performed:

```
temp = q -> link ;
q -> link = p -> link ;
p -> link = temp ;
s -> link = p ;

temp = p ;
p = q ;
q = temp ;

s = q ;
q = q -> link ;
start = p ;
```

You can trace these operations with the help of Figure 4-17.

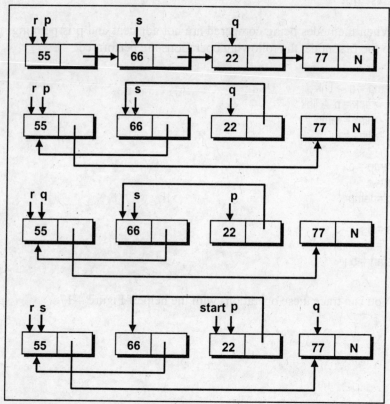

Figure 4-17. *Selection sort:* ***case (c).***

Case (d):

Lastly, when the nodes being compared are not adjacent and **p** is not pointing to the first node, the following operations are performed:

```
temp = q -> link ;
q -> link = p -> link ;
p -> link = temp ;
```

```
r -> link = q ;
s -> link = p ;

temp = p ;
p = q ;
q = temp ;

s = q ;
q = q -> link ;
```

You can trace these operations with the help of Figure 4-18.

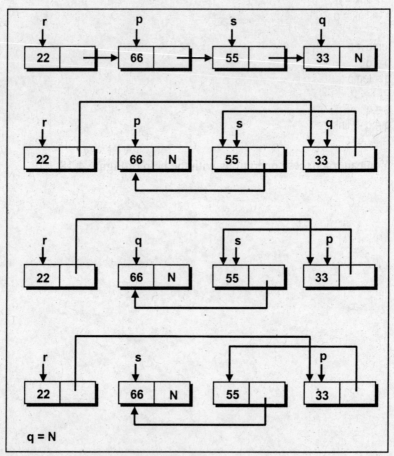

Figure 4-18. *Selection sort: case (d).*

If **p -> data** is not greater than **q -> data** then the only changes required are

```
s = q ;
q = q -> link ;
```

These statements are simply moving **s** and **q** one node down the list. Once the control comes out of the inner loop, we need to move **r** and **p** one node down the list.

Now let us understand the **bubble_sort( )** function. In **bubble_sort( ) p** and **q** point to the nodes being compared, **r** points to the node prior to the one pointed to by **p**. Lastly, **s** is used to point to the node up to which we have to make the comparisons. Initially, **p** and **r** are set to **start**, **q** is set to **p -> link** and **s** is set to **NULL**. The outer loop is controlled by the condition **s** != **start -> link** and the inner loop is controlled by the condition **p** != **s**.

Now while comparing the nodes there are only two cases to be tackled. These are:

(a) If **p** is pointing to the first node
(b) If **p** is not pointing to the first node

In the first case, the assignments that are carried out are given below:

```
temp = q -> link ;
q -> link = p ;
p -> link = temp ;

start = q ;
r = q ;
```

You can trace through these assignments using Figure 4-19.

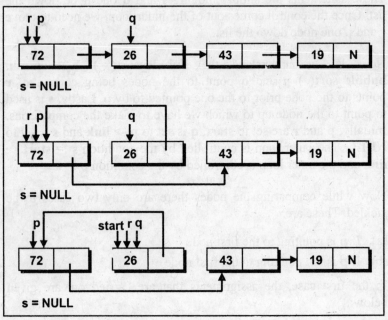

Figure 4-19. *Bubble Sort.*

On the other hand, when **p** is not pointing to **start**, the following operations should be performed:

```
temp = q -> link ;
q -> link = p ;
p -> link = temp ;

r -> link = q ;
r = q ;
```

Once again referring to Figure 4-20 would help you understand these operations easily.

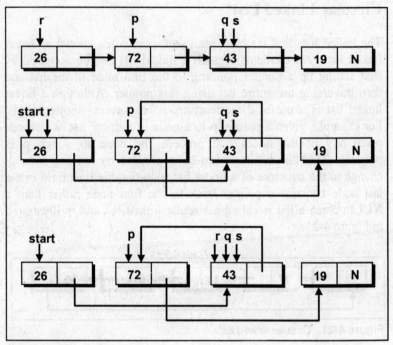

Figure 4-20. *Bubble sort.*

When the condition **p->data > q->data** becomes false, we need to store the address of node currently being pointed to by **p** in **r** and then shift **p** and **q** one node down the list.

During each iteration, of the outer loop, the biggest element gets stored at the end. This element naturally should not be used to carry out the comparisons during the next iteration of the outer loop. That is, during each iteration of the outer loop, the inner loop should be executed one time less. The pointer **s** is used to keep track of the node up to which the comparisons should be made during the next iteration.

Circular Linked List

The linked lists that we have seen so far are often known as linear linked lists. All elements of such a linked list can be accessed by first setting up a pointer pointing to the first node in the list and then traversing the entire list using this pointer. Although a linear linked list is a useful data structure, it has several shortcomings. For example, given a pointer **p** to a node in a linear list, we cannot reach any of the nodes that precede the node to which **p** is pointing. This disadvantage can be overcome by making a small change to the structure of a linear list such that the **link** field in the last node contains a pointer back to the first node rather than a NULL. Such a list is called a circular linked list and is illustrated in Figure 4-21.

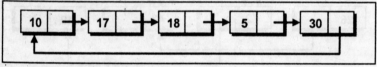

Figure 4-21. *Circular linked list.*

From any point in such a list it is possible to reach any other point in the list. If we begin at a given node and traverse the entire list, we ultimately end up at the starting point. A circular linked list does not have a first or last node. We must, therefore, establish a first and last node by convention. A circular linked list can be used to represent a stack and a queue. The following program implements a queue as a circular linked list.

```
#include <stdio.h>
#include <conio.h>
#include <alloc.h>

/* structure containing a data part and link part */
```

```
struct node
{
    int data ;
    struct node * link ;
} ;

void addcirq ( struct node **, struct node **, int ) ;
int delcirq ( struct node **, struct node ** ) ;
void cirq_display ( struct node * ) ;

void main( )
{
    struct node *front, *rear ;

    front = rear = NULL ;

    addcirq ( &front, &rear, 10 ) ;
    addcirq ( &front, &rear, 17 ) ;
    addcirq ( &front, &rear, 18 ) ;
    addcirq ( &front, &rear, 5 ) ;
    addcirq ( &front, &rear, 30 ) ;
    addcirq ( &front, &rear, 15 ) ;

    clrscr( ) ;

    printf ( "Before deletion:\n" ) ;
    cirq_display ( front ) ;

    delcirq ( &front, &rear ) ;
    delcirq ( &front, &rear ) ;
    delcirq ( &front, &rear ) ;

    printf ( "\n\nAfter deletion:\n" ) ;
    cirq_display ( front ) ;
}

/* adds a new element at the end of queue */
void addcirq ( struct node **f, struct node **r, int item )
```

```
{
    struct node *q ;

    /* create new node */
    q = malloc ( sizeof ( struct node ) ) ;
    q -> data = item ;

    /* if the queue is empty */
    if ( *f == NULL )
        *f = q ;
    else
        ( *r ) -> link = q ;

    *r = q ;
    ( *r ) -> link = *f ;
}


/* removes an element from front of queue */
int delcirq ( struct node **f, struct node **r )
{
    struct node *q ;
    int item ;

    /* if queue is empty */
    if ( *f == NULL )
        printf ( "queue is empty" ) ;
    else
    {
        if ( *f == *r )
        {
            item = ( *f ) -> data ;
            free ( *f ) ;
            *f = NULL ;
            *r = NULL ;
        }
        else
        {
            /* delete the node */
```

```
            q = *f ;
            item = q -> data ;
            *f = ( *f ) -> link ;
            ( *r ) -> link = *f ;
            free ( q ) ;
        }
        return ( item ) ;
    }
    return NULL ;
}

/* displays whole of the queue */
void cirq_display ( struct node *f )
{
    struct node *q = f, *p = NULL ;

    /* traverse the entire linked list */
    while ( q != p )
    {
        printf ( "%d ", q -> data ) ;

        q = q -> link ;
        p = f ;
    }
}
```

Output:

Before deletion:

10   17   18   5   30   15

After deletion:

5   30   15

The pointers **front** and **rear** point to the first node and the last node respectively. To begin with both the pointers **front** and **rear** are initialized to **NULL**. The functions defined in the program are discussed as follows:

Function *addcirq( )*

This function accepts three parameters. First parameter receives the address of the pointer to the first node (i.e. address of **front**), the second parameter receives the address of the pointer to the last node (i.e. address of **rear**). The third parameter is the **item** that holds the data that we need to add to the list.

Then memory is allocated for the new node whose address is stored in pointer **q**. Then the data, which is present in **item**, is stored in the **data** part of the new node.

Next a condition is checked, whether the new node is being added to an empty list. If the list is empty then the address of the node is stored in **front**. This is done through the statement

`*f = q ;`

After this the statement

`*r = q ;`

is executed which stores the address of the new node into **rear**. Thus both **front** and **rear** point to the same node.

Now the statement

`( *r ) -> link = *f ;`

is executed which stores the address of the **front** node in the **link** part of the **rear** node. This is done, because it is the property of a circular linked list that the link part of the last node should contain the address of the first node.

If the new node that is to be added is not the first node then the address present in the **link** part of the last node is overwritten with the address of the new node, which is done through the statement

(*r) -> link = q ;

Now the address of the new node is stored in the pointer **rear** through the statement

*r = q ;

and the address of the first node is stored in the **link** part of the new node. This done through the statement

(*r) -> link = *f ;

Figure 4-22 shows how to add a new node in the circular queue maintained as a linked list.

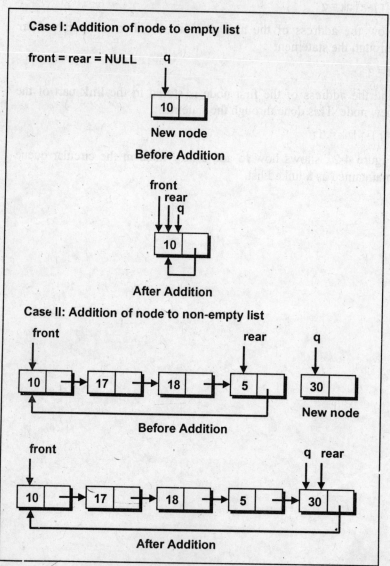

Figure 4-22. *Addition of a node in circular link list.*

Function *delcirq( )*

This function receives two parameters. The first parameter is the pointer to the **front** and the second is the pointer to the **rear**. Then a condition is checked whether the list is empty or not. If the list is empty then the control returns back to calling function.

If the list is not empty then it is checked whether the **front** and **rear** point to the same node or not. If they point to the same node then the memory occupied by the node is released and **front** and **rear** both are assigned a **NULL** value.

If **front** and **rear** are pointing to different nodes then the address of the first node is stored in a pointer **q**. Then the **front** pointer is made to point to the next node in the list i.e. to the node which is pointed by (***f**) -> **link**. Now the address of the **front** is stored in the **link** part of last node. Then the memory occupied by the node being deleted is released.

Figure 4-23 shows how the deletion of a node from the circular queue maintained as a linked list happens.

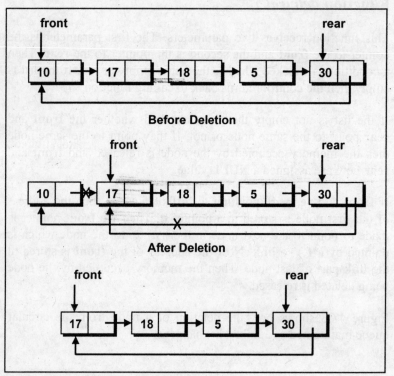

Figure 4-23. *Deletion of a node from circular link list.*

Function *cirq_display( )*

This function receives the pointer to the first node in the list as a parameter. Then **q** is also made to point to the first node in the list. This is done because the entire list is traversed using **q**. Another pointer **p** is set to **NULL** initially. Then through the loop the circular linked list is traversed till the time we do not reach the first node again. We would make the circle and reach the first node when **q** equals **p**.

First time through the loop **p** is assigned the address of the first node after **q** has been moved to the next node. Had we done this before the loop then the condition in the loop would have failed the first time itself.

A Few More Operations

If you think carefully you can list out so many operations that can be performed on a linked list. For example, concatenating one linked list at the end of another, deleting all nodes present in a linked list, modifying certain elements in a linked list, etc. Given below is a program for concatenation of linked list and erasing all nodes in the list.

```c
#include <stdio.h>
#include <conio.h>
#include <alloc.h>

struct node
{
    int data ;
    struct node *link ;
} ;

void append ( struct node **, int ) ;
void concat ( struct node **, struct node ** ) ;
void display ( struct node * ) ;
int count ( struct node * ) ;
struct node * erase ( struct node * ) ;

void main( )
{
    struct node *first, *second ;

    first = second = NULL ; /* empty linked lists */
```

```
        append ( &first, 1 ) ;
        append ( &first, 2 ) ;
        append ( &first, 3 ) ;
        append ( &first, 4 ) ;

        clrscr( ) ;
        printf ( "\nFirst List: " ) ;
        display ( first ) ;
        printf ( "\nNo. of elements in the first Linked List = %d", count ( first ) ) ;

        append ( &second, 5 ) ;
        append ( &second, 6 ) ;
        append ( &second, 7 ) ;
        append ( &second, 8 ) ;

        printf ( "\n\nSecond List: " ) ;
        display ( second ) ;
        printf ( "\nNo. of ele. ents in the second Linked List = %d",
                count ( second ) ) ;

        /* the result obtained after concatenation is in the first list */
        concat ( &first, &second ) ;

        printf ( "\n\nConcatenated List: " ) ;
        display ( first ) ;

        printf ( "\n\nNo. of elements in Linked List before erasing = %d",
                count ( first ) ) ;

        first = erase ( first ) ;
        printf ( "\nNo. of elements in Linked List after erasing = %d",
                count ( first ) ) ;
}

/* adds a node at the end of a linked list */
void append ( struct node **q, int num )
{
        struct node *temp ;
```

```
        temp = *q ;

        if ( *q == NULL )  /* if the list is empty, create first node */
        {
            *q = malloc ( sizeof ( struct node ) ) ;
            temp = *q ;
        }
        else
        {
            /* go to last node */
            while ( temp -> link != NULL )
                temp = temp -> link ;

            /* add node at the end */
            temp -> link = malloc ( sizeof ( struct node ) ) ;
            temp = temp -> link ;
        }

        /* assign data to the last node */
        temp -> data = num ;
        temp -> link = NULL ;
    }

    /* concatenates two linked lists */
    void concat ( struct node **p, struct node **q )
    {
        struct node *temp ;

        /* if the first linked list is empty */
        if ( *p == NULL )
            *p = *q ;
        else
        {
            /* if both linked lists are non-empty */
            if ( *q != NULL )
            {
                temp = *p ;  /* points to the starting of the first list */
```

```c
                    /* traverse the entire first linked list */
                    while ( temp -> link != NULL )
                        temp = temp -> link ;

                    temp -> link = *q ;  /* concatenate the second list after the
                                            first */
                }
            }
        }

/* displays the contents of the linked list */
void display ( struct node *q )
{
    printf ( "\n" ) ;

    /* traverse the entire linked list */
    while ( q != NULL )
    {
        printf ( "%d ", q -> data ) ;
        q = q -> link ;
    }
}

/* counts the number of nodes present in the linked list */
int count ( struct node *q )
{
    int c = 0 ;

    /* traverse the entire linked list */
    while ( q != NULL )
    {
        q = q -> link ;
        c++ ;
    }

    return c ;
}
```

```
/* erases all the nodes from a linked list */
struct node * erase ( struct node *q )
{
    struct node *temp ;

    /* traverse till the end erasing each node */
    while ( q != NULL )
    {
        temp = q ;
        q = q -> link ;
        free ( temp ) ;  /* free the memory occupied by the node */
    }

    return NULL ;
}
```

Output:

First List:
1 2 3 4
No. of elements in the first Linked List = 4

Second List:
5 6 7 8
No. of elements in the second Linked List = 4

Concatenated List:
1 2 3 4 5 6 7 8

No. of elements in Linked List before erasing = 8
No. of elements in Linked List after erasing = 0

Recursive Operations On Linked List

In C, it is possible for the functions to call themselves. A function is called 'recursive' if a statement within the body of a function calls the same function. Sometimes called 'circular definition', recursion is thus the process of defining something in terms of itself.

Some of the operations that are carried out on linked lists can be easily implemented using recursion. For example, finding out the number of nodes present in a linked list, comparing two linked lists, copying one linked list into another, adding a new node at the end of the linked list, etc. Given below are the programs for carrying out each of these operations. The programs have been suitably commented. Hence, we would omit the discussion about working of each of these programs.

(a) Program to find the number of nodes in the linked list using recursion

```c
#include <stdio.h>
#include <conio.h>
#include <alloc.h>

/* structure containing a data part and link part */
struct node
{
    int data ;
    struct node *link ;
} ;

void append ( struct node **, int ) ;
int length ( struct node * ) ;

void main( )
{
    struct node *p ;
    p = NULL ;  /* empty linked list */

    append ( &p, 1 ) ;
    append ( &p, 2 ) ;
```

```
        append ( &p, 3 ) ;
        append ( &p, 4 ) ;
        append ( &p, 5 ) ;

        clrscr( ) ;
        printf ( "Length of linked list = %d", length ( p ) ) ;
}

/* adds a node at the end of a linked list */
void append ( struct node **q. int num )
{
        struct node *temp ;
        temp = *q ;

        if ( *q == NULL )  /* if the list is empty, create first node */
        {
                *q = malloc ( sizeof ( struct node ) ) ;
                temp = *q ;
        }
        else
        {
                /* go to last node */
                while ( temp -> link != NULL )
                        temp = temp -> link ;

                /* add node at the end */
                temp -> link = malloc ( sizeof ( struct node ) ) ;
                temp = temp -> link ;
        }

        /* assign data to the last node */
        temp -> data = num ;
        temp -> link = NULL ;
}

/* counts the number of nodes in a linked list */
int length ( struct node *q )
{
```

```
        static int I ;

        /* if list is empty or if NULL is encountered */
        if ( q == NULL )
            return ( 0 ) ;
        else
        {
            /* go to next node */
            I = 1 + length ( q -> link ) ;
            return ( I ) ;
        }
}
```

Output:

Length of linked list = 5

(b)   Program to compare two linked lists using recursion

```
#include <stdio.h>
#include <conio.h>
#include <alloc.h>

struct node
{
    int data ;
    struct node *link ;
} ;

void append ( struct node **, int ) ;
int compare ( struct node *, struct node * ) ;

void main( )
{
    struct node *first, *second ;
    first = second = NULL ; /* empty linked lists */

    append ( &first, 1 ) ;
```

```
        append ( &first, 2 ) ;
        append ( &first, 3 ) ;

        append ( &second, 1 ) ;
        append ( &second, 2 ) ;
        append ( &second, 3 ) ;

        clrscr( ) ;
        if ( compare ( first, second ) )
            printf ( "Both linked lists are EQUAL" ) ;
        else
            printf ( "Linked lists are DIFFERENT" ) ;
    }

    /* adds a node at the end of a linked list */
    void append ( struct node **q, int num )
    {
        struct node *temp ;
        temp = *q ;

        if ( *q == NULL )   /* if the list is empty, create first node */
        {
            *q = malloc ( sizeof ( struct node ) ) ;
            temp = *q ;
        }
        else
        {
            /* go to last node */
            while ( temp -> link != NULL )
                temp = temp -> link ;

            /* add node at the end */
            temp -> link = malloc ( sizeof ( struct node ) ) ;
            temp = temp -> link ;
        }

        /* assign data to the last node */
        temp -> data = num ;
```

```
        temp -> link = NULL ;
}

/* compares 2 linked lists and returns 1 if linked lists are equal and 0 if
    unequal */
int compare ( struct node *q, struct node *r )
{
    static int flag ;

    if ( ( q == NULL ) && ( r == NULL ) )
        flag = 1 ;
    else
    {
        if ( q == NULL || r == NULL )
            flag = 0 ;

        if ( q -> data != r -> data )
            flag = 0 ;
        else
            compare ( q -> link, r -> link ) ;
    }
    return ( flag ) ;
}
```

Output:

Both linked lists are EQUAL

(c) Program to copy one linked list into another using recursion.

```
#include <stdio.h>
#include <conio.h>
#include <alloc.h>

/* structure containing a data part and link part */
struct node
{
```

```
        int data ;
        struct node *link ;
} ;

void append ( struct node **, int ) ;
void copy ( struct node *, struct node ** ) ;
void display ( struct node * ) ;

void main( )
{
    struct node *first, *second ;
    first = second = NULL ;  /* empty linked lists */

    append ( &first, 1 ) ;
    append ( &first, 2 ) ;
    append ( &first, 3 ) ;
    append ( &first, 4 ) ;
    append ( &first, 5 ) ;
    append ( &first, 6 ) ;
    append ( &first, 7 ) ;

    clrscr( ) ;
    display ( first ) ;

    copy ( first, &second ) ;

    display ( second ) ;
}

/* adds a node at the end of the linked list */
void append ( struct node **q, int num )
{
    struct node *temp ;
    temp = *q ;

    if ( *q == NULL )  /* if the list is empty, create first node */
    {
        *q = malloc ( sizeof ( struct node ) ) ;
```

```
        temp = *q ;
    }
    else
    {
        /* go to last node */
        while ( temp -> link != NULL )
            temp = temp -> link ;

        /* add node at the end */
        temp -> link = malloc ( sizeof ( struct node ) ) ;
        temp = temp -> link ;
    }

    /* assign data to the last node */
    temp -> data = num ;
    temp -> link = NULL ;
}

/* copies a linked list into another */
void copy ( struct node *q, struct node **s )
{
    if ( q != NULL )
    {
        *s = malloc ( sizeof ( struct node ) ) ;

        ( *s ) -> data = q -> data ;
        ( *s ) -> link = NULL ;

        copy ( q -> link, &( ( *s ) -> link ) ) ;
    }
}

/* displays the contents of the linked list */
void display ( struct node *q )
{
    printf ( "\n" ) ;

    /* traverse the entire linked list */
```

```
        while ( q != NULL )
        {
            printf ( "%d ", q -> data ) ;
            q = q -> link ;
        }
}
```

Output:

```
1 2 3 4 5 6 7
1 2 3 4 5 6 7
```

(d) Program to add a new node at the end of linked list using recursion.

```
#include <stdio.h>
#include <conio.h>
#include <alloc.h>

struct node
{
    int data ;
    struct node *link ;
} ;

void addatend ( struct node **, int ) ;
void display ( struct node * ) ;

void main( )
{
    struct node *p ;

    p = NULL ;

    addatend ( &p, 1 ) ;
    addatend ( &p, 2 ) ;
    addatend ( &p, 3 ) ;
```

```
    addatend ( &p, 4 ) ;
    addatend ( &p, 5 ) ;
    addatend ( &p, 6 ) ;
    addatend ( &p, 10 ) ;

    clrscr( ) ;
    display ( p ) ;
}

/* adds a new node at the end of the linked list */
void addatend ( struct node **s, int num )
{
    if ( *s == NULL )
    {
        *s = malloc ( sizeof ( struct node ) ) ;
        ( *s ) -> data = num ;
        ( *s ) -> link = NULL ;
    }
    else
        addatend ( &( ( *s ) -> link ), num ) ;
}

/* displays the contents of the linked list */
void display ( struct node *q )
{
    printf ( "\n" ) ;
    /* traverse the entire linked list */
    while ( q != NULL )
    {
        printf ( "%d ", q -> data ) ;
        q = q -> link ;
    }
}
```

Output:

1 2 3 4 5 6 10

Doubly Linked Lists

In the linked lists that we have used so far each node provides information about where is the next node in the list. It has no knowledge about where the previous node lies in memory. If we are at say the 15th node in the list, then to reach the 14th node we have to traverse the list right from the first node. To avoid this we can store in each node not only the address of next node but also the address of the previous node in the linked list. This arrangement is often known as a 'Doubly Linked List' and is shown in Figure 4-24.

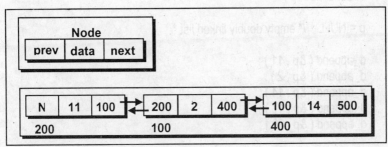

Figure 4-24. *Doubly linked list.*

The following program implements the Doubly Linked List (DLL).

```
#include <stdio.h>
#include <conio.h>
#include <alloc.h>

/* structure representing a node of the doubly linked list */
struct dnode
{
    struct dnode *prev ;
    int data ;
```

```
        struct dnode * next ;
} ;

void d_append ( struct dnode **, int ) ;
void d_addatbeg ( struct dnode **, int ) ;
void d_addafter ( struct dnode *, int , int ) ;
void d_display ( struct dnode * ) ;
int d_count ( struct dnode * ) ;
void d_delete ( struct dnode **, int ) ;

void main( )
{
    struct dnode *p ;

    p = NULL ; /* empty doubly linked list */

    d_append ( &p , 11 ) ;
    d_append ( &p , 2 ) ;
    d_append ( &p , 14 ) ;
    d_append ( &p , 17 ) ;
    d_append ( &p , 99 ) ;

    clrscr( ) ;
    d_display ( p ) ;
    printf ( "\nNo. of elements in the DLL = %d\n", d_count ( p ) ) ;

    d_addatbeg ( &p, 33 ) ;
    d_addatbeg ( &p, 55 ) ;

    d_display ( p ) ;
    printf ( "\nNo. of elements in the DLL = %d\n", d_count ( p ) ) ;

    d_addafter ( p, 4, 66 ) ;
    d_addafter ( p, 2, 96 ) ;

    d_display ( p ) ;
    printf ( "\nNo. of elements in the DLL = %d\n", d_count ( p ) ) ;
```

```
        d_delete ( &p, 55 ) ;
        d_delete ( &p, 2 ) ;
        d_delete ( &p, 99 ) ;

        d_display ( p ) ;
        printf ( "\nNo. of elements in the DLL = %d\n", d_count ( p ) ) ;
}

/* adds a new node at the end of the doubly linked list */
void d_append ( struct dnode **s, int num )
{
        struct dnode *r, *q = *s ;

        /* if the linked list is empty */
        if ( *s == NULL )
        {
            /*create a new node */
            *s = malloc ( sizeof ( struct dnode ) ) ;
            ( *s ) -> prev = NULL ;
            ( *s ) -> data = num ;
            ( *s ) -> next = NULL ;
        }
        else
        {
            /* traverse the linked list till the last node is reached */
            while ( q -> next != NULL )
                  q = q -> next ;

            /* add a new node at the end */
            r = malloc ( sizeof ( struct dnode ) ) ;
            r -> data = num ;
            r -> next = NULL ;
            r -> prev = q ;
            q -> next = r ;
        }
}

/* adds a new node at the begining of the linked list */
```

```
void d_addatbeg ( struct dnode **s, int num )
{
    struct dnode *q ;

    /* create a new node */
    q = malloc ( sizeof ( struct dnode ) ) ;

    /* assign data and pointer to the new node */
    q -> prev = NULL ;
    q -> data = num ;
    q -> next = *s ;

    /* make new node the head node */
    ( *s ) -> prev = q ;
    *s = q ;
}


/* adds a new node after the specified number of nodes */
void d_addafter ( struct dnode *q, int loc, int num )
{
    struct dnode *temp ;
    int i ;

    /* skip to desired portion */
    for ( i = 0 ; i < loc ; i++ )
    {
        q = q -> next ;
        /* if end of linked list is encountered */
        if ( q == NULL )
        {
            printf ( "\nThere are less than %d elements", loc );
            return ;
        }
    }

    /* insert new node */
    q = q -> prev ;
    temp = malloc ( sizeof ( struct dnode ) ) ;
```

```
        temp -> data = num ;
        temp -> prev = q ;
        temp -> next = q -> next ;
        temp -> next -> prev = temp ;
        q -> next = temp ;
}

/* displays the contents of the linked list */
void d_display ( struct dnode *q )
{
        printf ( "\n" ) ;

        /* traverse the entire linked list */
        while ( q != NULL )
        {
                printf ( "%2d\t", q -> data ) ;
                q = q -> next ;
        }
}

/* counts the number of nodes present in the linked list */
int d_count ( struct dnode * q )
{
        int c = 0 ;

        /* traverse the entire linked list */
        while ( q != NULL )
        {
                q = q -> next ;
                c++ ;
        }

        return c ;
}

/* deletes the specified node from the doubly linked list */
void d_delete ( struct dnode **s, int num )
{
```

```
       struct dnode *q = *s ;

       /* traverse the entire linked list */
       while ( q != NULL )
       {
           /* if node to be deleted is found */
           if ( q -> data == num )
           {
               /* if node to be deleted is the first node */
               if ( q == *s )
               {
                   *s = ( *s ) -> next ;
                   ( *s ) -> prev = NULL ;
               }
               else
               {
                   /* if node to be deleted is the last node */
                   if ( q -> next == NULL )
                       q -> prev -> next = NULL ;
                   else
                   /* if node to be deleted is any intermediate node */
                   {
                       q -> prev -> next = q -> next ;
                       q -> next -> prev = q -> prev ;
                   }
                   free ( q ) ;
               }
               return ;  /* return back after deletion */
           }
           q = q -> next ; /* go to next node */
       }
       printf ( "\n%d not found.", num ) ;
}
```

Output:

```
11   2   14   17   99
```

No. of elements in the DLL = 5

55   33   11   2   14   17   99
No. of elements in the DLL = 7

55   33   96   11   2   66   14   17   99
No. of elements in the DLL = 9

33   96   11   66   14   17
No. of elements in the DLL = 6

Let us now understand the different functions that we have defined in the program. Let us begin with the one that appends a new node at the end of a double linked list.

Function *d_append( )*

The **d_append( )** function adds a node at the end of the existing list. It also checks the special case of adding the first node if the list is empty.

This function accepts two parameters. The first parameter **s** is of type **struct dnode**** which contains the address of the pointer to the first node of the list or a **NULL** value in case of empty list. The second parameter **num** is an integer, which is to be added in the list.

To begin with we initialize **q** which is of the type **struct dnode** * with the value stored at **s**. This is done because using **q** the entire list is traversed if it is non-empty.

If the list is empty then the condition

if (*s == NULL)

gets satisfied. Now memory is allocated for the new node whose address is stored in *s (i.e. **p**). Using **s** a **NULL** value is stored in its **prev** and **next** links and the value of **num** is assigned to its **data** part.

If the list is non-empty then through the statements

```
while ( q -> next != NULL )
    q = q -> next ;
```

q is made to point to the last node of the list. Then memory is allocated for the node whose address is stored in **r**. A **NULL** value is stored in the **next** part of this node, because this is going to be last node. Now what remains to be done is to link this node with rest of the list. This is done through the statements

```
r -> prev = q ;
q -> next = r ·
```

The statement **r -> prev = q** makes the **prev** part of the new node **r** to point to the previous node **q**. The statement **q -> next = r** makes the **next** part of **q** to point to the last node **r**. This is shown in Figure 4-25.

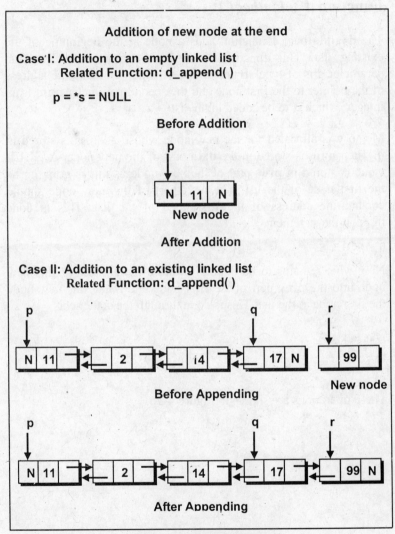

Figure 4-25. *Doubly linked list addition of a node.*

Function *d_addatbeg( )*

The **d_addatbeg( )** function adds a node at the beginning of the existing list. This function accepts two parameters. The first parameter **s** is of type **struct dnode**** which contains the address of the pointer to the first node and the second parameter **num** is an integer, which is to be added in the list.

Memory is allocated for the new node whose address is stored in **q**. Then **num** is stored in the **data** part of the new node. A **NULL** value is stored in **prev** part of the new node as this is going to be the first node of the list. The **next** part of this new node should contain the address of the first node of the list. This is done through the statement

```
q -> next = *s ;
```

Now what remains to be done is to store the address of this new node into the **prev** part of the first node and make this new node the first node in the list. This is done through the statements

```
( *s ) -> prev = q ;
*s = q ;
```

These operations are shown in Figure 4-26.

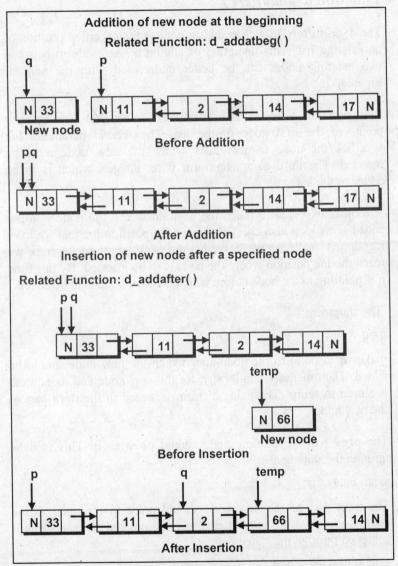

Figure 4-26. *Working of d_addatbeg( ) and d_addatbeg( )
functions.*

Function *d_addafter( )*

The **d_addafter( )** function adds a node at the specified position of an existing list. This operation of adding a new node in between two existing nodes can be better understood with the help of Figure 4-26.

This function accepts three parameters. The first parameter **q** points to the first node of the list. The second parameter **loc** specifies the node number after which the new node must be inserted. The third parameter **num** is an integer, which is to be added to the list.

A loop is executed to reach the position where the node is to be added. This loop also checks whether the position **loc** that we have mentioned, really occurs in the list or not. When the loop ends, we reach the **loc** position where the node is to be inserted. By this time **q** is pointing to the node before which the new node is to be added.

The statement

```
q = q -> prev ;
```

makes **q** to point to the node after which the new node should be added. Then memory is allocated for the new node and its address is stored in **temp**. The value of **num** is stored in the **data** part of the new node.

The **prev** part of the new node should point to **q**. This is done through the statement

```
temp -> prev = q ;
```

The **next** part of the new node should point to the node whose address is stored in the **next** part of node pointed to by **q**. This is achieved through the statement

```
temp -> next = q -> next ;
```

Now what remains to be done is to make **prev** part of the next node (node pointed by **q -> next**) to point to the new node. This is done through the statement

temp -> next -> prev = temp ;

At the end, we change the next part of the **q** to make it point to the new node, and this is done through the statement

q -> next = temp ;

Function *d_delete( )*

The function **d_delete( )** deletes a node from the list if the **data** part of that node matches **num**. This function receives two parameters. The first parameter is the address of the pointer to the first node and the second parameter is the number that is to be deleted.

We run a loop to traverse the list. Inside the loop the **data** part of each node is compared with the **num** value. If the **num** value matches the **data** part in the node then we need to check the position of the node to be deleted.

If it happens to be the first node, then the first node is made to point to the **next** part of the first node. This is done through the statement

*s = (*s) -> next ;

Then, a value **NULL** is stored in **prev** part of the second node, since it is now going to become the first node. This is done through the statement

(*s) -> prev = NULL ;

If the node to be deleted happens to be the last node, then a value **NULL** is stored in the **next** part of the second last node. This is done through the statements

```
if ( q -> next == NULL )
    q -> prev -> next = NULL ;
```

If the node to be deleted happens to be any intermediate node, then the address of the next node is stored in the **next** part of the previous node and the address of the previous node is stored in the **prev** part of the next node. This is done through the statements

```
q -> prev -> next = q -> next ;
q -> next -> prev = q -> prev ;
```

Finally the memory occupied by the node being deleted is released by calling the function **free( )**. Figure 4-27 shows the working of the **d_delete( )** function.

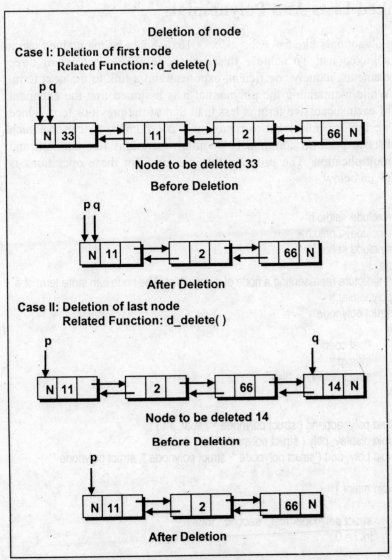

Figure 4-27. *Working of d_delete( ) function.*

Linked Lists And Polynomials

Polynomials like $5x^4 + 2x^3 + 7x^2 + 10x - 8$ can be maintained using a linked list. To achieve this each node should consist of three elements, namely coefficient, exponent and a link to the next term. While maintaining the polynomial it is assumed that the exponent of each successive term is less than that of the previous term. Once we build a linked list to represent a polynomial we can use such lists to perform common polynomial operations like addition and multiplication. The program that can perform these operations is given below.

```
#include <stdio.h>
#include <conio.h>
#include <alloc.h>

/* structure representing a node of a linked list. The node can store term of a
polynomial */
struct polynode
{
    float coeff ;
    int exp ;
    struct polynode *link ;
} ;

void poly_append ( struct polynode **, float, int ) ;
void display_poly ( struct polynode * ) ;
void poly_add ( struct polynode *, struct polynode *, struct polynode ** ) ;

void main( )
{
    struct polynode *first, *second, *total ;
    int i = 0 ;

    first = second = total = NULL ;  /* empty linked lists */
```

```
        poly_append ( &first, 1.4, 5 ) ;
        poly_append ( &first, 1.5, 4 ) ;
        poly_append ( &first, 1.7, 2 ) ;
        poly_append ( &first, 1.8, 1 ) ;
        poly_append ( &first, 1.9, 0 ) ;

        clrscr( ) ;
        display_poly ( first ) ;

        poly_append ( &second, 1.5, 6 ) ;
        poly_append ( &second, 2.5, 5 ) ;
        poly_append ( &second, -3.5, 4 ) ;
        poly_append ( &second, 4.5, 3 ) ;
        poly_append ( &second, 6.5, 1 ) ;

        printf ( "\n\n" ) ;
        display_poly ( second ) ;

        /* draws a dashed horizontal line */
        printf ( "\n" ) ;
        while ( i++ < 79 )
            printf ( "-" ) ;
        printf ( "\n\n" ) ;

        poly_add ( first, second, &total ) ;
        display_poly ( total ) ;  /* displays the resultant polynomial */
}

/* adds a term to a polynomial */
void poly_append ( struct polynode **q, float x, int y )
{
        struct polynode *temp ;
        temp = *q ;

        /* creates a new node if the list is empty */
        if ( *q == NULL )
        {
            *q = malloc ( sizeof ( struct polynode ) ) ;
```

```
            temp = *q ;
    }
    else
    {
        /* traverse the entire linked list */
        while ( temp -> link != NULL )
            temp = temp -> link ;

            /* create new nodes at intermediate stages */
            temp -> link = malloc ( sizeof ( struct polynode ) ) ;
            temp = temp -> link ;
    }

    /* assign coefficient and exponent */
    temp -> coeff = x ;
    temp -> exp = y ;
    temp -> link = NULL ;
}

/* displays the contents of linked list representing a polynomial */
void display_poly ( struct polynode *q )
{
    /* traverse till the end of the linked list */
    while ( q != NULL )
    {
        printf ( "%.1f x^%d  :  ", q -> coeff, q -> exp ) ;
        q = q -> link ;
    }

    printf ( "\b\b\b " ) ;  /* erases the last colon */
}

/* adds two polynomials */
void poly_add ( struct polynode *x, struct polynode *y, struct  polynode **s )
{
    struct polynode *z ;

    /* if both linked lists are empty */
```

```
if ( x == NULL && y == NULL )
    return ;

/* traverse till one of the list ends */
while ( x != NULL && y != NULL )
{
    /* create a new node if the list is empty */
    if ( *s == NULL )
    {
        *s = malloc ( sizeof ( struct polynode ) ) ;
        z = *s ;
    }
    /* create new nodes at intermediate stages */
    else
    {
        z -> link = malloc ( sizeof ( struct polynode ) ) ;
        z = z -> link ;
    }

    /* store a term of the larger degree polynomial */
    if ( x -> exp < y -> exp )
    {
        z -> coeff = y -> coeff ;
        z -> exp = y -> exp ;
        y = y -> link ;  /* go to the next node */
    }
    else
    {
        if ( x -> exp > y -> exp )
        {
            z -> coeff = x -> coeff ;
            z -> exp = x -> exp ;
            x = x -> link ;  /* go to the next node */
        }
        else
        {
            /* add the coefficients, when exponents are equal */
            if ( x -> exp == y -> exp )
```

```
                    {
                            /* assigning the added coefficient */
                            z -> coeff = x -> coeff + y -> coeff ;
                            z -> exp = x -> exp ;
                            /* go to the next node */
                            x = x -> link ;
                            y = y -> link ;
                    }
            }
        }
    }

    /* assign remaining terms of the first polynomial to the result */
    while ( x != NULL )
    {
        if ( *s == NULL )
        {
            *s = malloc ( sizeof ( struct polynode ) ) ;
            z = *s ;
        }
        else
        {
            z -> link = malloc ( sizeof ( struct polynode ) ) ;
            z = z -> link ;
        }

        /* assign coefficient and exponent */
        z -> coeff = x -> coeff ;
        z -> exp = x -> exp ;
        x = x -> link ;  /* go to the next node */
    }

    /* assign remaining terms of the second polynomial to the result */
    while ( y != NULL )
    {
        if ( *s == NULL )
        {
            *s = malloc ( sizeof ( struct polynode ) ) ;
```

```
            z = *s ;
        }
        else
        {
            z -> link = malloc ( sizeof ( struct polynode ) ) ;
            z = z -> link ;
        }

        /* assign coefficient and exponent */
        z -> coeff = y -> coeff ;
        z -> exp = y -> exp ;
        y = y -> link ;  /* go to the next node */
    }

    z -> link = NULL ;  /* assign NULL at end of resulting linked list */
}
```

Output:

1.4 x^5 : 1.5 x^4 : 1.7 x^2 : 1.8 x^1 : 1.9 x^0

1.5 x^6 : 2.5 x^5 : -3.5 x^4 : 4.5 x^3 : 6.5 x^1

1.5 x^6 : 3.9 x^5 : -2.0 x^4 : 4.5 x^3 : 1.7 x^2 : 8.3 x^1 : 1.9 x^0

In this program the **poly_append( )** function is called several times to build the two polynomials which are pointed to by the pointers **first** and **second**. Next the function **poly_add( )** is called to carry out the addition of two polynomials. In this function the linked lists representing the two polynomials are traversed till the end of one of them is reached. While doing this traversal the polynomials are compared on term by term basis. If the exponents of the two terms being compared are equal then their coefficients are added and the result is stored in the **third** polynomial. If the exponents of two terms are not equal then the term with the bigger exponent is added to the third polynomial. During the traversal if the end of one of the list is reached the control breaks out of the **while** loop. Now the remaining terms of that polynomial whose end has not been reached are simply appended to the resulting polynomial. Lastly, the terms of the resulting polynomials are displayed using the function **display_poly( )**.

Now a program to carry out multiplication of the two polynomials.

```
#include <stdio.h>
#include <conio.h>
#include <alloc.h>

/* structure representing a node of a linked list. The node can store a term of
   a polynomial */
struct polynode
{
    float coeff ;
    int exp ;
    struct polynode *link ;
} ;

void poly_append ( struct polynode **, float, int ) ;
void display_poly ( struct polynode * ) ;
void poly_multiply ( struct polynode *, struct polynode *, struct polynode ** ) ;
void padd ( float, int, struct polynode ** ) ;

void main( )
{
    struct polynode *first, *second, *mult ;
    int i = 1 ;

    first = second = mult = NULL ;  /* empty linked lists */

    poly_append ( &first, 3, 5 ) ;
    poly_append ( &first, 2, 4 ) ;
    poly_append ( &first, 1, 2 ) ;
```

```
    clrscr( ) ;
    display_poly ( first ) ;

    poly_append ( &second, 1, 6 ) ;
    poly_append ( &second, 2, 5 ) ;
    poly_append ( &second, 3, 4 ) ;

    printf ( "\n\n" ) ;
    display_poly ( second ) ;

    printf ( "\n" ) ;
    while ( i++ < 79 )
        printf ( "-" ) ;

    poly_multiply ( first, second, &mult ) ;
    printf ( "\n\n" ) ;
    display_poly ( mult ) ;
}

/* adds a term to a polynomial */
void poly_append ( struct polynode **q, float x, int y )
{
    struct polynode *temp ;
    temp = *q ;

    /* create a new node if the list is empty */
    if ( *q == NULL )
    {
        *q = malloc ( sizeof ( struct polynode ) ) ;
        temp = *q ;
    }
    else
    {
        /* traverse the entire linked list */
        while ( temp -> link != NULL )
            temp = temp -> link ;

        /* create new nodes at intermediate stages */
```

```
            temp -> link = malloc ( sizeof ( struct polynode ) ) ;
            temp = temp -> link ;
        }
        /* assign coefficient and exponent */
        temp -> coeff = x ;
        temp -> exp = y ;
        temp -> link = NULL ;
}

/* displays the contents of linked list representing a polynomial */
void display_poly ( struct polynode *q )
{
    /* traverse till the end of the linked list */
    while ( q != NULL )
    {
        printf ( "%.1f x^%d  :  ", q -> coeff, q -> exp ) ;
        q = q -> link ;
    }
    printf ( "\b\b\b " ) ;  /* erases the last colon(:) */
}

/* multiplies the two polynomials */
void poly_multiply ( struct polynode *x, struct polynode *y,
                    struct polynode **m )
{
    struct polynode *y1 ;
    float coeff1, exp1 ;

    y1 = y ;  /* point to the starting of the second linked list */

    if ( x == NULL && y == NULL )
        return :

    /* if one of the list is empty */
    if ( x == NULL )
        *m = y ;
    else
    {
```

```
            if ( y == NULL )
                *m = x ;
            else  /* if both linked lists exist */
            {
                /* for each term of the first list */
                while ( x != NULL )
                {
                    /* multiply each term of the second linked list with a
                       term of the first linked list */
                    while ( y != NULL )
                    {
                        coeff1 = x -> coeff * y -> coeff ;
                        exp1 = x -> exp + y -> exp ;
                        y = y -> link ;

                        /* add the new term to the resultant polynomial */
                        padd ( coeff1, exp1, m ) ;
                    }
                    y = y1 ;  /* reposition the pointer to the starting of
                                 the second linked list */
                    x = x -> link ;  /* go to the next node */
                }
            }
        }
}

/* adds a term to the polynomial in the descending order of the exponent */
void padd ( float c, int e, struct polynode **s )
{
    struct polynode *r, *temp = *s ;

    /* if list is empty or if the node is to be inserted before the first node */
    if ( *s == NULL || e > ( *s ) -> exp )
    {
        *s = r = malloc ( sizeof ( struct polynode ) ) ;
        ( *s ) -> coeff = c ;
        ( *s ) -> exp = e ;
        ( *s ) -> link = temp ;
```

```
        }
        else
        {
            /* traverse the entire linked list to search the position to insert a new
                node */
            while ( temp != NULL )
            {
                if ( temp -> exp == e )
                {
                    temp -> coeff += c ;
                    return ;
                }
                if ( temp -> exp > e && ( temp -> link -> exp < e ||
                                            temp -> link  == NULL ) )
                {
                    r = malloc ( sizeof ( struct polynode ) ) ;
                    r -> coeff = c ;
                    r -> exp = e ;
                    r -> link = temp -> link ;
                    temp -> link = r ;
                    return ;
                }
                temp = temp -> link ;  /* go to next node */
            }
            r -> link = NULL ;
            temp -> link = r ;
        }
    }
```

Output:

3.0 x^5 : 2.0 x^4 : 1.0 x^2

1.0 x^6 : 2.0 x^5 : 3.0 x^4

3.0 x^11 : 8.0 x^10 : 13.0 x^9 : 7.0 x^8 : 2.0 x^7 : 3.0 x^6

In this program once again the **poly_append( )** function is called to build the two polynomials. Followed by this, the **poly_multiply( )** function is called to carry out the multiplication of the two polynomials. In this function if it is found that both the linked lists (representing the two polynomials being multiplied) are non-empty then the control goes in a pair of **while** loops. Here each term of the second polynomial is multiplied with every term of the first polynomial. As this proceeds and a new term is built, the function **padd( )** is called to add this term to the resulting polynomial. In **padd( )** each term of the existing resulting polynomial is scanned to find whether there exists a term in this polynomial whose exponent is same as that of the term to be added. If it is so, then the corresponding coefficient of the existing polynomial is updated, otherwise the new term is simply appended to the end of the existing polynomial. Yet again the resulting polynomial is displayed using the function **display_poly( )**. The functions **poly_multiply( )** and **padd( )** are explained as follows:

Function *poly_multiply( )*

This function receives three parameters. The first two parameters **x** and **y** point to the lists that represent two polynomials that are to be multiplied. The third parameter is the address of the pointer of the resultant list where the result of the multiplication of the two lists would get stored.

Two variables **coeff1, exp1** are supposed to hold the value of coefficient and exponent of the current resultant node.

One more pointer is made to point to the second list such that each time after multiplication of all the terms of second list with the first term of first list, the pointer can be repositioned to the first node of the second list.

A condition is checked whether both the lists are empty or not. If both the lists are found to be empty then the control returns back.

If both the lists are not empty then a condition is checked whether either of the two lists is empty or not. If one of the two lists is found to be empty then the pointer of the resultant list is made to point to another list.

If both the lists exist then a **while** loop is executed which runs till the end of the first list (i.e. **x != NULL**). First time through this loop, each term of second list is multiplied with the first term of the first list. Then the pointer is again repositioned to the first term of the second list through the statement **y = y1**. The job of adding the resultant node to the resultant list is done through the function **padd( )**. This process is continued till we do not have multiplied each term of the first polynomial with the second polynomial.

Function *padd( )*

This function adds the node to the resultant list in the descending order of the exponents of the polynomial.

To begin with we initialize a structure pointer **temp** with a value *s, where *s is pointer to the first node of the resultant list. First time **padd( )** is called this value would be **NULL**.

Initially a condition is checked whether the resultant list is empty or not. If it is so then we need to add the first node. Hence memory is allocated for the new node and the value of coefficient and exponent is assigned to the coefficient and exponent part of the new node. **temp** which holds a **NULL** value to begin with is stored in the link part of the resultant new node.

When padd( ) is called to add the second node we need to compare the exponent value of the new node with that of the first node. If the exponent value of the new node is greater than the exponent value of the first node in the resultant list, then the new node is made the first node.

If both the above two conditions are false then the resultant list is traversed for searching the proper position where the new node is to be inserted. If the exponent of the same order already exists then simply the coefficient parts are added. If it does not exist then memory is allocated and a new node is inserted.

The process of searching the proper position to insert a node is exactly same as explained in the example of maintaining the linked list in ascending order, the only difference is that, there the list was maintained in ascending order and here it is maintained in descending order.

Exercise

[A] State whether the following statements are True or False:

(a) Linked list is used to store similar data.

(b) All nodes in the linked list must always be in non-contiguous memory locations.

(c) It is necessary that the **link** part of the last node in a linked list must contain **NULL**.

(d) In a singly linked list, if we lost the location of the first node : it is as good as having lost the entire linked list.

(e) Doubly linked list facilitates movement from one node to another in either direction.

(f) A doubly linked list will occupy less space as compared to a corresponding singly linked list.

(g) If we are to traverse from first node to last node it would be faster to do so if the linked list is singly linked instead of doubly linked.

(h) In a structure used to represent the node of a doubly linked list it is necessary that the structure elements are in the order backward link, data, forward link.

(i) If a pointer **p** is pointing to one of the nodes in a circular linked list, then moving the pointer to the next node would cause a memory leak.

[B] Answer the Following:

(a) Write a program to list the current directory in alphabetical order using a linked list.

Hints:

–   Use standard library functions **findfirst( )** and **findnext( )** in Turbo C to read the directory entries.

–   Define a structure **struct node**, which contains the standard structure **struct ffblk** defined in file "dos.h" as **data** part, and add another element **next** as **link** to the next node.

–   When all the directory entries are read and stored in the linked list, sort the linked list and then display the sorted linked list.

(b) Write a program that reads the name, age and salary of 10 persons and maintains them in a linked list sorted by name.

(c) There are two linked lists **A** and **B** containing the following data:

A: 3, 7, 10, 15, 16, 9, 22, 17, 32

B: 16, 2, 9, 13, 37, 8, 10, 1, 28

Write a program to create:

–   A linked list **C** that contains only those elements that are common in linked list **A** and **B**.

–   A linked list **D** which contains all elements of **A** as well as **B** ensuring that there is no repetition of elements.

(d) Assume a singly linked list containing integers. Write a function **move( )** which would move a node forward **n** positions in the linked list.

(e) Write in program to maintain a doubly linked circular linked list.

(f) There are two linked lists **A** and **B** containing the following data:

A: 7, 5, 3, 1, 20

B: 6, 25, 32, 11, 9

Write a function to combine the two lists such that the resulting list contains nodes in the following elements:

7, 6, 5, 25, 3, 32, 1, 11, 20, 9

You are not allowed to create any additional node while writing the function.

(g) A linked list contains some positive numbers and some negative numbers. Use this linked list write a program to create two more linked lists, one containing all positive numbers and the other containing all negative numbers.

(h) Create two linked lists to represent the following polynomials:

$3x^2y + 9xy^3 + 15\,xy + 3$
$13\,x^3y^2 + 7x^2y + 22\,xy + 9y^3$

Write a function **add( )** to add these polynomials and print the resulting linked list.

CHAPTER
FIVE

Sparse Matrices
Lean is better

7 1 percent of earth is occupied by water, leaving a meagerly 29
percent for land. It is only natural that we need to conserve the
available space. Nobody should occupy more space than what
they deserve to occupy, be it animals, man, plants or matrices.
There is no point in wasting costly space in computer's memory in

storing elements that do not deserve a place in it. Sparse matrix is the case in point.

If a lot of elements from a matrix have a value 0 then the matrix is known as a **sparse matrix**. There is no precise definition of when a matrix is sparse and when it is not, but it is a concept, which we can all recognise intuitively. If the matrix is sparse we must consider an alternate way of representing it rather than the normal row major or column major arrangement. This is because if majority of elements of the matrix are 0 then an alternative through which we can store only the non-zero elements and keep intact the functionality of the matrix can save a lot of memory space. Figure 5-1 shows a sparse matrix of dimension 7x7.

| | | COLUMN | | | | | |
		0	1	2	3	4	5	6
	0	0	0	0	5	0	0	0
	1	0	4	0	0	0	0	7
ROW	2	0	0	0	0	9	0	0
	3	0	3	0	2	0	0	0
	4	1	0	2	0	0	0	0
	5	0	0	0	0	0	0	0
	6	0	0	8	0	0	0	0

Figure 5-1. *Representation of a sparse matrix of dimension 7 x 7.*

A common way of representing non-zero elements of a sparse matrix is the 3-tuple forms. In this form each non-zero element is stored in a row, with the 1st and 2nd element of this row containing the row and column in which the element is present in the original matrix. The 3rd element in this row stores the actual value of the non-zero element. For example the 3-tuple representation of the sparse matrix shown in Figure 5-1 is shown below.

```
int spmat[10][3] = {
                7, 7, 9,
                0, 3, -5,
                1, 1, 4,
                1, 6, 7,
                2, 4, 9,
                3, 1, 3,
                3, 3, 2,
                4, 0, 11,
                4, 2, 2,
                6, 2, 8
               }
```

There are two ways in which information of a 3-tuple can be stored:

– Arrays
– Linked List

In both representations information about the non-zero elements is stored. However, as the number of non-zero elements in a sparse matrix may vary, it would be efficient to use a linked list to represent it.

Representation Of Sparse Matrix As An Array

Let us see a program that accepts elements of a sparse matrix and creates an array containing 3-tuples of non-zero elements present in the sparse matrix.

```c
#include <stdio.h>
#include <conio.h>
#include <alloc.h>
#define MAX1 3
#define MAX2 3

struct sparse
{
    int *sp ;
    int row ;
} ;

void initsparse ( struct sparse * ) ;
void create_array ( struct sparse * ) ;
void display ( struct sparse ) ;
int count ( struct sparse ) ;
void create_tuple ( struct sparse *, struct sparse ) ;
void display_tuple ( struct sparse ) ;
void delsparse ( struct sparse * ) ;

void main( )
{
    struct sparse s1, s2 ;
    int c ;

    clrscr( ) ;

    initsparse ( &s1 ) ;
    initsparse ( &s2 ) ;

    create_array ( &s1 ) ;
    printf ( "\nElements in Sparse Matrix: " ) ;
    display ( s1 ) ;

    c = count ( s1 ) ;
    printf ( "\n\nNumber of non-zero elements: %d", c ) ;

    create_tuple ( &s2, s1 ) ;
```

```
        printf ( "\n\nArray of non-zero elements: " ) ;
        display_tuple ( s2 ) ;

        delsparse ( &s1 ) ;
        delsparse ( &s2 ) ;

        getch( ) ;
}

/* initialises element of structure */
void initsparse ( struct sparse *p )
{
        p -> sp = NULL ;
}

/* dynamically creates the matrix of size MAX1 x MAX2 */
void create_array ( struct sparse *p )
{
        int n, i ;

        p -> sp = ( int * ) malloc ( MAX1 * MAX2 * sizeof ( int ) ) ;

        for ( i = 0 ; i < MAX1 * MAX2 ; i++ )
        {
                printf ( "Enter element no. %d: ", i ) ;
                scanf ( "%d", &n ) ;
                * ( p -> sp + i ) = n ;
        }
}

/* displays the contents of the matrix */
void display ( struct sparse p )
{
        int i ;

        /* traverses the entire matrix */
        for ( i = 0 ; i < MAX1 * MAX2 ; i++ )
        {
```

```
        /* positions the cursor to the new line for every new row */
        if ( i % MAX2 == 0 )
            printf ( "\n" ) ;
        printf ( "%d\t", * ( p.sp + i ) ) ;
    }
}

/* counts the number of non-zero elements */
int count ( struct sparse p )
{
    int cnt = 0, i ;

    for ( i = 0 ; i < MAX1 * MAX2 ; i++ )
    {
        if ( * ( p.sp + i ) != 0 )
            cnt++ ;
    }
    return cnt ;
}

/* creates an array that stores information about non-zero elements */
void create_tuple ( struct sparse *p, struct sparse s )
{
    int r = 0 , c = -1, l = -1, i ;

    p -> row = count ( s ) + 1 ;

    p -> sp = ( int * ) malloc ( p -> row * 3 * sizeof ( int ) ) ;
    * ( p -> sp + 0 ) = MAX1 ;
    * ( p -> sp + 1 ) = MAX2 ;
    * ( p -> sp + 2 ) = p -> row - 1 ;

    l = 2 ;

    for ( i = 0 ; i < MAX1 * MAX2 ; i++ )
    {
        c++ ;
```

```
        /* sets the row and column values */
        if ( ( ( i % MAX2 ) == 0 ) && ( i != 0 ) )
        {
            r++ ;
            c = 0 ;
        }

        /* checks for non-zero element
           row, column and non-zero element value
           is assigned to the matrix */
        if ( * ( s.sp + i ) != 0 )
        {
            l++ ;
            * ( p -> sp + l ) = r ;
            l++ ;
            * ( p -> sp + l ) = c ;
            l++ ;
            * ( p -> sp + l ) = * ( s.sp + i ) ;
        }
    }
}

/* displays the contents of 3-tuple */
void display_tuple ( struct sparse p )
{
    int i ;

    for ( i = 0 ; i < p.row * 3 ; i++ )
    {
        if ( i % 3 == 0 )
            printf ( "\n" ) ;
        printf ( "%d\t", * ( p.sp + i ) ) ;
    }
}

/* deallocates memory */
void delsparse ( struct sparse *p )
{
```

```
    free ( p -> sp ) ;
}
```

Output:

Enter element no. 0: 0
Enter element no. 1: 2
Enter element no. 2: 0
Enter element no. 3: 9
Enter element no. 4: 0
Enter element no. 5: 1
Enter element no. 6: 0
Enter element no. 7: 0
Enter element no. 8: -4

Elements in Sparse Matrix:
0   2   0
9   0   1
0   0   -4

Number of non-zero elements: 4

Array of non-zero elements:
3   3   4
0   1   2
1   0   9
1   2   1
2   2   -4

In this program we have designed a structure called **sparse**. In the **create_array( )** function, we have dynamically created a matrix of size **MAX1** x **MAX2**. The values for the matrix are accepted through keyboard. The **display( )** function displays the contents of the sparse matrix and the **count( )** function counts the total number of non-zero elements present in sparse matrix.

The **create_tuple( )** function creates a 2-D array dynamically. But, the question arises as how much space should get allocated for this array? Since each row in the 3-tuple form represents a non-zero element in the original array the new array should contain as many rows as the number of non-zero elements in the original matrix. From the 3-tuple form we must be able to build the original array. Hence the very first row in the new array should contain number of row, number of columns and number of non-zero elements in the original array. In the program we have determined the size of the new array through the following statements:

```
p -> row = count ( s ) + 1 ;
p -> sp = ( int * ) malloc ( row * 3 * sizeof ( int ) ) ;
```

In the first statement we have obtained the count of non-zero elements present in the given array. To that count we have added 1. The first row (i.e. 0th row) in this array stores the information about the total number of rows, columns and non-zero elements present in the given array. From second row (i.e. 1st row) onwards this array stores the row and column position of a non-zero element and the value of the non-zero element. Since the number of rows in the array depends on the number of non-zero elements in the given array we have created the array dynamically. The number of columns in this array would always be 3. The 0th column stores the row number of the non-zero element. The 1st column stores the column number of the non-zero element and the 2nd column stores the value of non-zero element.

Lastly, the **display_tuple( )** function displays the contents of 3-tuple.

Common Matrix Operations

Common matrix operations are addition, multiplication, transposition, etc. Let us see how these operations are carried out on a sparse matrix implemented as an array. Note that each program that we are going to discuss now consists of functions— **create_array( )**, **create_tuple( )**, **display( )**, **display_tuple( )** and **count( )**. We have already seen the working of these functions in previous program. Hence we shall discuss only the function(s) that perform given matrix operation.

Transpose Of A Sparse Matrix

Following program accepts elements of a sparse matrix, creates a 3-tuple form of non-zero elements present in the sparse matrix and then obtains a transpose of the sparse matrix from the 3-tuple form.

```
#include <stdio.h>
#include <conio.h>
#include <alloc.h>

#define MAX1 3
#define MAX2 3

struct sparse
{
    int *sp ;
    int row ;
} ;

void initsparse ( struct sparse * ) ;
void create_array ( struct sparse * ) ;
void display ( struct sparse ) ;
int count ( struct sparse ) ;
void create_tuple ( struct sparse *, struct sparse ) ;
void display_tuple ( struct sparse ) ;
void transpose ( struct sparse *, struct sparse ) ;
void display_transpose ( struct sparse ) ;
void delsparse ( struct sparse * ) ;
```

```
void main( )
{
    struct sparse s[3] ;
    int c, i ;

    for ( i = 0 ; i <= 2 ; i++ )
        initsparse ( &s[i] ) ;

    clrscr( ) ;

    create_array ( &s[0] ) ;

    printf ( "\nElements in Sparse Matrix: " ) ;
    display ( s[0] ) ;

    c = count ( s[0] ) ;
    printf ( "\n\nNumber of non-zero elements: %d", c ) ;

    create_tuple ( &s[1], s[0] ) ;
    printf ( "\n\nArray of non-zero elements: " ) ;
    display_tuple ( s[1] ) ;

    transpose ( &s[2], s[1] ) ;
    printf ( "\n\nTranspose of array: " ) ;
    display_transpose ( s[2] ) ;

    for ( i = 0 ; i <= 2 ; i++ )
        delsparse ( &s[i] ) ;

    getch( ) ;
}

/* initialises structure elements */
void initsparse ( struct sparse *p )
{
    p -> sp = NULL ;
}
```

```
/* dynamically creates the matrix of size MAX1 x MAX2 */
void create_array ( struct sparse *p )
{
    int n, i ;

    p -> sp = ( int * ) malloc ( MAX1 * MAX2 * sizeof ( int ) ) ;

    for ( i = 0 ; i < MAX1 * MAX2 ; i++ )
    {
        printf ( "Enter element no. %d:", i ) ;
        scanf ( "%d", &n ) ;

        * ( p -> sp + i ) = n ;
    }
}

/* displays the contents of the matrix */
void display ( struct sparse s )
{
    int i ;

    /* traverses the entire matrix */
    for ( i = 0 ; i < MAX1 * MAX2 ; i++ )
    {
        /* positions the cursor to the new line for every new row */
        if ( i % MAX2 == 0 )
            printf ( "\n" ) ;
        printf ( "%d\t", * ( s.sp + i ) ) ;
    }
}

/* counts the number of non-zero elements */
int count ( struct sparse s )
{
    int cnt = 0, i ;

    for ( i = 0 ; i < MAX1 * MAX2 ; i++ )
    {
```

```
            if ( * ( s.sp + i ) != 0 )
                cnt++ ;
    }
    return cnt ;
}
/* creates an array that stores information about non-zero elements */
void create_tuple ( struct sparse *p, struct sparse s )
{
    int r = 0 , c = -1, l = -1, i ;

    p -> row = count ( s ) + 1 ;

    p -> sp = ( int * ) malloc ( p -> row * 3 * sizeof ( int ) ) ;
    * ( p -> sp + 0 ) = MAX1 ;
    * ( p -> sp + 1 ) = MAX2 ;
    * ( p -> sp + 2 ) = p -> row - 1 ;

    l = 2 ;

    for ( i = 0 ; i < MAX1 * MAX2 ; i++ )
    {
        c++ ;

        /* sets the row and column values */
        if ( ( ( i % MAX2 ) == 0 ) && ( i != 0 ) )
        {
            r++ ;
            c = 0 ;
        }

        /* checks for non-zero element
           row, column and non-zero element value
           is assigned to the matrix */
        if ( * ( s.sp + i ) != 0 )
        {
            l++ ;
            * ( p -> sp + l ) = r ;
            l++ ;
```

```
            * ( p -> sp + l ) = c ;
            l++ ;
            * ( p -> sp + l ) = * ( s.sp + i ) ;
        }
    }
}

/* displays the contents of 3-tuple */
void display_tuple ( struct sparse p )
{
    int i ;

    for ( i = 0 ; i < p.row * 3 ; i++ )
    {
        if ( i % 3 == 0 )
            printf ( "\n" ) ;
        printf ( "%d\t", * ( p.sp + i ) ) ;
    }
}

/* obtains transpose of an array */
void transpose ( struct sparse *p, struct sparse s )
{
    int x, q, pos_1, pos_2, col, elem, c, y ;

    /* allocate memory */
    p -> sp = ( int * ) malloc ( s.row * 3 * sizeof ( int ) ) ;
    p -> row = s.row ;

    /* store total number of rows, cols
       and non-zero elements */
    * ( p -> sp + 0 ) = * ( s.sp + 1 ) ;
    * ( p -> sp + 1 ) = * ( s.sp + 0 ) ;
    * ( p -> sp + 2 ) = * ( s.sp + 2 ) ;

    col = * ( p -> sp + 1 ) ;
    elem = * ( p -> sp + 2 ) ;
```

```
if ( elem <= 0 )
    return ;

x = 1 ;

for ( c = 0 ; c < col ; c++ )
{
    for ( y = 1 ; y <= elem ; y++ )
    {
        q = y * 3 + 1 ;
        if ( * ( s.sp + q ) == c )
        {
            pos_2 = x * 3 + 0 ;
            pos_1 = y * 3 + 1 ;
            * ( p -> sp + pos_2 ) = * ( s.sp + pos_1 ) ;

            pos_2 = x * 3 + 1 ;
            pos_1 = y * 3 + 0 ;
            * ( p -> sp + pos_2 ) = * ( s.sp + pos_1 ) ;

            pos_2 = x * 3 + 2 ;
            pos_1 = y * 3 + 2 ;
            * ( p -> sp + pos_2 ) = * ( s.sp + pos_1 ) ;

            x++ ;
        }
    }
}
}

/* displays 3-tuple after transpose operation */
void display_transpose ( struct sparse p )
{
    int i ;

    for ( i = 0 ; i < p.row * 3 ; i++ )
    {
        if ( i % 3 == 0 )
```

```
            printf ( "\n" ) ;
        printf ( "%d\t", * ( p.sp + i ) ) ;
    }
}

/* deallocates memory */
void delsparse ( struct sparse *p )
{
    free ( p -> sp ) ;
}
```

Output:

Enter element no. 0:4
Enter element no. 1:0
Enter element no. 2:1
Enter element no. 3:0
Enter element no. 4:0
Enter element no. 5:3
Enter element no. 6:-2
Enter element no. 7:0
Enter element no. 8:0

Elements in Sparse Matrix:
```
4    0    1
0    0    3
-2   0    0
```

Number of non-zero elements: 4

Array of non-zero elements:
```
3    3    4
0    0    4
0    2    1
1    2    3
2    0    -2
```

Transpose of array:

```
3   3   4
0   0   4
0   2   -2
2   0   1
2   1   3
```

In the **transpose( )** function first we have allocated memory required to store the elements in the target 3-tuple. Next we have stored the total number of rows, columns and non-zero elements that this 3-tuple will hold. This is' achieved through the following three statements:

```
* ( p -> sp + 0 ) = * ( s.sp + 1 ) ;
* ( p -> sp + 1 ) = * ( s.sp + 0 ) ;
* ( p -> sp + 2 ) = * ( s.sp + 2 ) ;
```

Note that, here in **p -> sp**, the place where total number of rows should get stored we have stored total number of columns. Similarly in place where total number of columns should get stored we have stored total number of rows. This is because in case of transpose operation total number rows become equal to total number of columns and vice versa.

The transpose operation is carried out through a pair of **for** loops. The outer **for** loop runs till the non-zero elements of **col** number of columns (of source 3-tuple) are not scanned. In the inner **for** loop first we have obtained the position at which the column number of a non-zero element is stored (in the source 3-tuple) through the statement:

```
q = y * 3 + 1 ;
```

Then we have checked whether the column number of a non-zero element matches with the column number currently being considered i.e. **c**. If the two values match then the information is stored in the target 3-tuple through the statements given below:

```
pos_2 = x * 3 + 0 ;
pos_1 = y * 3 + 1 ;
* ( p -> sp + pos_2 ) = * ( s.sp + pos_1 ) ;
```

The variable **pos_2** is used for the target 3-tuple, to store the position at which data from source 3-tuple should get copied. Similarly, the variable **pos_1** is used for the source 3-tuple, to extract data from it. The third statement copies the column position of a non-zero element from source 3-tuple to the target 3-tuple. This column number gets stored at the row position in target 3-tuple.

On similar lines the row position of a non-zero element of source 3-tuple is copied at the column position of the target 3-tuple through the following statements:

```
pos_2 = x * 3 + 1 ;
pos_1 = y * 3 + 0 ;
* ( p -> sp + pos_2 ) = * ( s.sp + pos_1 ) ;
```

Finally, the non-zero value from source 3-tuple is copied to the target 3-tuple through the following statements:

```
pos_2 = x * 3 + 2 ;
pos_1 = y * 3 + 2 ;
* ( p -> sp + pos_2 ) = * ( s.sp + pos_1 ) ;
```

The target 3-tuple thus obtained is nothing but a transpose of an array that user has entered through **create_array( )** function. But the target 3-tuple stores the information of non-zero elements. The elements in this 3-tuple are then displayed by calling **display_transpose( )** function.

Addition Of Two Sparse Matrices

Let us now see a program that carries out addition of two sparse matrices represented in 3-tuple form. Here is the program...

```c
#include <stdio.h>
#include <conio.h>
#include <alloc.h>

#define MAX1 3
#define MAX2 3
#define MAXSIZE 9
#define BIGNUM 100

struct sparse
{
    int *sp ;
    int row ;
    int *result ;
} ;

void initsparse ( struct sparse * ) ;
void create_array ( struct sparse * ) ;
int count ( struct sparse ) ;
void display ( struct sparse ) ;
void create_tuple ( struct sparse *, struct sparse ) ;
void display_tuple ( struct sparse ) ;
void addmat ( struct sparse *, struct sparse, struct sparse ) ;
void display_result ( struct sparse ) ;
void delsparse ( struct sparse * ) ;

void main( )
{
    struct sparse s[5] ;
    int i ;

    clrscr( ) ;
```

```
        for ( i = 0 ; i <= 4 ; i++ )
        initsparse ( &s[i] ) ;

        create_array ( &s[0] ) ;

        create_tuple ( &s[1], s[0] ) ;
        display_tuple ( s[1] ) ;

        create_array ( &s[2] ) ;

        create_tuple ( &s[3], s[2] ) ;
        display_tuple ( s[3] ) ;

        addmat ( &s[4], s[1], s[3] ) ;

        printf ( "\nResult of addition of two matrices: " ) ;
        display_result ( s[4] ) ;

        for ( i = 0 ; i <= 4 ; i++ )
            delsparse ( &s[i] ) ;

        getch( ) ;
}

/* initialises structure elements */
void initsparse ( struct sparse *p )
{
        p -> sp = NULL ;
        p -> result = NULL ;
}

/* dynamically creates the matrix */
void create_array ( struct sparse *p )
{
        int n, i ;

        /* allocate memory */
        p -> sp = ( int * ) malloc ( MAX1 * MAX2 * sizeof ( int ) ) ;
```

```
/* add elements to the array */
for ( i = 0 ; i < MAX1 * MAX2 ; i++ )
{
        printf ( "Enter element no. %d: ", i ) ;
        scanf ( "%d", &n ) ;
        * ( p -> sp + i ) = n ;
}
}

/* displays the contents of the matrix */
void display ( struct sparse s )
{
    int i ;

    /* traverses the entire matrix */
    for ( i = 0 ; i < MAX1 * MAX2 ; i++ )
    {
        /* positions the cursor to the new line for every new row */
        if ( i % MAX2 == 0 )
            printf ( "\n" ) ;
        printf ( "%d\t", * ( s.sp + i ) ) ;
    }
}

/* counts the number of non-zero elements */
int count ( struct sparse s )
{
    int cnt = 0, i ;

    for ( i = 0 ; i < MAX1 * MAX2 ; i++ )
    {
        if ( * ( s.sp + i ) != 0 )
            cnt++ ;
    }
    return cnt ;
}
```

```
/* creates an array that stores information about non-zero elements */
void create_tuple ( struct sparse *p, struct sparse s )
{
    int r = 0 , c = -1, l = -1, i ;

    /* get the total number of non-zero elements
       and add 1 to store total no. of rows, cols, and non-zero values */
    p -> row = count ( s ) + 1 ;

    /* allocate memory */
    p -> sp = ( int * ) malloc ( p -> row * 3 * sizeof ( int ) ) ;

    /* store information about
       total no. of rows, cols, and non-zero values */
    * ( p -> sp + 0 ) = MAX1 ;
    * ( p -> sp + 1 ) = MAX2 ;
    * ( p -> sp + 2 ) = p -> row - 1 ;

    l = 2 ;

    /* scan the array and store info. about non-zero values
       in the 3-tuple */
    for ( i = 0 ; i < MAX1 * MAX2 ; i++ )
    {
        c++ ;

        /* sets the row and column values */
        if ( ( ( i % MAX2 ) == 0 ) && ( i != 0 ) )
        {
            r++ ;
            c = 0 ;
        }

        /* checks for non-zero element
           row, column and non-zero element value
           is assigned to the matrix */
        if ( * ( s.sp + i ) != 0 )
        {
```

```
                    I++ ;
                    * ( p -> sp + I ) = r ;
                    I++ ;
                    * ( p -> sp + I ) = c ;
                    I++ ;
                    * ( p -> sp + I ) = * ( s.sp + i ) ;
                }
            }
        }

/* displays the contents of the matrix */
void display_tuple ( struct sparse s )
{
    int i, j ;

    /* traverses the entire matrix */
    printf ( "\nElements in a 3-tuple: \n" ) ;

    j = ( * ( s.sp + 2 ) * 3 ) + 3 ;

    for ( i = 0 ; i < j ; i++ )
    {
        /* positions the cursor to the new line for every new row */
        if ( i % 3 == 0 )
            printf ( "\n" ) ;
        printf ( "%d\t", * ( s.sp + i ) ) ;
    }
    printf ( "\n" ) ;
}

/* carries out addition of two matrices */
void addmat ( struct sparse *p, struct sparse s1, struct sparse s2 )
{
    int i = 1, j = 1, k = 1 ;
    int elem = 1 ;
    int max, amax, bmax ;
    int rowa, rowb, cola, colb, vala, valb ;
```

```
/* get the total number of non-zero values
   from both the matrices */
amax = * ( s1.sp + 2 ) ;
bmax = * ( s2.sp + 2 ) ;
max = amax + bmax ;
/* allocate memory for result */
p -> result = ( int * ) malloc ( MAXSIZE * 3 * sizeof ( int ) `

while ( elem <= max )
{
    /* check if i < max. non-zero values
       in first 3-tuple and get the values */
    if ( i <= amax )
    {
        rowa = * ( s1.sp + i * 3 + 0 ) ;
        cola = * ( s1.sp + i * 3 + 1 ) ;
        vala = * ( s1.sp + i * 3 + 2 ) ;
    }
    else
        rowa = cola = BIGNUM ;

    /* check if j < max. non-zero values
       in secon 3-tuple and get the values */
    if ( j <= bmax )
    {
        rowb = * ( s2.sp + j * 3 + 0 ) ;
        colb = * ( s2.sp + j * 3 + 1 ) ;
        valb = * ( s2.sp + j * 3 + 2 ) ;
    }
    else
        rowb = colb = BIGNUM ;

    /* if row no. of both 3-tuple are same */
    if ( rowa == rowb )
    {
        /* if col no. of both 3-tuple are same */
        if ( cola == colb )
        {
```

```
                /* add tow non-zero values
                   store in result */
                * ( p -> result + k * 3 + 0 ) = rowa ;
                * ( p -> result + k * 3 + 1 ) = cola ;
                * ( p -> result + k * 3 + 2 ) = vala + valb ;
                i++ ;
                j++ ;
                max-- ;
        }

        /* if col no. of first 3-tuple is < col no. of
           second 3-tuple, then add info. as it is
           to result */
        if ( cola < colb )
        {
                * ( p -> result + k * 3 + 0 ) = rowa ;
                * ( p -> result + k * 3 + 1 ) = cola ;
                * ( p -> result + k * 3 + 2 ) = vala ;
                i++ ;
        }

        /* if col no. of first 3-tuple is > col no. of
           second 3-tuple, then add info. as it is
           to result */
        if ( cola > colb )
        {
                * ( p -> result + k * 3 + 0 ) = rowb ;
                * ( p -> result + k * 3 + 1 ) = colb ;
                * ( p -> result + k * 3 + 2 ) = valb ;
                j++ ;
        }
        k++ ;
}

/* if row no. of first 3-tuple is < row no. of
   second 3-tuple, then add info. as it is
   to result */
if ( rowa < rowb )
```

```
        {
            * ( p -> result + k * 3 + 0 ) = rowa ;
            * ( p -> result + k * 3 + 1 ) = cola ;
            * ( p -> result + k * 3 + 2 ) = vala ;
            i++ ;
            k++ ;
        }

        /* if row no. of first 3-tuple is > row no. of
           second 3-tuple, then add info. as it is
           to result */
        if ( rowa > rowb )
        {
            * ( p -> result + k * 3 + 0 ) = rowb ;
            * ( p -> result + k * 3 + 1 ) = colb ;
            * ( p -> result + k * 3 + 2 ) = valb ;
            j++ ;
            k++ ;
        }
        elem++ ;
    }

    /* add info about the total no. of rows,
       cols, and non-zero values that the resultant array
       contains to the result */
    * ( p -> result + 0 ) = MAX1 ;
    * ( p -> result + 1 ) = MAX2 ;
    * ( p -> result + 2 ) = max ;
}

/* displays the contents of the matrix */
void display_result ( struct sparse s )
{
    int i ;

    /* traverses the entire matrix */
    for ( i = 0 ; i < ( * ( s.result + 0 + 2 ) + 1 ) * 3 ; i++ )
    {
```

```
        /* positions the cursor to the new line for every new row */
        if ( i % 3 == 0 )
            printf ( "\n" ) ;
        printf ( "%d\t", * ( s.result + i ) ) ;
    }
}

/* deallocates memory */
void delsparse ( struct sparse *p )
{
    if ( p -> sp != NULL )
        free ( p -> sp ) ;
    if ( p -> result != NULL )
        free ( p -> result ) ;
}
```

Output:

Enter element no. 0: 1
Enter element no. 1: 0
Enter element no. 2: 2
Enter element no. 3: 0
Enter element no. 4: 3
Enter element no. 5: 0
Enter element no. 6: 4
Enter element no. 7: 0
Enter element no. 8: 0

Elements in a 3-tuple:

```
3    3    4
0    0    1
0    2    2
1    1    3
2    0    4
```
Enter element no. 1: 0
Enter element no. 2: 0
Enter element no. 3: 1

Enter element no. 4: 0
Enter element no. 5: 2
Enter element no. 6: 0
Enter element no. 7: 9
Enter element no. 8: 0

Elements in a 3-tuple:

```
3  3  3
1  0  1
1  2  2
2  1  9
```

Result of addition of two matrices:
```
3  3  7
0  0  1
0  2  2
1  0  1
1  1  3
1  2  2
2  0  4
2  1  9
```

The function **addmat( )** carries out addition of two sparse matrices. In this function firstly we have obtained the total number of non-zero elements that the target 3-tuple would hold. This has been achieved through the following statements:

```
amax = * ( s1.sp + 2 ) ;
bmax = * ( s2.sp + 2 ) ;
max = amax + bmax ;
```

Then we have allocated memory for the target 3-tuple that would store the result obtained from addition. Through a **while** loop we have carried out the addition operation. The variables **i** and **j** are used as counters for first 3-tuple (pointed to by **s1.sp**) and second

3-tuple (pointed to by **s2.sp**) respectively. Then we have retrieved the row number, column number and the non-zero value of ith and j^{th} non-zero element respectively. The following cases are considered while performing addition.

(a) If the row numbers as well as column numbers of the non-zero values retrieved from first and second 3-tuple (pointed to by s1.sp and s2.sp respectively) are same then we have added two non-zero values **vala** and **valb**. The row number **rowa**, column number **cola** and **vala + valb** is then copied to the target 3-tuple poited to by **result**.

(b) If column number of first 3-tuple is less than the column number of second 3-tuple, then we have added the information about the ith non-zero value of first 3-tuple to the target 3-tuple.

(c) If column number of first 3-tuple is greater than the column number of second 3-tuple, then we have added the information about the jth non-zero value of second 3-tuple to the target 3-tuple.

(d) If row number of first 3-tuple is less than the row number of second 3-tuple, then we have added the information about the ith non-zero value of first 3-tuple to the target 3-tuple.

(e) If row number of first 3-tuple is greater than the row number of second 3-tuple, then we have added the information about the jth non-zero value of second 3-tuple to the target 3-tuple.

Finally, the total number of rows, columns and non-zero values that the target 3-tuple holds is stored in the zeroth row of the target 3-tuple (pointed to by **result**). The function **display_result( )** displays result of the addition operation.

Multiplication Of Two Sparse Matrices

Now that we know how to obtain transpose of a sparse matrix and how to add two sparse matrices let us get into more complicated stuff. Following program carries out multiplication of two sparse matrices through their 3-tuple form.

```c
#include <stdio.h>
#include <conio.h>
#include <alloc.h>

#define MAX1 3
#define MAX2 3
#define MAXSIZE 20

#define TRUE 1
#define FALSE 2

struct sparse
{
    int *sp ;
    int row ;
    int *result ;
} ;

void initsparse ( struct sparse * ) ;
void create_array ( struct sparse * ) ;
int count ( struct sparse ) ;
void display ( struct sparse ) ;
void create_tuple ( struct sparse*, struct sparse ) ;
void display_tuple ( struct sparse ) ;
void prodmat ( struct sparse *, struct sparse, struct sparse ) ;
void searchina ( int *sp, int ii, int*p, int*flag ) ;
void searchinb ( int *sp, int jj, int colofa, int*p, int*flag ) ;
void display_result ( struct sparse ) ;
void delsparse ( struct sparse * ) ;
```

```
void main( )
{
    struct sparse s[5] ;
    int i ;

    clrscr( ) ;

    for ( i = 0 ; i <= 3 ; i++ )
        initsparse ( &s[i] ) ;

    create_array ( &s[0] ) ;

    create_tuple ( &s[1], s[0] ) ;
    display_tuple ( s[1] ) ;

    create_array ( &s[2] ) ;

    create_tuple ( &s[3], s[2] ) ;
    display_tuple ( s[3] ) ;

    prodmat ( &s[4], s[1], s[3] ) ;

    printf ( "\nResult of multiplication of two matrices: " ) ;
    display_result ( s[4] ) ;

    for ( i = 0 ; i <= 3 ; i++ )
        delsparse ( &s[i] ) ;

    getch( ) ;
}

/* initialises elements of structure */
void initsparse ( struct sparse *p )
{
    p -> sp = NULL ;
    p -> result = NULL ;
}
```

```c
/* dynamically creates the matrix */
void create_array ( struct sparse *p )
{
    int n, i ;

    /* allocate memory */
    p -> sp = ( int * ) malloc ( MAX1 * MAX2 * sizeof ( int ) ) ;

    /* add elements to the array */
    for ( i = 0 ; i < MAX1 * MAX2 ; i++ )
    {
        printf ( "Enter element no. %d: ", i ) ;
        scanf ( "%d", &n ) ;
        * ( p -> sp + i ) = n ;
    }
}

/* displays the contents of the matrix */
void display ( struct sparse s )
{
    int i ;

    /* traverses the entire matrix */
    for ( i = 0 ; i < MAX1 * MAX2 ; i++ )
    {
        /* positions the cursor to the new line for every new row */
        if ( i % 3 == 0 )
            printf ( "\n" ) ;
        printf ( "%d\t", * ( s.sp + i ) ) ;
    }
}

/* counts the number of non-zero elements */
int count ( struct sparse s )
{
    int cnt = 0, i ;

    for ( i = 0 ; i < MAX1 * MAX2 ; i++ )
```

```
    {
        if ( * ( s.sp + i ) != 0 )
            cnt++ ;
    }
    return cnt ;
}

/* creates an array that stores information about non-zero elements */
void create_tuple ( struct sparse *p, struct sparse s )
{
    int r = 0 , c = -1, l = -1, i ;

    /* get the total number of non-zero elements */
    p -> row = count ( s ) + 1 ;

    /* allocate memory */
    p -> sp = ( int * ) malloc ( p -> row * 3 * sizeof ( int ) ) ;

    /* store information about
       total no. of rows, cols, and non-zero values */
    * ( p -> sp + 0 ) = MAX1 ;
    * ( p -> sp + 1 ) = MAX2 ;
    * ( p -> sp + 2 ) = p -> row - 1 ;

    l = 2 ;

    /* scan the array and store info. about non-zero values
       in the 3-tuple */
    for ( i = 0 ; i < MAX1 * MAX2 ; i++ )
    {
        c++ ;

        /* sets the row and column values */
        if ( ( ( ( i % 3 ) == 0 ) && ( i != 0 ) )
        {
            r++ ;
            c = 0 ;
        }
```

```
                /* checks for non-zero element,
                    row, column and non-zero value
                    is assigned to the matrix */
                if ( * ( s.sp + i ) != 0 )
                {
                    l++ ;
                    * ( p -> sp + l ) = r ;
                    l++ ;
                    * ( p -> sp + l ) = c ;
                    l++ ;
                    * ( p -> sp + l ) = * ( s.sp + i ) ;
                }
            }
}

/* displays the contents of the matrix */
void display_tuple ( struct sparse s )
{
    int i, j ;

    /* traverses the entire matrix */
    printf ( "\nElements in a 3-tuple: " ) ;

    j = ( * ( s.sp + 2 ) * 3 ) + 3 ;

    for ( i = 0 ; i < j ; i++ )
    {
        /* positions the cursor to the new line for every new row */
        if ( i % 3 == 0 )
            printf ( "\n" ) ;
        printf ( "%d\t", * ( s.sp + i ) ) ;
    }
    printf ( "\n" ) ;
}

/* performs multiplication of sparse matrices */
void prodmat ( struct sparse *p, struct sparse a, struct sparse b )
{
```

```
int sum, k, position, posi, flaga, flagb, i , j ;
k = 1 ;

p -> result = ( int * ) malloc ( MAXSIZE * 3 * sizeof ( int ) ) ;

for ( i = 0 ; i < * ( a.sp + 0 * 3 + 0 ) ; i++ )
{
    for ( j = 0 ; j < * ( b.sp + 0 * 3 + 1 ) ; j++ )
    {
        /* search if an element present at ith row */
        searchina ( a.sp, i, &position, &flaga ) ;
        if ( flaga == TRUE )
        {
            sum = 0 ;

            /* run loop till there are element at ith row
                in first 3-tuple */
            while ( * ( a.sp + position * 3 + 0 ) == i )
            {
                /* search if an element present at ith col.
                    in second 3-tuple */
                searchinb ( b.sp, j, * ( a.sp + position * 3 + 1 ),
                        &posi, &flagb ) ;

                /* if found then multiply */
                if ( flagb == TRUE )
                    sum = sum + * ( a.sp + position * 3 + 2 ) *
                            * ( b.sp + posi * 3 + 2 ) ;
                position = position + 1 ;
            }
            /* add result */
            if ( sum != 0 )
            {
                * ( p -> result + k * 3 + 0 ) = i ;
                * ( p -> result + k * 3 + 1 ) = j ;
                * ( p -> result + k * 3 + 2 ) = sum ;
                k = k + 1 ;
            }
```

```
            }
        }
    }

    /* add total no. of rows, cols and non-zero values */
    * ( p -> result + 0 * 3 + 0 ) = * ( a.sp + 0 * 3 + 0 ) ;
    * ( p -> result + 0 * 3 + 1 ) = * ( b.sp + 0 * 3 + 1 ) ;
    * ( p -> result + 0 * 3 + 2 ) = k - 1 ;
}

/* searches if an element present at iith row */
void searchina ( int *sp, int ii, int *p, int *flag )
{
    int j ;
    *flag = FALSE ;
    for ( j = 1 ; j <= * ( sp + 0 * 3 + 2 ) ; j++ )
    {
        if ( * ( sp + j * 3 + 0 ) == ii )
        {
            *p = j ;
            *flag = TRUE ;
            return ;
        }
    }
}

/* searches if an element where col. of first 3-tuple
   is equal to row of second 3-tuple */
void searchinb ( int *sp, int jj, int colofa, int *p, int *flag )
{
    int j ;
    *flag = FALSE ;
    for ( j = 1 ; j <= * ( sp + 0 * 3 + 2 ) ; j++ )
    {
        if ( * ( sp + j * 3 + 1 ) == jj && * ( sp + j * 3 + 0 ) == colofa )
        {
            *p = j ;
            *flag = TRUE ;
```

```
                return ;
            }
        }
    }

    /* displays the contents of the matrix */
    void display_result ( struct sparse s )
    {
        int i ;

        /* traverses the entire matrix */
        for ( i = 0 ; i < ( * ( s.result + 0 + 2 ) + 1 ) * 3 ; i++ )
        {
            /* positions the cursor to the new line for every new row */
            if ( i % 3 == 0 )
                printf ( "\n" ) ;
            printf ( "%d\t", * ( s.result + i ) ) ;
        }
    }

    /* deallocates memory */
    void delsparse ( struct sparse *s )
    {
        if ( s -> sp != NULL )
            free ( s -> sp ) ;
        if ( s -> result != NULL )
            free ( s -> result ) ;
    }
```

Output:

Enter element no. 0: 0
Enter element no. 1: 4
Enter element no. 2: 1
Enter element no. 3: 0
Enter element no. 4: 0
Enter element no. 5: 1
Enter element no. 6: 1

Enter element no. 7: 0
Enter element no. 8: 0

Elements in a 3-tuple:

3	3	4
0	1	4
0	2	1
1	2	1
2	0	1

Enter element no. 0: 2
Enter element no. 1: 0
Enter element no. 2: 0
Enter element no. 3: 1
Enter element no. 4: 0
Enter element no. 5: 2
Enter element no. 6: 0
Enter element no. 7: 0
Enter element no. 8: 0

Elements in a 3-tuple:

3	3	3
0	0	2
1	0	1
1	2	2

Result of multiplication of two matrices:

3	3	3
0	0	4
0	2	8
2	0	2

In this program there are three functions **prodmat( ), searchina( ),
searchinb( )** which take part in the multiplication of two given
sparse matrices.

In the **prodmat( )** function first we have allocated memory
required to store the resultant 3-tuple. Then the multiplication is

carried out through a pair of **for** loops. The outer **for** loop runs for the number of times which is equal to the row dimension of first 3-tuple (pointed to by **a**), and the inner **for** loop runs for the number of times, which is equal to the column dimension of second 3-tuple (pointed to by **b**). Then we have called **searchina( )** function. This function checks whether or not an element is present in **a** at i^{th} row. If a non-zero element is there then this function sets **flaga** to **TRUE** and stores the position in **position** using which a non-zero element at i^{th} row is retrieved. Next, a **while** runs till there are elements at i^{th} row in **a**. Now, in this loop we have called **searchinb( )** function which searches for an element whose row number is equal to the column number of an element of **a** currently being considered and column number is equal to **j**. If a non-zero element is present then this function sets **flagb** to **TRUE** and stores position in **posi** using which a non-zero element is retrieved from **b**. The multiplication of two non-zero elements is carried out if **flagb** is **TRUE**. After termination of **while** loop the result of multiplication is stored to the target 3-tuple. Finally, the total number of rows, columns and non-zero values that the target 3-tuple holds is stored in its 0th row. Lastly, the result is displayed by calling **display_result( )** function.

Linked Representation Of A Sparse Matrix

Representing a sparse matrix as an array of 3-tuples suffers from one important limitation. When we carry out addition or multiplication it is not possible to predict beforehand how many elements in the resultant matrix would be non-zero. As a result, it is not possible to predict the size of the resultant matrix beforehand. Instead of an array we can represent the sparse matrix in the form of a linked list.

In the linked list representation a separate list is maintained for each column as well as each row of the matrix, i.e. if the matrix is of size 3 x 3, then there would be 3 lists for 3 columns and 3 lists for 3 rows. A node in a list stores the information about the non-zero element of the sparse matrix. The head node for a column list stores the column number, a pointer to the node, which comes first in the column, and a pointer to the next column head node. Thus the structure for column head node would be as shown below:

```
struct cheadnode
{
    struct node *down ;
    int colno ;
    struct cheadnode *next ;
} ;
```

A head node for a row list stores, a pointer to the node, which comes first in the row list, and a pointer to the next row head node. The structure for row head node would be as shown below:

```
struct rheadnode
{
    struct rheadnode *next ;
    int rowno ;
    struct node *right ;
} ;
```

A node on the other hand stores the row number, column number and the value of the non-zero element of the sparse matrix. It also stores a pointer to the node that is immediately to the right of the node in the row list as well as a pointer to the node that is immediately below the node in the column list. The structure for a node would be as shown below:

```
struct node
{
    int row ;
    int col ;
    int val ;
```

```
    struct node *down ;
    struct node *right ;
} ;
```

In addition to this a special node is used to store the total number of rows, total number of columns, a pointer to the first row head node and a pointer to the first column head node. The information stored in this special node is used for traversing the list. The structure of this special node would be as shown below:

```
struct spmat
{
    struct rheadnode *firstrow ;
    int noofrows ;
    int noofcols ;
    struct cheadnode *firstcol ;
} ;
```

If a particular column list is empty then the field **down** of the column head node would be NULL. Similarly if a row list is empty then the field **right** of the row head node would be empty. If a node is the last node in a particular column list or a particular row list then the field **down** or the field **right** of the node would be NULL.

Figure 5-2 gives pictorial representation of linked list of a sparse matrix of size 3 x 3.

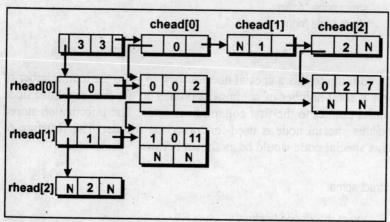

Figure 5-2. *Linked Representation of a sparse matrix.*

Let us now see a program that stores sparse matrix in the linked list form.

```c
#include <stdio.h>
#include <conio.h>
#include <alloc.h>

#define MAX1 3
#define MAX2 3

/* structure for col headnode */
struct cheadnode
{
    int colno ;
    struct node *down ;
    struct cheadnode *next ;
} ;

/* structure for row headnode */
struct rheadnode
```

```
{
    int rowno ;
    struct node * right ;
    struct rheadnode *next ;
} ;

/* structure for node to store element */
struct node
{
    int row ;
    int col ;
    int val ;
    struct node *right ;
    struct node *down ;
} ;

/* structure for special headnode */
struct spmat
{
    struct rheadnode *firstrow ;
    struct cheadnode *firstcol ;
    int noofrows ;
    int noofcols ;
} ;

struct sparse
{
    int *sp ;
    int row  ;
    struct spmat *smat ;
    struct cheadnode *chead[MAX2] ;
    struct rheadnode *rhead[MAX1] ;
    struct node *nd ;
} ;

void initsparse ( struct sparse * ) ;
void create_array ( struct sparse * ) ;
void display ( struct sparse ) ;
```

```
int count ( struct sparse ) ;
void create_triplet ( struct sparse *, struct sparse ) ;
void create_llist ( struct sparse * ) ;
void insert ( struct sparse *, struct spmat *, int, int, int ) ;
void show_llist ( struct sparse ) ;
void delsparse ( struct sparse * ) ;

void main( )
{
    struct sparse s1, s2 ;

    clrscr( ) ;

    initsparse ( &s1 ) ;
    initsparse ( &s2 ) ;

    create_array ( &s1 ) ;

    printf ( "\nElements in sparse matrix: " ) ;
    display ( s1 ) ;

    create_triplet ( &s2, s1 ) ;

    create_llist ( &s2 ) ;
    printf ( "\n\nInformation stored in linked list : " ) ;
    show_llist ( s2 ) ;

    delsparse ( &s1 ) ;
    delsparse ( &s2 ) ;

    getch( ) ;
}

/* initializes structure elements */
void initsparse ( struct sparse *p )
{
    int i ;
    /* create row headnodes */
```

```
    for ( i = 0 ; i < MAX1 ; i++ )
        p -> rhead[i] = ( struct rheadnode * ) malloc ( sizeof ( struct
                                                    rheadnode ) ) ;

    /* initialize and link row headnodes together */
    for ( i = 0 ; i < MAX1 - 1 ; i++ )
    {
        p -> rhead[i] -> next = p -> rhead[i + 1] ;
        p -> rhead[i] -> right = NULL ;
        p -> rhead[i] -> rowno = i ;
    }
    p -> rhead[i] -> right = NULL ;
    p -> rhead[i] -> next = NULL ;

    /* create col headnodes */
    for ( i = 0 ; i < MAX1 ; i++ )
        p -> chead[i] = ( struct cheadnode * ) malloc ( sizeof ( struct
cheadnode ) ) ;

    /* initialize and link col headnodes together */
    for ( i = 0 ; i < MAX2 - 1 ; i++ )
    {
        p -> chead[i] -> next = p -> chead[i + 1] ;
        p -> chead[i] -> down = NULL ;
        p -> chead[i] -> colno = i ;
    }
    p -> chead[i] -> down = NULL ;
    p -> chead[i] -> next = NULL ;

    /* create and initialize special headnode */
    p -> smat = ( struct spmat * ) malloc ( sizeof ( struct spmat ) ) ;
    p -> smat -> firstcol = p -> chead[0] ;
    p -> smat -> firstrow = p -> rhead[0] ;
    p -> smat -> noofcols = MAX2 ;
    p -> smat -> noofrows = MAX1 ;
}

/* creates, dynamically the matrix of size MAX1 x MAX2 */
```

```
void create_array ( struct sparse *p )
{
    int n, i ;

    p -> sp = ( int * ) malloc ( MAX1 * MAX2 * sizeof ( int ) ) ;

    /* get the element and store it */
    for ( i = 0 ; i < MAX1 * MAX2 ; i++ )
    {
        printf ( "Enter element no. %d: ", i ) ;
        scanf ( "%d", &n ) ;
        * ( p -> sp + i ) = n ;
    }
}

/* displays the contents of the matrix */
void display ( struct sparse s )
{
    int i ;

    /* traverses the entire matrix */
    for ( i = 0 ; i < MAX1 * MAX2 ; i++ )
    {
        /* positions the cursor to the new line for every new row */
        if ( i % MAX2 == 0 )
            printf ( "\n" ) ;
        printf ( "%d\t", * ( s.sp + i ) ) ;
    }
}

/* counts the number of non-zero elements */
int count ( struct sparse s )
{
    int cnt = 0, i ;

    for ( i = 0 ; i < MAX1 * MAX2 ; i++ )
    {
        if ( * ( s.sp + i ) != 0 )
```

```
            cnt++ ;
    }
    return cnt ;
}

/* creates an array of triplet containing info. about non-zero elements */
void create_triplet ( struct sparse *p, struct sparse s )
{
    int r = 0 , c = -1, l = -1, i ;

    p -> row = count ( s ) ;
    p -> sp = ( int * ) malloc ( p -> row * 3 * sizeof ( int ) ) ;

    for ( i = 0 ; i < MAX1 * MAX2 ; i++ )
    {
        c++ ;
        /* sets the row and column values */
        if ( ( ( i % MAX2 ) == 0 ) && ( i != 0 ) )
        {
            r++ ;
            c = 0 ;
        }

        /* checks for non-zero element. Row, column and
           non-zero element value is assigned to the matrix */

        if ( * ( s.sp + i ) != 0 )
        {
            l++ ;
            * ( p -> sp + l ) = r ;
            l++ ;
            * ( p -> sp + l ) = c ;
            l++ ;
            * ( p -> sp + l ) = * ( s.sp + i ) ;
        }
    }
}
```

```c
/* stores information of triplet in a linked list form */
void create_llist ( struct sparse *p )
{
    int j = 0, i ;
    for ( i = 0 ; i < p -> row ; i++, j+= 3 )
        insert ( p, p -> smat, * ( p -> sp + j ), * ( p -> sp + j + 1 ),
                                              * ( p -> sp + j + 2 ) ) ;

}

/* inserts element to the list */
void insert ( struct sparse *p, struct spmat *smat , int r, int c, int v )
{
    struct node *temp1, *temp2 ;
    struct rheadnode *rh ;
    struct cheadnode *ch ;
    int i, j ;

    /*  allocate and initialize memory for the node */
    p -> nd = ( struct node * ) malloc ( sizeof ( struct node ) ) ;
    p -> nd -> col = c ;
    p -> nd -> row = r ;
    p -> nd -> val = v ;

    /* get the first row headnode */
    rh = smat -> firstrow ;

    /* get the proper row headnode */
    for ( i = 0 ; i < r ; i++ )
        rh = rh -> next ;
    temp1 = rh -> right ;

    /* if no element added in a row */
    if ( temp1 == NULL )
    {
        rh -> right = p -> nd ;
        p -> nd -> right = NULL ;
    }
    else
```

```
{
    /* add element at proper position */
    while ( ( temp1 != NULL ) && ( temp1 -> col < c ) )
    {
        temp2 = temp1 ;
        temp1 = temp1 -> right ;
    }
    temp2 -> right = p -> nd ;
    p -> nd -> right = NULL ;
}

/* link proper col headnode with the node */
ch = p -> smat -> firstcol ;
for ( j = 0 ; j < c ; j++ )
    ch = ch -> next ;
temp1 = ch -> down ;

/* if col not pointing to any node */
if ( temp1 == NULL )
{
    ch -> down = p -> nd ;
    p -> nd -> down = NULL ;
}
else
{
    /* link previous node in column with next node in same column */
    while ( ( temp1 != NULL ) && ( temp1 -> row < r ) )
    {
        temp2 = temp1 ;
        temp1 = temp1 -> down ;
    }
    temp2 -> down = p -> nd ;
    p -> nd -> down = NULL ;
}
}

void show_llist ( struct sparse s )
{
```

```
        struct node *temp ;
        /* get the first row headnode */
        int r = s.smat -> noofrows ;
        int i ;

        printf ( "\n" ) ;

        for ( i = 0 ; i < r ; i++ )
        {
            temp = s.rhead[i] -> right ;
            if ( temp != NULL )
            {
                while ( temp -> right != NULL )
                {
                    printf ( "Row: %d Col: %d Val: %d\n", temp -> row,
                                                temp -> col, temp -> val ) ;
                    temp = temp -> right ;
                }
                if ( temp -> row == i )
                    printf ( "Row: %d Col: %d Val: %d\n", temp -> row,
                                                temp -> col, temp -> val ) ;
            }
        }
}

/* deallocates memory */
void delsparse ( struct sparse *p )
{
    int r = p -> smat -> noofrows ;
    struct rheadnode *rh ;
    struct node *temp1, *temp2 ;
    int i, c ;

    /* deallocate memeory of nodes by traversing rowwise */
    for ( i = r - 1 ; i >= 0 ; i-- )
    {
        rh = p -> rhead[i] ;
        temp1 = rh -> right ;
```

```
        while ( temp1 != NULL )
        {
                temp2 = temp1 -> right ;
                free ( temp1 ) ;
                temp1 = temp2 ;
        }
}

        /* deallocate memory of row headnodes */
        for ( i = r - 1 ; i >= 0 ; i-- )
                free ( p -> rhead[i] ) ;

        /* deallocate memory of col headnodes */
        c = p -> smat -> noofcols ;
        for ( i = c - 1 ; i >= 0 ; i-- )
                free ( p -> chead[i] ) ;
}
```

Output:

Enter element no. 0: 2
Enter element no. 1: 0
Enter element no. 2: 7
Enter element no. 3: 11
Enter element no. 4: 0
Enter element no. 5: 0
Enter element no. 6: 0
Enter element no. 7: 0
Enter element no. 8: 0

Elements in sparse matrix:
2   0   7
11   0   0
0   0   0

Information stored in linked list :
Row: 0 Col: 0 Val: 2
Row: 0 Col: 2 Val: 7

Row: 1 Col: 0 Val: 11

In this program first we have created a matrix of size **MAX1** x **MAX2**. The variable **s1** of the type **struct sparse** holds this matrix. Then as done in the previous programs we have created a triplet containing information about the non-zero elements of the matrix. The variable **s2** of the type **struct sparse** stores the triplet. Then we have called **create_llist( )** function to store the information in the form of a linked list.

In **create_llist( )** function through a **for** loop we have called **insert( )** function to add nodes to the linked list. The number of iterations in **for** loop depends on the total number of rows in the triplet. Note that the special node **smat**, an array **rhead** of row head nodes and an array **chead** of column head nodes has already been initialised in the function **initsparse( )** called after creating the variable **s2**. Let us now discuss how **insert( )** function adds node(s) to the linked list.

To the **insert( )** function we have passed a pointer **smat** to the special node, the row number **r**, column number **c** and the value **v** of the non-zero element. In this function first we have created a new node **nd**. Then we have initialized the field **row**, **col** and **val** of this node **nd** with the respective data. Then to place this node in the row list at a proper position, first we need to know the first row head node. This we have retrieved from the field **firstrow** of **smat**. Once we get the row head node, next job is to get the proper row head node for the node **nd** that is to be added in the row list. This has been done through a loop as shown below:

```
/* get the proper row head node */
for ( i = 0 ; i < r ; i++ )
    rh = rh -> next ;
```

The statement **temp1** = **rh** -> **right** stores the address of the first node in the row list (with row head node **rh**). If the row list is empty then **temp1** would be NULL. If so, then the node **nd** would be the first node in the row list and the field **right** of **rh** would be made to point to the node **nd**. But if **temp1** is not NULL, then we would be required to traverse the row list till we get a node that is the last node in the row list. The node in the row list whose right field stores NULL value and column number stored in **col** is less than the column number of **nd** would be the last node. The field **right** of such a node would then point to the node **nd**.

Next, this node **nd** should also get linked with the proper column head node. To do so first we should know the first column head node. We have retrieved the first column head node from **smat**. Through a **for** loop (as done in case of row list) we have retrieved the proper column head node **ch**. The field **down** of **ch** gives the address of the node, which is the first node in the column list currently being considered. If the column list is empty then **temp1** (that stores the address of first node in the column list) would be NULL. If so then the node **nd** would be the first node in the column list and the field **down** of **ch** would be made to point to the node **nd**.

However, if **temp1** is not NULL, then we would be required to traverse the column list to get a node which is the last node in the column list. The node in the column list whose **down** field stores NULL value and row number stored in **row** is less than the row number of **nd** would be the last node. The field **down** of such a node would then point to the node **nd**. Thus the nodes containing information about non-zero elements would get placed in the proper row list as well as column list.

To read and display the data stored in the linked list we have called function **show_llist( )**. Here we have traversed the list row wise. To traverse through row list first we should know the total number of row head nodes in the list. This we have retrieved from the field

noofrows of **smat**. The **for** loop runs for **r** times (where **r** stores **noofrows**). In every iteration of **for** loop we have traversed a row list (with row head node **rhead[i]**) till we get a node whose right field has got NULL value, and displayed the data of each node in the row list.

Other Forms Of A Sparse Matrix

A sparse matrix, which is also a square matrix, can fall in the following categories:

Diagonal	Where the non-zero elements are stored on the leading diagonal of the matrix.
Tridiagonal	Where the non-zero elements are placed below or above the leading diagonal.
Lower Triangular	Where the non-zero elements are placed below the leading diagonal.
Upper Triangular	Where the non-zero elements are placed above the leading diagonal.

Figure 5-3 illustrates these four matrices.

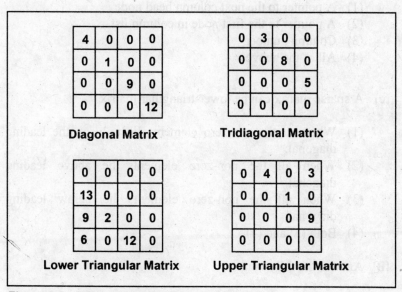

Figure 5-3. *Different forms of Sparse matrices.*

Exercise

[A] Pick up the correct alternative for each of the following questions:

(a) A matrix is called sparse when

    (1) Most of its elements are non-zero

    (2) Most of its elements are zero

    (3) All of its elements are non-zero

    (4) None of the above

(b) In the linked representation of a sparse matrix the head node for a column list stores

(1) A pointer to the next column head node
(2) A pointer to the first node in column list
(3) Column number
(4) All of the above

(c) A sparse matrix can be lower-triangular matrix

   (1) When all the non-zero elements lie only on the leading diagonal.
   (2) When all the non-zero elements lie above leading diagonal.
   (3) When all the non-zero elements lie below leading diagonal.
   (4) Both (3) and (4)

[B] Answer the following:

(a) Write a program to build a sparse matrix as an array. Write functions to check if the sparse matrix is a square, diagonal, lower triangular, upper triangular or tridiagonal matrix.

(b) Write a program to subtract two sparse matrices implemented as an array.

(c) Write a program to build a spare matrix as a linked list. The program should provide functions for following operations:
   (i)   Store an element when the row number, column number and the value is provided.
   (i)   Retrieve an element for given row and column number of the matrix.
   (ii) Add two sparse matrices
   (iii) Subtract two sparse matrices

CHAPTER
SIX

Stacks
Of Wad Of Notes

Be it items in a store, books in a library, or notes in a bank, the moment they become more than handful man starts stacking them neatly. It was natural, that when man started programming data, stack was one of the first structures that he thought of when faced with the problem of maintaining data in an orderly fashion. There is a small difference however, data in a

281

stack is consumed in an orderly fashion; same may not, be necessarily true in case of wads of nodes.

The linear data structure such as an array and a linked list allows us to insert and delete an element at any place in the list, either at the beginning or at the end or even in the middle. However, sometimes it is required to permit the addition or deletion of elements only at one end, that is either at the beginning or at the end. Stack and Queue are two types of data structures in which the addition or deletion of an element is done at end, rather than in the middle.

A Stack is a data structure in which addition of new element or deletion of an existing element always takes place at the same end. This end is often known as **top** of stack. This situation can be compared to a stack of plates in a cafeteria where every new plate added to the stack is added at the **top**. Similarly, every new plate taken off the stack is also from the **top** of the stack. The two changes that can be made to a stack are given special names. When an item is added to a stack, the operation is called **push**, and when an item is removed from the stack the operation is called **pop**. Stack is also called as last-in-first-out (LIFO) list. If the elements are added continuously to the stack it grows at one end. This is shown in Figure 6-1.

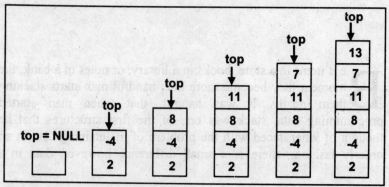

Figure 6-1. *Pictorial representation of stack after inserting elements.*

On deletion of elements the stack shrinks at the same end, as the elements at the top get removed. Figure 6-2 shows how the stack shrinks on deletion of elements.

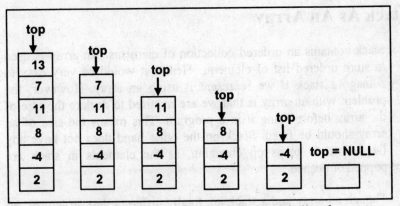

Figure 6-2. *Pictorial representation of stack after deletion of elements.*

Operations On Stack

A stack is generally implemented with two basic operations—push and pop. These are listed in Table 6-1.

Operation	Description
Push	Allows adding an element at the top of the stack.
Pop	Allows to remove an element from the top of the stack

Table 6-1. *Operations performed on stack.*

Before making use of stack in a program, it is very important to decide how to represent a stack. There are several ways of representing a stack. Let us see how efficient it is to use an array to represent a stack.

Stack As An Array

Stack contains an ordered collection of elements. An array is used to store ordered list of elements. Hence, it would be very easy to manage a stack if we represent it using an array. However, the problem with an array is that we are required to declare the size of the array before using it in a program. This means the size of an array should be fixed. Stack on the other hand does not have any fixed size. It keeps on changing, as the elements in stack are popped or pushed.

Though an array and a stack are totally different data structures, an array can be used to store the elements of a stack. We can declare the array with a maximum size large enough to manage a stack. As a result, the stack can grow or shrink within the space reserved for it. Let us see a program that implements a stack using an array.

```
#include <stdio.h>
#include <conio.h>

#define MAX 10

struct stack
{
    int arr[MAX] ;
    int top ;
} ;

void initstack ( struct stack * ) ;
void push ( struct stack *, int item ) ;
int pop ( struct stack * ) ;
```

```
void main( )
{
    struct stack s ;
    int i ;

    clrscr( ) ;

    initstack ( &s ) ;

    push ( &s, 11 ) ;
    push ( &s, 23 ) ;
    push ( &s, -8 ) ;
    push ( &s, 16 ) ;
    push ( &s, 27 ) ;
    push ( &s, 14 ) ;
    push ( &s, 20 ) ;
    push ( &s, 39 ) ;
    push ( &s, 2 ) ;
    push ( &s, 15 ) ;
    push ( &s, 7 ) ;

    i = pop ( &s ) ;
    printf ( "\n\nItem popped: %d", i ) ;

    i = pop ( &s ) ;
    printf ( "\nItem popped: %d", i ) ;

    i = pop ( &s ) ;
    printf ( "\nItem popped: %d", i ) ;

    i = pop ( &s ) ;
    printf ( "\nItem popped: %d", i ) ;

    i = pop ( &s ) ;
    printf ( "\nItem popped: %d", i ) ;

    getch( ) ;
}
```

```
/* intializes the stack */
void initstack ( struct stack *s )
{
    s -> top = -1 ;
}

/* adds an element to the stack */
void push ( struct stack *s, int item )
{
    if ( s -> top == MAX - 1 )
    {
        printf ( "\nStack is full." ) ;
        return ;
    }
    s -> top++ ;
    s -> arr[s ->top] = item ;
}

/* removes an element from the stack */
int pop ( struct stack *s )
{
    int data ;
    if ( s -> top == -1 )
    {
        printf ( "\nStack is empty." ) ;
        return NULL ;
    }
    data = s -> arr[s -> top] ;
    s -> top-- ;
    return data ;
}
```

Output:

Stack is full.

Item popped: 15

Item popped: 2
Item popped: 39
Item popped: 20
Item popped: 14

Here to begin with we have defined a structure called **stack**. The **push( )** and **pop( )** functions are used respectively to add and delete items from the top of the stack. The actual storage of stack elements is done in an array **arr**. The variable **top** is an index into that array. It contains a value where the addition or deletion is going to take place in the array, and thereby in the stack. To indicate that the stack is empty to begin with, the variable **top** is set with a value –1 by calling the function **initstack( )**.

Every time an element is added to stack, it is verified whether such an addition is possible at all. If it is not then the message 'Stack is full.' is reported. Since we have declared the array to hold 10 elements, the stack would be considered full if the value of **top** becomes equal to 9.

In **main( )** we have called **push( )** function to add 11 elements to the stack. The value of **top** would become 9 after adding 10 elements. As a result, the 11th element 7 would not get added to the stack. Lastly, we have removed few elements from the stack by calling the **pop( )** function.

Stack As A Linked List

In the earlier section we had used arrays to store the elements that get added to the stack. However, when implemented as an array it suffers from the basic limitation of an array—that its size cannot be increased or decreased once it is declared. As a result, one ends up reserving either too much space or too less space for an array and in turn for a stack. This problem can be overcome if we implement a stack using a linked list. In case of a linked stack we shall push and pop nodes from one end of a linked list.

The stack as linked list is represented as a singly connected list. Each node in the linked list contains the data and a pointer that gives location of the next node in the list. The node in the list is a structure as shown below:

```
struct node
{
    <data type> data ;
    node *link ;
};
```

where <data type> indicates that the data can be of any type like **int, float, char** etc, and **link,** is a pointer to the next node in the list. The pointer to the beginning of the list serves the purpose of the top of the stack. Figure 6-3 shows the linked list representation of a stack.

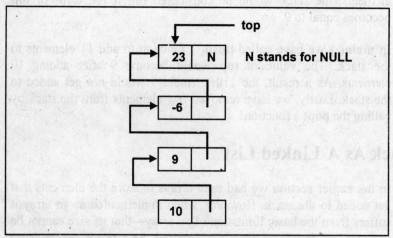

Figure 6-3. *Representation of stack as a linked list.*

Let us now see a program that implements stack as a linked list.

```
#include <stdio.h>
#include <conio.h>
#include <alloc.h>

/* structure containing data part and linkpart */
struct node
{
    int data ;
    struct node *link ;
} ;

void push ( struct node **, int ) ;
int pop ( struct node ** ) ;
void delstack ( struct node ** ) ;

void main( )
{
    struct node *s = NULL ;
    int i ;

    clrscr( ) ;

    push ( &s, 14 ) ;
    push ( &s, -3 ) ;
    push ( &s, 18 ) ;
    push ( &s, 29 ) ;
    push ( &s, 31 ) ;
    push ( &s, 16 ) ;

    i = pop ( &s ) ;
    printf ( "\nItem popped: %d", i ) ;

    i = pop ( &s ) ;
    printf ( "\nItem popped: %d", i ) ;

    i = pop ( &s ) ;
    printf ( "\nItem popped: %d", i ) ;
```

```
        delstack ( &s ) ;

        getch( ) ;
}

/* adds a new node to the stack as linked list */
void push ( struct node **top, int item )
{
        struct node *temp ;
        temp = ( struct node * ) malloc ( sizeof ( struct node ) ) ;

        if ( temp == NULL )
            printf ( "\nStack is full." ) ;

        temp -> data = item ;
        temp -> link = *top ;
        *top = temp ;
}

/* pops an element from the stack */
int pop ( struct node **top )
{
        struct node *temp ;
        int item ;

        if ( *top == NULL )
        {
            printf ( "\nStack is empty." ) ;
            return NULL ;
        }

        temp = *top ;
        item = temp -> data ;
        *top = ( *top ) -> link ;

        free ( temp ) ;
        return item ;
}
```

```
/* deallocates memory */
void delstack ( struct node **top )
{
    struct node *temp ;

    if ( *top == NULL )
        return ;

    while ( *top != NULL )
    {
        temp = *top ;
        *top = ( *top ) -> link ;
        free ( temp ) ;
    }
}
```

Output:

Item popped: 16
Item popped: 31
Item popped: 29

Here we have designed a structure called **node**. The variable **s** is a pointer to the structure **node**. Initially **s** is set to **NULL** to indicate that the stack is empty. In every call to the function **push( )** we are creating a new node dynamically. As long as there is enough space for dynamic memory allocation **temp** would never become **NULL**. If value of **temp** happens to be **NULL** then that would be the stage when stack would become full.

After, creating a new node, the pointer **s** should point to the newly created item of the list. Hence we have assigned the address of this new node to **s** using the pointer **top**. The stack as a linked list would grow as shown in Figure 6-4.

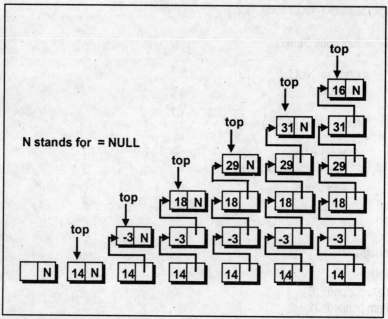

N stands for = NULL

Figure 6-4. *Stack as a linked list after insertion of elements.*

In the **pop( )** function, first we are checking whether or not a stack is empty. If the stack is empty then a message 'Stack is empty.' gets displayed. If the stack is not empty, then the topmost item gets removed from the list. The stack after removing three items from the list would be as shown in Figure 6-5.

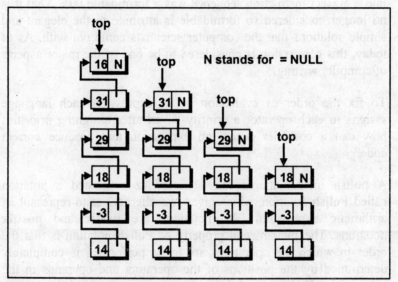

Figure 6-5. *Stack as a linked list after deletion of elements.*

Applications Of Stacks

The place where stacks are frequently used is in evaluation of arithmetic expression. An arithmetic expression consists of operands and operators. The operands can be numeric values or numeric variables. The operators used in an arithmetic expression represent the operations like addition, subtraction, multiplication, division and exponentiation.

When higher level programming languages came into existence one of the major hurdles faced by the computer scientists was to generate machine language instructions that would properly evaluate any arithmetic expression. To convert a complex assignment statement such as:

X = A / B + C * D − F * G / Q

into a correct instruction sequence was a formidable task. That it is no longer considered so formidable is attribute to the elegant and simple solutions that the computer scientists came out with. As of today, this conversion is considered to be one of the major aspects of compiler writing.

To fix the order of evaluation of an expression each language assigns to each operator a priority. Even after assigning priorities how can a compiler accept an expression and produce correct code?

A polish mathematician Jan Lukasiewicz suggested a notation called **Polish** notation, which gives two alternatives to represent an arithmetic expression. The notations are **prefix** and **postfix** notations. The fundamental property of **Polish** notation is that the order in which the operations are to be performed is completely determined by the positions of the operators and operands in the expression. Hence, parentheses are not required while writing expressions in **Polish** notation. Let us now discuss each of them.

While writing an arithmetic expression, the operator symbol is usually placed between two operands. For example,

A + B * C
A * B – C
A + B / C – D
A $ B + C

This way of representing arithmetic expressions is called **infix** notation. While evaluating an infix expression usually the following operator precedence is used:

- Highest priority: Exponentiation ($)
- Next highest priority: Multiplication (*) and Division (/)
- Lowest priority: Addition (+) and Subtraction (-)

If we wish to override these priorities we can do so by using a pair of parentheses as shown below.

```
( A + B ) * C
A * ( B - C )
( A + B ) / ( C - D )
```

The expressions within a pair of parentheses are always evaluated earlier than other operations.

In prefix notation the operator comes before the operands. For example, consider an arithmetic expression expressed in infix notation as shown below:

A + B

This expression in prefix form would be represented as follows:

+ A B

The same expression in postfix form would be represented as follows:

A B +

In postfix notation, the operator follows the two operands.

The prefix and postfix expressions have three features:

− The operand's maintain the same order as in the equivalent infix expression
− Parentheses are not needed to designate the expression unambiguously.
− While evaluating the expression the priority of the operators is irrelevant.

Infix To Prefix Conversion

Let us now see a program that would accept an expression in infix form and convert it to a prefix form.

```
#include <stdio.h>
#include <conio.h>
#include <string.h>
#include <ctype.h>
#define MAX 50

struct infix
{
    char target[MAX] ;
    char stack[MAX] ;
    char *s, *t ;
    int top, I ;
} ;

void initinfix ( struct infix * ) ;
void setexpr ( struct infix *, char * ) ;
void push ( struct infix *, char ) ;
char pop ( struct infix * ) ;
void convert ( struct infix * ) ;
int priority ( char c ) ;
void show ( struct infix ) ;

void main( )
{
    struct infix q ;
    char expr[MAX] ;

    clrscr( ) ;

    initinfix ( &q ) ;

    printf ( "\nEnter an expression in infix form: " ) ;
    gets ( expr ) ;

    setexpr ( &q, expr ) ;
    convert ( &q ) ;
```

```
    printf ( "The Prefix expression is: " ) ;
    show ( q ) ;

    getch( ) ;
}

/* initializes elements of structure variable */
void initinfix ( struct infix *pq )
{
    pq -> top = -1 ;
    strcpy ( pq -> target, "" ) ;
    strcpy ( pq -> stack, "" ) ;
    pq -> l = 0 ;
}

/* reverses the given expression */
void setexpr ( struct infix *pq, char *str )
{
    pq -> s = str ;
    strrev ( pq -> s ) ;
    pq -> l = strlen ( pq -> s ) ;
    *( pq -> target + pq -> l ) = '\0' ;
    pq -> t = pq -> target + ( pq -> l - 1 ) ;
}

/* adds operator to the stack */
void push ( struct infix *pq, char c )
{
    if ( pq -> top == MAX - 1 )
        printf ( "\nStack is full.\n" ) ;
    else
    {
        pq -> top++ ;
        pq -> stack[pq -> top] = c ;
    }
}

/* pops an operator from the stack */
```

```
char pop ( struct infix *pq )
{
    if ( pq -> top == -1 )
    {
        printf ( "Stack is empty\n" ) ;
            return -1 ;
    }
    else
    {
        char item = pq -> stack[pq -> top] ;
        pq -> top-- ;
        return item ;
    }
}

/* converts the infix expr. to prefix form */
void convert ( struct infix *pq )
{
    char opr ;

    while ( *( pq -> s ) )
    {
        if ( *( pq -> s ) == ' ' || *( pq -> s ) == '\t' )
        {
            pq -> s++   ;
            continue ;
        }

        if ( isdigit ( *( pq -> s ) ) || isalpha ( *( pq -> s ) ) )
        {
            while ( isdigit ( *( pq -> s ) ) || isalpha ( *( pq -> s ) ) )
            {
                *( pq -> t ) = *( pq -> s ) ;
                pq -> s++   ;
                pq -> t-- ;
            }
        }
```

```
if ( *( pq -> s ) == ')' )
{
    push ( pq, *( pq -> s ) ) ;
    pq -> s++   ;
}

if ( *( pq -> s ) == '*' || *( pq -> s ) == '+' ||
  *( pq -> s ) == '/' || *( pq -> s ) == '%' ||
  *( pq -> s ) == '-' || *( pq -> s ) == '$' )
{
    if ( pq -> top != -1 )
    {
        opr = pop ( pq ) ;

        while ( priority ( opr ) > priority ( *( pq -> s ) ) )
        {
            *( pq -> t ) = opr ;
            pq -> t-- ;
            opr = pop ( pq ) ;
        }
        push ( pq, opr ) ;
        push ( pq, *( pq -> s ) ) ;
    }
    else
        push ( pq, *( pq -> s ) ) ;
    pq -> s++   ;
}

if ( *( pq -> s ) == '(' )
{
    opr = pop ( pq ) ;
    while ( opr != ')' )
    {
        *( pq -> t ) = opr ;
        pq -> t-- ;
        opr = pop ( pq ) ;
    }
    pq -> s++   ;
```

```
        }
    }

    while ( pq -> top != -1 )
    {
        opr = pop ( pq ) ;
        *( pq -> t ) = opr ;
        pq -> t-- ;
    }
    pq -> t++ ;
}

/* returns the priotity of the operator */
int priority ( char c )
{
    if ( c == '$' )
        return 3 ;
    if ( c == '*' || c == '/' || c == '%' )
        return 2 ;
    else
    {
        if ( c == '+' || c == '-' )
            return 1 ;
        else
            return 0 ;
    }
}

/* displays the prefix form of given expr. */
void show ( struct infix pq )
{
    while ( *( pq.t ) )
    {
        printf ( " %c", *( pq.t ) ) ;
        pq.t++ ;
    }
}
```

Output:

Enter an expression in infix form: 4 $ 2 * 3 - 3 + 8 / 4 / (1 + 1)
Stack is empty
The Prefix expression is: + - * $ 4 2 3 3 / / 8 4 + 1 1

In this program we have designed a structure called **infix**. It contains two character arrays **target** and **stack** that store the prefix expression (string) and the operators (that would be pushed onto the stack) respectively. The two **char** pointers **s** and **t** are used in the conversion process. The variable **top** stores the index of the item at the topmost position in the stack and **l** stores the length of the infix expression entered by the user.

During the course of program execution, the user enters an arithmetic expression as string (consisting of digits, alphabets and operators). The function **setexpr( )** reverses this expression and stores it in a string pointed to by **s**. Thus, if the expression entered by the user is

4 $ 2 * 3 - 3 + 8 / 4 / (1 + 1)

then on reversing this string **s** would point to the string

) 1 + 1 (/ 4 / 8 + 3 - 3 * 2 $ 4

The **setexpr( )** function also makes the **char** pointer **t** to point to (**l** -1)th memory location in the **target** string.

Next the function **convert( )** gets called. This is the function in which the given infix expression gets converted to prefix expression. In this function, we are scanning every character of the string pointed to by **s** in a **while** loop. Following steps are performed depending on the type of character scanned:

(a) If the character scanned happens to be a space then that character is skipped.

(b) If character scanned is a digit or an alphabet, it is added to the target string at a position pointed to by **t**.

(c) If the character scanned is a closing parentheses then it is added to the stack by calling the **push( )** function.

(d) If the character scanned happens to be an operator, then firstly the topmost element from the stack is retrieved. Then, through a **while** loop, the priorities of the character scanned (i.e. ***(p -> s)**) and the character popped **opr** are compared. Following steps are now performed as per the precedence rule.

  (i) If priority of **opr** is higher than the character scanned, then **opr** gets added to the target string.

  (ii) If **opr** has lower or the same priority than the character scanned, then the loop gets terminated. **opr** gets pushed back to the stack. Then, the character scanned is also pushed to the stack.

(e) If the character scanned happens to be an opening parenthesis, then the operators entered into the stack are retrieved through a loop. The loop continues till it does not encounter a closing parenthesis. The operators popped are added to the target string.

In the **convert( )** function we have called functions like **push( )**, **pop( )** and **priority( )**. The **push( )** function adds a character to the stack, whereas the **pop( )** function removes the topmost item from the stack.

The **priority( )** function returns the priority of operators used in the infix expression. The exponentiation operation represented by $ has got the highest precedence. Addition and subtraction has got lower precedence. The function actually returns integers like 3 for $, 2 for * or /, 1 for + and - and 0 for any other character.

The **while** loop in the **convert( )** gets terminated if the string **s** is exhausted. But, then some operators are still there in the stack, which should get added to the prefix string. This job is done once the control reaches outside the **while** loop in the **convert( )**

function. Lastly, the converted expression is displayed using the **show( )** function.

The steps performed in the conversion of a sample infix expression 4 $ 2 * 3 - 3 + 8 / 4 / (1 + 1) to a prefix expression are shown in Table 6-2.

Infix Expression: 4 $ 2 * 3 - 3 + 8 / 4 / (1 + 1)

Reversed Infix Expression:) 1 + 1 (/ 4 / 8 + 3 - 3 * 2 $ 4

Char. Scanned	Stack	Prefix Expression
)	)	
1	)	1
+	) +	1
1	) +	1 1
(	Empty	+ 1 1
/	/	+ 1 1
4	/	4 + 1 1
/	/ /	4 + 1 1
8	/ /	8 4 + 1 1
+	+	/ / 8 4 + 1 1
3	+	3 / / 8 4 + 1 1
-	+ -	3 / / 8 4 + 1 1
3	+ -	3 3 / / 8 4 + 1 1
*	+ - *	3 3 / / 8 4 + 1 1
2	+ - *	2 3 3 / / 8 4 + 1 1
$	+ - * $	2 3 3 / / 8 4 + 1 1
4	+ - * $	4 2 3 3 / / 8 4 + 1 1
	Empty	+ - * $ 4 2 3 3 / / 8 4 + 1 1

Table 6-2. *Conversion of Infix to Prefix form.*

Infix To Postfix Conversion

Let us now see a program that converts an arithmetic expression given in an infix form to a postfix form.

```
#include <stdio.h>
#include <conio.h>
#include <string.h>
#include <ctype.h>

#define MAX 50

struct infix
{
    char target[MAX] ;
    char stack[MAX] ;
    char *s, *t ;
    int top ;
} ;

void initinfix ( struct infix * ) ;
void setexpr ( struct infix *, char * ) ;
void push ( struct infix *, char ) ;
char pop ( struct infix * ) ;
void convert ( struct infix * ) ;
int priority ( char ) ;
void show ( struct infix ) ;

void main( )
{
    struct infix p ;
    char expr[MAX] ;

    initinfix ( &p ) ;

    clrscr( ) ;
```

```
        printf ( "\nEnter an expression in infix form: " ) ;
        gets ( expr ) ;

        setexpr ( &p, expr ) ;
        convert ( &p ) ;

        printf ( "The postfix expression is: " ) ;
        show ( p ) ;

        getch( ) ;
}

/* initializes structure elements */
void initinfix ( struct infix *p )
{
        p -> top = -1 ;
        strcpy ( p -> target, "" ) ;
        strcpy ( p -> stack, "" ) ;
        p -> t = p -> target ;
        p -> s = "" ;
}

/* sets s to point to given expr. */
void setexpr ( struct infix *p, char *str )
{
        p -> s = str ;
}

/* adds an operator to the stack */
void push ( struct infix *p, char c )
{
        if ( p -> top == MAX )
                printf ( "\nStack is full.\n" ) ;
        else
        {
                p -> top++ ;
                p -> stack[p -> top] = c ;
        }
```

```
}

/* pops an operator from the stack */
char pop ( struct infix *p )
{
    if ( p -> top == -1 )
    {
        printf ( "\nStack is empty.\n" ) ;
        return -1 ;
    }
    else
    {
        char item = p -> stack[p -> top] ;
        p -> top-- ;
        return item ;
    }
}

/* converts the given expr. from infix to postfix form */
void convert ( struct infix *p )
{
    char opr ;

    while ( *( p -> s ) )
    {
        if ( *( p -> s ) == ' ' || *( p -> s ) == '\t' )
        {
            p -> s++ ;
            continue ;
        }
        if ( isdigit ( *( p -> s ) ) || isalpha ( *( p -> s ) ) )
        {
            while ( isdigit ( *( p -> s ) ) || isalpha ( *( p -> s ) ) )
            {
                *( p -> t ) = *( p -> s ) ;
                p -> s++ ;
                p -> t++ ;
            }
```

```
    }
    if ( *( p -> s ) == '(' )
    {
        push ( p, *( p -> s ) ) ;
        p -> s++ ;
    }

    if ( *( p -> s ) == '*' || *( p -> s ) == '+' || *( p -> s ) == '/' ||
      *( p -> s ) == '%' || *( p -> s ) == '-' || *( p -> s ) == '$' )
    {
        if ( p -> top != -1 )
        {
            opr = pop ( p ) ;
            while ( priority ( opr ) >= priority ( *( p -> s ) ) )
            {
                *( p -> t ) = opr ;
                p -> t++ ;
                opr = pop ( p ) ;
            }
            push ( p, opr ) ;
            push ( p, *( p -> s ) ) ;
        }
        else
            push ( p, *( p -> s ) ) ;
        p -> s++ ;
    }

    if ( *( p -> s ) == ')' )
    {
        opr = pop ( p ) ;
        while ( ( opr ) != '(' )
        {
            *( p -> t ) = opr ;
            p -> t++ ;
            opr = pop ( p ) ;
        }
        p -> s++ ;
    }
```

```
    }

    while ( p -> top != -1 )
    {
        char opr = pop ( p ) ;
        *( p -> t ) = opr ;
        p -> t++ ;
    }

    *( p -> t ) = '\0' ;
}

/* returns the priority of an operator */
int priority ( char c )
{
    if ( c == '$' )
        return 3 ;
    if ( c == '*' || c == '/' || c == '%' )
        return 2 ;
    else
    {
        if ( c == '+' || c == '-' )
            return 1 ;
        else
            return 0 ;
    }
}

/* displays the postfix form of given expr. */
void show ( struct infix p )
{
    printf ( " %s", p.target ) ;
}
```

Output:

Enter an expression in infix form: 4 $ 2 * 3 - 3 + 8 / 4 / (1 + 1

Stack is empty.
The postfix expression is: 42$3*3-84/11+/+

This program too contains a structure called **infix**. The elements **target** and **stack** are used to store the postfix string and to maintain the stack respectively. The **char** pointers **s** and **t** are used to store intermediate results while converting an infix expression to a postfix form. The variable **top** points to the top of the stack.

During the course of program execution, the user enters an arithmetic expression (consisting of digits, alphabets and operators). The function **setexpr( )** assigns the base address of the string to **char** pointer **s**. Note that, here we have not reversed the original infix expression, as we did in case of infix to prefix conversion.

Next, the function **convert( )** gets called. This function converts the given infix expression to postfix expression. As done in previous program of infix to prefix conversion, here too we have scanned every character of the string in a **while** loop till we do not reach the end of string pointed to by **s**. Following steps are performed depending on the type of character scanned.

(a) If the character scanned happens to be a space then that character is skipped.

(b) If character scanned is a digit or an alphabet, it is added to the target string pointed to by **t**.

(c) If the character scanned is a closing parentheses then it is added to the stack by calling **push( )** function.

(d) If the character scanned happens to be an operator, then firstly, the topmost element from the stack is retrieved. Through a **while** loop, the priorities of the character scanned (i.e.***(p -> s)**) and the character popped **opr** are compared. Then following steps are performed as per the precedence rule.

(i) If **opr** has higher or same priority as the character scanned, then **opr** is added to the target string.

(ii) If **opr** has lower precedence than the character scanned, then the loop is terminated. **opr** is pushed back to the stack. Then, the character scanned (***(p -> s))** is also added to the stack.

(e) If the character scanned happens to be an opening parentheses, then the operators present in the stack are **retrieved** through a loop. The loop continues till it does not encounter a closing parentheses. The operators popped, are added to the target string pointed to by **t**.

In the **convert( )** function we have called functions like **push( )**, **pop( )**, **priority( )**. The working of these functions is same as discussed in previous program.

The **while** loop in the **convert( )** gets terminated if the string **s** is exhausted. But, then some operators are still there in the stack, which should get added to the prefix string. This job would be done in the **show( )** function. At first look the prefix form of an infix expression appears to be a mirror image of the postfix form. But, this is not true. If observed carefully, there is a difference between a prefix and postfix form.

The steps performed in the conversion of a sample infix expression 4 $ 2 * 3 - 3 + 8 / 4 / (1 + 1) to a postfix expression are shown in Table 6-3.

Infix Expression: 4 $ 2 * 3 - 3 + 8 / 4 / (1 + 1)

Char Scanned	Stack Contents	Postfix Expression
4	Empty	4
$	$	4
2	$	4 2
*	*	4 2 $
3	*	4 2 $ 3
-	-	4 2 $ 3 *
3	-	4 2 $ 3 * 3
+	+	4 2 $ 3 * 3 -
8	+	4 2 $ 3 * 3 - 8
/	+ /	4 2 $ 3 * 3 - 8
4	+ /	4 2 $ 3 * 3 - 8 4
/	+ /	4 2 $ 3 * 3 - 8 4 /
(	+ / (	4 2 $ 3 * 3 - 8 4 /
1	+ / (	4 2 $ 3 * 3 - 8 4 / 1
+	+ / (+	4 2 $ 3 * 3 - 8 4 / 1
1	+ / (+	4 2 $ 3 * 3 - 8 4 / 1 1
)	+ /	4 2 $ 3 * 3 - 8 4 / 1 1 +
	Empty	4 2 $ 3 * 3 - 8 4 / 1 1 + / +

Table 6-3. *Conversion of Infix to Postfix form.*

Postfix To Prefix Conversion

Let us now see a program that converts an expression in postfix form to a prefix form.

```
#include <stdio.h>
#include <conio.h>
#include <string.h>

#define MAX 50

struct postfix
{
    char stack[MAX][MAX], target[MAX] ;
    char temp1[2], temp2[2] ;
    char str1[MAX], str2[MAX], str3[MAX] ;
    int i, top ;
} ;

void initpostfix ( struct postfix * ) ;
void setexpr ( struct postfix *, char * ) ;
void push ( struct postfix *, char * ) ;
void pop ( struct postfix *, char * ) ;
void convert ( struct postfix * ) ;
void show ( struct postfix ) ;

void main( )
{
    struct postfix q ;
    char expr[MAX] ;

    clrscr( ) ;

    initpostfix ( &q ) ;

    printf ( "\nEnter an expression in postfix form: " ) ;
    gets ( expr ) ;

    setexpr ( &q, expr ) ;
    convert ( &q ) ;

    printf ( "The Prefix expression is: " ) ;
    show ( q ) ;
```

```
        getch( ) ;
}

/* initializes the elements of the structure */
void initpostfix ( struct postfix *p )
{
    p -> i = 0 ;
    p -> top = -1 ;
    strcpy ( p -> target, "" ) ;
}

/* copies given expr. to target string */
void setexpr ( struct postfix *p, char *c )
{
    strcpy ( p -> target, c ) ;
}

/* adds an operator to the stack */
void push ( struct postfix *p, char *str )
{
    if ( p -> top == MAX - 1 )
        printf ( "\nStack is full." ) ;
    else
    {
        p -> top++ ;
        strcpy ( p -> stack[p -> top], str ) ;
    }
}

/* pops an element from the stack */
void pop ( struct postfix *p, char *a )
{
    if ( p -> top == -1 )
        printf ( "\nStack  is empty." ) ;
    else
    {
        strcpy ( a, p -> stack[p -> top] ) ;
        p -> top-- ;
```

```
        }
    }

    /* converts given expr. to prefix form */
    void convert ( struct postfix *p )
    {
        while ( p -> target[p -> i] != '\0' )
        {
            /* skip whitespace, if any */
            if ( p -> target[p -> i] == ' ' )
                p -> i++ ;
            if( p -> target[p -> i] == '%' || p -> target[p -> i] == '*' ||
                p -> target[p -> i] == '-' || p -> target[p -> i] == '+' ||
                p -> target[p -> i] == '/' || p -> target[p -> i] == '$' )
            {
                pop ( p, p -> str2 ) ;
                pop ( p, p -> str3 ) ;
                p -> temp1[0] = p -> target[ p -> i] ;
                p -> temp1[1] = '\0' ;
                strcpy ( p -> str1, p -> temp1 ) ;
                strcat ( p -> str1, p -> str3 ) ;
                strcat ( p -> str1, p -> str2 ) ;
                push ( p, p -> str1 ) ;
            }
            else
            {
                p -> temp1[0] = p -> target[p -> i] ;
                p -> temp1[1] = '\0' ;
                strcpy ( p -> temp2, p -> temp1 ) ;
                push ( p, p -> temp2 ) ;
            }
            p -> i++ ;
        }
    }

    /* displays the prefix form of expr. */
    void show ( struct postfix p )
    {
```

```
        char *temp = p.stack[0] ;
        while ( *temp )
        {
            printf ( "%c ", *temp ) ;
            temp++ ;
        }
}
```

Output:

Enter an expression in postfix form: 4 2 $ 3 * 3 - 8 4 / 1 1 + / +
The Prefix expression is: + - * $ 4 2 3 3 / / 8 4 + 1 1

In this program the structure **postfix** contains character arrays like **temp1, temp2, str1, str2, str3** to store the intermediate results. The character arrays **stack** and **target** are used to maintain the stack and to store the final string in the prefix form respectively.

In the **convert( )** function the string containing expression in postfix form is scanned through a **while** loop till the string **target** is not exhausted. Following steps are performed depending on the type of character scanned.

(a) If the character scanned is a space then that character is skipped.

(b) If the character scanned contains a digit or an alphabet, it is pushed to the stack by calling **push( )** function.

(c) If the character scanned contains an operator, then the topmost two elements are popped from the stack. These two elements are then stored in the array **temp1**. A temporary string **temp2** containing the operator and the two operands is formed. This temporary string is then pushed on the stack.

The postfix form that is converted to prefix form is stored at the 0th position in the stack. Finally, the **show( )** function displays the prefix form. The steps performed in the conversion of a sample postfix expression 4 2 $ 3 * 3 - 8 4 / 1 1 + / + to its equivalent prefix expression is demonstrated in Table 6-4.

Postfix Expression: 4 2 $ 3 * 3 - 8 4 / 1 1 + / +	
Char. Scanned	**Stack Contents**
4	4
2	4 2
$	$ 4 2
3	$ 4 2 3
*	* $ 4 2 3
3	* $ 4 2 3, 3
-	- * $ 4 2 3 3
8	- * $ 4 2 3 3, 8
4	- * $ 4 2 3 3, 8, 4
/	- * $ 4 2 3 3, / 8 4
1	- * $ 4 2 3 3, / 8 4, 1
1	- * $ 4 2 3 3, / 8 4, 1, 1
+	- * $ 4 2 3 3, / 8 4, + 1 1
/	- * $ 4 2 3 3, / / 8 4 + 1 1
+	+ - $ 4 2 3 3 / / 8 4 + 1 1

Table 6-4. *Conversion of Infix to Postfix form.*

Postfix To Infix Conversion

Let us now see a program to convert an expression in postfix form to an infix form.

```
#include <stdio.h>
#include <conio.h>
#include <string.h>

#define MAX 50

struct postfix
{
    char stack[MAX][MAX], target[MAX] ;
    char temp1[2], temp2[2] ;
    char str1[MAX], str2[MAX], str3[MAX] ;
    int i, top ;
} ;

void initpostfix ( struct postfix * ) ;
void setexpr ( struct postfix *, char * ) ;
void push ( struct postfix *, char * ) ;
void pop ( struct postfix *, char * ) ;
void convert ( struct postfix * ) ;
void show ( struct postfix ) ;

void main( )
{
    struct postfix q ;
    char expr[MAX] ;

    clrscr( ) ;

    initpostfix ( &q ) ;

    printf ( "\nEnter an expression in postfix form: " ) ;
    gets ( expr ) ;

    setexpr ( &q, expr ) ;
    convert ( &q ) ;

    printf ( "The infix expression is: " ) ;
    show ( q ) ;
```

```
        getch( ) ;
}

/* initializes structure elements */
void initpostfix ( struct postfix *p )
{
    p -> i = 0 ;
    p -> top = -1 ;
    strcpy ( p -> target, "" ) ;
}

/* copies given expression to target string */
void setexpr ( struct postfix *p, char *c )
{
    strcpy ( p -> target, c ) ;
}

/* adds an expr. to the stack */
void push ( struct postfix *p, char *str )
{
    if ( p -> top == MAX - 1 )
        printf ( "\nStack is full." ) ;
    else
    {
        p -> top++ ;
        strcpy ( p -> stack[p -> top], str ) ;
    }
}

/* pops an expr. from the stack */
void pop ( struct postfix *p, char *a )
{
    if ( p -> top == -1 )
        printf ( "\nStack  is empty." ) ;
    else
    {
        strcpy ( a, p -> stack[p -> top] ) ;
        p -> top-- ;
```

```
        }
}

/* converts given expr. to infix form */
void convert ( struct postfix *p )
{
    while ( p -> target[p -> i] )
    {
        /* skip whitespace, if any */
        if( p -> target[p -> i] == ' ' )
            p -> i++ ;
        if ( p -> target[p -> i] == '%' || p -> target[p -> i] == '*' ||
             p -> target[p -> i] == '-' || p -> target[p -> i] == '+' ||
             p -> target[p -> i] == '/' || p -> target[p -> i] == '$' )
        {
            pop ( p, p -> str2 ) ;
            pop ( p, p -> str3 ) ;
            p -> temp1[0] = p -> target[p -> i] ;
            p -> temp1[1] = '\0' ;
            strcpy ( p -> str1, p -> str3 ) ;
            strcat ( p -> str1, p -> temp1 ) ;
            strcat ( p -> str1, p -> str2 ) ;
            push ( p, p -> str1 ) ;
        }
        else
        {
            p -> temp1[0] = p -> target[p -> i] ;
            p -> temp1[1] = '\0' ;
            strcpy ( p -> temp2, p -> temp1 ) ;
            push ( p, p -> temp2 ) ;
        }
        p -> i++ ;
    }
}

/* displays the expression */
void show ( struct postfix p )
{
```

```
    char *t ;
    t = p.stack[0] ;
    while ( *t )
    {
        printf ( "%c ", *t ) ;
        t++ ;
    }
}
```

Output:

Enter an expression in postfix form: 4 2 $ 3 * 3 - 8 4 / 1 1 + / +
The infix expression is: 4 $ 2 * 3 - 3 + 8 / 4 / 1 + 1

This program is similar to the one discussed in previous section 'Postfix To Prefix Conversion', except for a small difference in the **convert( )** function. Since, this program is to convert a postfix form to an infix form, the operator would get placed between the two operands. The steps that are performed in the **convert( )** function are given below:

(a) The **while** loop runs as long as the string **target** is not exhausted.

(b) If the character scanned happens to be a space then that character is skipped.

(c) If the character scanned is a digit or an alphabet, it is added to the stack by calling **push( )** function.

(d) If the character scanned is an operator, then the topmost two elements (operands) are popped from the stack. A temporary string containing an operand-operator-operand is formed. This temporary string is then pushed on the stack.

The postfix form converted to an infix form, is stored at the 0th position in the stack. Finally, the **show( )** function displays the infix form. The steps carried out in converting a sample postfix expression to an infix expression are demonstrated in Table 6-5.

Postfix Expression: 4 2 $ 3 * 3 - 8 4 / 1 1 + / +	
Char. Scanned	**Stack Contents**
4	4
2	4, 2
$	4 $ 2
3	4 $ 2, 3
*	4 $ 2 * 3
3	4 $ 2 * 3, 3
-	4 $ 2 * 3 – 3
8	4 $ 2 * 3 – 3, 8
4	4 $ 2 * 3 – 3, 8, 4
/	4 $ 2 * 3 – 3, 8 / 4
1	4 $ 2 * 3 – 3, 8 / 4, 1
1	4 $ 2 * 3 – 3, 8 / 4, 1, 1
+	4 $ 2 * 3 – 3, 8 / 4 , 1 + 1
/	4 $ 2 * 3 – 3, 8 / 4 / 1 + 1
+	4 $ 2 * 3 – 3 + 8 / 4 / 1 + 1

Table 6-5. *Conversion of Postfix to Infix form.*

Evaluation Of Postfix Expression

The virtue of postfix notation is that it enables easy evaluation of expressions. To begin with, the need for parentheses is eliminated. Secondly, the priority of the operators is no longer relevant. The expression can be evaluated by making a left to right scan, stacking operands, and evaluating operators using as operands the correct elements from the stack and finally placing the result onto the stack. This evaluation is much simpler than attempting a direct evaluation of infix notation. Let us now see a program to evaluate a postfix expression.

```
#include <stdio.h>
#include <conio.h>
#include <stdlib.h>
#include <math.h>
#include <ctype.h>

#define MAX 50

struct postfix
{
    int stack[MAX] ;
    int top, nn ;
    char *s ;
} ;

void initpostfix ( struct postfix * ) ;
void setexpr ( struct postfix *, char * ) ;
void push ( struct postfix *, int ) ;
int pop ( struct postfix * ) ;
void calculate ( struct postfix * ) ;
void show ( struct postfix ) ;

void main( )
{
    struct postfix q ;
    char expr[MAX] ;

    clrscr( ) ;

    initpostfix ( &q ) ;
```

```
        printf ( "\nEnter postfix expression to be evaluated: " ) ;
        gets ( expr ) ;

        setexpr ( &q, expr ) ;
        calculate ( &q ) ;
        show ( q ) ;

        getch( ) ;
}

/* initializes structure elements */
void initpostfix ( struct postfix *p )
{
    p -> top = -1 ;
}

/* sets s to point to the given expr. */
void setexpr ( struct postfix *p, char *str )
{
    p -> s = str ;
}

/* adds digit to the stack */
void push ( struct postfix *p, int item )
{
    if ( p -> top == MAX - 1 )
        printf ( "\nStack is full." ) ;
    else
    {
        p -> top++ ;
        p -> stack[p -> top] = item ;
    }
}

/* pops digit from the stack */
int pop ( struct postfix *p )
{
    int data ;
```

```
if ( p -> top == -1 )
{
    printf ( "\nStack is empty." ) ;
        return NULL ;
}

data = p -> stack[p -> top] ;
p -> top-- ;

return data ;
}

/* evaluates the postfix expression */
void calculate( struct postfix *p )
{
    int n1, n2, n3 ;
    while ( *( p -> s ) )
    {
        /* skip whitespace, if any */
        if ( *( p -> s ) == ' ' || *( p -> s ) == '\t' )
        {
            p -> s++ ;
            continue ;
        }

        /* if digit is encountered */
        if ( isdigit ( *( p -> s ) ) )
        {
            p -> nn = *( p -> s ) - '0' ;
            push ( p, p -> nn ) ;
        }
        else
        {
            /* if operator is encountered */
            n1 = pop ( p ) ;
            n2 = pop ( p ) ;
            switch ( *( p -> s ) )
            {
```

```
                    case '+' :
                        n3 = n2 + n1 ;
                        break ;

                    case '-' :
                        n3 = n2 - n1 ;
                        break ;

                    case '/' :
                        n3 = n2 / n1 ;
                        break ;

                    case '*' :
                        n3 = n2 * n1 ;
                        break ;

                    case '%' :
                        n3 = n2 % n1 ;
                        break ;

                    case '$' :
                        n3 = pow ( n2 , n1 ) ;
                        break ;

                    default :
                        printf ( "Unknown operator" ) ;
                        exit ( 1 ) ;
                }

                push ( p, n3 ) ;
        }
        p -> s++ ;
    }
}

/* displays the result */
void show ( struct postfix p )
{
```

```
    p.nn = pop ( &p ) ;
    printf ( "Result is: %d", p.nn ) ;
}
```

Output:

Enter postfix expression to be evaluated: 4 2 $ 3 * 3 - 8 4 / 1 1 + / +
Result is: 46

In this program the structure **postfix** contains an integer array **stack**, to store the intermediate results of the operations and **top** to store the position of the topmost element in the stack. The evaluation of the expression gets performed in the **calculate( )** function.

During the course of execution, the user enters an arithmetic expression in the postfix form. In the **calculate( )** function, this expression would get scanned character by character. If the character scanned is an operand, then first it is converted to a digit form (from string form), and then it is pushed onto the stack. If the character scanned is a blank space, then it is skipped. If the character scanned is an operator, then the top two elements from the stack are retrieved. An arithmetic operation is performed between the two operands. The type of arithmetic operation i.e. addition, subtraction or multiplication etc. depends on the operator scanned from the sting **s**. The result is then pushed back onto the **stack**. These steps are repeated as long as the string **s** is not exhausted. The **show( )** function displays the final result. These steps can be better understood if you go through the evaluation of a sample postfix expression shown in Table 6-6.

Postfix Expression: 4 2 $ 3 * 3 - 8 4 / 1 1 + / +

Char. Scanned	Stack Contents
4	4
2	4, 2
$	16
3	16, 3
*	48
3	48, 3
-	45
8	45, 8
4	45, 8, 4
/	45, 2
1	45, 2, 1
1	45, 2, 1, 1
+	45, 2, 2
/	45, 1
+	46 (Result)

Table 6-6. *Evaluation of Postfix expression.*

Exercise

[A] Fill in the blanks:

(a) A stack is a data structure in which addition of new element or deletion of an existing element always takes place at an end called _____.

(b) The data structure stack is also called _____ structure.

(c) In _____ notation the operators precedes the two operands.

(d) In _____ notation the operator follows the two operands.

[B] Pick up the correct alternative for each of the following questions:

(a) Adding an element to the stack means
  (1) Placing an element at the front end
  (2) Placing an element at the top
  (3) Placing an element at the rear end
  (4) None of the above

(b) Pushing an element to a stack means
  (1) Removing an element from the stack
  (2) Searching a given element in the stack
  (3) Adding a new element to the stack
  (4) Sorting the elements in the stack

(c) Popping an element from the stack means
  (1) Removing an element from the stack
  (2) Searching a given element in the stack
  (3) Adding a new element to the stack
  (4) Sorting the elements in the stack

[C] Write programs for the following:

(a) Copying contents of one stack to another.

(b) To check whether a string of opening and closing parenthesis is well formed or not.

[D] Transform the following infix expressions into their equivalent postfix expressions:

```
( A - B ) * ( D / E )
( A + B ^ D ) / ( E - F ) + G
A * ( B + D ) / E - F * ( G + H / K )
( A + B ) * ( C - D ) $ E * F
( A + B ) * ( C $ ( D - E ) + F ) / G ) $ ( H - J )
```

[E] Transform the following infix expressions into their equivalent prefix expressions:

```
( A - B ) * ( D / E )
( A + B ^ D ) / ( E - F ) + G
A * ( B + D ) / E - F * ( G + H / K )
```

[F] Transform each of the following prefix expression to infix.

```
+ A - B C
+ + A - * $ B C D / + E F * G H I
+ - $ A B C * D ** E F G
```

[G] Transform each of the following postfix expression to infix.

```
A B C + -
A B - C + D E F - + $
A B C D E - + $ * E F * -
```

Other Titles of Interest by Y.P. Kanetkar

- C COLUMN COLLECTION
- C PEARLS
- C PROJECTS (W/CD)
- C#.NET FUNDAS (W/CD)
- C++.NET FUNDAS (W/CD)
- DATA STRUCTURE THROUGH C (W/CD)
- DATA STRUCTURE THROUGH C++ (W/CD)
- DIRECTX GAME PROGRAMMING FUNDAS (W/CD)
- EXPLORING C
- Go Embedded (W/CD) NEW
- GRAPHICS UNDER C
- INTRODUCTION TO OOPS & C++
- LET US C - 8th Ed.
- LET US C SOLUTIONS - 8th Ed.
- LET US C++
- PROGRAMMING EXPERTISE IN BASIC
- TEST YOUR C SKILL -2nd Ed.
- TEST YOUR C++ SKILLS
- TEST YOUR C# .NET SKILLS NEW
- TEST YOUR UNIX SKILLS
- TEST YOUR VB.NET SKILLS PART I
- TEST YOUR VB.NET SKILLS PART II
- UNDERSTANDING POINTERS IN C
- UNDOCUMENTED DOS THROUGH C
- UNIX SHELL PROGRAMMING
- VC++ GEMS (W/CD)
- VC++, COM AND BEYOND (W/CD)
- VISUAL C++ PROGRAMMING
- VISUAL C++ PROJECTS (W/CD)
- WORKING WITH C (FOR DOE - A & B LEVEL)
- WRITING TSR'S THROUGH C
- WRITING WINDOWS DEVICE DRIVERS (W/CD)
- BPB LET US C (HINDI)

CHAPTER
SEVEN

Queues
Await Your Turn

W hether it is a railway reservation counter, a movie theatre
or print jobs submitted to a network printer there is only
one way to bring order to chaos—form a queue. If you
await your turn patiently there is a more likelihood that you would
get a better service.

Queue is a linear data structure that permits insertion of new element at one end and deletion of an element at the other end. The end at which the deletion of an element take place is called **front**, and the end at which insertion of a new element can take place is called **rear**. The deletion or insertion of elements can take place only at the **front** or **rear** end of the list respectively.

The first element that gets added into the queue is the first one to get removed from the list. Hence, queue is also referred to as first-in-first-out (FIFO) list. The name 'queue' comes from the everyday use of the term. Consider a queue of people waiting at a bus stop. Each new person who comes takes his or her place at the end of the line, and when the bus comes, the people at the front of the line board first. The first person in the line is the first person to leave. Figure 7-1 gives a pictorial representation of a queue.

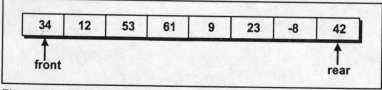

Figure 7-1. *Pictorial representation of a queue.*

In Figure 7-1, 34 is the first element and 42 is the last element added to the queue. Similarly, 34 would be the first element to get removed and 42 would be the last element to get removed.

Applications of queue as a data structure are even more common than applications of stacks. While performing tasks on a computer, it is often necessary to wait one's turn before having access to some device or process. Within a computer system there may be queues of tasks waiting for the line printer, or for access to disk storage, or in a time-sharing system for use of the CPU. Within a single program, there may be multiple requests to be kept in a queue, or one task may create other tasks, which must be done in turn by keeping them in a queue.

Let us now discuss how a queue can be represented in order to use it in a program.

Representation Of A Queue As An Array

Queue, being a linear data structure can be represented in various ways such as arrays and linked lists. Representing a queue as an array would have the same problem that we discussed in case of stacks. An array is a data structure that can store a fixed number of elements. The size of an array should be fixed before using it. Queue, on the other hand keeps on changing as we remove elements from the front end or add new elements at the rear end. Declaring an array with a maximum size would solve this problem. The maximum size should be large enough for a queue to expand or shrink. Figure 7-2 shows the representation of a queue as an array.

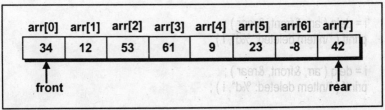

Figure 7-2. *Representation of a queue as an array.*

Let us now see a program that implements queue as an array.

```
#include <stdio.h>
#include <conio.h>

#define MAX 10
```

```c
void addq ( int *, int, int *, int * ) ;
int delq ( int *, int *, int * ) ;
void main( )
{
    int arr[MAX] ;
    int front = -1, rear = -1, i ;

    clrscr( ) ;

    addq ( arr, 23, &front, &rear ) ;
    addq ( arr, 9, &front, &rear ) ;
    addq ( arr, 11, &front, &rear ) ;
    addq ( arr, -10, &front, &rear ) ;
    addq ( arr, 25, &front, &rear ) ;
    addq ( arr, 16, &front, &rear ) ;
    addq ( arr, 17, &front, &rear ) ;
    addq ( arr, 22, &front, &rear ) ;
    addq ( arr, 19, &front, &rear ) ;
    addq ( arr, 30, &front, &rear ) ;
    addq ( arr, 32, &front, &rear ) ;

    i = delq ( arr, &front, &rear ) ;
    printf ( "\nItem deleted: %d", i ) ;

    i = delq ( arr, &front, &rear ) ;
    printf ( "\nItem deleted: %d", i ) ;

    i = delq ( arr, &front, &rear ) ;
    printf ( "\nItem deleted: %d", i ) ;

    getch( ) ;
}

/* adds an element to the queue */
void addq ( int *arr, int item, int *pfront, int *prear )
{
    if ( *prear == MAX - 1 )
```

```
    {
        printf ( "\nQueue is full." ) ;
        return ;
    }

    ( *prear )++ ;
    arr[*prear] = item ;

    if ( *pfront == -1 )
        *pfront = 0 ;
}

/* removes an element from the queue */
int delq ( int *arr, int *pfront, int *prear )
{
    int data ;

    if ( *pfront == -1 )
    {
        printf ( "\nQueue is Empty." ) ;
        return NULL ;
    }

    data = arr[*pfront] ;
    arr[*pfront] = 0 ;
    if ( *pfront == *prear )
        *pfront = *prear = -1 ;
    else
        ( *pfront )++ ;

    return  data ;
}
```

Output:

Queue is full.
Item deleted: 23

Item deleted: 9
Item deleted: 11

Here we have used an array **arr** to maintain the queue. We have also declared two variables **front** and **rear** to monitor the two ends of the queue. The initial values of **front** and **rear** are set to -1, which indicate that the queue is empty. The functions **addq( )** and **delq( )** are used to perform add and delete operations on the queue.

While adding a new element to the queue, first it would be ascertained whether such an addition is possible or not. Since the array indexing begins with 0 the maximum number of elements that can be stored in the queue are **MAX** - 1. If these many elements are already present in the queue then it is reported to be full. If the element can be added to the queue then the value of the variable **rear** is incremented using the pointer **prear** and the new item is stored in the array. The addition of an element to the queue has been illustrated in Figure 7-3.

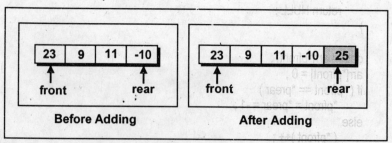

Figure 7-3. *Adding an element to a queue.*

If the item being added to the queue is the first element (i.e. if the variable **front** has a value -1) then as soon as the item is added to the queue **front** is set to 0 indicating that the queue is no longer empty.

Let us now see how the **delq( )** function works. Before deleting an element from the queue it is first ascertained whether there are any elements available for deletion. If not, then the queue is reported as empty. Otherwise, an element is deleted form **arr[*pfront]**. The deletion of an element is illustrated in Figure 7-4.

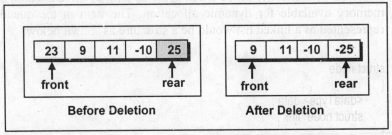

Figure 7-4. *Representation of queue after deleting an element.*

Imagine a case where we add 5 elements to the queue. Value of **rear** would now be 4. Suppose we have not deleted any elements from the queue, then at this stage the value of **front** would be 0. Now suppose we go on deleting elements from the queue. When the fifth element is deleted the queue would fall empty. To make sure that another attempt to delete should be met with an 'empty queue' message, in such a case **front** and **rear** both are reset to -1 to indicate emptiness of the queue.

But this program has got some limitations. Suppose we go on adding elements to the queue till the entire array gets filled. At this stage the value of rear would be **MAX** - 1. Now if we delete 5 elements from the queue, at the end of these deletions the value of **front** would be 5. If now we attempt to add a new element to the queue then it would be reported as full even though in reality the first five slots of the queue are empty. To overcome this situation we can implement a queue as a circular queue, which would be discussed later in this chapter.

Representation Of A Queue As A Linked-List

Queue can also be represented using a linked list. As discussed earlier, linked lists do not have any restrictions on the number of elements it can hold. Space for the elements in a linked list is allocated dynamically, hence it can grow as long as there is enough memory available for dynamic allocation. The item in the queue represented as a linked list would be a structure as shown below:

```
struct node
{
    <dataType> data ;
    struct node *link ;
} ;
```

where dataType represents the type of data such as an **int, float, char**, etc. Figure 7-5 shows the representation of a queue as a linked list.

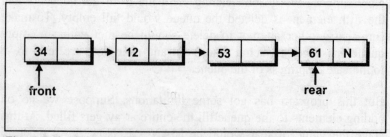

Figure 7-5. *Representation of a queue as a linked list.*

Let us now see a program that implements the queue as a linked list.

```
#include <stdio.h>
#include <conio.h>
```

```c
struct node
{
    int data ;
    struct node *link ;
} ;

struct queue
{
    struct node *front ;
    struct node *rear ;
} ;

void initqueue ( struct queue * ) ;
void addq ( struct queue *, int ) ;
int delq ( struct queue * ) ;
void delqueue ( struct queue * ) ;

void main( )
{
    struct queue a ;
    int i ;

    clrscr( ) ;

    initqueue ( &a ) ;

    addq ( &a, 11 ) ;
    addq ( &a, -8 ) ;
    addq ( &a, 23 ) ;
    addq ( &a, 19 ) ;
    addq ( &a, 15 ) ;
    addq ( &a, 16 ) ;
    addq ( &a, 28 ) ;

    i = delq ( &a ) ;
    printf ( "\nItem extracted: %d", i ) ;

    i = delq ( &a ) ;
```

```
        printf ( "\nItem extracted: %d", i ) ;

        i = delq ( &a ) ;
        printf ( "\nItem extracted: %d", i ) ;

        delqueue ( &a ) ;

        getch( ) ;
}

/* initialises data member */
void initqueue ( struct queue *q )
{
        q -> front = q -> rear = NULL ;
}

/* adds an element to the queue */
void addq ( struct queue *q, int item )
{
        struct node *temp ;

        temp = ( struct node * ) malloc ( sizeof ( struct node ) ) ;
        if ( temp == NULL )
            printf ( "\nQueue is full." ) ;

        temp -> data = item ;
        temp -> link = NULL ;

        if ( q -> front == NULL )
        {
            q -> rear = q -> front = temp ;
            return ;
        }

        q -> rear -> link = temp ;
        q -> rear = q -> rear -> link ;
}
```

```c
/* removes an element from the queue */
int delq (. struct queue * q )
{
    struct node *temp ;
    int item ;

    if ( q -> front == NULL )
    {
        printf ( "\nQueue is empty." ) ;
        return NULL ;
    }

    item = q -> front  -> data ;
    temp = q -> front ;
    q -> front = q -> front -> link ;
    free ( temp ) ;
    return item ;
}

/* deallocates memory */
void delqueue ( struct queue *q )
{
    struct node *temp ;

    if ( q -> front == NULL )
        return ;

    while ( q -> front != NULL )
    {
        temp = q -> front ;
        q -> front = q -> front -> link ;
        free ( temp ) ;
    }
}
```

Output:

Item extracted: 11
Item extracted: -8
Item extracted: 23

In this program the structure **queue** contains two data members **front** and **rear**, both are of the type pointers to the structure **node**. To begin with, the queue is empty hence both **front** and **rear** are set to **NULL**.

The **addq( )** function adds a new element at the rear end of the list. If the element added is the first element, then both **front** and **rear** are made to point to the new node. However, if the element added is not the first element then only **rear** is made to point to the new node, whereas **front** continues to point to the first node in the list.

The **delq( )** function removes an element from the list which is at the front end of the list. Removal of an element from the list actually deletes the node to which **front** is pointing. After deletion of a node, **front** is made to point to the next node that comes in the list, whereas **rear** continues to point to the last node in the list.

The function **delqueue( )** is called before the function **main( )** comes to an end. This is done because the memory allocated for the existing nodes in the list must be de-allocated.

Circular Queues

The queue that we implemented using an array suffers from one limitation. In that implementation there is a possibility that the queue is reported as full (since **rear** has reached the end of the array), even though in actuality there might be empty slots at the beginning of the queue. To overcome this limitation we can implement the queue as a circular queue. Here as we go on adding elements to the queue and reach the end of the array, the next element is stored in the first slot of the array (provided it is free). More clearly, suppose an array **arr** of **n** elements is used to implement a circular queue. Now if we go on adding elements to the queue we may reach **arr[n-1]**. We cannot add any more elements to the queue since we have reached the end of the array. Instead of reporting the queue as full, if some elements in the queue have been deleted then there might be empty slots at the beginning of the queue. In such a case these slots would be filled by new elements being added to the queue. In short just because we have reached the end of the array the queue would not be reported as full. The queue would be reported as full only when all the slots in the array stand occupied. Figure 7-6 shows the pictorial representation of a circular queue.

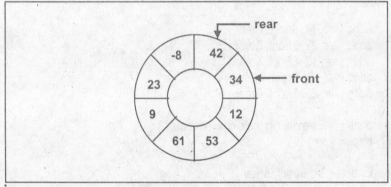

Figure 7-6. *Pictorial representation of a circular queue.*

Let us now see a program that performs the addition and deletion operation on a circular queue.

```
#include <stdio.h>
#include <conio.h>
```

```
#define MAX 10

void addq ( int *, int, int *, int * ) ;
int delq ( int *, int *, int * ) ;
void display ( int * ) ;

void main( )
{
    int arr[MAX] ;
    int i, front, rear ;

    clrscr( ) ;

    /* initialise data member */
    front = rear = -1 ;
    for ( i = 0 ; i < MAX ; i++ )
        arr[i] = 0 ;

    addq ( arr, 14, &front, &rear ) ;
    addq ( arr, 22, &front, &rear ) ;
    addq ( arr, 13, &front, &rear ) ;
    addq ( arr, -6, &front, &rear ) ;
    addq ( arr, 25, &front, &rear ) ;

    printf ( "\nElements in the circular queue: " ) ;
    display ( arr ) ;

    i = delq ( arr, &front, &rear ) ;
    printf ( "Item deleted: %d", i ) ;

    i = delq ( arr, &front, &rear ) ;
    printf ( "\nItem deleted: %d", i ) ;

    printf ( "\nElements in the circular queue after deletion: " ) ;
    display ( arr ) ;

    addq ( arr, 21, &front, &rear ) ;
    addq ( arr, 17, &front, &rear ) ;
```

```
        addq ( arr, 18, &front, &rear ) ;
        addq ( arr, 9, &front, &rear ) ;
        addq ( arr, 20, &front, &rear ) ;

        printf ( "Elements in the circular queue after addition: " ) ;
        display ( arr ) ;

        addq ( arr, 32, &front, &rear ) ;

        printf ( "Elements in the circular queue after addition: " ) ;
        display ( arr ) ;

        getch( ) ;
}

/* adds an element to the queue */
void addq ( int *arr, int item, int *pfront, int *prear )
{
        if ( ( *prear == MAX - 1 && *pfront == 0 ) || ( *prear + 1 == *pfront ) )
        {
                printf ( "\nQueue is full." ) ;
                return ;
        }

        if ( *prear == MAX - 1 )
                *prear = 0 ;
        else
                ( *prear )++ ;

        arr[*prear] = item ;

        if ( *pfront == -1 )
                *pfront = 0 ;
}

/* removes an element from the queue */
int delq ( int *arr, int *pfront, int *prear )
{
```

```
    int data ;

    if ( *pfront == -1 )
    {
        printf ( "\nQueue is empty." ) ;
        return NULL ;
    }

    data = arr[*pfront] ;
    arr[*pfront] = 0 ;

    if ( *pfront == *prear )
    {
        *pfront = -1 ;
        *prear = -1 ;
    }
    else
    {
        if ( *pfront == MAX - 1 )
            *pfront = 0 ;
        else
            ( *pfront )++ ;
    }
    return data ;
}

/* displays element in a queue */
void display ( int * arr )
{
    int i ;
    printf ( "\n" ) ;
    for ( i = 0 ; i < MAX ; i++ )
        printf ( "%d\t", arr[i] ) ;
    printf ( "\n" ) ;
}
```

Output:

Elements in the circular queue:
14   22   13   -6   25   0   0   0   0   0

Item deleted: 14
Item deleted: 22
Elements in the circular queue after deletion:
0   0   13   -6   25   0   0   0   0   0

Elements in the circular queue after addition:
0   0   13   -6   25   21   17   18   9   20

Elements in the circular queue after addition:
32   0   13   -6   25   21   17   18   9   20

Here the array **arr** is used to store the elements of the circular queue. The functions **addq( )** and **delq( )** are used to add and remove the elements from the queue respectively. The function **display( )** displays the existing elements of the queue. The initial values of **front** and **rear** are set to -1, which indicates that the queue is empty.

In **main( )**, first we have called the **addq( )** function 5 times to insert elements in the circular queue. In this function, following cases are considered before adding an element to the queue.

(a) First we have checked whether or not the array is full. The message 'Queue is full' gets displayed if **front** and **rear** are in adjacent locations with **rear** following the **front**.

(b) If the value of **front** is -1 then it indicates that the queue is empty and the element to be added would be the first element in the queue. The values of **front** and **rear** in such a case are set to 0 and the new element gets placed at the 0th position.

(c) It may also happen that some of the positions at the front end of the array are vacant. This happens if we have deleted some elements from the queue, when the value of **rear** is **MAX** - 1 and the value of **front** is greater than 0. In such a case the value of **rear** is set to 0 and the element to be added is added at this position.

(d) The element is added at the rear position in case the value of **front** is either equal to or greater than 0 and the value of **rear** is less than **MAX** - 1.

Thus, after adding 5 elements the value of **front** and **rear** become 0 and 4 respectively. The **display( )** function displays the elements in the queue. Figure 7-7 shows the pictorial representation of a circular queue after adding 5 elements

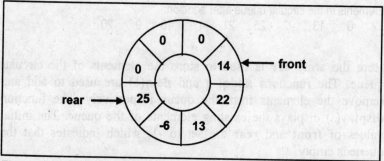

Figure 7-7. *Pictorial representation of circular queue after addition of 5 elements.*

Next we have called **delq( )** function twice to remove 2 elements from the queue. The following conditions are checked while deleting an element.

(a) First we have checked whether or not the queue is empty. The value of **front** in our case is 4, hence an element at the **front** position would get removed.

(b) Next, we have checked if the value of **front** has become equal to **rear**. If it has, then the element we wish to remove is the only element of the queue. On removal of this element the queue would become empty and hence the values of **front** and **rear** are set to -1.

On deleting an element from the queue the value of **front** is set to 0 if it is equal to **MAX - 1**. Otherwise **front** is simply increment by 1. Figure 7-8 shows the pictorial representation of a circular queue after deleting two elements from the queue.

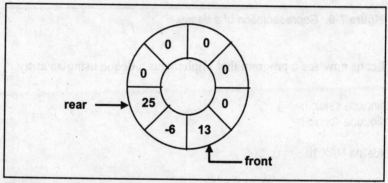

Figure 7-8. *Pictorial representation a circular queue after deleting two elements from the queue.*

Further calls to **addq( )** function adds elements 21, 17, 18, 9, and 20 to the queue. The value of **front** and **rear** at this stage becomes 2 and **MAX - 1** respectively. One more call to **addq( )** function changes the value of **rear** from **MAX - 1** to 0 and the element gets added at the 0th position.

Deque

The word **deque** is a short form of double-ended queue and defines a data structure in which items can be added or deleted at either the front or rear end, but no changes can be made elsewhere in the list. Thus a deque is a generalization of both a stack and a queue. Figure 7-9 shows the representation of a deque.

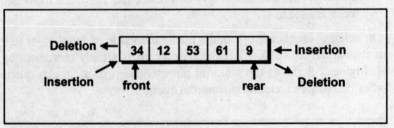

Figure 7-9. *Representation of a deque.*

Let us now see a program that implements a deque using an array.

```c
#include <stdio.h>
#include <conio.h>

#define MAX 10

void addqatbeg ( int *, int, int *, int * ) ;
void addqatend ( int *, int, int *, int * ) ;
int delqatbeg ( int *, int *, int * ) ;
int delqatend ( int *, int *, int * ) ;
void display ( int * ) ;
int count ( int * ) ;

void main( )
{
    int arr[MAX] ;
    int front, rear, i, n ;

    clrscr( ) ;

    /* initialises data members */
    front = rear = -1 ;
    for ( i = 0 ; i < MAX ; i++ )
        arr[i] = 0 ;
```

```
addqatend ( arr, 17, &front, &rear ) ;
addqatbeg ( arr, 10, &front, &rear ) ;
addqatend ( arr, 8, &front, &rear ) ;
addqatbeg ( arr, -9, &front, &rear ) ;
addqatend ( arr, 13, &front, &rear ) ;
addqatbeg ( arr, 28, &front, &rear ) ;
addqatend ( arr, 14, &front, &rear ) ;
addqatbeg ( arr, 5, &front, &rear ) ;
addqatend ( arr, 25, &front, &rear ) ;
addqatbeg ( arr, 6, &front, &rear ) ;
addqatend ( arr, 21, &front, &rear ) ;
addqatbeg ( arr, 11, &front, &rear ) ;

printf ( "\nElements in a deque: " ) ;
display ( arr ) ;

n = count ( arr ) ;
printf ( "\nTotal number of elements in deque: %d", n ) ;

i = delqatbeg ( arr, &front, &rear ) ;
printf ( "\nItem extracted: %d", i ) ;

i = delqatbeg ( arr, &front, &rear ) ;
printf ( "\nItem extracted:%d", i ) ;

i = delqatbeg ( arr, &front, &rear ) ;
printf ( "\nItem extracted:%d", i ) ;

i = delqatbeg ( arr, &front, &rear ) ;
printf ( "\nItem extracted: %d", i ) ;

printf ( "\nElements in a deque after deletion: " ) ;
display ( arr ) ;

addqatend ( arr, 16, &front, &rear ) ;
addqatend ( arr, 7, &front, &rear ) ;

printf ( "\nElements in a deque after addition: " ) ;
```

```
        display ( arr ) ;

        i = delqatend ( arr, &front, &rear ) ;
        printf ( "\nItem extracted: %d", i ) ;

        i = delqatend ( arr, &front, &rear ) ;
        printf ( "\nItem extracted: %d", i ) ;

        printf ( "\nElements in a deque after deletion: " ) ;
        display ( arr ) ;

        n = count ( arr ) ;
        printf ( "\nTotal number of elements in deque: %d", n ) ;

        getch( ) ;
}

/* adds an element at the beginning of a deque */
void addqatbeg ( int *arr, int item, int *pfront, int *prear )
{
        int i, k, c ;

        if ( *pfront == 0 && *prear == MAX - 1 )
        {
                printf ( "\nDeque is full.\n" ) ;
                return ;
        }

        if ( *pfront == -1 )
        {
                *pfront = *prear = 0 ;
                arr[*pfront] = item ;
                return ;
        }

        if ( *prear != MAX - 1 )
        {
                c = count ( arr ) ;
```

```
        k = *prear + 1 ;
        for ( i = 1 ; i <= c ; i++ )
        {
            arr[k] = arr[k - 1] ;
            k-- ;
        }
        arr[k] = item ;
        *pfront = k ;
        ( *prear )++ ;
    }
    else
    {
        ( *pfront )-- ;
        arr[*pfront] = item ;
    }
}

/* adds an element at the end of a deque */
void addqatend ( int *arr, int item, int *pfront, int *prear )
{
    int i, k ;

    if ( *pfront == 0 && *prear == MAX - 1 )
    {
        printf ( "\nDeque is full.\n" ) ;
        return ;
    }

    if ( *pfront == -1 )
    {
        *prear = *pfront = 0 ;
        arr[*prear] = item ;
        return ;
    }

    if ( *prear == MAX - 1 )
    {
        k = *pfront - 1 ;
```

```
        for ( i = *pfront - 1 ; i < *prear ; i++ )
        {
            k = i ;
            if ( k == MAX - 1 )
                    arr[k] = 0 ;
            else
                    arr[k] = arr[i + 1] ;
        }
        ( *prear )-- ;
        ( *pfront )-- ;
    }
    ( *prear )++ ;
    arr[*prear] = item ;
}

/* removes an element from the *pfront end of deque */
int delqatbeg ( int *arr, int *pfront, int *prear )
{
    int item ;

    if ( *pfront == -1 )
    {
        printf ( "\nDeque is empty.\n" ) ;
        return 0 ;
    }

    item = arr[*pfront] ;
    arr[*pfront] = 0 ;

    if ( *pfront == *prear )
        *pfront = *prear = -1 ;
    else
        ( *pfront )++ ;

    return item ;
}

/* removes an element from the *prear end of the deque */
```

```
int delqatend ( int *arr, int *pfront, int *prear )
{
    int item ;

    if ( *pfront == -1 )
    {
        printf ( "\nDeque is empty.\n" ) ;
        return 0 ;
    }

    item = arr[*prear] ;
    arr[*prear] = 0 ;
    ( *prear )-- ;
    if ( *prear == -1 )
        *pfront = -1 ;
    return item ;
}

/* displays elements of a deque */
void display ( int *arr )
{
    int i ;

    printf ( "\n front->" ) ;
    for ( i = 0 ; i < MAX ; i++ )
        printf ( "\t%d", arr[i] ) ;
    printf ( " <-rear" ) ;
}

/* counts the total number of elements in deque */
int count ( int *arr )
{
    int c = 0, i ;

    for ( i = 0 ; i < MAX ; i++ )
    {
        if ( arr[i] != 0 )
            c++ ;
```

```
    }
    return c ;
}
```

Output:

Deque is full.

Deque is full.

```
Elements in a deque:
 front->    6    5    28   -9   10   17   8   13
14    25 <-rear
Total number of elements in deque: 10
Item extracted: 6
Item extracted:5
Item extracted:28
Item extracted: -9
Elements in a deque after deletion:
 front->    0    0    0    0    10   17   8   13
14    25 <-rear
Elements in a deque after addition:
 front->    0    0    10   17   8    13   14   25
16    7 <-rear
Item extracted: 7
Item extracted: 16
Elements in a deque after deletion:
 front->    0    0    10   17   8    13   14   25
0    0 <-rear
Total number of elements in deque: 6
```

Here we have used an array of integers called **arr** to hold the elements of a deque. The variables **front** and **rear** are used to monitor the front end and the rear end of the deque.

We have called **addqatbeg( )** and **addqatend( )** functions alternately to add elements at the beginning and at the end of the deque respectively. Let us discuss how the elements get added at the front or rear end of the deque.

First we have called **addqatend( )** function. In this function we have checked whether or not the deque is full. A message 'Deque is full' gets displayed if the deque is full. Next we have checked whether the element to be added is the first element. The element that we wish to add indeed is the first element of the deque. Hence the values of **front** and **rear** are set to 0 and the element 17 is placed in the deque. Figure 7-10 shows the representation of a deque after adding one element.

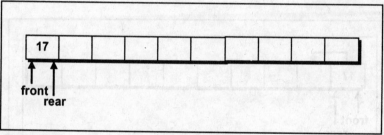

Figure 7-10. *Deque after addition of first element.*

Next we have called **addqatbeg( )** function to add an element at the front end of the deque. In this function too, before adding the element we have checked two conditions. First whether or not the deque is full and the second whether the element to be added is first element of the deque. In our case both the conditions would evaluate to false, since the deque is not full as holds one element— 17. Now, the element 10 should get added at the 0th position, but that position is already occupied by element 17. To make 0th position vacant we need to shift 17 to the right. This would be possible if there is any vacant place available to the right of the element 17. In other words, this would be possible if the value of

rear is less than **MAX**. Since, 17 is the only element added to the deque so far, it would get shifted one place to the right and the element 10 would now occupy the 0th place.

To shift the element(s) to the right, first we have obtained the total number of elements present in the deque by calling the **count( )** function. Next we have obtained the position of the last element in the deque, i.e. the element at the rear end of the deque. Then, through a loop we have shifted the elements one place to the right. The new element is then placed at the vacant place that comes immediately to the left of the element (to which **front** is pointing). Figure 7-11 gives the pictorial representation of how element gets shifted to the right and then a new element gets added at the vacant place.

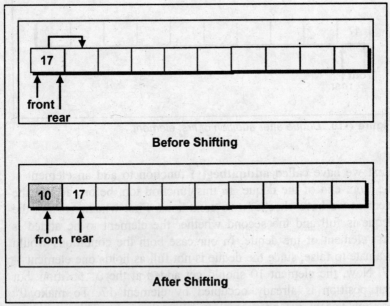

Figure 7-11. *Shifting of element(s) in a deque while adding element at the beginning.*

At this stage the value of **front** and **rear** would be 0 and 1 respectively. Then we have added several elements to the deque. After adding the element 6 values of **front** and **rear** would become 0 and 9 respectively. Figure 7-12 shows deque after adding all the 10 elements. Trying to add any more elements to the deque at this stage would display the message 'Deque is full'. We have called **display( )** function to display all the elements in a deque.

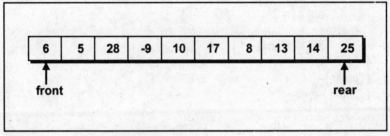

Figure 7-12. *Deque containing 10 elements.*

Now, let us discuss the functions **delqatbeg( )** and **delqatend( )**. The **delqatbeg( )** function removes an element from the **front** position. After removing an element **front** stores the index of next element in the deque. Hence we have incremented the value of **front** by 1. In the function **delqatend( )** on removing element at the end, **rear** should store the index of the element that occupies the position to the left of the element being deleted. Hence we have decremented the value of **rear** by 1.

Imagine a situation when the value of **rear** has reached **MAX** - 1 and the value of **front** is greater than 0, say 4 for example (after deleting first 4 elements). This would be the stage where the deque is not full. But, it would not be possible to add an element at the **rear** end of the deque. To do so the elements would be required to be shifted one position to the left. In **addqatend( )** function this ituation is handled as follows.

```
int i, k ;

if ( *prear == MAX - 1 )
{
    k = *pfront - 1 ;
    for ( i = *pfront - 1 ; i < *prear ; i++ )
    {
        k = i ;
        if ( k == MAX - 1 )
            arr[ k ] = 0 ;
        else
            arr[ k ] = arr[ i + 1 ] ;
    }
    ( *prear )-- ;
    ( *pfront )-- ;
}
```

If the condition given in the code snippet evaluates to **true** then the value of a temporary variable **k** is set to **front - 1**. Thus, if value of **front** were 4 then **k** would be 3. Then, through **for** loop the elements are shifted one position to the left. The new element is then added at the end of the deque. Figure 7-13 illustrates shifting of elements to the left and placing a new element at the end of the deque.

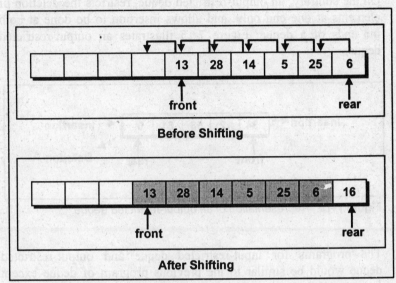

front
rear

Before Shifting

front
rear

After Shifting

Figure 7-13. *Shifting of elements to add a new element at the end.*

There are two variations of a deque. These are:

- Input-restricted deque
- Output-restricted deque

An Input restricted deque restricts the insertion of elements at one end only, but the deletion of elements can be done at both the ends of a queue. Figure 7-14 illustrates an input-restricted deque.

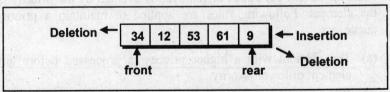

Deletion ← | 34 | 12 | 53 | 61 | 9 | ← Insertion
front   rear   → Deletion

Figure 7-14. *Representation of an input-restricted deque.*

On the contrary, an output-restricted deque, restricts the deletion of elements at one end only, and allows insertion to be done at both the ends of a deque. Figure 7-15 illustrates an output-restricted deque.

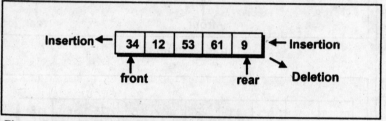

Figure 7-15. *Representation of an output-restricted deque.*

The programs for input-restricted deque and output-restricted deque would be similar to the previous program of deque except for a small difference. The program for the input-restricted deque would not contain the function **addqatbeg( )**. Similarly, the program for the output-restricted deque would not contain the function **delatbeg( )**.

Priority Queue

A priority queue is a collection of elements where the elements are stored according to their priority levels. The order in which the elements should get added or removed is decided by the priority of the element. Following rules are applied to maintain a priority queue.

(a) The element with a higher priority is processed before any element of lower priority.

(b) If there are elements with the same priority, then the element added first in the queue would get processed.

Priority queues are used for implementing job scheduling by the operating system where jobs with higher priorities are to be processed first. Another application of priority queues is simulation systems where priority corresponds to event times.

Array Implementation Of A Priority Queue

Like stacks and queues even a priority queue can be represented using an array. However, if an array is used to store elements of a priority queue, then insertion of elements to the queue would be easy, but deletion of elements would be difficult. This is because while inserting elements in the priority queue they are not inserted in an order. As a result, deleting an element with the highest priority would require examining the entire array to search for such an element. Moreover, an element in a queue can be deleted from the front end only.

There is no satisfactory solution to this problem. However, it would be more efficient if we store the elements in a priority queue in an ordered manner. Each element in an array can have following structure.

```
struct data
{
    <dataType> item ;
    int priority ;
    int order ;
} ;
```

where **dataType** would be data type of the item like **int**, **char**, etc., **priority** would be the priority number of the element and **order** would be the order in which the element has been added to the queue.

Given below is a program that implements the priority queue using an array.

```c
#include <stdio.h>
#include <conio.h>

#define MAX 5

struct data
{
    char job[MAX] ;
    int prno ;
    int ord ;
} ;

struct pque
{
    struct data d[MAX] ;
    int front ;
    int rear ;
} ;

void initpque ( struct pque * ) ;
void add ( struct pque *, struct data ) ;
struct data delete ( struct pque * ) ;

void main( )
{
    struct pque q ;
    struct data dt, temp ;
    int i, j = 0 ;

    clrscr( ) ;

    initpque ( &q ) ;

    printf ( "Enter Job description (max 4 chars) and its priority\n" ) ;
```

```
        printf ( "Lower the priority number, higher the priority\n" ) ;
        printf ( "Job     Priority\n" ) ;

        for ( i = 0 ; i < MAX ; i++ )
        {
            scanf ( "%s %d", &dt.job, &dt.prno ) ;
            dt.ord = j++ ;
            add ( &q, dt ) ;
        }
        printf ( "\n" ) ;

        printf ( "Process jobs prioritywise\n" ) ;
        printf ( "Job\tPriority\n" ) ;

        for ( i = 0 ; i < MAX ; i++ )
        {
            temp  = delete ( &q ) ;
            printf ( "%s\t%d\n", temp.job, temp.prno ) ;
        }
        printf ( "\n" ) ;

        getch( ) ;
    }

    /* initialises data members */
    void initpque ( struct pque *pq )
    {
        int i ;

        pq -> front = pq -> rear = -1 ;
        for ( i = 0 ; i < MAX ; i++ )
        {
            strcpy ( pq -> d[i].job, '\0' ) ;
            pq -> d[i].prno = pq -> d[i].ord = 0 ;
        }
    }

    /* adds item to the priority queue */
```

```c
void add ( struct pque *pq, struct data dt )
{
    struct data temp ;
    int i, j ;

    if ( pq -> rear == MAX - 1 )
    {
        printf ( "\nQueue is full." ) ;
        return ;
    }

    pq -> rear++ ;
    pq -> d[pq -> rear] = dt ;

    if ( pq -> front == -1 )
        pq -> front = 0 ;

    for ( i = pq -> front ; i <= pq -> rear ; i++ )
    {
        for ( j = i + 1 ; j <= pq -> rear ; j++ )
        {
            if ( pq -> d[i].prno > pq -> d[j].prno )
            {
                temp = pq -> d[i] ;
                pq -> d[i] = pq -> d[j] ;
                pq -> d[j] = temp ;
            }
            else
            {
                if ( pq -> d[i].prno == pq -> d[j].prno )
                {
                    if ( pq -> d[i].ord > pq -> d[j].ord )
                    {
                        temp = pq -> d[i] ;
                        pq -> d[i] = pq -> d[j] ;
                        pq -> d[j] = temp ;
                    }
                }
            }
```

```
            }
         }
      }
}

/* removes item from priority queue */
struct data  delete ( struct pque *pq )
{
    struct data  t ;
    strcpy ( t.job, "" ) ;
    t.prno = 0 ;
    t.ord = 0 ;

    if ( pq -> front == -1 )
    {
        printf ( "\nQueue is Empty.\n" ) ;
        return t ;
    }

    t = pq -> d[pq -> front] ;
    pq -> d[pq -> front] = t ;
    if ( pq -> front == pq -> rear )
        pq -> front = pq -> rear = -1 ;
    else
        pq -> front++ ;

    return t ;
}
```

Output:

```
Enter Job description (max 4 chars) and its priority
Lower the priority number, higher the priority
Job    Priority
TYPE   4
SWAP   3
COPY   5
PRNT   1
```

SWAP   3

Process jobs priority wise
Job   Priority
PRNT   1
SWAP   3
SWAP   3
TYPE   4
COPY   5

Here the structure **pque** contains an array **d** to hold the elements of the priority queue. The element in the array is a structure holding information about the job to be processed, priority of the job, and the order in which the element is added. The function **add( )** adds the element to the priority queue, whereas, the function **remove( )** deletes an element with the highest priority from the queue.

In **main( )** through a **for** loop, we have added 5 elements to the priority queue. In **addq( )** function, the element **dt** gets added to the queue at the rear end. Suppose the first element to be added to the queue holds data as {TYPE, 4, 1}. After adding this element the value of **front** and **rear** would be 0. Next, in this function we have arranged the elements in ascending order of their priorities. Suppose the second element to be added to the queue is {SWAP, 3, 2}. The priority of the second element is lower than the element at the 0th position in the queue. Hence the second element would get placed at 0th position and the element at 0th position would occupy first position. Figure 7-16 shows the priority queue after adding two elements.

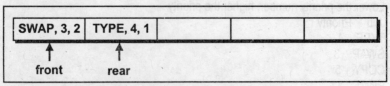

Figure 7-16. *Priority queue after adding two elements.*

In case there are two elements with the same priority, then the elements are arranged according to their order number in which they were entered. Thus, the elements in the priority queue are arranged priority wise and within the same priority as per the order of entry. Figure 7-17 shows priority queue after adding fifth element.

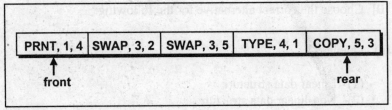

Figure 7-17. *Priority queue with 5 elements.*

Next, in order to process the information with the highest priority we have called **remove( )** function. In this function the element at the **front** is removed.

Exercise

[A] Fill in the blanks:

(a) For a queue built using an array and containing **n** elements, the value of **front** would be _____ and **rear** would be _____.

(b) In a circular queue implemented using an array and holding 5 elements, if **front** is equal to **3** and **rear** is equal to **4**, then the new element would get placed at ____ position.

(c) A queue is called _____ when addition as well as deletion of elements can take place at both the ends.

(d) An _____ is a queue in which insertion of an element takes place at one end only but deletion occurs at both the ends.

(e) An _____ is a queue in which insertion of an element takes place at both the ends but deletion occurs at one end only.

[B] Choose the correct alternative for the following:

(a) Queue is a

(1) Linear data structure
(2) Non-linear data structure
(3) Both (1) and (2)
(4) None of the above

(b) The end at which a new element gets added to a queue is called

(1) front
(2) rear
(3) top
(4) bottom

(c) The end from which an element gets removed from the queue is called

(1) front
(2) rear
(3) top
(4) bottom

(d) Queue is also called

(1) Last-In-First-Out data structure
(2) First-In-Last-Out data structure
(3) First-In-First-Out data structure
(4) Last-In-Last-Out data structure

[C] Write programs for the following:

(a) Write a program to represent a deque using linked list. Also write functions to add and delete elements from the deque.

(b) Suppose there are several jobs to be performed with each job having a priority value of 1, 2, 3, 4, etc. Write a program that receives the job descriptions and the priorities. Create as many queues as the number of priorities and queue up the jobs into appropriate queues. For example, suppose the priorities are 1, 2, 3, and 4 and the data to be entered is as follows:

ABC, 2, XYZ, 1, PQR, 1, RTZ, 3, CBZ, 2, QQQ, 3, XXX, 4, RRR, 1

Then arrange these jobs as shown below:

Q1: XYZ, 1, PQR, 1, RRR, 1

Q2: ABC, 2, CBZ, 2

Q3: RTZ, 3, QQQ, 3

Q4: XXX, 4

The order of processing should be: Q1, Q2, Q3, Q4. Write a program to simulate the above problem.

(c) Write a menu-driven program to simulate processing of batch jobs by a computer system. The scheduling of these jobs should be handled using a priority queue. The program should allow user to add or remove items from the queue. It should also display current status i.e. the total number of items in the queue.

(d) Write a program to copy one queue to another when the queue is implemented as a linked list.

(e) Specify which of the following applications would be suitable for a First-In-First-Out queue.

(1) A program is to keep track of patients as they check into a clinic, assigning them to doctors on a first-come, first-served basis.

(2) An inventory of parts is to be processed by part number.

(3) A dictionary of words used by spelling checker is to be created.

(4) Customers are to take numbers at a bakery and be served in order when their numbers come up.

CHAPTER

EIGHT

Trees

Herbs, shrubs, bushes and trees

Nature is man's best teacher. In every walk of life man has looked and explored the nature, learnt his lessons and then applied the knowledge that nature offered him to solve every-day problems that he faced at work-place. It isn't without reason that there are data structures like Trees, Binary Trees, Search Trees, AVL Trees, Forests, etc.

The data structures that we have seen so far (such as linked lists, stacks and queues) were linear data structures. As against this, trees are non-linear data structures. Trees are encountered frequently in everyday life.

In a linked list each node has a link which points to another node. In a tree structure, however, each node may point to several other nodes (which may then point to several other nodes, etc.). Thus a tree is a very flexible and powerful data structure that can be used for a wide variety of applications. For example, suppose we wish to use a data structure to represent a person and all of his or her descendants. Assume that the person's name is **Rahul** and that he has 3 children, **Sanjay**, **Sameer** and **Nisha**. Also suppose that **Sameer** has 3 children, **Abha**, **Ajit** and **Madhu** and **Nisha** has one child **Neha**. We can represent **Rahul** and his descendants quite naturally with the tree structure shown in Figure 8-1.

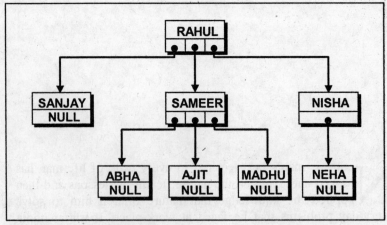

Figure 8-1. *A Tree Structure.*

Notice that each tree node contains a name for data and one or more pointers to the other tree nodes.

Although the nodes in a general tree may contain any number of pointers to the other tree nodes, a large number of data structures have at the most two pointers to the other tree nodes. This type of a tree is called a **binary tree**.

Binary Trees

Let us begin our study of binary trees by discussing some basic concepts and terminology. A simple binary tree is shown in Figure 8-2.

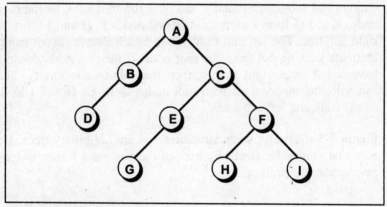

Figure 8-2. *Binary tree.*

Here are a few definitions:

A binary tree: A binary tree consists of a finite set of elements that can be partitioned into three distinct sub-sets called the **root**, the **left** and the **right sub-tree**. If there are no elements in the binary tree it is called an empty binary tree.

Node: Each element present in a binary tree is called a **node** of that tree.

Root: The element that represents the base node of the tree is called the **root** of the tree.

The left and **right sub-trees:** Apart from the root, the other two sub-sets of a binary tree are binary trees. They are called the **left** and **right sub-trees** of the original tree. Any of these sub-sets can be empty.

The tree shown in Figure 8-2 consists of nine nodes. This tree has a root node **A**, a left sub-tree formed by nodes **B, D** and the right sub-tree formed by nodes **C, E, F, G, H** and **I**. The left sub-tree is itself a binary with **B** as the root node, **D** as the left sub-tree and an empty right sub-tree. Similarly, the right sub-tree has **C** as the root node, **E** and **G** form its left sub-tree and nodes **F, H** and **I** form its right sub-tree. The left and right sub-trees are always shown using branches coming out from the root node. If the root node doesn't have a left or a right branch then that sub-tree is empty. For example, the binary trees with root nodes as **D, G, H** and **I** have empty right and left sub-trees.

Figure 8-3 illustrates some structures that are not binary trees. Be sure that you understand why each of them is not a binary tree as per the above definition.

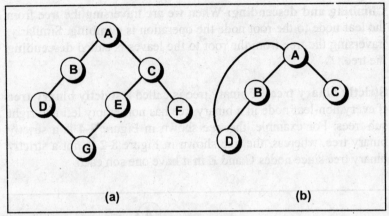

(a)   (b)

Figure 8-3. *Trees that are not binary trees.*

Let us now look at some more definitions that are used in association with binary trees.

Father and son: Suppose **A** is the root node of a binary tree and **B** is the root of its left or right sub-tree. In this case **A** is said to be the **father** of **B** and **B** is said to be the **left** or **right son** of **A**.

Leaf node: A node that does not have any sons (such as **D, G, H,** or **I** shown in Figure 8-2) is called a **leaf** node.

Ancestor and descendant: A node **A** is said to be an **ancestor** of node **B** if **A** is either the father of **B** or the father of some ancestor of **B**. For example, in the tree shown in Figure 8-2, **A** is an ancestor of **C**. A node **B** is said to be a **left descendant** of node **A** if **B** is either the left son of **A** or a descendant of the left son of **A**. In a similar fashion we can define the right descendant.

Unlike natural trees, the tree data structures are depicted with root node at the top and the leaves at the bottom. The common convention used about direction is "down" from the root node to leaf nodes and "up" from leaf node to root node.

Climbing and descending: When we are traversing the tree from the leaf node to the root node the operation is **climbing**. Similarly, traversing the tree from the root to the leaves is called **descending** the tree.

Strictly binary tree: A binary tree is called a **strictly binary tree** if every non-leaf node in a binary tree has non-empty left and right sub-trees. For example, the tree shown in Figure 8-4 is a strictly binary tree, whereas, the tree shown in Figure 8-2 is not a strictly binary tree since nodes **C** and **E** in it have one son each.

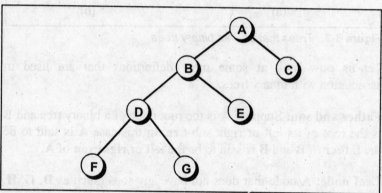

Figure 8-4. *Strictly binary tree.*

Degree: The number of nodes connected to a particular node is called the **degree** of that node. For example, in Figure 8-4 the node containing data **D** has a degree 3. The degree of a leaf node is always one.

Level: The root node of the tree has level 0. The level of any other child node is one more than the level of its father. For example, in the binary tree shown in Figure 8-2, node **E** is at level 2 and node **H** is at level 3.

Depth: The maximum level of any leaf node in the tree is called the **depth** of the binary tree. For example, the depth of the tree shown in Figure 8-2 is 3.

Complete binary tree: A strictly binary tree all of whose leaf nodes are at the same level is called a complete binary tree. Figure 8-5 illustrates the complete binary tree. The depth of this tree is 2.

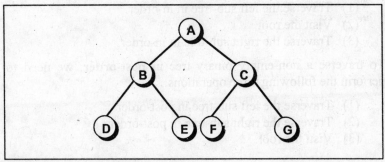

Figure 8-5. *Complete binary tree.*

Traversal Of A Binary Tree

The traversal of a binary tree involves visiting each node in the tree exactly once. In several applications involving a binary tree we need to go to each node in the tree systematically. In a linear list, nodes can be visited in a systematic manner from beginning to end. However, such an order is not possible while traversing a tree. There are three methods commonly used for binary tree traversal. These methods are known as **in-order** traversal, **pre-order** traversal and **post-order** traversal. The methods differ primarily in the order in which they visit the root node the nodes in the left sub-tree and the nodes in the right sub-tree. Note that a binary tree is of recursive nature, i.e. each sub-tree is a binary tree itself. Hence the functions used to traverse a tree using these methods can use recursion.

To traverse a non-empty binary tree in **pre-order**, we need to perform the following three operations:

    (1) Visit the root.
    (2) Traverse the left sub-tree in pre-order.
    (3) Traverse the right sub-tree in pre-order

To traverse a non-empty binary tree in **in-order**, we need to perform the following three operations:

    (1) Traverse the left sub-tree in in-order.
    (2) Visit the root.
    (3) Traverse the right sub-tree in in-order.

To traverse a non-empty binary tree in **post-order**, we need to perform the following three operations:

    (1) Traverse the left sub-tree in post-order.
    (2) Traverse the right sub-tree in post-order.
    (3) Visit the root.

In all the three methods nothing needs be done to traverse an empty binary tree.

Representation Of A Binary Trees In Memory

The structure of each node of a binary tree contains the data field, a pointer to the left child and a pointer to the right child. Figure 8-6 shows this structure.

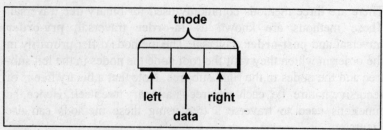

Figure 8-6. *Node of a binary tree.*

This structure can be defined as follows:

```
sturct tnode
{
    struct tnode *left ;
    int data ;
    struct tnode *right ;
} ;
```

There are two ways by which we can represent a binary tree.

(a) Linked representation of a binary tree

(b) Array representation of a binary tree

Both these ways are discussed below.

Linked Representation Of Binary Trees

Binary trees can be represented by links, where each node contains the address of the left child and the right child. These addresses are nothing but kinks to the left and right child respectively. A node that does not have a left or a right child contains a **NULL** value in its link fields. Figure 8-7 shows the linked representation of a binary tree.

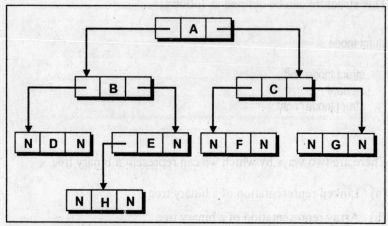

Figure 8-7. *Linked representation of a Binary tree.*

In Figure 8-7, the link fields of node **C** contain the address of the nodes **F** and **G**. The left link field of node **E** contains the address of the node **H**. Similarly the right link contains a **NULL** value as there is only one (left) child of node **E**.

The node **D**, **F**, **G** and **H** contain a **NULL** value in both their link fields, as these are the leaf nodes.

Array Representation Of Binary Trees

When a binary tree is represented by arrays three separate arrays are required. One array **arr** stores the data fields of the trees. The other two arrays **lc** and **rc** represents the left child and right child of the nodes. Figure 8-8 shows these three arrays, which represents the tree that is shown in Figure 8-7.

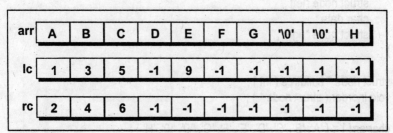

Figure 8-8. *Array representation of a binary tree.*

The array **lc** and **rc** contains the index of the array **arr** where the data is present. If the node does not have any left child or right child then the element of the array **lc** or **rc** contains a value –1. The 0th element of the array **arr** that contains the data is always the root node of the tree. Some elements of the array **arr** contain '\0' which represents an empty child.

Let us understand this with the help of an example. Suppose we want to find the left and right child of the node **E.** Then we need to find the value present at index 4 in array **lc** and **rc** since **E** is present at index 4 in the array **arr**. The value present at index 4 in the array **lc** is 9, which is the index position of node **H** in the array **arr.** So the left child of the node **E** is **H.** The right child of the node **E** is empty because the value present at index 4 in the array **rc** is –1.

Following program shows how a binary tree can be represented using arrays.

```
#include <stdio.h>
#include <conio.h>
#include <alloc.h>

struct node
{
```

```
        struct node *left ;
        char data ;
        struct node *right ;
} ;

struct node * buildtree ( int ) ;
void inorder ( struct node * ) ;

char arr[ ] = { 'A', 'B', 'C', 'D', 'E', 'F', 'G', '\0', '\0', 'H' } ;
int  lc[ ] = { 1,  3,  5,  -1,  9, -1, -1,  -1,  -1, -1 } ;
int  rc[ ] = { 2,  4,  6,  -1, -1, -1, -1,  -1,  -1, -1 } ;

void main( )
{
        struct node *root ;

        clrscr( ) ;

        root = buildtree ( 0 ) ;
        printf ( "In-order Traversal:\n" ) ;
        inorder ( root ) ;

        getch( ) ;
}
struct node * buildtree ( int index )
{
        struct node *temp = NULL ;
        if ( index != -1 )
        {
                temp = ( struct node * ) malloc ( sizeof ( struct node ) ) ;
                temp -> left = buildtree ( lc[index] ) ;
                temp -> data = arr[index] ;
                temp -> right = buildtree ( rc[index] ) ;
        }
        return temp ;
}
```

```
void inorder ( struct node *root )
{
    if ( root != NULL )
    {
        inorder ( root -> left ) ;
        printf ( "%c\t", root -> data ) ;
        inorder ( root -> right ) ;
    }
}
```

Output:

In-order Traversal:
D   B   H   E   A   F   C   G

The function **buildtree( )** is called by passing a value 0 and is received in an integer variable **index** which indicates the 0th element of the array **arr** (the root node). In the function a condition is checked, whether **index** is -1. If it is, then it indicates that the particular node doesn't have any child. But if the index is not -1 then memory is allocated for a new node. The data from the array **arr** is stored in data part of the new node. Finally, a recursive call is made for the left and right child of the new node, by passing the corresponding index values from the arrays **lc** and **rc**.

The function **inorder( )** is called to traverse the tree in in-order traversal. This function receives only one parameter as the address of the root node. Then a condition is checked whether the pointer is **NULL**. If the pointer is not **NULL** then a recursive call is made first for the left child and then for the right child. The values passed are the addresses of the left and right children that are present in the pointers **left** and **right** respectively. In-between these two calls the data of the current node is printed.

We can also represent a binary tree using one single array. For this, numbers are given to each node starting from the root node— 0 to root node, 1 to the left node of the first level, then 2 to the second node from left of the first level and so on. In other words, the nodes are numbered from left to right level by level from top to bottom. Figure 8-9(a) shows the numbers given to each node in the tree. Note that while numbering the nodes of the tree, empty nodes are also taken into account.

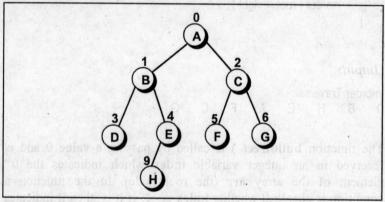

Figure 8-9(a). *Numbering of nodes.*

Figure 8-9(b) shows the array representation of the tree that is shown in Figure 8-9(a).

	a[0]	a[1]	a[2]	a[3]	a[4]	a[5]	a[6]	a[7]	a[8]	a[9]
a	A	B	C	D	E	F	G	'\0'	'\0'	H

a[10]	a[11]	a[12]	a[13]	a[14]	a[15]	a[16]	a[17]	a[18]	a[19]	a[20]
'\0'	'\0'	'\0'	'\0'	'\0'	'\0'	'\0'	'\0'	'\0'	'\0'	'\0'

Figure 8-9(b). *Array representation of a Binary tree.*

It can be observed that if **n** is the number given to the node then its left child occurs at the position **(2n + 1)** and right child at **(2n + 2)**.

If any node doesn't have a left or a right child then an empty node is assumed and a value '\0' is stored at that index in the array.

Following program shows how a binary tree can be represented as an array using the method discussed above.

```c
#include <stdio.h>
#include <conio.h>
#include <alloc.h>

struct node
{
    struct node *left ;
    char data ;
    struct node *right ;
} ;

struct node * buildtree ( int ) ;
void inorder ( struct node * ) ;

char a[ ] = {
                'A', 'B', 'C', 'D', 'E', 'F', 'G', '\0', '\0', 'H', '\0',
                '\0', '\0', '\0', '\0', '\0', '\0', '\0', '\0', '\0', '\0'
            } ;

void main( )
{
    struct node *root ;

    clrscr( ) ;

    root = buildtree ( 0 ) ;
    printf ( "In-order Traversal:\n" ) ;
    inorder ( root ) ;

    getch( ) ;
}
```

```
struct node * buildtree ( int n )
{
    struct node *temp = NULL ;
    if ( a[n] != '\0' )
    {
        temp = ( struct node * ) malloc ( sizeof ( struct node ) ) ;
        temp -> left = buildtree ( 2 * n + 1 ) ;
        temp -> data = a[n] ;
        temp -> right = buildtree ( 2 * n + 2 ) ;
    }
    return temp ;
}

void inorder ( struct node *root )
{
    if ( root != NULL )
    {
        inorder ( root -> left ) ;
        printf ( "%c\t", root -> data ) ;
        inorder ( root -> right ) ;
    }
}
```

Output:

In-order Traversal:
D   B   H   E   A   F   C   G

In the above program the working of functions **inorder( )** and
buildtree( ) is same as what we saw in the last program except for
a small change in the function **buildtree( )**. Here, the condition is
checked that the value present at particular index is '\0'. If it is not
'\0' then the recursive calls are made for the left and right child.
Instead of three arrays only one array is maintained and hence the
value of index passed to recursive call is **2 * n + 1** and **2 * n + 2**
for the left and right child respectively.

Binary Search Trees

Many algorithms that use binary trees proceed in two phases. The first phase builds a binary tree, and the second traverses the tree. As an example of such an algorithm, consider the following sorting method. Given a list of numbers in an input file, we wish to print them in ascending order. As we read the numbers, they can be inserted into a binary tree such as the one shown in Figure 8-10. When a number is compared with the contents of a node in the tree, a left branch is taken if the number is smaller than the contents of the node and a right branch if it is greater or equal to the contents of the node. Thus if the input list is

20 17 6 8 10 7 18 13 12 5

then the binary tree shown in Figure 8-10 is produced.

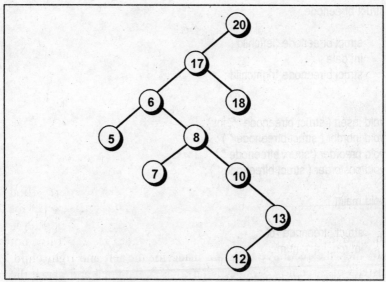

Figure 8-10. *Binary search tree.*

Such a binary tree has the property that all the elements in the left sub-tree of a node **n** are less than the contents of **n**. And all the elements in the right sub-tree of **n** are greater than or equal to the contents of **n**.

A binary tree that has these properties is called a **Binary Search Tree**. If a binary search tree is traversed in in-order (left, root, and right) and the contents of each node are printed as the node is visited, the numbers are printed in ascending order. Convince yourself that this is the case for the binary search tree shown in Figure 8-10. The program to implement this algorithm is as follows:

```
#include <stdio.h>
#include <conio.h>
#include <alloc.h>
struct btreenode
{
    struct btreenode *leftchild ;
    int data ;
    struct btreenode *rightchild ;
} ;

void insert ( struct btreenode **, int ) ;
void inorder ( struct btreenode * ) ;
void preorder ( struct btreenode * ) ;
void postorder ( struct btreenode * ) ;

void main( )
{
    struct btreenode *bt ;
    int req, i = 1, num ;

    bt = NULL ;  /* empty tree */

    clrscr( ) ;
    printf ( "Specify the number of items to be inserted: " ) ;
```

```
        scanf ( "%d", &req ) ;

        while ( i++ <= req )
        {
            printf ( "Enter the data: " ) ;
            scanf ( "%d", &num ) ;
            insert ( &bt, num ) ;
        }

        printf ( "\nIn-order   Traversal: " ) ;
        inorder ( bt ) ;

        printf ( "\nPre-order  Traversal: " ) ;
        preorder ( bt ) ;

        printf ( "\nPost-order Traversal: " ) ;
        postorder ( bt ) ;
}

/* inserts a new node in a binary search tree */
void insert ( struct btreenode **sr, int num )
{
    if ( *sr == NULL )
    {
        *sr = malloc ( sizeof ( struct btreenode ) ) ;

        ( *sr ) -> leftchild = NULL ;
        ( *sr ) -> data = num ;
        ( *sr ) -> rightchild = NULL ;
        return ;
    }
    else  /* search the node to which new node will be attached */
    {
        /* if new data is less, traverse to left */
        if ( num < ( *sr ) -> data )
            insert ( &( ( *sr ) -> leftchild ), num ) ;
        else
            /* else traverse to right */
```

```
                insert ( &( ( *sr ) -> rightchild ), num ) ;
    }
    return ;
}

/* traverse a binary search tree in a LDR (Left-Data-Right) fashion */
void inorder ( struct btreenode *sr )
{
    if ( sr != NULL )
    {
        inorder ( sr -> leftchild ) ;

        /* print the data of the node whose leftchild is NULL or the path
           has already been traversed */
        printf ( "\t%d", sr -> data ) ;

        inorder ( sr -> rightchild ) ;
    }
    else
        return ;
}

/* traverse a binary search tree in a DLR (Data-Left-right) fashion */
void preorder ( struct btreenode *sr )
{
    if ( sr != NULL )
    {
        /* print the data of a node */
        printf ( "\t%d", sr -> data ) ;
        /* traverse till leftchild is not NULL */
        preorder ( sr -> leftchild ) ;
        /* traverse till rightchild is not NULL */
        preorder ( sr -> rightchild ) ;
    }
    else
        return ;
}
```

```
/* traverse a binary search tree in LRD (Left-Right-Data) fashion */
void postorder ( struct btreenode *sr )
{
    if ( sr != NULL )
    {
        postorder ( sr -> leftchild ) ;
        postorder ( sr -> rightchild ) ;
        printf ( "\t%d", sr -> data ) ;
    }
    else
        return ;
}
```

Output:

Specify the number of items to be inserted: 5
Enter the data: 1
Enter the data: 2
Enter the data: 3
Enter the data: 4
Enter the data: 5

In-order Traversal: 1   2   3   4   5
Pre-order Traversal: 1   2   3   4   5
Post-order Traversal: 5   4   3   2   1

In the above program the working of the function **inorder( )** is exactly the same as the last program. The functions **preorder( )** and **postorder( )** work in the same manner except for a small difference. In case of the function **preorder( )** initially data is printed then the recursive calls are made for the left and right children. On the other hand, in case of **postorder( )** firstly the recursive calls for left and right children are made and then the data is printed.

In the function **insert( )** two arguments are passed—one is the pointer to the node of the tree and the other is the data that is to be inserted. Initially, the pointer to the node contains a **NULL** value, which indicates an empty tree. Then a condition is checked whether the pointer is **NULL**. If it is **NULL** then a new node is created and the data that is to be inserted is stored in its data part. The left and right child of this new node is set with a **NULL** value, as this is always going to be the leaf node.

In the **else** block, i.e. if the current node is not empty then the data of the current node is compared with the data that is to be inserted. If the data that is to be inserted is found to be smaller than the data of the current node then a recursive call is made to **insert( )** function by passing the address of the node of the left sub-tree, otherwise the address of the node of right sub-tree is passed. So at one stage in the recursive call the node is found to be empty, which is the place where the new node is to be inserted.

Operations On A Binary Search Tree

There are many operations that can be performed on binary search trees. Searching, insertion and deletion of a node are the most basic operations that are required to maintain a tree. Let us now discuss these operations in detail.

Searching Of A Node In A BST

To search any node in a binary tree, initially the data that is to be searched is compared with the data of the root node. If the data is equal to the data of the root node then the searching is successful. If the data is found to be greater than the data of the root node then the searching process proceeds in the right sub-tree of the root node, otherwise, searching process proceeds in the left sub-tree of the root node.

Same procedure is repeated for the left or right sub-tree until the data is found. While searching the data if the leaf node of tree is reached and the data is not found then it is concluded that the data is not present in the tree.

Consider Figure 8-10 and suppose the data that is to be searched is 8. Initially 8 is compared with root node which holds a value 20 and since 8 is less than 20 the searching would proceed in the left sub-tree. Now 8 is compared 17 and since 8 is less than 17 the searching would proceed in the left sub-tree of the node which holds a value 17. Next, 8 is compared with 6 and since 8 is greater than 6 the searching proceeds in the right sub-tree of the node which holds a value 6. Now 8 is compared with the node which holds a value 8 and since 8 is found the searching process ends here.

Insertion Of A Node In A BST

To insert any node into a BST, initially the data that is to be inserted is compared with the data of the root node. If the data is found to be greater than or equal to the data of the root node then the new node is inserted in the right sub-tree of the root node, otherwise, the new node is inserted in the left sub-tree of the root node.

Now the root node of the right or left sub-tree is taken and its data is compared with the data that is to be inserted and the same procedure is repeated. This is done till the left or the right sub-tree where the new node is to be inserted is found to be empty. Finally, the new node is made the appropriate child of this current node.

Figure 8-12 shows how a new node is inserted into a binary search tree.

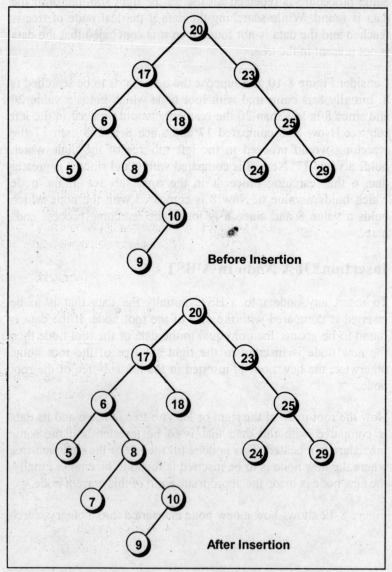

Figure 8-12. *Insertion of a node in a binary search tree (BST).*

Suppose the new node that is to be inserted holds a value 7 in its data field. To find the appropriate position of this new node in the tree, initially it is compared with the root node, which holds a value 20. Since 7 is less than 20, the searching of appropriate position of new node will be done in the left sub-tree. Now 7 is compared with 17 and since 7 is less than 17 the searching of appropriate position of new node will be done in the left sub-tree of the node that holds a value 17. Next 7 is compared with 6 and since 7 is greater than 6 the searching of appropriate position of new node is done in the right sub-tree of the node that holds a value 6. Now 7 is compared with 8 and since 7 is less than 8 the searching of appropriate position of the new node is done in the left sub-tree of the node that holds a value 8. But since this left sub-tree is empty the new node is made the left child of the node that holds a value 8.

Deletion From A Binary Tree

In addition to techniques for inserting data in a binary tree and traversing the tree, practical examples call for deleting data from the binary tree. Assuming that we will pass the specified data item that we wish to delete to a **delete( )** function, there are four possible cases that we need to consider:

(a) No node in the tree contains the specified data.

(b) The node containing the data has no children.

(c) The node containing the data has exactly one child.

(d) The node containing the data has two children.

Case (a):

Here, we merely need to print the message that the data item is not present in the tree.

Case (b):

In this case since the node to be deleted has no children the memory occupied by this should be freed and either the left link or the right link of the parent of this node should be set to **NULL**. Which of these to set to **NULL** depends upon whether the node being deleted is a left child or a right child of its parent.

Case (c):

In this case since the node to be deleted has one child the solution is again rather simple. We have to adjust the pointer of the parent of the node to be deleted such that after deletion it points to the child of the node being deleted. This is shown in Figure 8-13.

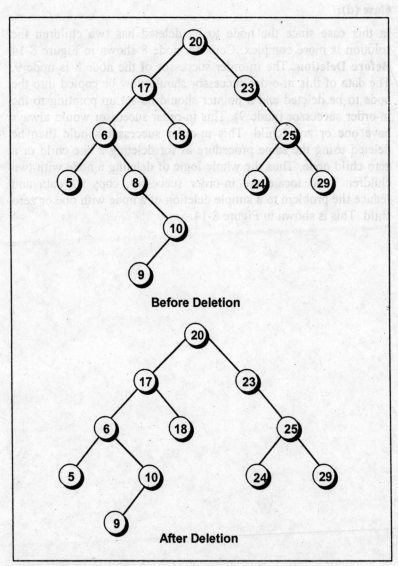

Figure 8-13. *Deletion of a node that has only one child.*

Case (d):

In this case since the node to be deleted has two children the solution is more complex. Consider node 8 shown in Figure 8-14 **Before Deletion**. The in-order successor of the node 8 is node 9. The data of this in-order successor should now be copied into the node to be deleted and a pointer should be set up pointing to the in-order successor (node 9). This in-order successor would always have one or zero child. This in-order successor should then be deleted using the same procedure as for deleting a one child or a zero child node. Thus the whole logic of deleting a node with two children is to locate the in-order successor, copy its data and reduce the problem to a simple deletion of a node with one or zero child. This is shown in Figure 8-14.

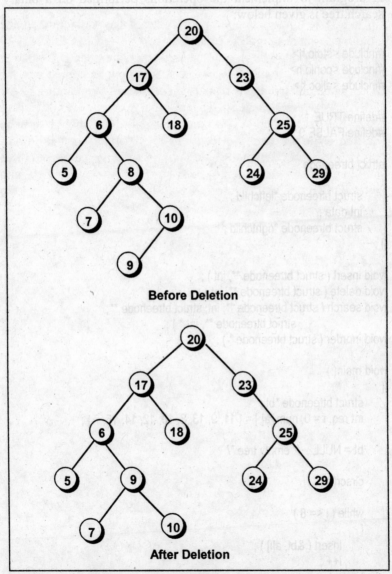

Before Deletion

After Deletion

Figure 8-14. *Deletion of a node that has both left and right child.*

A program to implement the operations performed on a binary search tree is given below:

```c
#include <stdio.h>
#include <conio.h>
#include <alloc.h>

#define TRUE 1
#define FALSE 0

struct btreenode
{
    struct btreenode *leftchild ;
    int data ;
    struct btreenode *rightchild ;
} ;

void insert ( struct btreenode **, int ) ;
void delete ( struct btreenode **, int ) ;
void search ( struct btreenode **, int, struct btreenode **,
                    struct btreenode **, int * ) ;
void inorder ( struct btreenode * ) ;

void main( )
{
    struct btreenode *bt ;
    int req, i = 0, num, a[ ] = { 11, 9, 13, 8, 10, 12, 14, 15, 7 } ;

    bt = NULL ;  /* empty tree */

    clrscr( ) ;

    while ( i <= 8 )
    {
        insert ( &bt, a[i] ) ;
        i++ ;
    }
```

```
    clrscr( ) ;
    printf ( "Binary tree before deletion:\n" ) ;
    inorder ( bt ) ;

    delete ( &bt, 10 ) ;
    printf ( "\nBinary tree after deletion:\n" ) ;
    inorder ( bt ) ;

    delete ( &bt, 14 ) ;
    printf ( "\nBinary tree after deletion:\n" ) ;
    inorder ( bt ) ;

    delete ( &bt, 8 ) ;
    printf ( "\nBinary tree after deletion:\n" ) ;
    inorder ( bt ) ;

    delete ( &bt, 13 ) ;
    printf ( "\nBinary tree after deletion:\n" ) ;
    inorder ( bt ) ;
}

/* inserts a new node in a binary search tree */
void insert ( struct btreenode **sr, int num )
{
    if ( *sr == NULL )
    {
        *sr = malloc ( sizeof ( struct btreenode ) ) ;

        ( *sr ) -> leftchild = NULL ;
        ( *sr ) -> data = num ;
        ( *sr ) -> rightchild = NULL ;
    }
    else  /* search the node to which new node will be attached */
    {
        /* if new data is less, traverse to left */
        if ( num < ( *sr ) -> data )
            insert ( &( ( *sr ) -> leftchild ), num ) ;
        else
```

```
                /* else traverse to right */
                insert ( &( ( *sr ) -> rightchild ), num ) ;
        }
}

/* deletes a node from the binary search tree */
void delete ( struct btreenode **root, int num )
{
    int found ;
    struct btreenode *parent, *x, *xsucc ;

    /* if tree is empty */
    if ( *root == NULL )
    {
        printf ( "\nTree is empty" ) ;
        return ;
    }

    parent = x = NULL ;

    /* call to search function to find the node to be deleted */
    search ( root, num, &parent, &x, &found ) ;

    /* if the node to deleted is not found */
    if ( found == FALSE )
    {
        printf ( "\nData to be deleted, not found" ) ;
        return ;
    }

    /* if the node to be deleted has two children */
    if ( x -> leftchild != NULL && x -> rightchild != NULL )
    {
        parent = x ;
        xsucc = x -> rightchild ;

        while ( xsucc -> leftchild != NULL )
        {
```

```
            parent = xsucc ;
            xsucc = xsucc -> leftchild ;
        }

        x -> data = xsucc -> data ;
        x = xsucc ;
    }

    /* if the node to be deleted has no child */
    if ( x -> leftchild == NULL && x -> rightchild == NULL )
    {
        if ( parent -> rightchild == x )
            parent -> rightchild = NULL ;
        else
            parent -> leftchild = NULL ;

        free ( x ) ;
        return ;
    }

    /* if the node to be deleted has only rightchild */
    if ( x -> leftchild == NULL && x -> rightchild != NULL )
    {
        if ( parent -> leftchild == x )
            parent -> leftchild = x -> rightchild ;
        else
            parent -> rightchild = x -> rightchild ;

        free ( x ) ;
        return ;
    }

    /* if the node to be deleted has only left child */
    if ( x -> leftchild != NULL && x -> rightchild == NULL )
    {
        if ( parent -> leftchild == x )
            parent -> leftchild = x -> leftchild ;
        else
```

```
                parent -> rightchild = x -> leftchild ;

        free ( x ) ;
        return ;
    }
}

/*returns the address of the node to be deleted, address of its parent and
    whether the node is found or not */
void search ( struct btreenode **root, int num, struct btreenode **par, struct
        btreenode **x, int *found )
{
    struct btreenode *q ;

    q = *root ;
    *found = FALSE ;
    *par = NULL ;

    while ( q != NULL )
    {
        /* if the node to be deleted is found */
        if ( q -> data == num )
        {
            *found = TRUE ;
            *x = q ;
            return ;
        }

        *par = q ;

        if ( q -> data > num )
            q = q -> leftchild ;
        else
            q = q -> rightchild ;
    }
}

/* traverse a binary search tree in a LDR (Left-Data-Right) fashion */
```

```
void inorder ( struct btreenode *sr )
{
    if ( sr != NULL )
    {
        inorder ( sr -> leftchild ) ;

        /* print the data of the node whose leftchild is NULL or the path  has
           already been traversed */
        printf ( "%d\t", sr -> data ) ;

        inorder ( sr -> rightchild ) ;
    }
}
```

Output:

Binary tree before deletion:
7   8   9   10   11   12   13   14   15
Binary tree after deletion:
7   8   9   11   12   13   14   15
Binary tree after deletion:
7   8   9   11   12   13   15
Binary tree after deletion:
7   9   11   12   13   15
Binary tree after deletion:
7   9   11   12   15

In the above program the working of the functions **insert( )** and **inorder( )** is exactly the same as what we saw in the previous program. The function **search( )** searches for the given number in the tree and returns the address of the node where the number is found, address of its parent and an integer value which holds either **TRUE** or **FALSE** (0 or 1) depending upon whether the number is found or not.

The function **search( )** receives five parameters. The first parameter **root** is the address of the root node of the tree, second parameter **num** is the number that is to be searched, the third and fourth parameters (**par** and **x**) are the pointers to the addresses of the parent of the node where data is found and the address of the node itself, respectively, and the last parameter **found** is the integer value indicating whether the element is found or not.

In the **insert( )** function initially the variable pointed by **found** is set to a **FALSE** value and the value of **par** is set to **NULL**, because if the node is not found then the pointer pointed by **par** should hold a **NULL** value. Then a **while** loop is executed with a condition **q != NULL** where **q** holds the address of the root node. Inside the **while** loop a condition is checked for the data to be searched. If the data is found then a **TRUE** value is stored in the variable pointed by **found** and the address of the current node is stored in **x**. If the data is found in the first iteration then the value of **par** is **NULL**, since it has no parent.

If the data is not found in the first iteration then inside the **while** loop the address of the current node is stored in **par** and then the data is compared with the data present in the current node. If the data of the current node is greater than the data which is to be searched then **q** will hold the address of the left sub-tree of the current node otherwise it will hold the address of the right sub-tree of the current node. This way any function that calls **search( )** gets the address of the node where the node is present and the address of its parent.

In the function **delete( )** two parameters are received. The first is the address of the root node and other is the number that is to be deleted. Initially, a condition is checked whether the root node is empty. If it is then a message will be displayed and the control will be returned back, otherwise the function **search( )** is called with **NULL** values stored in the two pointer variables **parent** and **x**.

If the data that is to be deleted is not found then the last argument passed to function **search( )** holds a value **FALSE**. Hence, after the call to function **search( )** a condition is checked whether **found == FALSE**. If it is equal to **FALSE** then it indicates that the data is not present in the tree. So an appropriate message will be displayed and control will be returned back.

If the data that is to be deleted is found then the following four cases would arise:

(a) the node has two children

(b) the node has no child

(c) the node has only right child

(d) the node has only left child

Case (a): Node to be deleted has two children

In this case, initially the address of the node that is to be deleted is stored in the pointer **parent**. But by doing so the address of the parent node that is to be deleted is lost. We don't mind doing so, because we are not interested in storing any address or a **NULL** value in the left or right child of the parent node. What we need to do is to find out the in-order successor of the node that is to be deleted. For this the address of the right child of the node that is to be deleted is stored in a pointer variable **xsucc**. Then a **while** loop is executed where a condition is checked whether the left child of **xsucc** is **NULL**. If it is not then the address of the **xsucc** is stored in the **parent** and the left child of the **xsucc** is stored in the **xsucc**. As a result, at the end of the **while** loop the value present in **xsucc** is the address of the in-order successor of the node that is to be deleted and will always either have only one child or no child.

After the **while** loop the value present in the in-order successor is copied into the data that is to be deleted. Finally, the address of the in-order successor is stored in **x**, which is the node that is to be deleted. So the logic of deleting the node which has two children is converted to the case of deleting the node which has only one or no child, which are discussed below:

Case (b): Node to be deleted has no child

Since both the children of node that is to be deleted hold a **NULL** value what needs to be done is store a **NULL** value in the respective child of the parent. This is done by checking the condition **parent -> rightchild == x**. If the right child of the parent node is equal to the value in the node to be deleted, then a **NULL** value is stored in the **rightchild** of the **parent,** otherwise, it is stored in the **leftchild**. Finally the memory occupied by the node to be deleted is released and control is returned.

Case (c): Node to be deleted has only right child

Here a condition is checked whether the node that is to be deleted is the left child of its parent, this is done through the statement

if (parent -> leftchild == x)

If this condition is true then the address of the **rightchild** of the node that is to be deleted is stored in the **leftchild** of the **parent** node, otherwise in the **rightchild** of the **parent** node. Then the memory occupied by the node to be deleted is released and control is returned.

Case (d): Node to be deleted has only left child

The action taken here is similar to case (c) discussed above.

Applications Of Binary Trees

There are many applications of a Binary tree. For example, whenever we want to take the two-way decisions, binary trees are the best option. One such application is a Binary Search Tree, which we have already discussed. Binary trees can also be used to represent expressions as discussed below.

Representing Expressions In Binary Trees

The arithmetic expressions represented as binary trees are known as **expression trees**. The root node is operator and the left and right children are operands. In case of unary operators the left child is absent and the right child is the operand. Since there is no operator available for exponent in C, the operator $ is used to denote exponent. Generally, nodes appearing in circular shape denote the operators and nodes appearing in square shape are used for operands. For example, Figure 8-15 shows a tree for the expression

$$A * B + C * D + E$$

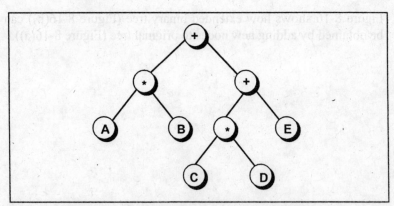

Figure 8-15. *Expression represented as a binary tree.*

When the expression tree is traversed in pre-order then the prefix form of the expression is obtained. Similarly, when the expression tree is traversed in post-order then the postfix form of the expression is obtained. In the same way we get the infix form of the expression when the tree is traversed in in-order. But the parentheses present in the original arithmetic expression cannot be obtained back from the in-order traversal of the binary tree. This is because the structure of the binary tree itself decides the order of the evaluation of the tree.

Extended Binary Tree

A binary tree can be converted to an extended binary tree by adding new nodes to its leaf nodes and to the nodes that have only one child. These new nodes are added in such a way that all the nodes in the resultant tree have either zero or two children. The extended tree is also known as a **2-tree**. The nodes of the original tree are called **internal** nodes and the new nodes that are added to binary tree, to make it an extended binary tree are called **external** nodes.

Figure 8-16 shows how extended binary tree (Figure 8-16(b)) can be obtained by adding new nodes to original tree (Figure 8-16(a)).

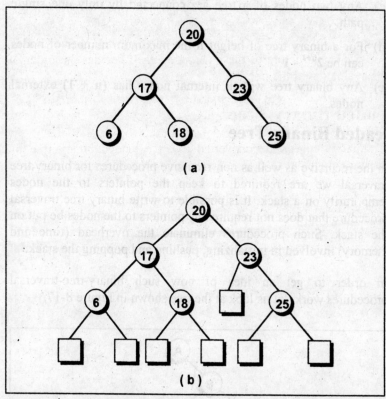

Figure 8-16. *Binary tree converted to an extended binary tree.*

In Figure 8-16, all the nodes with circular shape are internal nodes and all the nodes with square shape are external nodes.

A few points to note...

(a) If a tree has **n** nodes then the number of branches it has is **(n - 1)**.

(b) Except the root node every node in a tree has exactly one parent.

(c) Any two nodes of a tree are connected by only one single path.

(d) For a binary tree of height **h** the maximum number of nodes can be $2^{h+1} - 1$.

(e) Any binary tree with **n** internal nodes has **(n + 1)** external nodes.

Threaded Binary Tree

In the recursive as well as non-recursive procedures for binary tree traversal we are required to keep the pointers to the nodes temporarily on a stack. It is possible to write binary tree traversal procedure that does not require any pointers to the nodes be put on the stack. Such procedures eliminate the overhead (time and memory) involved in initializing, pushing and popping the stack.

In order to get an idea of how such binary-tree-traversal procedures work, let us look at the tree shown in Figure 8-17.

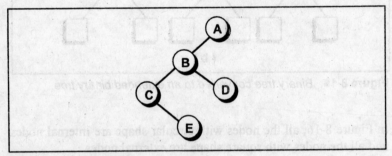

Figure 8-17. *Binary tree.*

Here, first we follow the left pointers until we reach node **C**, without, however, pushing the pointers to **A**, **B** and **C** onto a stack. For in-order traversal the data for node **C** is then printed, after which **C**'s right pointer is followed to node **E**. Then the data from node **E** is printed. The next step in our in-order traversal is to go back to node **B** and print its data; however, we did not save any pointers. But suppose that when we created the tree we had replaced the **NULL** right pointer of node **E** with a pointer back to node **B**. We could then easily follow this pointer back to node **B**. This is shown in Figure 8-18.

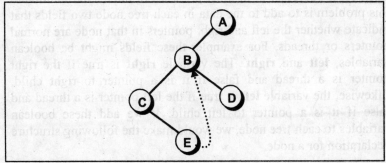

Figure 8-18. *Threaded binary tree.*

Similarly, suppose we replace the **NULL** right pointer of **D** with a pointer back up to **A**, as shown in Figure 8-19. Then after printing the data in **D**, we can easily jump up to **A** and print its data.

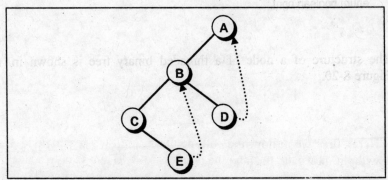

Figure 8-19. *Threaded binary tree.*

The pointers that point in-order successor of a node are called **right threads**. Each **right thread** replaces a normal right pointer in a tree node. Likewise, we can have **left threads** that point to the in-order predecessor of a node.

Threads suffer from one problem—we need to know whether a pointer is a normal pointer to a child or a thread that points back to an in-order successor or in-order predecessor node. One solution to this problem is to add to the data in each tree node two fields that indicate whether the left and right pointers in that node are normal pointers or threads. For example, these fields might be boolean variables, **left** and **right**. The variable **right** is true if the right pointer is a thread and false if it is a pointer to right child. Likewise, the variable **left** is true if the left pointer is a thread and false if it is a pointer to left child. If we add these boolean variables to each tree node, we would make the following structure declaration for a node.

```
struct thtree
{
    enum boolean left ;
    struct thtree *leftchild ;
    int data ;
    struct thtree *rightchild ;
    enum boolean right ;
};
```

The structure of a node of a threaded binary tree is shown in Figure 8-20.

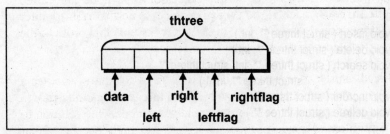

Figure 8-20. *Node of a threaded binary tree.*

Thus each node would contain data, a left pointer, a true or false value for left thread, a right pointer and a true or false value for right thread.

The program to implement a threaded binary tree is given below. The program shows how to insert nodes in a threaded binary tree, delete nodes from it and traverse it in in-order traversal.

```
#include <stdio.h>
#include <conio.h>
#include <alloc.h>

enum boolean
{
    false = 0,
    true = 1
};

struct thtree
{
    enum boolean isleft ;
    struct thtree *left ;
    int data ;
    struct thtree *right ;
    enum boolen isright ;
```

```
} ;

void insert ( struct thtree **, int ) ;
void delete ( struct thtree **, int ) ;
void search ( struct thtree **, int, struct thtree **,
                    struct thtree **, int * ) ;
void inorder ( struct thtree * ) ;
void deltree ( struct thtree ** ) ;

void main( )
{
    struct thtree *th_head ;

    th_head = NULL ;  /* empty tree */

    insert ( &th_head, 11 ) ;
    insert ( &th_head, 9 ) ;
    insert ( &th_head, 13 ) ;
    insert ( &th_head, 8 ) ;
    insert ( &th_head, 10 ) ;
    insert ( &th_head, 12 ) ;
    insert ( &th_head, 14 ) ;
    insert ( &th_head, 15 ) ;
    insert ( &th_head, 7 ) ;

    clrscr( ) ;
    printf ( "Threaded binary tree before deletion:\n" ) ;
    inorder ( th_head ) ;

    delete ( &th_head, 10 ) ;
    printf ( "\nThreaded binary tree after deletion:\n" ) ;
    inorder ( th_head ) ;

    delete ( &th_head, 14 ) ;
    printf ( "\nThreaded binary tree after deletion:\n" ) ;
    inorder ( th_head ) ;

    delete ( &th_head, 8 ) ;
```

```
        printf ( "\nThreaded binary tree after deletion:\n" ) ;
        inorder ( th_head ) ;

        delete ( &th_head, 13 ) ;
        printf ( "\nThreaded binary tree after deletion:\n" ) ;
        inorder ( th_head ) ;

        deltree ( &th_head ) ;

        getch( ) ;
}

/* inserts a node in a threaded binary tree */
void insert ( struct thtree **s, int num )
{
        struct thtree *p, *z, *head = *s ;

        /* allocating a new node */
        z = malloc ( sizeof ( struct thtree ) ) ;

        z -> isleft = true ;  /* indicates a thread */
        z -> data = num ;  /* assign new data */
        z -> isright = true ;  /* indicates a thread */

        /* if tree is empty */
        if ( *s == NULL )
        {
                head = malloc ( sizeof ( struct thtree ) ) ;

                /* the entire tree is treated as a left sub-tree of the head node */
                head -> isleft = false ;
                head -> left = z ;  /* z becomes leftchild of the head node */
                head -> data = -9999 ;  /* no data */
                head -> right = head ;  /* right link will always be pointing
                                                to itself */
                head -> isright = false ;

                *s = head ;
```

```
            z -> left = head ;  /* left thread to head */
            z -> right = head ;  /* right thread to head */
    }
    else  /* if tree is non-empty */
    {
        p = head -> left ;

        /* traverse till the thread is found attached to the head */
        while ( p != head )
        {
            if ( p -> data > num )
            {
                if ( p -> isleft != true )  /* checking for a thread */
                    p = p -> left ;
                else
                {
                    z -> left = p -> left ;
                    p -> left = z ;
                    p -> isleft = false ;  /* indicates a link */
                    z -> isright = true ;
                    z -> right = p ;
                    return ;
                }
            }
            else
            {
                if ( p -> data < num )
                {
                    if ( p -> isright != true )
                        p = p -> right ;
                    else
                    {
                        z -> right = p -> right ;
                        p -> right = z ;
                        p -> isright = false ;  /* indicates a link */
                        z -> isleft = true ;
                        z -> left = p ;
```

```
                        return ;
                    }
                }
            }
        }
    }
}

/* deletes a node from the binary search tree */
void delete ( struct thtree **root, int num )
{
    int found ;
    struct thtree *parent, *x, *xsucc ;

    /* if tree is empty */
    if ( *root == NULL )
    {
        printf ( "\nTree is empty" ) ;
        return ;
    }

    parent = x = NULL ;

    /* call to search function to find the node to be deleted */
    search ( root, num, &parent, &x, &found ) ;

    /* if the node to deleted is not found */
    if ( found == false )
    {
        printf ( "\nData to be deleted, not found" ) ;
        return ;
    }

    /* if the node to be deleted has two children */
    if ( x -> isleft == false && x -> isright == false )
    {
        parent = x ;
        xsucc = x -> right ;
```

```c
        while ( xsucc -> isleft == false )
        {
            parent = xsucc ;
            xsucc = xsucc -> left ;
        }

        x -> data = xsucc -> data ;
        x = xsucc ;
    }

    /* if the node to be deleted has no child */
    if ( x -> isleft == true && x -> isright == true )
    {
        /* if node to be deleted is a root node */
        if ( parent == NULL )
        {
            ( *root ) -> left = *root ;
            ( *root ) -> isleft = true ;

            free ( x ) ;
            return ;
        }

        if ( parent -> right == x )
        {
            parent -> isright = true ;
            parent -> right = x -> right ;
        }
        else
        {
            parent -> isleft = true ;
            parent -> left = x -> left ;
        }

        free ( x ) ;
        return ;
    }
```

```
/* if the node to be deleted has only rightchild */
if ( x -> isleft == true && x -> isright == false )
{
     /* node to be deleted is a root node */
     if ( parent == NULL )
     {
          ( *root ) -> left = x -> right ;
          free ( x ) ;
          return ;
     }

     if ( parent -> left == x )
     {
          parent -> left = x -> right ;
          x -> right -> left = x -> left ;
     }
     else
     {
          parent -> right = x -> right ;
          x -> right -> left = parent ;
     }

     free ( x ) ;
     return ;
}

/* if the node to be deleted has only left child */
if ( x -> isleft == false && x -> isright == true )
{
     /* the node to be deleted is a root node */
     if ( parent == NULL )
     {
          parent = x ;
          xsucc = x -> left ;

          while ( xsucc -> right == false )
          xsucc = xsucc -> right ;
```

```
                xsucc -> right = *root ;

                ( *root ) -> left = x -> left ;

                free ( x ) ;
                return ;
        }

        if ( parent -> left == x )
        {
                parent -> left = x -> left ;
                x -> left -> right = parent ;
        }
        else
        {
                parent -> right = x -> left ;
                x -> left -> right = x -> right ;
        }

        free ( x ) ;
        return ;
    }
}

/* returns the address of the node to be deleted, address of its parent and
        whether the node is found or not */
void search ( struct thtree **root, int num, struct thtree **par,
                        struct thtree **x, int *found )
{
        struct thtree *q ;

        q = ( *root ) -> left ;
        *found = false ;
        *par = NULL ;

        while ( q != *root )
        {
```

```
        /* if the node to be deleted is found */
        if ( q -> data == num )
        {
            *found = true ;
            *x = q ;
            return ;
        }

        *par = q ;

        if ( q -> data > num )
        {
            if ( q -> isleft == true )
            {
                *found = false ;
                x = NULL ;
                return ;
            }
            q = q -> left ;
        }
        else
        {
            if ( q -> isright == true )
            {
                *found = false ;
                *x = NULL ;
                return ;
            }
            q = q -> right ;
        }
    }
}

/* traverses the threaded binary tree in inorder */
void inorder ( struct thtree *root )
{
    struct thtree *p ;
```

```
        p = root -> left ;

        while ( p != root )
        {
            while ( p -> isleft == false )
                p = p -> left ;

            printf ( "%d\t", p -> data ) ;

            while ( p -> isright == true )
            {
                p = p -> right ;

                if ( p == root )
                    break ;

                printf ( "%d\t", p -> data ) ;

            }
            p = p -> right ;
        }
    }

    void deltree ( struct thtree **root )
    {
        while ( ( ( *root ) -> left != *root )
            delete ( root, ( *root ) -> left -> data ) ;
    }
```

Output:

Threaded binary tree before deletion:
7   8   9   10   11   12   13   14   15
Threaded binary tree after deletion:
7   8   9   11   12   13   14   15
Threaded binary tree after deletion:
7   8   9   11   12   13   15
Threaded binary tree after deletion:

```
7   9   11   12   13   15
```
Threaded binary tree after deletion:
```
7   9   11   12   15
```

Now, a brief explanation about the program. We have used an enumerated data type **boolean** to store information whether the thread is present or not. If **left** is true it means that there is a left thread and the node has no left child, if **right** is true it shows the presence of right thread and the node has no right child.

To insert a new node in a threaded tree, the **insert( )** function is called which first checks for the empty tree. If the tree is found to be empty a head node is created and the node is joined as its left sub-tree with both links converted to threads by making **left** and **right** both true and **leftchild** and **rightchild** pointing back to the head node. Otherwise, the node is inserted into the tree so that a threaded binary search tree is created.

Deletion of a node from the threaded binary tree is similar to that of a normal binary tree. That is, we have to identify the four possibilities about the node being deleted:

(a) No node in the tree contains the specified data.

(b) The node has no children.

(c) The node has exactly one child.

(d) The node has two children.

The treatment given to these possibilities is same as the one discussed in the previous section on binary trees except for some minor readjustment of threads.

The threaded binary tree's in-order traversal is different than a normal tree in the sense that we do not have to stack the pointers to nodes visited earlier so as to reach them later. This is avoided by using the threads to ancestors. The procedure to achieve this is as follows:

This procedure begins by first going to the left sub-tree of the head node using the statement

p = root -> leftchild ;

* then through a **while** loop we follow the leftmost pointers until a thread to a predecessor is found. On encountering this thread we print the data for the leftmost node. Next, through another **while** loop we check the boolean value of the right thread. If this value is true, we follow the thread back up to the ancestor node and print this ancestor node's data. This way we continue to move up till the right thread is true. When the right thread is found to be false we again proceed by going to the right child and checking it's left sub-tree.

As we follow these steps we are sometimes likely to reach the head node, and that is the time to stop the procedure. This is what is being achieved from the statements

if (p == root)
    break ;

Reconstruction Of A Binary Tree

If we know the sequence of nodes obtained through in-order/pre-order/post-order traversal it may not be feasible to reconstruct the binary tree. This is because two different binary trees may yield same sequence of nodes when traversed using post-order traversal. Similarly in-order or pre-order traversal of different binary trees may yield the same sequence of nodes. However, we can construct a unique binary tree if the result of in-order and pre-order traversal are available. Let us understand this with the help of following set of in-order and pre-order traversal results:

In-order traversal: 4, 7, 2, 8, 5, 1, 6, 9, 3

Pre-order traversal: 1, 2, 4, 7, 5, 8, 3, 6, 9

We know that the first value in the pre-order traversal gives us the root of the binary tree. So the node with data 1 becomes the root of the binary tree. In in-order traversal, initially the left sub-tree is traversed then the root node and then the right sub-tree. So the data before 1 in the in-order list (i.e. 4, 7, 2, 8, 5) forms the left sub-tree and the data after 1 in the in-order list (i.e. 6, 9, 3) forms the right sub-tree. In Figure 8-21(a) the structure of tree is shown after separating the tree in left and right sub-trees.

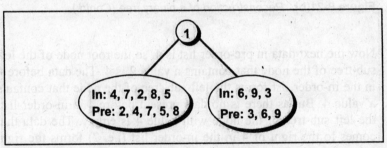

Figure 8-21(a). *Reconstruction of a binary tree.*

Now the next data in pre-order list is 2 so the root node of the left sub-tree is 2. Hence the data before 2 in the in-order list (i.e. 4, 7) forms the left sub-tree of the node that contains a value 2. The data that comes to the right of 2 in the in-order list (i.e. 8, 5) forms the right sub-tree of the node with value 2. Figure 8-21(b) shows structure of tree after expanding the left and right sub-tree of the node that contains a value 2.

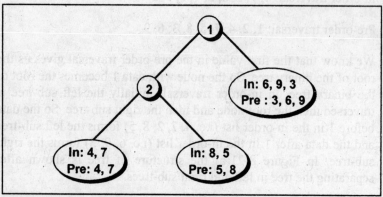

Figure 8-21(b). *Reconstruction of a binary tree (Contd.).*

Now the next data in pre-order list is 4, so the root node of the left sub-tree of the node that contains a value 2 is 4. The data before 4 in the in-order list forms the left sub-tree of the node that contains a value 4. But as there is no data present before 4 in in-order list, the left sub-tree of the node with value 4 is empty. The data that comes to the right of 4 in the in-order list (i.e. 7) forms the right sub-tree of the node that contains a value 4. Figure 8-21(c) shows structure of tree after expanding the left and right sub-tree of the node that contains a value 4.

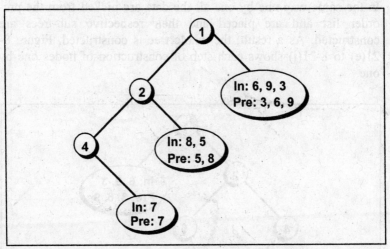

Figure 8-21(c). *Reconstruction of a binary tree (Contd.).*

Since we are now left with only one value 7 in both the pre-order and in-order form we simply represent it with a node as shown in Figure 8-21(d).

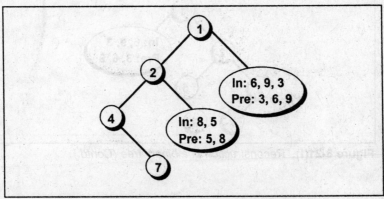

Figure 8-21(d). *Reconstruction of a binary tree (Contd.).*

In the same way one by one all the data are picked from the pre-order list and are placed and their respective sub-trees are constructed. As a result, the whole tree is constructed. Figure 8-21(e) to 8-21(i) shows each step of construction of nodes one by one.

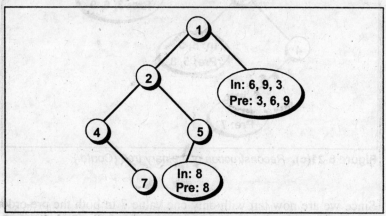

Figure 8-21(e). *Reconstruction of a binary tree (Contd.).*

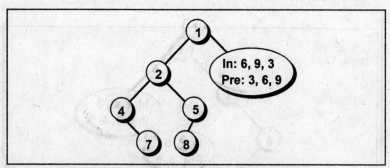

Figure 8-21(f). *Reconstruction of a binary tree (Contd.).*

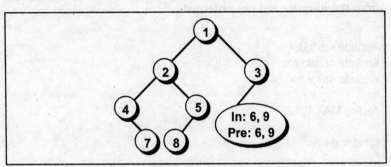

Figure 8-21(g). *Reconstruction of a binary tree (Contd.).*

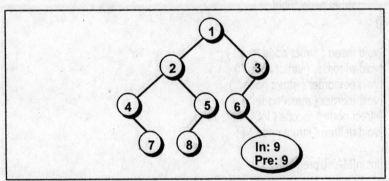

Figure 8-21(h). *Reconstruction of a binary tree (Contd.).*

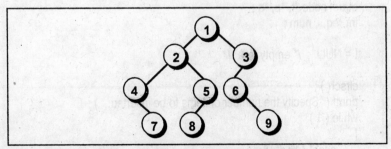

Figure 8-21(i). *Reconstruction of a binary tree (Contd.).*

Here is the program that shows how to reconstruct a binary tree from the in-order and pre-order list.

```c
#include <stdio.h>
#include <conio.h>
#include <alloc.h>

#define MAX 101

struct node
{
    struct node *left ;
    int data ;
    struct node *right ;
} ;

void insert ( struct node **, int ) ;
void preorder ( struct node * ) ;
void postorder ( struct node * ) ;
void inorder ( struct node * ) ;
struct node * recons ( int *, int *, int ) ;
void deltree ( struct node * ) ;

int in[MAX], pre[MAX], x ;

void main( )
{
    struct node *t, *p, *q ;
    int req, i, num ;

    t = NULL ; /* empty tree */

    clrscr( ) ;
    printf ( "Specify the number of items to be inserted: " ) ;
    while ( 1 )
    {
        scanf ( "%d", &req ) ;
```

```
        if ( req >= MAX || req <= 0 )
            printf ( "\nEnter number between 1 to 100.\n" ) ;
        else
            break ;
    }

    for ( i = 0 ; i < req ; i++ )
    {
        printf ( "Enter the data: " ) ;
        scanf ( "%d", &num ) ;
        insert ( &t, num ) ;
    }

    printf ( "\nIn-order   Traversal:\n" ) ;
    x = 0 ;
    inorder ( t ) ;

    printf ( "\nPre-order  Traversal:\n" ) ;
    x = 0 ;
    preorder ( t ) ;

    printf ( "\nPost-order Traversal:\n" ) ;
    x = 0 ;
    postorder ( t ) ;

    deltree ( t ) ;
    t = NULL ;
    t = recons ( in, pre, req ) ;

    printf ( "\n\nAfter reconstruction of the binary tree.\n" ) ;

    x = 0 ;
    printf ( "\nIn-order   Traversal:\n" ) ;
    inorder ( t ) ;

    x = 0 ;
    printf ( "\nPre-order  Traversal:\n" ) ;
    preorder ( t ) ;
```

```
        x = 0 ;
        printf ( "\nPost-order Traversal:\n" ) ;
        postorder ( t ) ;

        deltree ( t ) ;
        getch( ) ;
}

/* inserts a new node in a binary search tree */
void insert ( struct node **sr, int num )
{
    if ( *sr == NULL )
    {
        *sr = ( struct node * ) malloc ( sizeof ( struct node ) ) ;

        ( *sr ) -> left = NULL ;
        ( *sr ) -> data = num ;
        ( *sr ) -> right = NULL ;
        return ;
    }
    else  /* search the node to which new node will be attached */
    {
        /* if new data is less, traverse to left */
        if ( num < ( *sr ) -> data )
            insert ( &( ( *sr ) -> left ), num ) ;
        else
            /* else traverse to right */
            insert ( &( ( *sr ) -> right ), num ) ;
    }
}

void preorder ( struct node *t )
{
    if ( t != NULL )
    {
        printf ( "%d\t", pre[x++]= t -> data ) ;
        preorder ( t -> left ) ;
        preorder ( t -> right ) ;
```

```
        }
}

void postorder ( struct node *t )
{
    if ( t != NULL )
    {
        postorder ( t -> left ) ;
        postorder ( t -> right ) ;
        printf ( "%d\t", t -> data ) ;
    }
}

void inorder ( struct node *t )
{
    if ( t != NULL )
    {
        inorder ( t -> left ) ;
        printf ( "%d\t", in[x++]= t -> data ) ;
        inorder ( t -> right ) ;
    }
}

struct node * recons ( int *inorder, int *preorder, int noofnodes )
{
    struct node *temp, *left, *right ;
    int tempin[100], temppre[100], i, j ;

    if ( noofnodes == 0 )
        return NULL ;

    temp = ( struct node * ) malloc ( sizeof ( struct node ) ) ;
    temp -> data = preorder[0] ;
    temp -> left = NULL ;
    temp -> right = NULL ;

    if ( noofnodes == 1 )
        return temp ;
```

```
    for ( i = 0 ; inorder[i] != preorder[0] ; )
        i++ ;

    if ( i > 0 )
    {
        for ( j = 0 ; j <= i ; j++ )
            tempin[j] = inorder[j] ;

        for ( j = 0 ; j < i ; j++ )
            temppre[j] = preorder[j + 1] ;
    }

    left = recons ( tempin, temppre, i ) ;
    temp -> left = left ;

    if ( i < noofnodes - 1 )
    {
        for ( j = i ; j < noofnodes - 1 ; j++ )
        {
            tempin[j - i] = inorder[j + 1] ;
            temppre[j - i] = preorder[j + 1] ;
        }
    }

    right = recons ( tempin, temppre, noofnodes - i - 1 ) ;
    temp -> right = right ;

    return temp ;
}

void deltree ( struct node *t )
{
    if ( t != NULL )
    {
        deltree ( t -> left ) ;
        deltree ( t -> right ) ;
    }
    free ( t ) ;
```

}

Output:

Specify the number of items to be inserted: 5
Enter the data: 1
Enter the data: 2
Enter the data: 3
Enter the data: 4
Enter the data: 5

In-order Traversal:
1   2   3   4   5
Pre-order Traversal:
1   2   3   4   5
Post-order Traversal:
5   4   3   2   1

After reconstruction of the binary tree.

In-order Traversal:
1   2   3   4   5
Pre-order Traversal:
1   2   3   4   5
Post-order Traversal:
5   4   3   2   1

Initially data is received, tree is constructed and is traversed in in-order, pre-order and post-order traversal. While traversing the tree two arrays **pre[ ]** and **in[ ]** are constructed to store the sequence of nodes. Then through the function **deltree( )** the tree is deleted and a **NULL** value is stored in **t** which is pointer to tree. Then a function **recons( )** is called to reconstructs the tree from the arrays **pre[ ]** and **in[ ]**. This function returns a pointer to the root node of the reconstructed tree. Finally, again the tree is traversed in in-order, pre-order and post-order traversal to verify the reconstruction of the tree.

The working of the function **deltree( )** is straight-forward. It checks whether the value of **t** is **NULL.** If it is not, two recursive calls are made one for the left child of the current node and the other for the right child. After the control returns from the recursive calls the memory occupied by the current node is released.

The function **recons( )** receives three parameters. First and second are the pointers to the in-order and pre-order arrays respectively. The third is the number of nodes that a particular tree or sub-tree has. Inside the function two local arrays **tempin** and **temppre** are created, to store the values of in-order and pre-order sub-trees respectively. Then a condition is checked whether the number of nodes is 0. If it is then a **NULL** value is returned. If it is not 0 then memory is allocated for a new node and its address is stored in a pointer **temp.** The element present at the 0th index in pre-order list is going to be the root node of the tree, hence, it is stored in the **data** part of the new node. A **NULL** value is stored in left and right child of the new node. Then a condition is checked whether number of node is equal to 1. If it is 1, then the value of **temp** is returned which holds the address of the new node. If the sub-tree contains more than one node then a **for** loop is executed which finds the index of the first node of the pre-order list in the in-order list. This is done because the left and right sub-trees are needs to be separated and stored in **tempin** and **temppre** arrays.

In order to separate the left and right sub-tree it is checked whether the index of the first node of the pre-order list in the in-order list is more than 0. If it is then the respective children of the left sub-tree from the in-order and pre-order list are stored in the **tempin** and **temppre** respectively. Then a recursive call is made to **recons( )** function to build the left sub-tree. This time the address returned by the function **recons( )** is going to be address of the root node of the left sub-tree for the current node. Hence, it is stored in the **left** part of the current node. Similarly, a recursive call is made for the right sub-tree, after storing the values of the respective children of the right sub-tree from the in-order and pre-order list in **tempin** and **temppre** respectively. This time the address returned by the function **recons( )** is going to be the address of the root node of the right sub-tree for the current node. Hence it is stored in the right part of the current node. Finally, the address of the current node is returned which is stored in **temp**.

General Trees

A general tree can have any number of nodes. The children of a node are called as **siblings** of each other. In other words, if a particular node has four children, then the second, third and fourth child of that node are the siblings of the first child. Figure 8-22 shows a general tree.

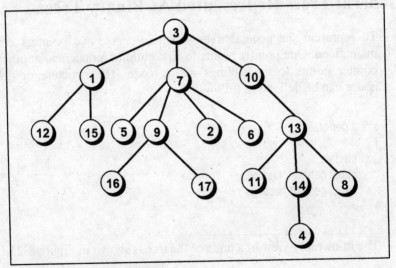

Figure 8-22. *A general tree.*

In Figure 8-22, the nodes containing values 9, 2, 6 are siblings of the node that contains a value 5.

While representing any tree it is necessary to have as many pointers in the node as the number of children that node has. However, each node in a general tree is likely to have different number of children. For example, some nodes may have 2 children, some may have 5 and some may have 4 children. Hence the structure of a node of a general tree should be declared in such a way that it contains variable number of pointers. This is practically impossible.

To overcome this problem the maximum children occurring in any node in a general tree can be counted and then the structure with those many pointers can be declared. This however would lead to wastage of a large number of pointers. A better solution for this problem is to represent the general trees as binary trees.

General Trees Represented As Binary Trees

To represent the general trees as binary trees, two pointers are maintained. One pointer points to first child of a node and another pointer points to the siblings of the node. The structure of the nodes can be defined as follows:

```
struct general
{
    int data ;
    struct general *firstchild ;
    struct general *siblings ;
} ;
```

The in-memory view of a node of the tree is shown in Figure 8-23.

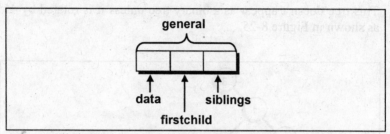

Figure 8-23. *Node of a general tree represented as binary tree.*

While representing a general tree as a binary tree, the pointer to the first child of a particular node is made the left child of that node and the right child is the pointer to the siblings of the node. Thus while representing a general tree any node has only two children. Hence, a general tree can be represented as a binary tree. Figure 8-24 shows the binary presentation of general tree in Figure 8-22.

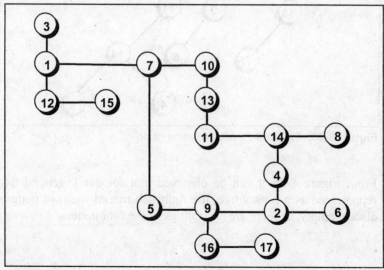

Figure 8-24. *General tree represented as a binary tree.*

This tree doesn't appear as a binary tree unless it is rotated by 45°
as shown in Figure 8-25.

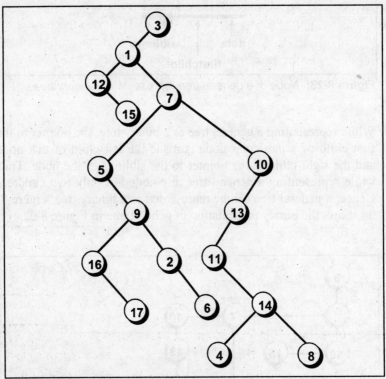

Figure 8-25. *Figure 8-22 after rotation of 45°*

From Figure 8-25 it can be observed that for every general tree
represented as a binary tree, the right sub-tree of the root node is
always empty, as there are no siblings of the root node.

Forest

Forest is a set of several trees that are not linked to each other in any way. Forest can be represented as a binary tree. Initially the left most tree is represented as a binary tree exactly in the same way as explained in the previous section. Then the second tree is made the right child of the root node of the first tree and the third tree is made the right child of the root node of the second tree. Figure 8-26 shows how a forest can be represented as a binary tree.

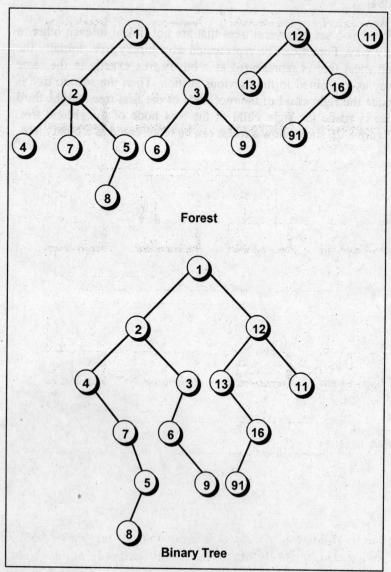

Forest

Binary Tree

Figure 8-26. *Forest represented as a binary tree.*

AVL Trees

Searching in a binary search tree is efficient if the heights of both left and right sub-trees of any node are equal. However, frequent insertions and deletions in a BST is likely to make it unbalanced. The efficiency of searching is ideal if the difference between the heights of left and right sub-trees of all the nodes in a binary search tree is at the most one. Such a binary search tree is called as a **Balanced Binary Tree**. It was invented in the year 1962 by two Russian mathematicians—G. M. Adelson-Velskii and E. M. Landis. Hence such trees are also known as AVL trees. Figure 8-27 shows some examples of AVL trees.

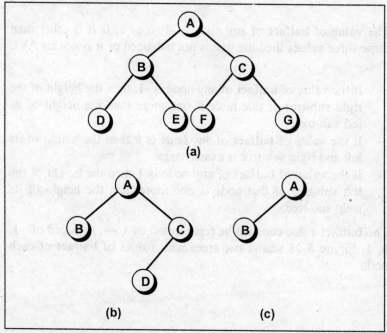

(a)

(b)   (c)

Figure 8-27. *AVL trees.*

To represent a node of an AVL tree four fields are required—one for data, two for storing the address of the left and right child and an additional field is required to hold the balance factor. The **balance factor** of any node is calculated by subtracting the height of the right sub-tree of the node from the height of the left sub-tree. The structure of a node of an AVL tree is given below:

```
struct AVL
{
    struct AVL * left ;
    int data ;
    struct AVL * right ;
    int balfact ;
} ;
```

The value of **balfact** of any node is -1, 0 or 1. If it is other than these three values then the tree is not balanced or it is not an AVL tree.

- If the value of **balfact** of any node is **-1**, then the height of the right sub-tree of that node is one more than the height of its left sub-tree.
- If the value of **balfact** of any node is **0** then the height of its left and right sub-tree is exactly same.
- If the value of **balfact** of any node is **1** then the height of the left sub-tree of that node is one more than the height of its right sub-tree.

The **balfact** value can also be represented by \, —, / instead of **-1, 0, 1**. Figure 8-28 shows two trees with values of **balfact** of each node.

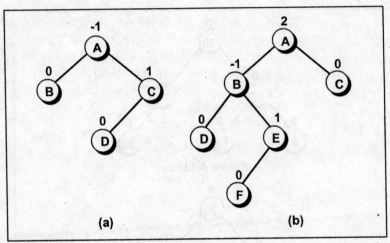

Figure 8-28. *Balance factor of trees*

Here, the tree (a) is an AVL tree, whereas (b) is not.

Insertion Of A Node In An AVL Tree

We can insert a new node in an AVL tree by finding its appropriate position. But insertion of a new node involves certain overheads since the tree may become unbalanced due to the increase in its height.

If the new node is inserted as a child of any non-leaf node then there will be no effect on its balance, as the height of the tree does not increase. This is shown in Figure 8-29.

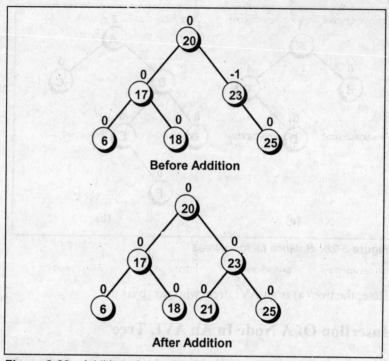

Before Addition

After Addition

Figure 8-29. *Addition of a new node to a non-leaf node of an AVL tree.*

If the new node is inserted as a child of leaf node then there is possibility that the tree may become unbalanced. This depends upon whether the node is inserted to a left sub-tree or to a right sub-tree, which in turn changes the balance factor of the nodes.

If the new node is inserted as a child of leaf node of sub-tree (left or right) of shorter height then there will be no effect on the balance of an AVL tree. Figure 8-30 shows the insertion of new node in the sub-tree of shorter height.

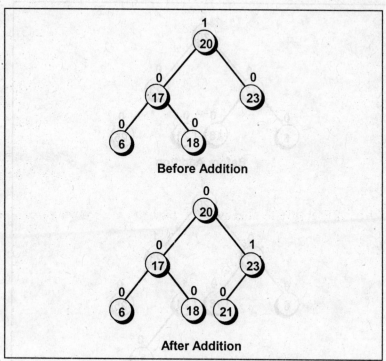

Figure 8-30. *Addition of a new node to a sub-tree of shorter height.*

If the height of the left and the right sub-tree is same then the insertion of a new node on any of the leaf node does not disturb the balance of an AVL tree. In this case even if the height of a sub-tree increases by one there will be no effect on the balance of the tree. Figure 8-31 shows how increase in height of one sub-tree doesn't affect the balance of the tree.

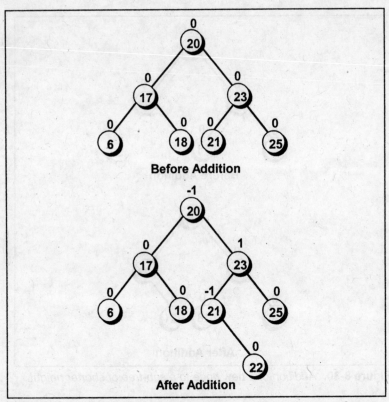

Figure 8-31. *Addition of a new node to one of the sub-trees of same height.*

If the new node is inserted as a child of the leaf node of taller sub-tree (left or right) then the AVL tree becomes unbalanced and the tree no longer remains an AVL tree. This is shown in Figure 8-32.

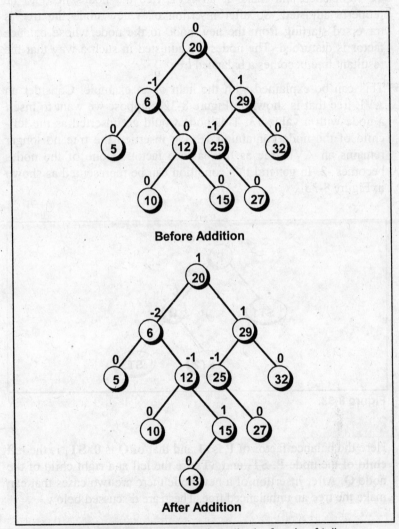

Before Addition

After Addition

Figure 8-32. *Addition of a new node to the leaf node of taller sub-tree.*

To re-balance and make it an AVL tree the nodes need to be properly adjusted. So after insertion of a new node the tree is traversed starting from the new node to the node whose balance factor is disturbed. The nodes are adjusted in such a way that the resultant tree becomes a balanced tree.

This can be explained with the help of an example. Consider an AVL tree that is shown in Figure 8-32. Suppose we want to insert a node with a value **13**. This node would get inserted as the left-child of the node containing **15**. On insertion the tree no longer remains an AVL tree as the balance factor of one of the nodes becomes -2. In general this condition can be represented as shown in Figure 8-33.

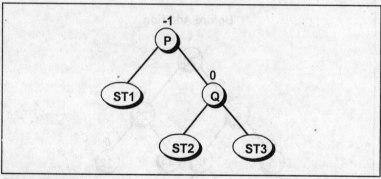

Figure 8-33.

Here the balance factor of **P** is **-1** and that of **Q** is **0**. **ST₁** is the left child of the node **P**. **ST₂** and **ST₃** are the left and right child of the node **Q**. After insertion of a new node there are two cases that can make the tree an unbalanced tree. These are discussed below.

(a) The new node is inserted as a child (left or right) of the leaf node of sub-tree **ST₃**. This is shown in Figure 8-34.

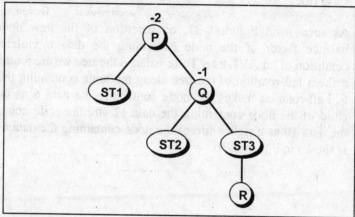

Figure 8-34.

(b) The new node is inserted as a child (left or right) of the leaf node of sub-tree **ST₂**. This is shown in Figure 8-35.

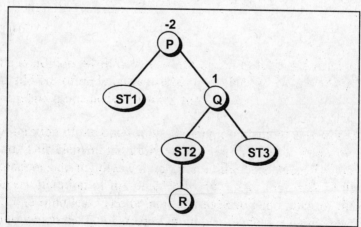

Figure 8-35.

Let us now see how to achieve the balance in both these cases.

Case (a):

As seen from Figure 8-32, on insertion of the new node the balance factor of the node containing the data **6** violates the condition of an AVL tree. To re-balance the tree we are required to make a left-rotation of the tree along the node containing the data **6**. Left-rotation makes the node containing the data **6** as the left child of the node containing the data **12** and the node containing the data **10** as a right child of the node containing the data **6**. This is shown in Figure 8-36.

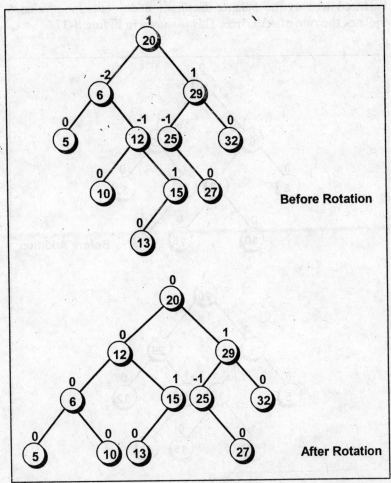

Before Rotation

After Rotation

Figure 8-36. *Left Rotation.*

Case (b):

Now suppose instead of **13** we insert a node with value **11**. This new node would get inserted as the right child of the node containing s value **10**. After this the tree no longer remains a balanced tree as the balance factor of node containing value **6** violates the rule of AVL tree. This is shown in Figure 8-37.

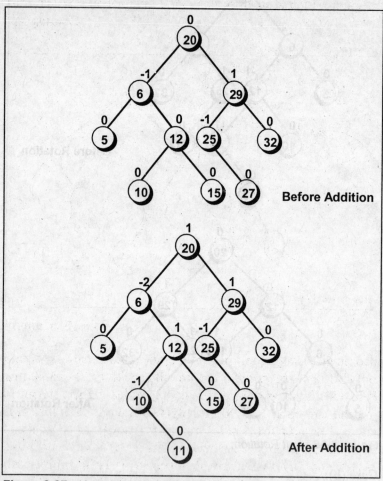

Before Addition

After Addition

Figure 8-37. How tree becomes unbalanced after addition of new node.

To re-balance the tree we are required to make initially a right-rotation of the tree along the node containing a value **12**. Right-rotation makes node **10** the right child of node **6**. Node **12** becomes the right child of node **10** and node **11** becomes the left child of node **12**. This is shown in Figure 8-38.

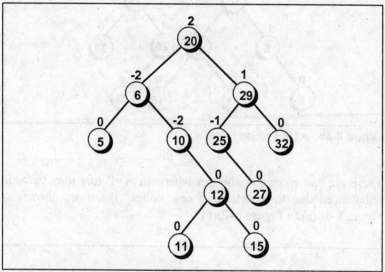

Figure 8-38. *After First Rotation.*

But even now the tree is not balanced and hence, the tree is rotated to left along the node **6**. As a result node **10** becomes the left child of the node **20**. The node **6** becomes the left child of the node **10**. Since, there is no left child for node **10** the right child of node **6** is empty. Thus finally the tree becomes a balanced binary tree or an AVL tree. This procedure of rotating the tree, first to right and then to the left is known as **double rotation**. Figure 8-39 shows the resultant tree that is an AVL tree.

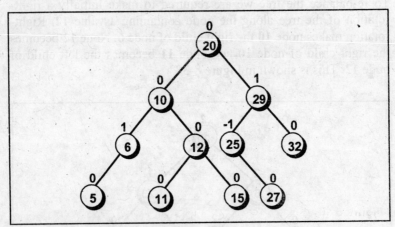

Figure 8-39. *After second rotation.*

There are two more possibilities where an AVL tree may become unbalanced due to insertion of new nodes. These are shown in Figure 8-40(a) to Figure 8-40(c).

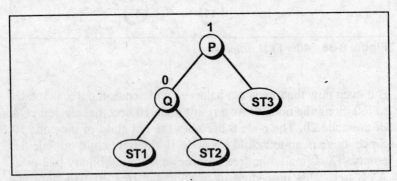

Figure 8-40(a).

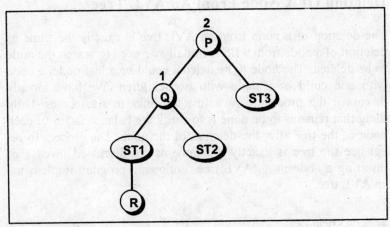

Figure 8-40(b).

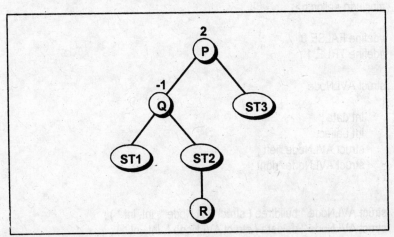

Figure 8-40(c).

To balance the tree shown in Figure 8-40(b) only a right rotation is required and to balance the tree that is shown in Figure 8-40(c) a double rotation is required—initially a left rotation and then a right rotation.

Deletion Of A Node From An AVL Tree

The deletion of a node from an AVL tree is exactly the same as deletion of a node from a BST. Initially we need to search the node to be deleted. The node to be deleted could be a leaf node, a node with one child or a node with two children. We have already discussed the procedure to adjust the links in such cases. Only thing that remains to be done is to check the balance factor of each node of the tree after the deletion of the node. The process to re-balance the tree is exactly the same as we discussed in case of inserting a node in an AVL tree. Following program implements an AVL tree.

```
#include <stdio.h>
#include <conio.h>
#include <alloc.h>

#define FALSE 0
#define TRUE 1

struct AVLNode
{
    int data ;
    int balfact ;
    struct AVLNode *left ;
    struct AVLNode *right ;
} ;

struct AVLNode * buildtree ( struct AVLNode *, int, int * ) ;
struct AVLNode * deldata ( struct AVLNode *, int, int * ) ;
struct AVLNode * del ( struct AVLNode *, struct AVLNode *, int * ) ;
struct AVLNode * balright ( struct AVLNode *, int * ) ;
struct AVLNode * balleft ( struct AVLNode *, int * ) ;
void display ( struct AVLNode * ) ;
void deltree ( struct AVLNode * ) ;

void main( )
```

```
{
    struct AVLNode *avl = NULL ;
    int h ;

    clrscr( ) ;

    avl = buildtree ( avl, 20, &h ) ;
    avl = buildtree ( avl, 6, &h ) ;
    avl = buildtree ( avl, 29, &h ) ;
    avl = buildtree ( avl, 5, &h ) ;
    avl = buildtree ( avl, 12, &h ) ;
    avl = buildtree ( avl, 25, &h ) ;
    avl = buildtree ( avl, 32, &h ) ;
    avl = buildtree ( avl, 10, &h ) ;
    avl = buildtree ( avl, 15, &h ) ;
    avl = buildtree ( avl, 27, &h ) ;
    avl = buildtree ( avl, 13, &h ) ;

    printf ( "\nAVL tree:\n" ) ;
    display ( avl ) ;

    avl = deldata ( avl, 20, &h ) ;
    avl = deldata ( avl, 12, &h ) ;

    printf ( "\nAVL tree after deletion of a node:\n" ) ;
    display ( avl ) ;

    deltree ( avl ) ;

    getch( ) ;
}

/* inserts an element into tree */
struct AVLNode * buildtree ( struct AVLNode *root, int data, int *h )
{
    struct AVLNode *node1, *node2 ;

    if ( !root )
```

```
{
    root = ( struct AVLNode * ) malloc ( sizeof ( struct AVLNode ) ) ;
    root -> data = data ;
    root -> left = NULL ;
    root -> right = NULL ;
    root -> balfact = 0 ;
    *h = TRUE ;
    return ( root ) ;
}

if ( data < root -> data )
{
    root -> left = buildtree ( root -> left, data, h ) ;
    /* If left subtree is higher */
    if ( *h )
    {
        switch ( root -> balfact )
        {
            case 1:
                node1 = root -> left ;
                if ( node1 -> balfact == 1 )
                {
                    printf ( "\nRight rotation along %d.", root -> data ) ;
                    root -> left = node1 -> right ;
                    node1 -> right = root ;
                    root -> balfact = 0 ;
                    root = node1 ;
                }
                else
                {
                    printf ( "\nDouble rotation, left along %d",
                            node1 -> data ) ;
                    node2 = node1 -> right ;
                    node1 -> right = node2 -> left ;
                    printf ( " then right along %d.\n", root -> data ) ;
                    node2 -> left = node1 ;
                    root -> left = node2 -> right ;
                    node2 -> right = root ;
```

```
                    if ( node2 -> balfact == 1 )
                        root -> balfact = -1 ;
                    else
                        root -> balfact = 0 ;
                    if ( node2 -> balfact == -1 )
                        node1 -> balfact = 1 ;
                    else
                        node1 -> balfact = 0 ;
                    root = node2 ;
                }
                root -> balfact = 0 ;
                *h = FALSE ;
                break ;

            case 0:
                root -> balfact = 1 ;
                break ;

            case -1:
                root -> balfact = 0 ;
                *h = FALSE ;
            }
        }
    }

    if ( data > root -> data )
    {
        root -> right = buildtree ( root -> right, data, h ) ;
        /* If the right subtree is higher */
        if ( *h )
        {
            switch ( root -> balfact )
            {
                case 1:
                    root -> balfact = 0 ;
                    *h = FALSE ;
                    break ;
```

```
            case 0:
                root -> balfact = -1 ;
                break;

            case -1:
                node1 = root -> right ;
                if ( node1 -> balfact == -1 )
                {
                    printf ( "\nLeft rotation along %d.", root -> data ) ;
                    root -> right = node1 -> left ;
                    node1 -> left = root ;
                    root -> balfact = 0 ;
                    root = node1 ;
                }
                else
                {
                    printf ( "\nDouble rotation, right along %d",
                            node1 -> data ) ;
                    node2 = node1 -> left ;
                    node1 -> left = node2 -> right ;
                    node2 -> right = node1 ;
                    printf ( " then left along %d.\n", root -> data ) ;
                    root -> right = node2 -> left ;
                    node2 -> left = root ;

                    if ( node2 -> balfact == -1 )
                        root -> balfact = 1 ;
                    else
                        root -> balfact = 0 ;
                    if ( node2 -> balfact == 1 )
                        node1 -> balfact = -1 ;
                    else
                        node1 -> balfact = 0 ;
                    root = node2 ;
                }
                root -> balfact = 0 ;
                *h = FALSE ;
    }
```

```
        }
    }
    return ( root ) ;
}

/* deletes an item from the tree */
struct AVLNode * deldata ( struct AVLNode *root, int data, int *h )
{
    struct AVLNode *node ;

    if ( !root )
    {
        printf ( "\nNo such data." ) ;
        return ( root ) ;
    }
    else
    {
        if ( data < root -> data )
        {
            root -> left = deldata ( root -> left, data, h ) ;
            if ( *h )
                root = balright ( root, h ) ;
        }
        else
        {
            if ( data > root -> data )
            {
                root -> right = deldata ( root -> right, data, h ) ;
                if ( *h )
                    root = balleft ( root, h ) ;
            }
            else
            {
                node = root ;
                if ( node -> right == NULL )
                {
                    root = node -> left ;
                    *h = TRUE ;
```

```
                    free ( node ) ;
            }
            else
            {
                if ( node -> left == NULL )
                {
                    root = node -> right ;
                    *h = TRUE ;
                    free ( node ) ;
                }
                else
                {
                    node -> right = del ( node -> right, node, h ) ;
                    if ( *h )
                        root = balleft ( root, h ) ;
                }
            }
        }
    }
    return ( root ) ;
}

struct AVLNode * del ( struct AVLNode *succ, struct AVLNode *node, int *h )
{
    struct AVLNode *temp = succ ;
    if ( succ -> left != NULL )
    {
        succ -> left = del ( succ -> left, node, h ) ;
        if ( *h )
            succ = balright ( succ, h ) ;
    }
    else
    {
        temp = succ ;
        node -> data = succ -> data ;
        succ = succ -> right ;
        free ( temp ) ;
```

```
        *h = TRUE ;
    }
    return ( succ ) ;
}

/* balances the tree, if right sub-tree is higher */
struct AVLNode * balright ( struct AVLNode *root, int *h )
{
    struct AVLNode *node1, *node2 ;

    switch ( root -> balfact )
    {
        case 1:
            root -> balfact = 0 ;
            break;

        case 0:
            root -> balfact = -1 ;
            *h  = FALSE ;
            break;

        case -1:
            node1 = root -> right ;
            if ( node1 -> balfact <= 0 )
            {
                printf ( "\nLeft rotation along %d.", root -> data ) ;
                root -> right = node1 -> left ;
                node1 -> left = root ;
                if ( node1 -> balfact == 0 )
                {
                    root -> balfact = -1 ;
                    node1 -> balfact = 1 ;
                    *h = FALSE ;
                }
                else
                {
                    root -> balfact = node1 -> balfact = 0 ;
                }
```

```
                    root = node1 ;
                }
                else
                {
                    printf ( "\nDouble rotation, right along %d", node1 -> data );
                    node2 = node1 -> left ;
                    node1 -> left = node2 -> right ;
                    node2 -> right = node1 ;
                    printf ( " then left along %d.\n", root -> data );
                    root -> right = node2 -> left ;
                    node2 -> left = root ;

                    if ( node2 -> balfact == -1 )
                        root -> balfact = 1 ;
                    else
                        root -> balfact = 0 ;
                    if ( node2 -> balfact == 1 )
                        node1 -> balfact = -1 ;
                    else
                        node1 -> balfact = 0 ;
                    root = node2 ;
                    node2 -> balfact = 0 ;
                }
        }
        return ( root ) ;
}

/* balances the tree, if left sub-tree is higher */
struct AVLNode * balleft ( struct AVLNode *root, int *h )
{
        struct AVLNode *node1, *node2 ;

        switch ( root -> balfact )
        {
            case -1:
                root -> balfact = 0 ;
                break ;
```

```
case 0:
    root -> balfact = 1 ;
    *h = FALSE ;
    break ;

case 1:
    node1 = root -> left ;
    if ( node1 -> balfact >= 0 )
    {
        printf ( "\nRight rotation along %d.", root -> data ) ;
        root -> left = node1 -> right ;
        node1 -> right = root ;
        if ( node1 -> balfact == 0 )
        {
            root -> balfact = 1 ;
            node1 -> balfact = -1 ;
            *h = FALSE ;
        }
        else
        {
            root -> balfact = node1 -> balfact = 0 ;
        }
        root = node1 ;
    }
    else
    {
        printf ( "\nDouble rotation, left along %d", node1 -> data ) ;
        node2 = node1 -> right ;
        node1 -> right = node2 -> left ;
        node2 -> left = node1 ;
        printf ( " then right along %d.\n", root -> data ) ;
        root -> left = node2 -> right ;
        node2 -> right = root ;

        if ( node2 -> balfact == 1 )
            root -> balfact = -1 ;
        else
            root -> balfact = 0 ;
```

```
                    if ( node2-> balfact == -1 )
                        node1 -> balfact = 1 ;
                    else
                        node1 -> balfact = 0 ;
                    root = node2 ;
                    node2 -> balfact = 0 ;
            }
    }
    return ( root ) ;
}

/* displays the tree in-order */
void display ( struct AVLNode *root )
{
    if ( root != NULL )
    {
        display ( root -> left ) ;
        printf ( "%d\t", root -> data ) ;
        display ( root -> right ) ;
    }
}

/* deletes the tree */
void deltree ( struct AVLNode *root )
{
    if ( root != NULL )
    {
        deltree ( root -> left ) ;
        deltree ( root -> right ) ;
    }
    free ( root ) ;
}
```

Output:

Left rotation along 6.
AVL tree:

```
5    6    10   12   13   15   20   25   27   29
32
```
AVL tree after deletion of a node:
```
5    6    10   13   15   25   27   29   32
```

In the program initially eleven nodes are created and then two nodes are deleted. After deletion of the node since the tree becomes unbalanced, it is balanced by doing appropriate rotations. The functions **buildtree( )**, **del( )** and **display( )** are called from **main( )** to add, delete and display the nodes. These functions in turn calls functions like **deldata( )**, **balleft( )** and **balright( )**. Finally, a function **deltree( )** is called that deletes the entire tree by releasing the memory occupied by tree.

The function **buildtree( )** is used to add a new node to the tree. It receives three parameters; the first is the address of root node of the tree or sub-tree to which the new node is to be added. The second is an integer that holds the data of the node that is to be added and the third is the address of a variable that is used as a flag to check whether there is a need for balancing the tree after addition of the new node.

In the function **buildtree( )** it is checked whether **root** is NULL. If it is, then the tree is empty and the new node is going to be the first node. Now memory is allocated for a new node. Next, data is stored in the data part, NULL in the left and right part of the node and a value 0 is assigned to its **balfact** field as at this point the new node it going to be the leaf node.

If the tree is non-empty then the new node is added as a child of the leaf node. To determine whether the new node should be a left child or right child it is checked whether the data of the new node is less than the data of the current node. If it is, then a recursive call is made to function **buildtree( )** by passing the address of the left sub-tee. If the left sub-tree is empty then the new node is made the left child of the current node. Then using **if (*h)** it is checked whether there is a need for balancing.

If balancing needs to be done then a **switch-case** is applied on the **balfact** of the current node. If the **balfact** of current node is 1 (left sub-tree of current node is higher) then it is checked whether the **balfact** of left child of current node is 1. If it is, then simply a right rotation is required along the current node, otherwise a double rotation is required. After rotation, **balfact** of current node is assigned a value 0 and a **FALSE** value is stored in the flag variable pointed to by **h**. If **balfact** of current node is 0, **balfact** is simply assigned a value 1. If **balfact** of current node is –1, then **balfact** is assigned a value 0 and a **FALSE** value is stored in the flag variable pointed to by **h**.

There is one more possibility—the data of the new node is greater than data of the current node. If it is, then a recursive call is made to function **buildtree( )** by passing the address of the right child of the current node. Here too the **switch-case** is applied if the height of the right sub-tree is higher, and appropriate rotation is applied, if needed. Finally, the address of the current node is returned.

The function **deldata( )** works similar to the function **buildtree( )**. Here also the recursive call is made for either left or right child depending upon the data to be deleted. If data is found then its in-order successor is searched and a call is made to function **del( )** which deletes the node. The functions **balleft( )** and **balright( )** are called to balance the tree after deletion of the node.

The function **display( )** is nothing but in-order traversal of the tree which we have already discussed.

2-3 Trees

The basic idea behind maintaining a search tree is to make the insertion, deletion and searching operations efficient. In AVL trees the searching operation is efficient. However, insertion and deletion involves rotation that makes the operation complicated. To eliminate this complication a data structure called 2-3 tree can be used. To build a 2-3 tree there are certain rules that need to be followed. These rules are as follows:

(a) All the non-leaf nodes in a 2-3 tree must always have two or three non-empty child nodes that are again 2-3 trees.

(b) The level of all the leaf nodes must always be the same.

(c) One single node can contain either one or two values.

(d) If any node has two children (left and right) then that node contains single data. The data occurring on left sub-tree of that node is less than the data of the node and the data occurring on right sub-tree of that node is greater than the data of the node.

(e) If any node has three children (left, middle and right), then that node contains two data values, say i and j, where i < j. The data of all the nodes on the left sub-tree are less than i. The data of all the nodes on the middle sub-tree are greater than i but less than j and the data of all the nodes on the right sub-tree are greater than j.

Figure 8-41 shows a 2-3 tree.

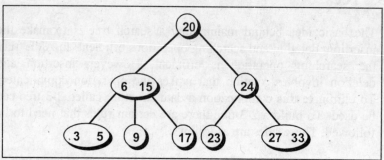

Figure 8-41. *A 2-3 tree.*

The structure of a node of a 2-3 tree is as follows:

```
struct twothree
{
    int count ;
    int data[3] ;
    struct twothree * child[4] ;
};
```

Here, the array **data** has 3 elements even though any node of the tree contains maximum two values. Also, the array **child** has 4 elements even though any node of the tree has maximum three children. The reason behind this is explained in the section "Insertion Of A Value In A 2-3 Tree" later.

Searching For A Value In A 2-3 Tree

The process of searching data in a 2-3 tree starts from the root node of the tree. Consider Figure 8-41. Suppose we want to search the value **17**. It is first compared with the root node of the tree i.e. **20**. Since **17** is less than **20** the comparison will proceed in the left sub-tree of the tree, i.e. the node which contains two data values, **6** and **15**. Since **17** is greater than **6**, it is compared with **15** and as **17** is greater than **15** too, the comparison process will proceed in the right sub-tree of the node containing **6** and **15**. Here, since the right sub-tree contains the value **17**, the search is successful.

Insertion Of A Value In A 2-3 Tree

Let us now try to understand the process of insertion of a value in a 2-3 tree. To insert a value in a 2-3 tree we first need to search the position where the value can be inserted, then the value and the node in which the value is to be inserted are adjusted. The 2-3 tree grows in the reverse direction. This is a bit odd, hence let us understand this with the help of an example.

Consider the tree shown in Figure 8-41 and suppose we want to insert a value **2**. To insert the value, first we need to search the appropriate position for the value. To search the position the method that we had already seen is followed. The searching process will terminate at the leaf node that contains the data **3** and **5**. The actual insertion process starts here. The value that is to be inserted i.e. **2**, is added to this node. So the node now contains the values **2**, **3** and **5**. This is shown in Figure 8-42.

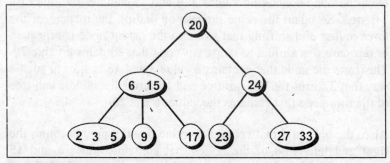

Figure 8-42. *Addition of a new value.*

Adding **2** to the node that already contains **3** and **5** violates the definition of a 2-3 tree. To again make it a 2-3 tree, the median of the three values **2**, **3** and **5** is taken and that value is shifted to the parent of this node. In our case, the median value happens to be **3**, which is moved up to the parent node. As a result the parent node now contains **3**, **6** and **15**. Also, the node containing **2** and **5** is now split into two different nodes containing values **2** and **5**. These two nodes are then attached as first and second child of the parent node containing the data **3**, **6** and **15**. This is shown in Figure 8-43.

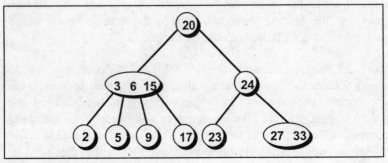

Figure 8-43. *Addition of a value.*

Now the node containing values **3**, **6** and **15** violates the rule of a 2-3 tree. So again the same process of finding the median of the three values and shifting that value to the parent node is repeated. In our case **6** is shifted to its parent node that contains a value **20**. This time the node that contains a value **3** and **15** is split in such a way that **3** forms the left sub-tree and **15** forms the middle sub-tree of the root node that contains the values **6** and **20**.

Also, the old child that contains a value **5** and **9** now becomes the right and left child of the nodes that contains values **3** and **15** respectively. The process of inserting the new value to the 2-3 tree ceases here as all the nodes satisfy the conditions of a 2-3 tree. The final 2-3 tree is shown in Figure 8-44.

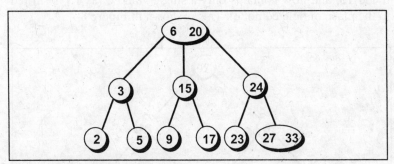

Figure 8-44. *Addition of a value.*

From Figure 8-44 it is clear that during the process of insertion some node may contain three data values and four children. This is merely an intermediate step. Hence, while defining the structure of the node of a 2-3 tree it is necessary to declare an array of three elements for data values and an array of four elements for pointers to child nodes.

Deletion Of A Value From A 2-3 Tree

Deletion of a value from a 2-3 tree is exactly opposite to insertion. In case of insertion the node where the data is to be inserted is split if it already contains maximum number of values (i.e. two values). But in case of deletion, two nodes are merged if the node of the value to be deleted contains minimum number of values (i.e. only one value).

Let us understand this with the help of an example. Consider the tree shown in Figure 8-41. Suppose the node that contains a value **17** is to be deleted. Its parent holds the values **6** and **15**, and **15** is predecessor of **17**. Hence **17** is replaced by **15** and is then merged with its sibling, i.e. with **9**. Then the node that contains **9** and **15** is made the right child of the node that initially contained the values

6 and **15**, and now contains only a single value **6** (as **15** is shifted to the place of deleted node). This is shown in Figure 8-45.

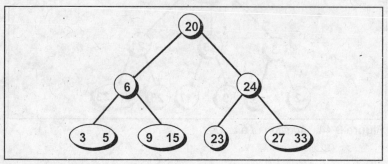

Figure 8-45. *2-3 tree after deletion of a value.*

B-Trees

The number of values that a particular node of a binary search tree or an AVL tree can hold is only one. On the other hand a 2-3 tree can contain at the most two values per node. To improve the efficiency of operations performed on a tree we need to reduce the height of the tree. Another problem arises when the data is stored in secondary storage medium. The time required to access the data from a secondary storage medium is very high. Hence if we access the data less number of times, less would be the time required to perform an operation. If a node contains more number of values then at a time more values can be accessed from the secondary medium. To improve the efficiency of tree operations Multi-way Search trees can be used.

Multi-Way Search Trees

A multi-way tree of order **n** is a tree in which any node may contain maximum **n - 1** values and can have maximum of **n** children. Order of a tree as we have seen earlier, is the maximum number of the child nodes that a particular node has. In a multi-way tree of order **4** (or a **4-way** tree) any node can contain maximum three values and four children. Figure 8-46 shows a multi-way tree of order **4**.

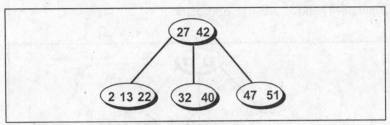

Figure 8-46. *Multi-way tree of order 4.*

Definition Of B-Tree

B-tree is a multi-way search tree of order **n** that satisfies the following conditions:

(a)   All the non-leaf nodes (except the root node) have at least **n/2** children and at the most **n** children.

(b)   The non-leaf root node may have at the most **n** non-empty child and at least two child nodes.

(c)   A B-tree can exist with only one node i.e. the root node containing no child.

(d)   If a node has **n** children then it must have **n - 1** values. All the values of a particular node are in increasing order.

(e)   All the values that appear on the left most child of a node are smaller than the first value of that node. All the values that appear on the right most child of a node are greater than the last value of that node.

(f) If **x** and **y** are any two i^{th} and $(i+1)^{th}$ values of a node, where **x** < **y**, then all the values appearing on the $(i+1)^{th}$ sub-tree of that node are greater than **x** and less than **y**.

(g) All the leaf nodes should appear on the same level.

Figure 8-47 shows a B-tree of order **3**.

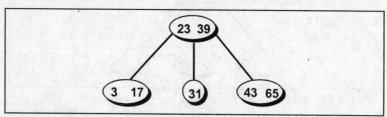

Figure 8-47. *B-tree of order 3.*

From Figure 8-47 it can be observed that a B-tree of order **3** is a 2-3 tree.

The structure of a node of a B-tree is similar to the structure of a node of 2-3 tree. This structure is given below:

```
struct btnode
{
    int count ;
    int value[MAX + 1] ;
    struct btnode *child[MAX + 1] ;
} ;
```

Here **count** represents the number of children that a particular node has. The values of a node stored in the array **value**. The addresses of child nodes are stored in the **child** array. The **MAX** macro signifies the maximum number of values that a particular node can contain.

Searching Of A Value In A B-Tree

Searching for a value **k** in a B-tree is exactly similar to searching for a value in a 2-3 tree. To begin with the value **k** is compared with the first value **key[0]** of the root node. If they are same then the search is complete. If **k** is less than **key[0]** then the search is done in the first child node or sub-tree of the root node. If **k** is greater than **key[0]** then it is compared with **key[1]**. If **k** is greater than **k[0]** and smaller than **key[1]** then **k** is searched in the second child node or sub-tree of the root node. If **k** is greater than the last value **key[i]** of the root node then searching is done in the last child node or sub-tree of the root node.

If **k** is searched in any of the child nodes or sub-tree of the root node then the same procedure of searching is repeated for that particular node or sub-tree.

If the value **k** is found in the tree then the search is successful. The address of the node in which **k** is present and the position of the value **k** in that node is returned. If the value **k** is not found in the tree, then the search is unsuccessful.

Insertion Of A Value In A B-Tree

Let us now try to understand the process of insertion of a value in a B-tree. To insert a value in a B-tree firstly we need to search the position of the node where the value can be inserted and then the value and the node are adjusted if required. The node where the new value is to be inserted would always be the leaf node.

Suppose a value **k** is to be inserted in a B-tree of order **4**. Here the maximum number of values that any node may have is **3**. After searching for the appropriate leaf node to insert the value **k**, the values present at that particular leaf node is counted. This leads to two possibilities:

(a) The leaf node is not full (doesn't contain **3** values).

(b) The leaf node is full (contains **3** values).

Different methods are used for inserting new value in these two cases. These are explained below:

Case (a):

If the leaf node is not full then the value is inserted at its appropriate position in the node and the insertion procedure ends. Let us understand this with the help of an example.

Consider Figure 8-46. Suppose we intend to add a value **37** to the tree. For this firstly the node where this value can be inserted is searched. In our case it is the leaf node that contains the values **32** and **40**. Since this node contains only two values the third value can be added and hence the insertion procedure ends here. The value **37** is inserted in between **32** and **40** because the values of any node of a B-tree should always appear in ascending order. Figure 8-48 shows the tree after insertion of the value **37**.

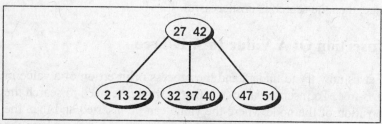

Figure 8-48. *Addition of a value to a B-tree of order 4.*

Case (b):

If the leaf node is full, then that node is split into two nodes. If **m** is the order of the tree then any node is always split after the value **m/2-1**. As a result, the first part of the node contains the first **m/2-1** values and **m/2** children if any, and the second part of the node contains the last **m-m/2** values and **m-m/2+1** children, if any. Then the **(m/2)**th value is moved up to the parent node and the new value is appropriately attached to one of the two split nodes. If the parent node is full then the same procedure is repeated.

Let us understand this with the help of an example. Consider the tree shown in Figure 8-48. Suppose the value that is to be inserted is **19**. To begin with, the node in which **19** can be inserted is searched. In our case it is the node that contains values **2**, **13** and **22**. Since this node already contains three values no more values can be added to this node. Hence the node is split after the value **4 / 2 - 1** (since order of the tree is **4**). As a result, the first part of the node contains the first value (i.e. **2**) and has two children that are as yet empty. The second part of the node contains the last value **22** and has two children, which too are empty. The value **13** is moved up to the parent node and the new value **19** is attached to second split node, as it is greater than **13**.

Finally, these two split nodes are made the first and second children of the node containing the values **13**, **27** and **42**. This is shown in Figure 8-49.

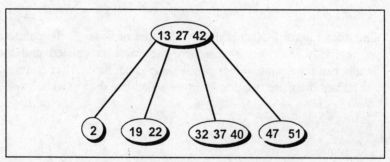

Figure 8-49. *Addition of a value to B-tree of order 4.*

Deletion Of A Value From A B-Tree

Deletion of a value from the B-tree is similar to insertion. Initially, we need to find the node from which the value is to be deleted. After the deletion of the value, we need to check, whether the tree still maintains the property of the B-tree or not. Let us try to understand this with the help of an example.

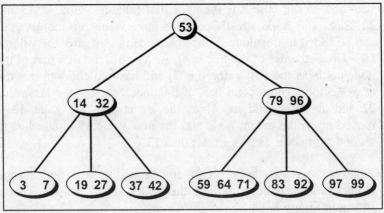

Figure 8-50. *A B-tree of order 5.*

Consider Figure 8-50 that shows a B-tree of order **5**. To delete a value firstly its node is searched, the value is deleted and the number of remaining values in the node is counted. After counting the values there are two possibilities, which are discussed below:

Case A:

The number of values is greater than or equal to the minimum number of values required (i.e. **2**) for a B-tree of order **5**.

Consider Figure 8-50 and suppose we want to delete the value **64**. On deleting this value the number of values that are left in the node are **2,** which satisfy the condition of a B-tree. Hence the deletion process comes to an end. Figure 8-51 shows the B-tree after the deletion of the value **64.**

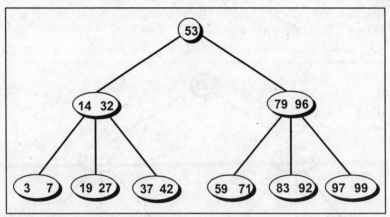

Figure 8-51. *B-tree after deletion of value 64.*

Case B:

The number of values is less than the minimum number of values required (i.e. **2**) for a B-tree of order **5**. Here again there are two possibilities, which are discussed below:

Case (a):

The left or right sibling of the node from which the value is deleted contains more than the required minimum number of values.

Here the value of its (node from which the value is deleted) parent is moved to the node and a value from its sibling (left or right which contains more number of values than the required minimum values) is moved to its parent. This can be understood with the help of following example.

Consider the B-tree shown in Figure 8-50 and suppose we want to delete the value **92**. After deleting the value **92**, value **79** is moved from its parent to the node from where the value is deleted. Then the value **71** is moved from its left sibling to its parent. The deletion process ends here as all the nodes satisfy the condition of B-tree. This is shown in Figure 8-52.

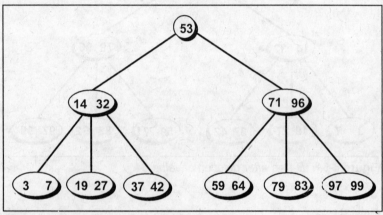

Figure 8-52. *B-tree after deletion of a value.*

Case (b):

The left or right sibling of the node from which the value is deleted contains exactly the required minimum number of values.

Here the value of its (node from which the value is deleted) parent is moved to the node and the node is merged with its sibling. If the parent also contains the minimum number of values then the same procedure of merging the node with its sibling is applied. Let us understand this with the help of an example.

Consider the B-tree that is shown in Figure 8-52 and suppose we want to delete the value **42**. After deletion of the value **42** the node contains only one value **37**. So value **32** is copied from its parent and it is merged with its left sibling that contains values **19** and **27**. As a result the node now contains four values **19, 27, 32** and **37**. This is shown in Figure 8-53.

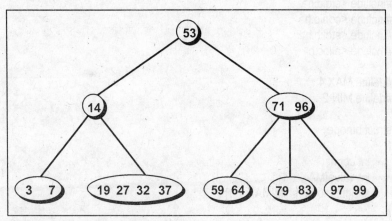

Figure 8-53. *B-tree after merging.*

Now the parent node contains only one value **14**. So the value **53** is copied from its parent and is merged with its right sibling that contains values **71** and **96**. As a result, the node now contains four values **14, 53, 71** and **96**. The deletion process ends here as all the nodes satisfy the condition of B-tree. This is shown in Figure 8-54.

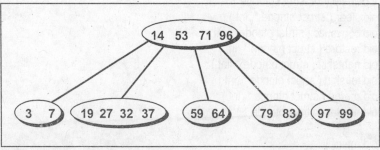

Figure 8-54. *B-tree after merging.*

Let us now put all the theory that we learnt into practice. Here is a program that implements B-tree of order 5.

```c
#include <stdio.h>
#include <conio.h>
#include <stdlib.h>
#include <alloc.h>

#define MAX 4
#define MIN 2

struct btnode
{
    int count ;
    int value[MAX + 1] ;
    struct btnode *child[MAX + 1] ;
} ;

struct btnode * insert ( int, struct btnode * ) ;
int setval ( int, struct btnode *, int *, struct btnode ** ) ;
struct btnode * search ( int, struct btnode *, int * ) ;
int searchnode ( int, struct btnode *, int * ) ;
void fillnode ( int, struct btnode *, struct btnode *, int ) ;
void split ( int, struct btnode *, struct btnode *,
                      int, int *, struct btnode ** ) ;
struct btnode * delete ( int, struct btnode * ) ;
int delhelp ( int, struct btnode * ) ;
void clear ( struct btnode *, int ) ;
void copysucc ( struct btnode *, int ) ;
void restore ( struct btnode *, int ) ;
void rightshift ( struct btnode *, int ) ;
void leftshift ( struct btnode *, int ) ;
void merge ( struct btnode *, int ) ;
void display ( struct btnode * ) ;

void main( )
{
```

```
    struct node *root ;
    root = NULL ;

    clrscr( ) ;

    root = insert ( 27, root ) ;
    root = insert ( 42, root ) ;
    root = insert ( 22, root ) ;
    root = insert ( 47, root ) ;
    root = insert ( 32, root ) ;
    root = insert ( 2, root ) ;
    root = insert ( 51, root ) ;
    root = insert ( 40, root ) ;
    root = insert ( 13, root ) ;

    printf ( "B-tree of order 5:\n" ) ;
    display ( root ) ;

    root = delete ( 22, root ) ;
    root = delete ( 11, root ) ;

    printf ( "\n\nAfter deletion of values:\n" ) ;
    display ( root ) ;

    getch( ) ;
}

/* inserts a value in the B-tree*/
struct btnode * insert ( int val, struct btnode *root )
{
    int i ;
    struct btnode *c, *n ;
    int flag ;

    flag = setval ( val, root, &i, &c ) ;
    if ( flag )
    {
        n = ( struct btnode * ) malloc ( sizeof ( struct btnode ) ) ;
```

```
            n -> count = 1 ;
            n -> value [1] = i ;
            n -> child [0] = root ;
            n -> child [1] = c ;
            return n ;
        }
        return root ;
}

/* sets the value in the node */
int setval ( int val, struct btnode *n, int *p, struct btnode **c )
{
    int k ;
    if ( n == NULL )
    {
        *p = val ;
        *c = NULL ;
        return 1 ;
    }
    else
    {
        if ( searchnode ( val, n, &k ) )
            printf ( "\nKey value already exists.\n" ) ;
        if ( setval ( val, n -> child [k], p, c ) )
        {
            if ( n -> count < MAX )
            {
                fillnode ( *p, *c, n, k ) ;
                return 0 ;
            }
            else
            {
                split ( *p, *c, n, k, p, c ) ;
                return 1 ;
            }
        }
        return 0 ;
    }
```

```
}

/* searches value in the node */
struct btnode * search ( int val, struct btnode *root, int *pos )
{
    if ( root == NULL )
        return NULL ;
    else
    {
        if ( searchnode ( val, root, pos ) )
            return root ;
        else
            return search ( val, root -> child [*pos], pos ) ;
    }
}

/* searches for the node */
int searchnode ( int val, struct btnode *n, int *pos )
{
    if ( val < n -> value [1] )
    {
        *pos = 0 ;
        return 0 ;
    }
    else
    {
        *pos = n -> count ;
        while ( ( val < n -> value [*pos] ) && *pos > 1 )
            ( *pos )-- ;
        if ( val == n -> value [*pos] )
            return 1 ;
        else
            return 0 ;
    }
}

/* adjusts the value of the node */
```

```c
void fillnode ( int val, struct btnode *c, struct btnode *n, int k )
{
    int i ;
    for ( i = n -> count ; i > k ; i-- )
    {
        n -> value [i + 1] = n -> value [i] ;
        n -> child [i + 1] = n -> child [i] ;
    }
    n -> value [k + 1] = val ;
    n -> child [k + 1] = c ;
    n -> count++ ;
}

/* splits the node */
void split ( int val, struct btnode *c, struct btnode *n,
                int k, int *y, struct btnode **newnode )
{
    int i, mid ;

    if ( k <= MIN )
        mid = MIN ;
    else
        mid = MIN + 1 ;

    *newnode = ( struct btnode * ) malloc ( sizeof ( struct btnode ) ) ;

    for ( i = mid + 1 ; i <= MAX ; i++ )
    {
        ( *newnode ) -> value [i - mid] = n -> value [i] ;
        ( *newnode ) -> child [i - mid] = n -> child [i] ;
    }

    ( *newnode ) -> count = MAX - mid ;
    n -> count = mid ;

    if ( k <= MIN )
        fillnode ( val, c, n, k ) ;
    else
```

```
                fillnode ( val, c, *newnode, k - mid ) ;

        *y = n -> value [n -> count] ;
        ( *newnode ) -> child [0] = n -> child [n -> count] ;
        n -> count-- ;
}

/* deletes value from the node */
struct btnode * delete ( int val, struct btnode *root )
{
        struct btnode * temp ;
        if ( ! delhelp ( val, root ) )
                printf ( "\nValue %d not found.", val ) ;
        else
        {
                if ( root -> count == 0 )
                {
                        temp = root ;
                        root = root -> child [0] ;
                        free ( temp ) ;
                }
        }
        return root ;
}

/* helper function for delete( ) */
int delhelp ( int val, struct btnode *root )
{
        int i ;
        int flag ;
        if ( root == NULL )
                return 0 ;
        else
        {
                flag = searchnode ( val, root, &i ) ;
                if ( flag )
                {
                        if ( root -> child [i - 1] )
```

```
            {
                copysucc ( root, i ) ;
                flag = delhelp ( root -> value [i], root -> child [i] ) ;
                if ( !flag )
                    printf ( "\nValue %d not found.", val ) ;
            }
            else
                clear ( root, i ) ;
        }
        else
            flag = delhelp ( val, root -> child [i] ) ;

        if ( root -> child [i] != NULL )
        {
            if ( root -> child [i] -> count < MIN )
                restore ( root, i ) ;
        }
        return flag ;
    }
}

/* removes the value from the node and adjusts the values */
void clear ( struct btnode *node, int k )
{
    int i ;
    for ( i = k + 1 ; i <= node -> count ; i++ )
    {
        node -> value [i - 1] = node -> value [i] ;
        node -> child [i - 1] = node -> child [i] ;
    }
    node -> count-- ;
}

/* copies the successor of the value that is to be deleted */
void copysucc ( struct btnode *node, int i )
{
    struct btnode *temp ;
```

```
    temp = node -> child [i] ;

    while ( temp -> child[0] )
        temp = temp -> child [0] ;

    node -> value [i] = temp -> value [1] ;
}

/* adjusts the node */
void restore ( struct btnode *node, int i )
{
    if ( i == 0 )
    {
        if ( node -> child [1] -> count > MIN )
            leftshift ( node, 1 ) ;
        else
            merge ( node, 1 ) ;
    }
    else
    {
        if ( i == node -> count )
        {
            if ( node -> child [i - 1] -> count > MIN )
                rightshift ( node, i ) ;
            else
                merge ( node, i ) ;
        }
        else
        {
            if ( node -> child [i - 1] -> count > MIN )
                rightshift ( node, i ) ;
            else
            {
                if ( node -> child [i + 1] -> count > MIN )
                    leftshift ( node, i + 1 ) ;
                else
                    merge ( node, i ) ;
            }
        }
```

```
            }
        }
}

/* adjusts the values and children while shifting the value from parent to right
   child */
void rightshift ( struct btnode *node, int k )
{
    int i ;
    struct btnode *temp ;

    temp = node -> child [k] ;

    for ( i = temp -> count ; i > 0 ; i-- )
    {
        temp -> value [i + 1] = temp -> value [i] ;
        temp -> child [i + 1] = temp -> child [i] ;
    }

    temp -> child [1] = temp -> child [0] ;
    temp -> count++ ;
    temp -> value [1] = node -> value [k] ;

    temp = node -> child [k - 1] ;
    node -> value [k] = temp -> value [temp -> count] ;
    node -> child [k] -> child [0] = temp -> child [temp -> count] ;
    temp -> count-- ;
}

/* adjusts the values and children while shifting the value from parent to left
   child */
void leftshift ( struct btnode *node, int k )
{
    int i ;
    struct btnode *temp ;

    temp = node -> child [k - 1] ;
    temp -> count++ ;
```

```
        temp -> value [temp -> count] = node -> value [k] ;
        temp -> child [temp -> count] = node -> child [k] -> child [0] ;

        temp = node -> child [k] ;
        node -> value [k] = temp -> value [1] ;
        temp -> child [0] = temp -> child [1] ;
        temp -> count-- ;

        for ( i = 1 ; i <= temp -> count ; i++ )
        {
            temp -> value [i] = temp -> value [i + 1] ;
            temp -> child [i] = temp -> child [i + 1] ;
        }
}

/* merges two nodes */
void merge ( struct btnode *node, int k )
{
    int i ;
    struct btnode *temp1, *temp2 ;

    temp1 = node -> child [k] ;
    temp2 = node -> child [k - 1] ;
    temp2 -> count++ ;
    temp2 -> value [temp2 -> count] = node -> value [k] ;
    temp2 -> child [temp2 -> count] = node -> child [0] ;

    for ( i = 1 ; i <= temp1 -> count ; i++ )
    {
        temp2 -> count++ ;
        temp2 -> value [temp2 -> count] = temp1 -> value [i] ;
        temp2 -> child [temp2 -> count] = temp1 -> child [i] ;
    }
    for ( i = k ; i < node -> count ; i++ )
    {
        node -> value [i] = node -> value [i + 1] ;
        node -> child [i] = node -> child [i + 1] ;
    }
```

```
        node -> count-- ;
        free ( temp1 ) ;
}

/* displays the B-tree */
void display ( struct btnode *root )
{
    int i ;

    if ( root != NULL )
    {
        for ( i = 0 ; i < root -> count ; i++ )
        {
            display ( root -> child [i] ) ;
            printf ( "%d\t", root -> value [i + 1] ) ;
        }
        display ( root -> child [i] ) ;
    }
}
```

Output:

```
B-tree of order 5:
2    13   22   27   32   40   42   47   51
Value 11 not found.

After deletion of values:
2    13   27   32   40   42   47   51
```

In the program, from **main( )** three functions are called—**insert( )**, **delete( )** and **display( )**. These functions in turn calls several functions like **leftshift( )**, **rightshift( )**, **delhelp( )**, etc. The function **insert( )** is used to insert a value in the tree. The function **delete( )** is used to delete a value from the tree and the function **display( )** is used to display the list in ascending order.

The function **insert( )** receives two parameters—the address of the root node and the value that is to inserted. This function in turn calls a function **setval( )** which returns a value 0 if the new value is inserted in the tree, otherwise it returns a value 1. If it returns 1 then memory is allocated for new node, the variable **count** is assigned a value 1 and the new value is inserted in the node. Then the addresses of the child nodes are stored in **child** pointers and finally the address of the node is returned.

The function **setval( )** receives four parameters. The first is the value that is to be inserted, second is the address of the node (root node, if called for the first time), third is an integer pointer that points to a local flag variable defined in the function **insert( )** and last parameter is a pointer to pointer to the child node that will be set in a function (**split( )** or **fillnode( )**) called from this function. The function **setval( )** returns a flag value that indicates whether the value is inserted or not. If the node is empty then this function returns a value 1. If the node is not empty then this function calls a function **searchnode( )** that checks whether the value already exists in the tree. If the value already exists then a suitable message is displayed. Then a recursive call is made to the function **setval( )** for the child of the node. If this time the function returns a value 1 it means the value is not inserted. Then a condition is checked whether the node is full or not. If the node is not full then a function **fillnode( )** is called that fills the value in the node hence at this point a value 0 is returned. If the node is full then a function **split( )** called that splits the existing node. At this point a value 1 is returned to add the current value to the new node.

The function **search( )** receives three parameters. The first parameter is the value to be searched, second is the address of the node from where the search is to be performed and third is the address of a variable that is used to store the position of the value once found. Initially a condition is checked whether the address of the node being searched is NULL. If it is, then simply a NULL value is returned. Otherwise, a function **searchnode( )** is called which actually searches the given value. If the search is successful the address of the node in which the value is found is returned. If the search is unsuccessful then a recursive call is made to the **search( )** function for the child of the current node.

The function **searchnode( )** receives three parameters. The first parameter is the value that is to be searched. The second parameter is the address of the node in which the search is to be performed and third is a pointer **pos** that holds the address of a variable in which the position of the value that once found is stored. This function returns a value 0 if the search in unsuccessful and 1 if it is successful. In this function initially it is checked whether the value that is to be searched is less than the very first value of the node. If it is then it indicates that the value is not present in the current node. Hence, a value 0 is assigned in the variable that is pointed to by **pos** and 0 is returned, as the search is unsuccessful.

If the value to be searched is not less than the first value of the node then the value of the **count** is stored in the variable pointed to by **pos**. Then a **while** loop is executed till the time a value, let's say **x** (which is greater than the value that is to be searched) is found. Inside the loop each time the position of the value that is pointed to by **pos** is decrement by one. This is done in order to find the position of the value that is less than **x**. Hence, outside the loop it is checked whether the value that is to be searched is equal to the value present at the position stored in the variable pointed by **pos**. If it is then a value 1 is returned, as the search if successful otherwise a value 0 is returned.

The function **fillnode( )** receives four parameters. The first is the value that is to be inserted. The second is the address of the child node of the new value that is to be inserted. The third is the address of the node in which the new value is to be inserted. The last parameter is the position of the node where the new value is to be inserted. In the function **fillnode( ),** initially, a **for** loop is executed which shifts all the value and their respective children one place to right. Once outside the loop the new value and its child is stored at the appropriate position and the variable **count** is increment by 1.

The function **split( )** receives six parameters. The first four parameters are exactly the same as in the case of function **fillnode( )**. The fifth parameter is a pointer to variable that holds the value from where the node is split. The last parameter is a pointer to pointer of the new node created at the time of split. In this function firstly it is checked whether the new value that is to be inserted is inserted at a position less than or equal to the minimum values required in a node. If the condition is satisfied then the node is split at the position **MIN** (the minimum required values of a node). Otherwise, the node is split at one position more than **MIN**. Then dynamically memory is allocated for a new node. Next, a **for** loop is executed which copies into the new node the values and children that occur on the right side of the value from where the old node is split. Outside the loop the values of **count** of new node and old node are set. The function **fillnode( )** is called by passing the address of the new node or old node depending upon whether the new value is inserted to new node or old node. The value from which the node is split is assigned to the variable that is pointed to by **y**. Finally, the child of the node from which the node is split is made the first child of the new node and then the value of old node is decrement by 1.

The function **delete( )** receives two parameters. First is the value that is to be deleted second is the address of the root node. This function calls another helper function **delhelp( )** which returns a value 0 if the deletion of the value is unsuccessful, 1 otherwise. If it is unsuccessful then the appropriate message is displayed. Otherwise, a condition is checked whether the **count** is 0. If it is, then it indicates that the node from which the value is deleted is the last value. Hence, the first child of the node is itself made the node and the original node is deleted. Finally, the address of the new root node is returned.

The function **delhelp( )** receives two parameters. First is the value to be deleted and the second is the address of the node from which it is to be deleted. Initially it is checked whether the node is NULL. If it is, then a value 0 is returned. Otherwise, a call to function **searchnode( )** is made. If the value is found then another condition is checked to see whether there is any child to the value that is to be deleted. If so, then a function **copysucc( )** is called which copies the successor of the value to be deleted and then a recursive call is made to the function **delhelp( )** for the value that is to be deleted and its child. If data is not found then the appropriate message is displayed. If the child is empty then a call to function **clear( )** is made which deletes the value. If the **searchnode( )** function fails then a recursive call is made to function **delhelp( )** by passing the address of the child. Then a condition is checked whether the child of the node that is searched is empty or not. If is not empty, then another condition is checked to see whether the value present at this child is less than the minimum required value. If so, then a function **restore( )** is called to merge the child with its siblings. Finally, the value of the **flag** is returned which is set as a returned value of the function **searchnode( )**.

The function **clear( )** receives two parameters. First is the address of the node from which the value is to be deleted and second is the position of the value that is to be deleted. This function simply shifts the values one place to the left from the position where the value that is to be deleted is present. Hence, the value that is to be deleted is overwritten with its successor value.

The function **copysucc( )** receives two parameters. First is the address of the node where the successor is to be copied and second is the position of the value that is overwritten with its successor. Initially, the address of the first child of current node is copied into a temporary variable and a **while** loop is executed till the time the leaf node is not reached. Inside the loop each time the address of the first child of a node is assigned to the temporary variable so that the leaf node is reached. Finally, outside the loop the first value of the leaf node is assigned to the value that is to be deleted.

The function **restore( )** receives two parameters. First is the node that is to be restored and second is the position of the value from where the values are restored. If second parameter is 0, then another condition is checked to find out whether the values present at the first child are more than the required minimum number of values. If so, then a function **leftshift( )** is called by passing the address of the node and a value 1 signifying that the value of this node is to be left shifted from the first value. If the condition is not satisfied then a function **merge( )** is called for merging the two children of the node.

If the node that is to be restored is not restored from the first position then in the **else** block of outer **if** another condition is checked. This time the position of the value from where the values are restored is compared with the maximum number of values that a particular node can contain. If it matches then another condition is checked whether the child of the node contains more than the minimum required values of a node. If this condition is also satisfied then a function **rightshift( )** is called, otherwise, the function **merge( )** is called. This time the second value passed to the function is the not 1 but **i** which holds the position from where the values are shifted or merged.

If the node that is to be restored is not restored from the positions 1 and **count** then there is **else** block where the condition is checked for the minimum number of values for the previous child. If it is satisfied then the function **rightshift( )** is called, otherwise, the condition for next child is checked. If this is satisfied then the function **leftshift( )** is called, otherwise, the function **merge( )** is called.

The function **rightshift( )** receives two parameters. First is the address of the node from where the value is shifted to its child and second is the position **k** of the value that is to be shifted. The address of the child of value present at position **k** is copied into a temporary variable **temp**. Then the value and the child pointed by **temp** are shifted one position to the right. The first child of the child node is made the second child and the value present at the position **k** is copied to its child after incrementing the **count** of the child. Finally, the value from the child which is present at the position $k - 1$ is shifted to the parent node and the last child of the $(k -1)^{th}$ child is made the first child of the kth child. Then the **count** of the $(k -1)^{th}$ child is decremented by one.

The function **leftshift( )** receives two parameters. Both the parameters are exactly same as that of function **rightshift( )**. The working of the function is exactly opposite to the working of **rigthshift( )**.

The function **merge( )** receives two parameters. First is the address of the node from which the value is to be copied to the child and second is the position of the value. In this function two temporary variables **temp1** and **temp2** are defined to hold the addresses of the two children of the value that is to be copied. Initially the value of the node is copied to its child. Then the first child of the node is made the respective child of the node where the value is copied. Then two **for** loops are executed, out of which first copies all the values and children of one child to the other child. The second loop shifts the value and child of the node from where the value is copied. Then the **count** of the node from where the node is copied is decremented. Finally, the memory occupied by the second node is released by calling **free( )**.

The function **display( )** receives only one parameter—the address of the node. If the tree/node is non-empty then a **for** loop is executed **count** number of times, i.e. as many times as the number of values present in the node. Inside the **for** loop there is a recursive call to the function **display( )**. The argument passed is the address of the first child node in the first iteration, second child node in the second iteration and so on. After the recursive call the value of the current node is printed. Outside the **for** loop there is again a recursive call to **display( )** function. This time the argument passed to this function is the address of the last child of the current node. This is done because the **for** loop executes only the count number of times and hence the last child is not traversed.

Priority Queue

In a priority queue all the elements are assigned some priority. The order in which the elements could be deleted or processed from the priority queue depends upon this priority. The element with the highest priority is accessed then the element with the second priority and so on. The elements with the same priority are accessed in the order in which they were added to the queue.

Operating system uses priority queue for scheduling jobs where jobs with higher priority are processed first. Priority queue is also used in time-sharing systems where the programs with high priority are processed first and a standard queue is formed for the programs with the same priority. A priority queue can be implemented using a heap as we would see in a later section.

Heap

Heap is a complete binary tree. There are two types of heaps. If the value present at any node is greater than all its children then such a tree is called as the **max-heap** or **descending heap**. In case of a **min-heap** or **ascending heap** the value present in any node is smaller than all its children. Figure 8-55 shows a descending heap.

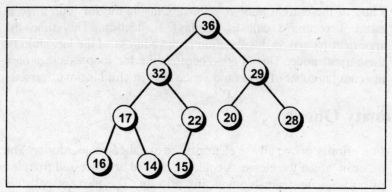

Figure 8-55. *Max-heap or descending heap.*

Priority Queue Represented As A Heap

We have seen how a binary tree can be represented by one-dimensional array. The nodes are numbered as **0** for root node, then from left to right at each level as **1, 2**, etc. For an **i**th node its left and right child exist at **(2i + 1)**th and **(2i + 2)**th position respectively. Same is the case with heap, if the index of the root is considered as **1** then the left and right child of **i**th node are present at **(2i)**th and **(2i + 1)**th position respectively and the parent node is present at **(i/2)**th index in the array. Figure 8-56 shows an array **a** that represents the heap shown in Figure 8-55.

	a[0]	a[1]	a[2]	a[3]	a[4]	a[5]	a[6]	a[7]
a	1000	36	32	29	17	22	20	28

	a[8]	a[9]	a[10]	a[11]	a[12]	a[13]	a[14]	a[15]
	16	14	15	'\0'	'\0'	'\0'	'\0'	'\0'

Figure 8-56. *Heap represented as an array.*

The root node of the tree starts from the index **1** of the array. The **0**[th] element is called as the sentinel value that is a maximum value and is not the node of the tree. It can be any number, like say 1000. This value is required because while addition of new node certain operations are performed in a loop and to terminate the loop the sentinel value is used.

The operations that can be performed on a heap are insertion of a node, deletion of a node and replacement of a node. On performing these operations the tree may not satisfy the heap properties and hence must be re-constructed.

Insertion Of A Node In A Heap

To insert an element to the heap, the node is inserted after the last element in the array and is compared with its parent that is present at $(i/2)^{th}$ position. If it is found to be greater than its parent then they are exchanged. This procedure is repeated till the element is placed at its appropriate place. Let us understand this with the help of an example. Suppose a node that contains a value **24** is inserted in the tree that is shown in Figure 8-55.

Firstly, the value is inserted at index **11** in the array, as the tree has **10** nodes. Then **24** is compared with its parent **22** and since **24** is greater than **22** they are exchanged. This is shown in Figure 8-57.

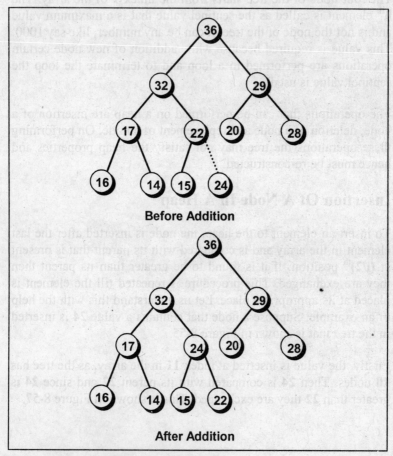

Before Addition

After Addition

Figure 8-57. *Addition of a node to a heap.*

Now the element **24** is compared with its new parent **32** and since **24** is less than **32** they are not exchanged. The insertion process ends here and it is the final position of the node **24** in the tree.

Replacement Of A Node In A Heap

To replace the node of highest priority (i.e. the root node), the new value is inserted at the root of the node. Then it is compared with its children. If it is smaller, then it is exchanged with the child that is greater among them. Let us understand this with the help of an example.

Suppose the value present in the root node in Figure 8-55 (i.e. **36**) is replaced with **5**. Then it is compared with its children **32** and **29**. Since **5** is smaller than these values it is exchanged with the greatest value (i.e. **32**), so the tree now becomes as shown in Figure 8-58.

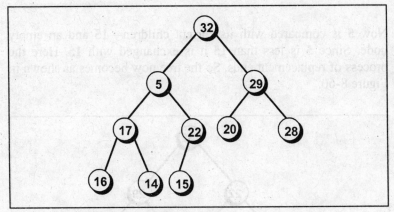

Figure 8-58. *Replacing a value in a heap.*

Now **5** is compared with its current children **17** and **22** and since **5** is less than these values it is exchanged with the greatest value (i.e. **22**), so the tree now becomes as shown in Figure 8-59.

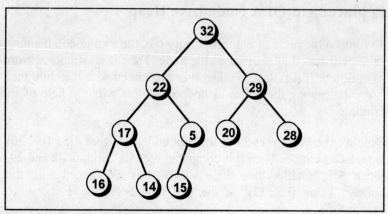

Figure 8-59. *Exchanging the values.*

Now **5** is compared with its current children—**15** and an empty node. Since **5** is less than **15** it is exchanged with **15**. Here the process of replacement ends. So the tree now becomes as shown in Figure 8-60.

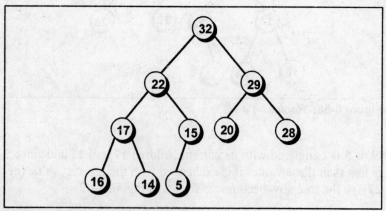

Figure 8-60. *Exchanging the values.*

Deletion Of A Node From A Heap

Suppose the tree from which the node is to be deleted contains **n** nodes. Also the node that is to be deleted is always of the highest priority (i.e. the root node). Firstly, the element present at the index **n** in the array is stored at the 1st position in the array and maximum index value of the array is decremented by one. Then the heap is restored as in the case of replace operation. Let us understand this with the help of an example.

Suppose we want to delete a value from the heap shown in Figure 8-55. For this the value 15 is copied at the index 1 in the array and then heap is restored. Figures 8-61(a) to 8-61(c) shows steps involved in restoring the heap.

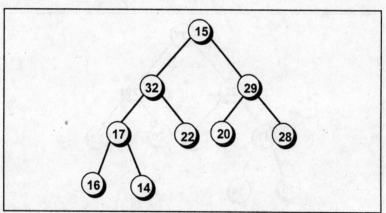

Figure 8-61(a). *Deletion of a node from a heap.*

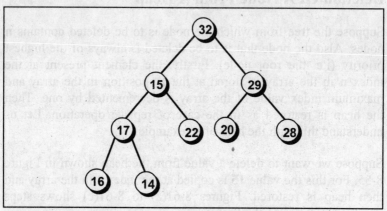

Figure 8-61(b). *Deletion of a node from a heap.*

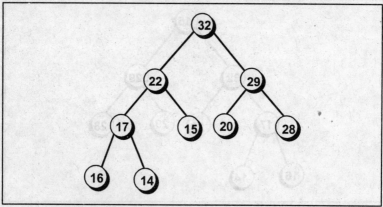

Figure 8-61(c). *Deletion of a node from a heap.*

Construction Of A Heap

Heap can be constructed from an array. To begin with a tree is constructed. If the tree doesn't satisfy heap properties then it is converted into a heap by adjusting nodes.

Adjustment of nodes starts from the level one less than the maximum level of the tree (as the leaf nodes are always heap). Each sub-tree of that particular level is made a heap. Then all the sub-trees at the level two less than the maximum level of tree are made heaps. This procedure is repeated till the root node. As a result the final tree becomes a heap.

Let us understand this with the help of example. Consider an array **arr** that contains **15** elements given below:

7, 10, 25, 17, 23, 27, 16, 19, 37, 42, 4, 33, 1, 5, 11

The tree that can be constructed from the array is shown in Figure 8-62.

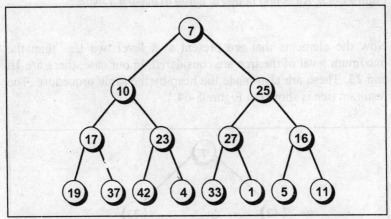

Figure 8-62. *Tree built from an array.*

To make it a heap initially the elements that are present at a level one less than the maximum level of the tree are taken into consideration. In our case, these are **17, 23, 27** and **16**. They are converted to heaps in the same way as replacing the node of a heap. The resultant tree is shown in Figure 8-63.

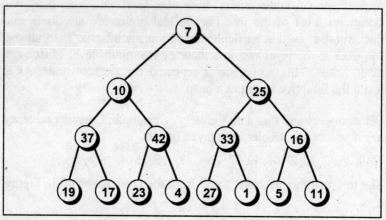

Figure 8-63. *Restoring nodes of a tree to make it a heap.*

Now the elements that are present at a level two less than the maximum level of the tree are considered. In our case, these are **10** and **25**. These are also made the heap by the same procedure. The resultant tree is shown in Figure 8-64.

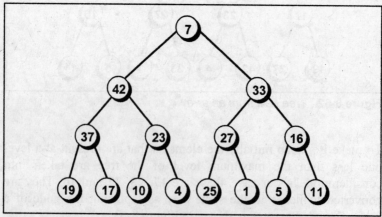

Figure 8-64. *Restoring nodes of a tree to make it a heap.*

Similarly, each time one level is decremented and all the sub-trees at that level are converted to heaps. As a result, finally the entire tree gets converted to a heap as shown in Figure 8-65.

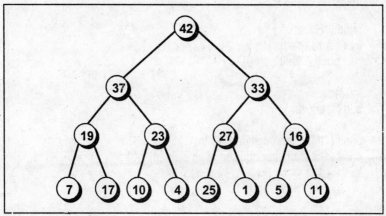

Figure 8-65. *Heap.*

Following program implements all the operations that can be performed on a heap.

```
#include <stdio.h>
#include <conio.h>

void restoreup ( int, int * ) ;
void restoredown ( int, int *, int ) ;
void makeheap ( int *, int ) ;
void add ( int, int *, int * ) ;
int replace ( int, int *, int ) ;
int del ( int *, int * ) ;

void main( )
{
        int arr [20] = { 1000, 7, 10, 25, 17, 23, 27, 16,
```

```
                          19, 37, 42, 4, 33, 1, 5, 11 } ;
     int i, n = 15 ;

     clrscr( ) ;
     makeheap ( arr, n ) ;

     printf ( "Heap:\n" ) ;
     for ( i = 1 ; i <= n ; i++ )
         printf ( "%d\t", arr [i] ) ;

     i = 24 ;
     add ( i, arr, &n ) ;

     printf ( "\n\nElement added %d.\n", i ) ;
     printf ( "\nHeap after addition of an element:\n" ) ;
     for ( i = 1 ; i <= n ; i++ )
         printf ( "%d\t", arr [i] ) ;

     i = replace ( 2, arr, n ) ;
     printf ( "\n\nElement replaced %d.\n", i ) ;
     printf ( "\nHeap after replacement of an element:\n" ) ;
     for ( i = 1 ; i <= n ; i++ )
         printf ( "%d\t", arr [i] ) ;

     i = del ( arr, &n ) ;
     printf ( "\n\nElement deleted %d.\n", i ) ;
     printf ( "\nHeap after deletion of an element:\n" ) ;
     for ( i = 1 ; i <= n ; i++ )
         printf ( "%d\t", arr [i] ) ;

     getch( ) ;
}

void restoreup ( int i, int *arr )
{
     int val ;
     val = arr [i] ;
     while ( arr [i / 2] <= val )
```

```
        {
            arr [i] = arr [i / 2] ;
            i = i / 2 ;
        }
        arr [i] = val ;
}

void restoredown ( int pos, int *arr, int n )
{
        int i, val ;
        val = arr [pos] ;
        while ( pos <= n / 2 )
        {
            i = 2 * pos ;
            if ( ( i < n ) && ( arr [i] < arr [i + 1] ) )
                i++ ;
            if ( val >= arr [i] )
                break ;
            arr [pos] = arr [i] ;
            pos = i ;
        }
        arr [pos] = val ;
}

void makeheap ( int *arr, int n )
{
        int i ;
        for ( i = n / 2 ; i >= 1 ; i-- )
            restoredown ( i, arr, n ) ;
}

void add ( int val, int *arr, int *n )
{
        ( *n ) ++ ;
        arr [*n] = val ;
        restoreup ( *n, arr ) ;
}
int replace ( int i, int *arr, int n )
```

```
{
    int r = arr [1] ;
    arr [1] = i ;
    for ( i = n / 2 ; i >= 1 ; i-- )
        restoredown ( i, arr, n ) ;
    return r ;
}

int del ( int *arr, int *n )
{
    int val ;
    val = arr [1] ;
    arr [1] = arr [*n] ;
    ( *n ) -- ;
    restoredown ( 1, arr, *n ) ;
    return val ;
}
```

Output:

Heap:
```
42   37   33   19   23   27   16   7   17   10
4    25   1    5    11
```

Element added 24.

Heap after addition of an element:
```
42   37   33   24   23   27   16   19   17   10
4    25   1    5    11   7
```

Element replaced 42.

Heap after replacement of an element:
```
37   24   33   19   23   27   16   7   17   10
4    25   1    5    11   2
```

Element deleted 37.

Heap after deletion of an element:
33 24 27 19 23 25 16 7 17 10
4 2 1 5 11

From **main( )** the function **makeheap( )** is called which builds the heap. Then by calling functions like **add( )**, **replace( )** and **del( )** operations like addition, deletion and replacement of the new node are performed on the heap.

The function **makeheap( )** receives two parameters—first is the base address of the array which holds the values of the nodes and second is the number of nodes in the tree. In **makeheap( )** a **for** loop is executed which restores the heap by calling the function **restoredown( )**. The loop is started from the $(n/2)^{th}$ element as all the nodes present above the index **n/2** are leaf nodes and they are always the heap.

The function **restoredown( )** receives three parameters. First is the index of the node from where the heap needs to be restored. Second is the base address of the array that holds the values of the nodes and third is the total number of the nodes in the heap. The value present at the particular position from where the heap needs to be restored is stored in a temporary variable **val**.

A **while** loop is executed till the time the index of the array reaches **n / 2**. As we discussed earlier this is the maximum position above which all the nodes are heap as all of them are leaf nodes. Inside the **while** loop for each node the position of its left child is calculated which is stored in **i**. Then a condition is checked whether **i** is less than **n** and the left child of the current node is less than the right child. If both the conditions are true then the index **i** is increased by one, as we intend to store the value of child that is greater amongst them. Then another condition is checked to see whether the value of the node from where the heap needs to be restores is greater than or equal to the value of the left or right child of the current node. If it is, then the **while** loop is terminated.

If the loop continues then the value of the respective child (left or right) is stored in the place of current node. Finally, the index of the child is stored in position of the current node, so that in the next iteration of **while** loop the whole procedure is repeated for its respective child.

Once outside the **while** loop the value present in the temporary variable **val** is stored in the array at position **pos,** where **pos** is the position of the node for which the heap is restored.

The function **add( )** receives three parameters—first is the value that is to be added, second is the base address of the array and third is a pointer to variable that holds maximum index of the array.

To begin with, using the pointer, the maximum index of array is incremented by one. Then the new value is stored at the highest position in the array. Finally, a function **restoreup( )** is called which restores the heap up, so that the new value is placed at its appropriate position in the heap.

The function **restoreup( )** is the counter-part of the function **restoredown( )**. It receives two parameters—first is the total number of nodes present in the heap and second is the base address of the array. Initially, the new value that is added is stored in a temporary variable **val**. Then a **while** loop is executed by checking the condition whether the value present at the parent node is less than the current value. If it is, then the value present at its parent is stored in the current node. Then the index **i** is assigned a value of its parent's index i.e. **i / 2**. As a result, at the end of **while** loop the value present in **i** is the index where the new value needs to be added. Hence, outside the **while** loop the value present in **val** is stored in the array at the ith index.

The function **replace( )** receives three parameters. First is the value that is to be added, second is the base address of the array, and the third is the total number of the nodes present in the heap.

Initially, the value present at index **1** is stored in a temporary variable **r**. This is the root node of the heap, as the node that is replaced is always the root node. Then the new value is added at the root node and a **for** loop is executed which restores the heap down for each and every node from one level less than the height of the tree. Finally, the value of the node which is replaced is returned.

The function **del( )** receives two parameters—first is the base address of the array and second is the address of the variable that holds the total number of nodes present in the heap. The value that is to be deleted is always the root node, hence the value present at the index **1** is stored in a temporary variable **val**. The value present at the maximum index is stored at the index **1**, the value of maximum index is decremented by one and then the heap is restored. Finally, the value that is deleted is returned.

Exercise

[A] State whether the following statements are True or False:

(a) A binary tree whose non-leaf nodes have left and the right child is a complete binary tree.

(b) The number of nodes attached to a particular node in a tree is called the degree of the node.

(c) To reconstruct a unique binary tree the in-order and pre-order lists are required.

(d) The balance factor of a node in an AVL tree is 1 if the height of the left sub-tree is one less than the height of the right sub-tree.

[B] Fill in the blanks:

(a) In a threaded binary tree the address of the in-order predecessor and in-order successor are stored in _____ and _____ child of the leaf node respectively.

(b) In any node of B-tree of order **n** the minimum required values and children are _____ and _____ respectively.

(c) In a heap if the largest element is present at the root node then it is called as the _____ heap.

[C] Answer the Following:

(a) Write a program that finds the height of a binary tree.

(b) Write a program that counts the number of nodes in a binary tree and the number of leaf nodes in a binary tree.

(c) Given a binary tree, create another binary tree that is mirror image of the given tree.

(d) Write a program that implements the non-recursive form of the functions **inorder( )**, **preorder( )** and **postorder( )**.

(e) Write a program that maintains a dictionary of words as a binary tree.

(f) Given any number, find whether that number is present in the binary tree. If present then find the level at which it is present.

(g) Given two binary trees, write a program that finds whether

- the two binary trees are similar

- the two binary trees are mirror images of each other.

(h) Write a program that finds the number of nodes in a binary tree at each level.

(i) Write a program that traverses a binary tree level by level, from left towards right.

(j) Write a function to insert a node **t** as a left child of any node **s** in a threaded binary tree.

CHAPTER
NINE

Searching And Sorting

Seek Me Out, Sort Me Out

I t would be an interesting statistic to find out how much time pre computer age generations spent in searching things and arranging them in an order. What a colossal waste it must have been to do these things manually. When history of computing is written 'searching' and 'sorting' would be right there at the top, as entities responsible for changing the way people do work.

We often spend time in searching some thing or the other. If the data is kept properly in some sorted order then searching becomes very easy. Think of searching a word's meaning from an unordered list of words and then you will appreciate the way dictionary is designed. In this chapter we are going to discuss different types of searching and sorting methods. Let us being with searching.

Searching

Searching is an operation which finds the location of a given element in a list. The search is said to be successful or unsuccessful depending on whether the element that is to be searched is found or not. Here, we will discuss two standard searching methods—Linear search and Binary search.

Linear Search

This is the simplest method of searching. In this method, the element to be found is sequentially searched in the list. This method can be applied to a sorted or an unsorted list. Searching is case of a sorted list starts from 0th element and continues until the element is found or an element whose value is greater (assuming the list is sorted in ascending order) than the value being searched is reached. As against this, searching in case of unsorted list starts from the 0th element and continues until the element is found or the end of list is reached.

Let us now try to understand this with the help of example. Consider the array shown in Figure 9-1.

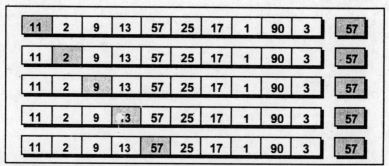

Figure 9-1. *Linear search in an unsorted array.*

The array shown in figure consists of 10 numbers. Suppose the element that is to be searched is 57. So 57 is compared with all the elements starting with 0th element and the searching process ends either when 57 is found or the list ends.

The performance of linear search algorithm can be measured by counting the comparisons done to find out an element. The number of comparisons is **O(n)**.

Following program implements linear search method for an unsorted array.

```c
#include <stdio.h>
#include <conio.h>

void main( )
{
    int arr[10] = { 11, 2, 9, 13, 57, 25, 17, 1, 90, 3 } ;
    int i, num ;

    clrscr( ) ;

    printf ( "Enter number to search: " ) ;
```

```
scanf ( "%d", &num ) ;

for ( i = 0 ; i <= 9 ; i++ )
{
    if ( arr[i] == num )
        break ;
}

if ( i == 10 )
    printf ( "Number is not present in the array." ) ;
else
    printf ( "The number is at position %d in the array.", i ) ;

getch( ) ;
}
```

Output:

Enter number to search: 57
The number is at position 4 in the array.

In the program, **num** is the number that is to be searched in the array **arr**. Inside the **for** loop each time **arr[i]** is compared with **num**. If any element is equal to **num** then that's the position of element where the number being searched is found. Hence **break** is applied to the **for** loop.

In case of a sorted list, searching of element starts from the 0th element. Searching ends when the element is found or any element of the list is found to be greater than the element to be searched. This is shown in Figure 9-2.

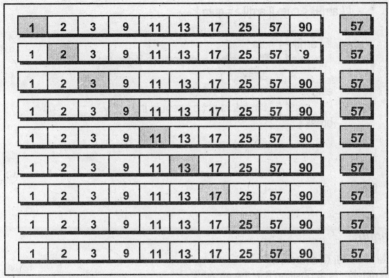

Figure 9-2. *Linear search in a sorted array.*

The following program implements linear search on a sorted array.

```
#include <stdio.h>
#include <conio.h>

void main( )
{
    int arr[10] = { 1, 2, 3, 9, 11, 13, 17, 25, 57, 90 } ;
    int i, num ;

    clrscr( ) ;

    printf ( "Enter number to search: " ) ;
    scanf ( "%d", &num ) ;

    for ( i = 0 ; i <= 9 ; i++ )
```

```
    {
        if ( arr[9] < num || arr[i] >= num )
        {
            if ( arr[i] == num )
                printf ( "The number is at position %d in the
                            array.", i ) ;
            else
                printf ( "Number is not present in the array." ) ;
            break ;
        }
    }

    getch( ) ;
}
```

Output:

Enter number to search: 57
The number is at position 8 in the array.

Here, inside the **for** loop it is checked whether **arr[9]** is less than
num or **arr[i]** is greater than or equal to **num**. If the condition is
satisfied then again a condition is checked whether **arr[i]** is equal
to **num**. Depending upon the condition the desired message will be
printed. In either case the **for** loop is terminated because there is
no point in searching the element further (as the array **arr** is in
sorted order).

The number of comparisons in case of sorted list might be less as
compared to the unsorted list because the search need not always
continue till the end of the list.

Binary Search

Binary search method is very fast and efficient. This method
requires that the list of elements be in sorted order.

)

In this method, to search an element we compare it with the element present at the center of the list. If it matches then the search is successful. Otherwise, the list is divided into two halves: one from 0th element to the center element (first half), and another from center element to the last element (second half). As a result, all the elements in first half are smaller than the center element, whereas, all the elements in second half are greater than the center element.

The searching will now proceed in either of the two halves depending upon whether the element is greater or smaller than the center element. If the element is smaller than the center element then the searching will be done in the first half, otherwise in the second half.

Same process of comparing the required element with the center element and if not found then dividing the elements into two halves is repeated for the first half or second half. This procedure is repeated till the element is found or the division of half parts gives one element. Let us understand this with the help of Figure 9-3.

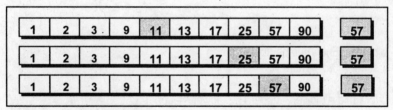

Figure 9-3. *Binary search.*

Suppose an array **arr** consists of 10 sorted numbers and 57 is element that is to be searched. The binary search method when applied to this array works as follows:

(a) 57 is compared with the element present at the center of the list (i.e. 11). Since 57 is greater than 11, the searching is restricted only to the second half of the array.

(b) Now 57 is compared with the center element of the second half of array (i.e. 25). Here again 57 is greater than 25 so the searching now proceed in the elements present between the 25 and the last element 90.

(c) This process is repeated till 57 is found or no further division of sub-array is possible.

The maximum number of comparisons in binary search is limited to $\log_2 n$. Following program implements binary search algorithm for a sorted array.

```c
#include <stdio.h>
#include <conio.h>

void main( )
{
    int arr[10] = { 1, 2, 3, 9, 11, 13, 17, 25, 57, 90 } ;
    int mid, lower = 0 , upper = 9, num, flag = 1 ;

    clrscr( ) ;

    printf ( "Enter number to search: " ) ;
    scanf ( "%d", &num ) ;

    for ( mid = ( lower + upper ) / 2 ; lower <= upper ;
        mid = ( lower + upper ) / 2 )
    {
        if ( arr[mid] == num )
        {
            printf ( "The number is at position %d in the array.",
                    mid ) ;
            flag = 0 ;
            break ;
```

```
        }
        if ( arr[mid] > num )
            upper = mid - 1 ;
        else
            lower = mid + 1 ;
    }

    if ( flag )
        printf ( "Element is not present in the array." ) ;

    getch( ) ;
}
```

Output:

Enter number to search: 57
The number is at position 8 in the array.

In the program each time through the loop **arr[mid]** is compared with **num** as **mid** holds the index of the middle element of array. If **num** is found then the search ends. If it is not found, then for further searching it is checked whether **num** is present in lower half or upper half of the array. If **num** is found to be smaller than the middle element then **mid − 1** is made the upper limit, keeping lower limit as it is. Otherwise **mid + 1** is made the lower limit of searching, keeping the upper limit as it is. During each iteration the value of **mid** is calculated, as **mid = (lower + upper) / 2**.

Comparison Of Linear Search And Binary Search

Consider the following set of elements:

1, 2, 3, 9, 11, 13, 17, 25, 57, 90

Suppose we want to search 25 in the above set of numbers. Table 9-1 shows number of comparisons required in both the methods.

Method	Number Of Comparisons
Linear search	8
Binary search	3

Table 9-1. *Comparison between linear search and binary search.*

The table clearly shows that how fast a binary search algorithm works. The advantage of the binary search method is that, in each iteration it reduces the number of elements to be searched from **n** to **n/2**. On the other hand, linear search method checks sequentially for every element, which makes it inefficient.

The disadvantage of binary search is that it works only on sorted lists. So when searching is to be performed on unsorted list then linear search is the only option.

Sorting

Sorting means arranging a set of data in some order. There are different methods that are used to sort the data in ascending or descending order. These methods can be divided into two categories. They are as follows:

Internal Sorting

If all the data that is to be sorted can be accommodated at a time in memory then internal sorting methods are used.

External Sorting

When the data to be sorted is so large that some of the data is present in the memory and some is kept in auxiliary memory (hard disk, floppy, tape, etc.), then external sorting methods are used. Let us begin with internal sorting methods.

Internal Sorting

There are different types of internal sorting methods. We will discuss some of the standard methods that are generally used. The following methods sort the data is ascending order. With a minor change we can also sort the data in descending order.

Bubble Sort

In this method, to arrange elements in ascending order, to begin with the 0th element is compared with the 1st element. If it is found to be greater than the 1st element then they are interchanged. Then the 1st element is compared with the 2nd element, if it is found to be greater, then they are interchanged. In the same way all the elements (excluding last) are compared with their next element and are interchanged if required. This is the first iteration and on completing this iteration the largest element gets placed at the last position. Similarly, in the second iteration the comparisons are made till the last but one element and this time the second largest element gets placed at the second last position in the list. As a result, after all the iterations the list becomes a sorted list. This can be explained with the help of Figure 9-4

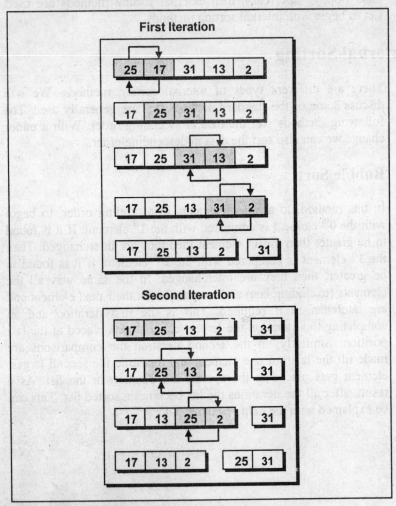

Figure 9-4. Bubble sort at work.

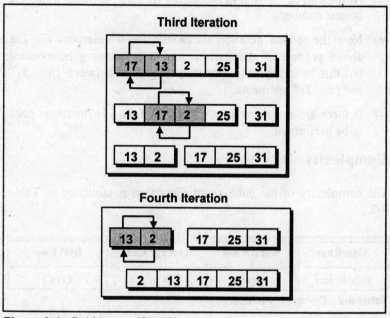

Figure 9-4. *Bubble sort (Contd.).*

Suppose an array **arr** consists of 5 numbers. The bubble sort algorithm works as follows:

(a) In the first iteration the 0th element 25 is compared with 1st element 17 and since 25 is greater than 17, they are interchanged.

(b) Now the 1st element 25 is compared with 2nd element 31. But 25 being less than 31 they are not interchanged.

(c) This process is repeated until $(n - 2)^{nd}$ element is compared with $(n - 1)^{th}$ element. During the comparison if $(n - 2)^{nd}$ element is found to be greater than the $(n - 1)^{th}$, then they are interchanged, otherwise not.

(d) At the end of the first iteration, the $(n-1)^{th}$ element holds the largest number.

(e) Now the second iteration starts with the 0th element 17. The above process of comparison and interchanging is repeated but this time the last comparison is made between $(n-3)^{rd}$ and $(n-2)^{nd}$ elements.

(f) If there are **n** number of elements then **(n - 1)** iterations need to be performed.

Complexity

The complexity of the bubble sort algorithm is tabulated in Table 9-2.

Algorithm	Worst Case	Average Case	Best Case
Bubble sort	$O(n^2)$	$O(n^2)$	$O(n^2)$

Table 9-2. *Complexity of bubble sort.*

The following program implements the bubble sort algorithm:

```
#include <stdio.h>
#include <conio.h>

void main( )
{
    int arr[5] = { 25, 17, 31, 13, 2 } ;
    int i, j, temp ;

    clrscr( ) ;

    printf ( "Bubble sort.\n" ) ;
    printf ( "\nArray before sorting:\n") ;
```

```
    for ( i = 0 ; i <= 4 ; i++ )
        printf ( "%d\t", arr[i] ) ;

    for ( i = 0 ; i <= 3 ; i++ )
    {
        for ( j = 0 ; j <= 3 - i ; j++ )
        {
            if ( arr[j] > arr[j + 1] )
            {
                temp = arr[j] ;
                arr[j] = arr[j + 1] ;
                arr[j + 1] = temp ;
            }
        }
    }

    printf ( "\n\nArray after sorting:\n" ) ;

    for ( i = 0 ; i <= 4 ; i++ )
        printf ( "%d\t", arr[i] ) ;

    getch( ) ;
}
```

Output:

Bubble sort.

Array before sorting:
25   17   31   13   2

Array after sorting:
2   13   17   25   31

The elements compared in bubble sort are always adjacent. Hence each time the elements compared are **arr[j]** and **arr[j + 1]**. If the element **arr[j]** is found to be greater than **arr[j + 1]** then they are interchanged. If we wish to arrange the numbers in descending order then the only change that we are required to make is in the condition, as shown below:

```
if ( arr[j] < arr[j + 1] )
{
    /* exchange arr[j] with arr[j + 1] */
}
```

Selection Sort

This is the simplest method of sorting. In this method, to sort the data in ascending order, the 0th element is compared with all other elements. If the 0th element is found to be greater than the compared element then they are interchanged. So after the first iteration the smallest element is placed at the 0th position. The same procedure is repeated for the 1st element and so on. This can be explained with the help of Figure 9-5.

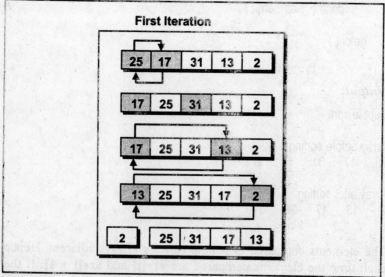

Figure 9-5. *Selection sort.*

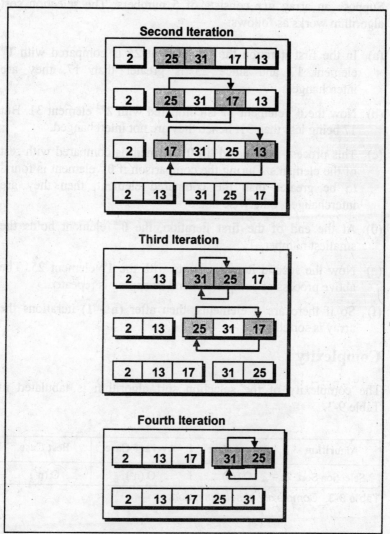

Figure 9-5. *Selection sort (Contd.).*

Suppose an array **arr** consists of 5 numbers. The selection sort algorithm works as follows:

(a) In the first iteration the 0th element 25 is compared with 1st element 17 and since 25 is greater than 17, they are interchanged.

(b) Now the 0th element 17 is compared with 2nd element 31. But 17 being less than 31, hence they are not interchanged.

(c) This process is repeated till 0th element is compared with rest of the elements. During the comparison if 0th element is found to be greater than the compared element, then they are interchanged, otherwise not.

(d) At the end of the first iteration, the 0th element holds the smallest number.

(e) Now the second iteration starts with the 1st element 25. The above process of comparison and swapping is repeated.

(f) So if there are **n** elements, then after **(n - 1)** iterations the array is sorted.

Complexity

The complexity of the selection sort algorithm is tabulated in Table 9-3.

Algorithm	Worst Case	Average Case	Best Case
Selection Sort	$O(n^2)$	$O(n^2)$	$O(n^2)$

Table 9-3. *Complexity of selection sort.*

Here the number of interchanges and assignments depend on the original order of the elements in the array **arr**, but the sum of these does not exceed a factor of n^2.

The following program sorts the list using selection sort algorithm.

```c
#include <stdio.h>
#include <conio.h>

void main( )
{
    int arr[5] = { 25, 17, 31, 13, 2 } ;
    int i, j, temp ;

    clrscr( ) ;

    printf ( "Selection sort.\n" ) ;
    printf ( "\nArray before sorting:\n") ;

    for ( i = 0 ; i <= 4 ; i++ )
        printf ( "%d\t", arr[i] ) ;

    for ( i = 0 ; i <= 3 ; i++ )
    {
        for ( j = i + 1 ; j <= 4 ; j++ )
        {
            if ( arr[i] > arr[j] )
            {
                temp = arr[i] ;
                arr[i] = arr[j] ;
                arr[j] = temp ;
            }
        }
    }

    printf ( "\n\nArray after sorting:\n") ;

    for ( i = 0 ; i <= 4 ; i++ )
        printf ( "%d\t", arr[i] ) ;

    getch( ) ;
```

}

Output:

Selection sort.

Array before sorting:
25   17   31   13   2

Array after sorting:
2   13   17   25   31

Here, **arr[i]** is compared with **arr[j]**. If the element **arr[i]** is found to be greater than **arr[j]** then they are interchanged. The value of **j** is starting from **i + 1**, as we need to compare any element with its next element, till the last element of array.

Quick Sort

Quick sort is a very popular sorting method. The name comes from the fact that, in general, quick sort can sort a list of data elements significantly faster than any of the common sorting algorithms. This algorithm is based on the fact that it is faster and easier to sort two small arrays than one larger one. The basic strategy of quick sort is to divide and conquer.

If you were given a large stack of papers bearing the names of the students to sort them by name, you might use the following approach. Pick a splitting value, say L (known as **pivot** element) and divide the stack of papers into two piles, A-L and M-Z (note that the two piles will not necessarily contain the same number of papers). Then take the first pile and sub-divide it into two piles, A-F and G-L. The A-F pile can be further broken down into A-C and D-F. This division process goes on until the piles are small enough to be easily sorted. The same process is applied to the M-Z pile. Eventually all the small sorted piles can be stacked one on top of the other to produce an ordered set of papers.

This strategy is based on recursion—on each attempt to sort the stack of papers the pile is divided and then the same approach is used to sort each smaller piles (a smaller case).

Quick sort is also known as **partition exchange sort**. The quick sort procedure can be explained with the help of Figure 9-6. In Figure 9-6 the element that is indicated by '*' is the pivot element and the element that is indicated by '—' is the element whose position is finalized.

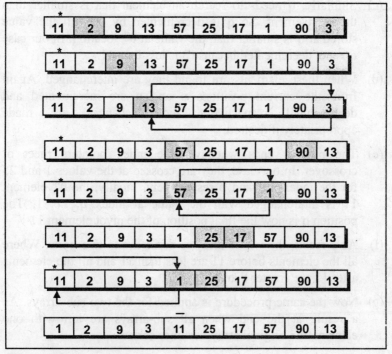

Figure 9-6. *Quick sort.*

Suppose an array **arr** consists of **10** distinct elements. The quick sort algorithm works as follows:

(a) In the first iteration, we will place the 0th element 11 at its final position and divide the array. Here, 11 is the pivot element. To divide the array, two index variables, **p** and **q**, are taken. The indexes are initialized in such a way that, **p** refers to the 1st element 2 and **q** refers to the $(n - 1)^{th}$ element 3.

(b) The job of index variable **p** is to search an element that is greater than the value at 0th location. So **p** is incremented by one till the value stored at **p** is greater than 0th element. In our case it is incremented till 13, as 13 is greater that 11.

(c) Similarly, **q** needs to search an element that is smaller than the 0th element. So **q** is decremented by one till the value stored at **q** is smaller than the value at 0th location. In our case **q** is not decremented because 3 is less than 11.

(d) When these elements are found they are interchanged. Again from the current positions **p** and **q** are incremented and decremented respectively and exchanges are made appropriately if desired.

(e) The process ends whenever the index pointers meet or crossover. In our case, they are crossed at the values 1 and 25 for the indexes **q** and **p** respectively. Finally, the 0th element 11 is interchanged with the value at index **q**, i.e. 1. The position **q** is now the final position of the pivot element 11.

(f) As a result, the whole array is divided into two parts. Where all the elements before 11 are less than 11 and all the elements after 11 are greater than 11.

(g) Now the same procedure is applied for the two sub-arrays. As a result, at the end when all sub-arrays are left with one element, the original array becomes sorted.

Here, it is not necessary that the pivot element whose position is to be finalized in the first iteration must be the 0th element. It can be any other element as well.

Complexity

The complexity of the quick sort algorithm is tabulated in Table 9-4:

Algorithm	Worst Case	Average Case	Best Case
Quick Sort	$O(n^2)$	$\log_2 n$	$\log_2 n$

Table 9-4. *Complexity of quick sort.*

The program given below implements the Quick sort algorithm.

```
#include <stdio.h>
#include <conio.h>

void quicksort ( int *, int, int ) ;
int split ( int *, int, int ) ;

void main( )
{
    int arr[10] = { 11, 2, 9, 13, 57, 25, 17, 1, 90, 3 } ;
    int i ;

    clrscr( ) ;

    printf ( "Quick sort.\n" ) ;
    printf ( "\nArray before sorting:\n") ;

    for ( i = 0 ; i <= 9 ; i++ )
        printf ( "%d\t", arr[i] ) ;
```

```
        quicksort ( arr, 0, 9 ) ;
        printf ( "\nArray after sorting:\n") ;

        for ( i = 0 ; i <= 9 ; i++ )
            printf ( "%d\t", arr[i] ) ;

        getch( ) ;
}

void quicksort ( int a[ ], int lower, int upper )
{
    int i ;
    if ( upper > lower )
    {
        i = split ( a, lower, upper ) ;
        quicksort ( a, lower, i - 1 ) ;
        quicksort ( a, i + 1, upper ) ;
    }
}

int split ( int a[ ], int lower, int upper )
{
    int i, p, q, t ;

    p = lower + 1 ;
    q = upper ;
    i = a[lower] ;

    while ( q >= p )
    {
        while ( a[p] < i )
            p++ ;

        while ( a[q] > i )
            q-- ;

        if ( q > p )
```

```
        {
            t = a[p] ;
            a[p] = a[q] ;
            a[q] = t ;
        }
    }

    t = a[lower] ;
    a[lower] = a[q] ;
    a[q] = t ;

    return q ;
}
```

Output:

Quick sort.

Array before sorting:
11   2   9   13   57   25   17   1   90   3

Array after sorting:
1   2   3   9   11   13   17   25   57   90

The arguments being passed to the function **quicksort( )** would reflect the part of the array that is being currently processed. We will pass the first and last indexes that define the part of the array to be processed on this call. The initial call to **quicksort( )** would contain the arguments 0 and 9, since there are 10 integers in our array.

In the function **quicksort( )**, a condition is checked whether **upper** is greater than **lower**. If the condition is satisfied then only the array will be split into two parts, otherwise, the control will simply be returned. To split the array into two parts the function **split( )** is called.

In the function **split( )**, to start with the two variables **p** and **q** are taken which are assigned with the values **lower + 1** and **upper**. Then a **while** loop is executed that checks whether the indexes **p** and **q** crosses each other. If they are not crossed then inside the **while** loop two more nested **while** loops are executed to increase the index **p** and decrease the index **q** to their appropriate places. Then it is checked whether **q** is greater than **p**. If so, then the elements present at **p**th ant **q**th positions are interchanged.

Finally, when the control returns to the function **quicksort( )** two recursive calls are made to function **quicksort( )**. This is done to sort the two split sub-arrays. As a result after all the recursive calls when the control reaches the function **main( )** the arrays becomes sorted.

The efficiency of the quick sort method can be improved by:

(h) Choosing a better pivot element.

(i) Using better algorithm for small sub-lists.

(j) Eliminating recursion.

Insertion Sort

Insertion sort is implemented by inserting a particular element at the appropriate position. In this method, the first iteration starts with comparison of **1**st element with the **0**th element. In the second iteration **2**nd element is compared with the **0**th and **1**st element. In general, in every iteration an element is compared with all elements before it. During comparison if is found that the element in question can be inserted at a suitable position then space is created for it by shifting the other elements one position to the right and inserting the element at the suitable position. This procedure is repeated for all the elements in the array. Let us understand this with the help of Figure 9-7.

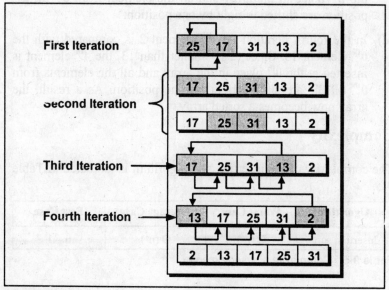

Figure 9-7. *Insertion sort.*

Following points explains the algorithm of insertion sort for an array **arr** of 5 elements:

(a) In the first iteration the 1st element 17 is compared with the 0th element 25. Since 17 is smaller than 25, 17 is inserted at 0th place. The 0th element 25 is shifted one position to the right.

(b) In the second iteration, the 2nd element 31 and 0th element 17 are compared. Since 31 is greater than 17, nothing is done. Then the 2nd element 31 is compared with the 1st element 25. Again no action is taken as 25 is less than 31.

(c) In the third iteration, the 3rd element 13 is compared with the 0th element 17. Since, 13 is smaller than 17, 13 is inserted at the 0th place in the array and all the element from 0th till 2nd position are shifted to right by one position.

(d) In the fourth iteration the 4th element 2 is compared with the 0th element 13. Since, 2 is smaller than 13, the 4th element is inserted at the 0th place in the array and all the elements from 0th till 3rd are shifted right by one position. As a result, the array now becomes a sorted array.

Complexity

The complexity of the insertion sort algorithm is tabulated in Table 9-5.

Algorithm	Worst Case	Average Case	Best Case
Insertion sort	$O(n^2)$	$O(n^2)$	$n - 1$

Table 9-5. *Complexity of insertion sort.*

The following program implements the insertion sort algorithm:

```c
#include <stdio.h>
#include <conio.h>

void main( )
{
    int arr[5] = { 25, 17, 31, 13, 2 } ;
    int i, j, k, temp ;

    clrscr( ) ;

    printf ( "Insertion sort.\n" ) ;
    printf ( "\nArray before sorting:\n") ;

    for ( i = 0 ; i <= 4 ; i++ )
        printf ( "%d\t", arr[i] ) ;
```

```
for ( i = 1 ; i <= 4 ; i++ )
{
    for ( j = 0 ; j < i ; j++ )
    {
        if ( arr[j] > arr[i] )
        {
            temp = arr[j] ;
            arr[j] = arr[i] ;

            for ( k = i ; k > j ; k-- )
                arr[k] = arr[k - 1] ;

            arr[k + 1] = temp ;
        }
    }
}

printf ( "\n\nArray after sorting:\n") ;

for ( i = 0 ; i <= 4 ; i++ )
    printf ( "%d\t", arr[i] ) ;

getch( ) ;
}
```

Output:

Insertion sort.

Array before sorting:
25   17   31   13   2

Array after sorting:
2   13   17   25   31

In the program the outer **for** loop is starting from 1 and the inner is from 0, because we need to compare the elements first till the **1ˢᵗ** element, then till the **2ⁿᵈ** element, then till **3ʳᵈ** and so on. There is one more **for** loop inside the **if**, which shifts all the elements one position to right.

Binary Tree Sort

Binary tree sort uses a binary search tree (BST). In this method, each element is scanned from the input list and placed in its proper position in a binary tree. In a binary tree each element is known as a node.

To place an element in its proper position, the element is compared with the node element. If this element is less than the element in the node, then it is placed in the left branch. If the element is greater than or equal to the node then it is placed in the right branch. Now if we access the elements according to in-order traversal (left, root, right) we would get the elements in ascending order.

Let's understand this in more details. Suppose **arr** is an array that consists of 10 distinct elements. The elements are as follows:

11, 2, 9, 13, 57, 25, 17, 1, 90, 3

The tree that can be built from these elements is shown in Figure 9-8.

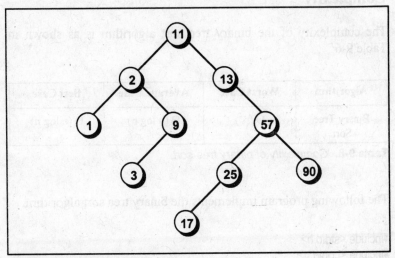

Figure 9-8. *Binary Search Tree.*

The binary tree sort algorithm works as follows:

(a) To construct the binary search tree, we start with the **0**th element 11. It is made the root of the tree.

(b) While inserting the .1st element, i.e. 2, 2 is compared with its root element 11. Since 2 is less than 11 it is made the left child of the root node 11.

(c) While inserting the **2**nd element of the list, i.e. 13, 13 is compared with the root element 11. Since 13 is greater than 11 it is made the right child of the root node 11.

(d) Similarly, all the elements are placed in their proper position in the binary search tree using the above procedure.

(e) Now to get the elements in the sorted order, the tree is traversed in in-order. The in-order traversal of the binary search tree lists the elements in ascending order.

Complexity

The complexity of the binary tree sort algorithm is as shown in Table 9-6:

Algorithm	Worst Case	Average Case	Best Case
Binary Tree Sort	$O(n^2)$	$O(n \log n)$	$O(n \log n)$

Table 9-6. *Complexity of binary tree sort.*

The following program implements the binary tree sort algorithm.

```
#include <stdio.h>
#include <conio.h>
#include <alloc.h>

struct btreenode
{
    struct btreenode *leftchild ;
    int data ;
    struct btreenode *rightchild ;
} ;

void insert ( struct btreenode **, int ) ;
void inorder ( struct btreenode * ) ;

void main( )
{
    struct btreenode *bt ;
    int arr[10] = { 11, 2, 9, 13, 57, 25, 17, 1, 90, 3 } ;
    int i ;

    bt = NULL ;
```

```
        clrscr( ) ;

        printf ( "Binary tree sort.\n" ) ;

        printf ( "\nArray:\n" ) ;
        for ( i = 0 ; i <= 9 ; i++ )
            printf ( "%d\t", arr[i] ) ;

        for ( i = 0 ; i <= 9 ; i++ )
            insert ( &bt, arr[i] ) ;

        printf ( "\n In-order traversal of binary tree:\n" ) ;
        inorder ( bt ) ;

        getch( ) ;
}

void insert ( struct btreenode **sr, int num )
{
        if ( *sr == NULL )
        {
            *sr = malloc ( sizeof ( struct btreenode ) ) ;

            ( *sr ) -> leftchild = NULL ;
            ( *sr ) -> data = num ;
            ( *sr ) -> rightchild = NULL ;
        }
        else
        {
            if ( num < ( *sr ) -> data )
                insert ( &( ( *sr ) -> leftchild ), num ) ;
            else
                insert ( &( ( *sr ) -> rightchild ), num ) ;
        }
}

void inorder ( struct btreenode *sr )
{
```

```
if ( sr != NULL )
{
    inorder ( sr -> leftchild ) ;
    printf ( "%d\t", sr -> data ) ;
    inorder ( sr -> rightchild ) ;
}
}
```

Output:

Binary tree sort.

Array:
11   2   9   13   57   25   17   1   90   3

In-order traversal of binary tree:
1   2   3   9   11   13   17   25   57   90

In the function **insert( )** two parameters are passed—one is the pointer to the node of the tree and the other is the data that is to be inserted. Initially the pointer to the node contains a **NULL** value, which indicates an empty tree. A condition is checked whether the pointer is **NULL**. If it is **NULL** then a new node is created and the data that is to be inserted is stored in its data part. The left and right child of this new node are set with a **NULL** value, as the node being inserted is always going to be the leaf node.

If the tree or sub-tree is not empty then the data of the current node is compared with the data that is to be inserted. If the data that is to be inserted is found to be smaller than the data of the current node then a recursive call is made to the **insert( )** function by passing the address of the node of the left sub-tree, otherwise the address of the node of right sub-tree is passed. At one stage in the recursive call the tree is found to be empty, which is the place where the new node gets inserted.

The function **inorder( )** is called to traverse the tree as per the in-order traversal. This function receives address of the root node as the parameter. Then a condition is checked whether the pointer is **NULL**. If the pointer is not **NULL** then a recursive call is made first for the left child and then for the right child. The values passed are the address of the left and right children that are present in the pointers **left** and **right** respectively. In between these two calls the data of the current node is printed.

The drawback of the binary tree sort is that additional space is required for building the tree.

Heap Sort

In this method, a tree structure called heap is used. A heap is type of a binary tree. An ordered balanced binary tree is called a **min-heap** where the value at the root of any sub-tree is less than or equal to the value of either of its children. An ordered balanced binary tree is called a **max-heap** when the value at the root of any sub-tree is more than or equal to the value of either of its children. It is not necessary that the two children must be in some order. Sometimes the value in left child may be more than the value at right child and some other times it may be the other way round.

Heap sort is basically an improvement over the binary tree sort. It does not create nodes as in case of binary tree sort. Instead it builds a heap by adjusting the position of elements within the array itself.

Basically, there are two phases involved in sorting the elements using heap sort algorithm. They are as follows:

(a) Construct a heap by adjusting the array elements.
(b) Repeatedly eliminate the root element of the heap by shifting it to the end of the array and then restore the heap structure with remaining elements.

The root element of a max-heap is always the largest element. The sorting ends when all the root element of each successive heap has been moved to the end of the array (i.e. when the tree is exhausted). The resulting array now contains a sorted list.

Lets us try to understand this in more detail. Suppose an array consists of **n** number of distinct elements in memory, then the heap sort algorithm works as follows:

(a) To begin with, a heap is built by moving the elements to proper positions within the array. For detailed explanation of 'how to build a heap' refer Chapter 8.

(b) In the second phase the root element is eliminated from the heap by moving it to the end of the array.

(c) The balance elements may not be a heap. So again steps (a) and (b) are repeated for the balance elements. The procedure is continued till all the elements are eliminated.

Note that for eliminating the element from the heap we need to merely decrement the maximum index value of the array by one. The elements are eliminated in decreasing order for a max-heap and in increasing order for a min-heap.

Let us now understand this procedure with the help of an example. Suppose the array **arr** that is to be sorted contains the following elements:

11, 2, 9, 13, 57, 25, 17, 1, 90, 3

The first step now is to create a heap from the array elements. For this imagine a binary tree that can be built from the array elements (Figure 9-9). The zeroth element would be the root element and left and right child of any element **arr[i]** would be at **arr[2 * i + 1]** and **arr[2 * i + 2]** respectively. Note that while writing the program we do not physically construct this binary tree by establishing the link between the nodes. Instead we imagine this tree and then readjust the array elements to form a heap.

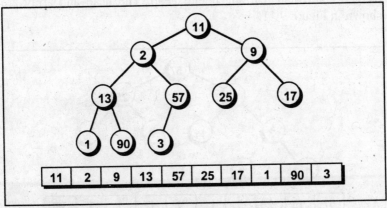

Figure 9-9. *Array and its equivalent binary tree.*

Now the heap is build from the binary tree. The heap and the array are shown in Figure 9-10.

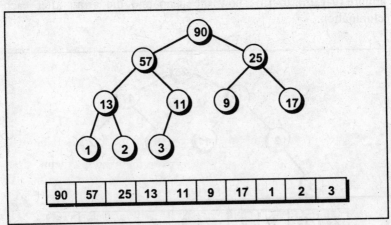

Figure 9-10. *Heap build from a binary tree.*

Now the root element 90 is moved to the last location by exchanging it with 3. Finally, 90 is eliminated from the heap by reducing the maximum index value of the array by 1. The balance elements are then rearranged into heap. The heap and array are shown in Figure 9-11.

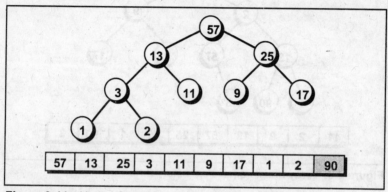

Figure 9-11. *Heap after eliminating root element 90.*

Similarly, one by one the root element of the heap is eliminated Figure 9-12(a) to (h) show the heap and the array after each elimination.

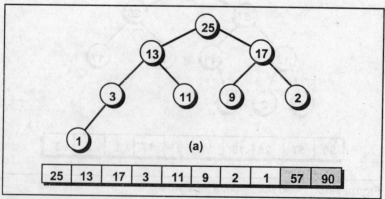

Figure 9-12. *Heap after eliminating root element 57.*

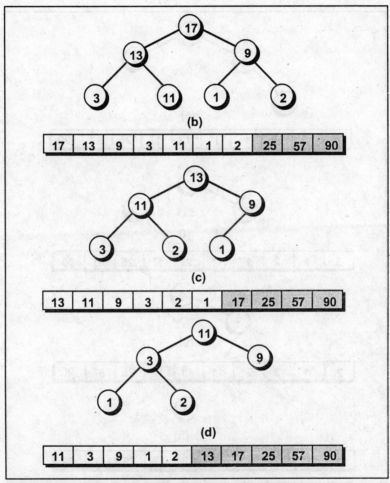

Figure 9-12. *(Contd.) Heap on eliminating successive root elements.*

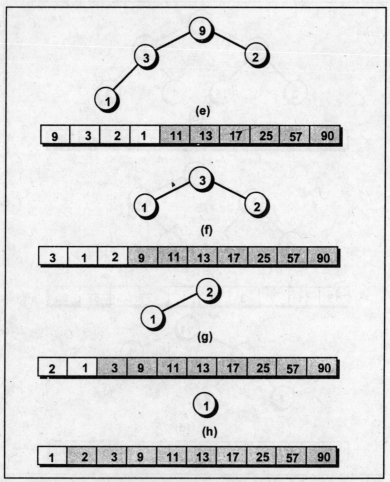

Figure 9-12. *(Contd.) Heap on eliminating successive root elements.*

Complexity

The complexity of the heap sort algorithm is tabulated in Table 9-7.

Algorithm	Worst Case	Average Case	Best Case
Heap Sort	O (n log n)	O (n log n)	O (n log n)

Table 9-7. Complexity of heap sort.

The following program implements the heap sort algorithm:

```c
#include <stdio.h>
#include <conio.h>

void makeheap ( int [ ], int ) ;
void heapsort ( int [ ], int ) ;

void main( )
{
    int arr[10] = { 11, 2, 9, 13, 57, 25, 17, 1, 90, 3 } ;
    int i ;

    clrscr( ) ;
    printf ( "\nHeap Sort" ) ;
    makeheap ( arr, 10 ) ;

    printf ( "\nBefore Sorting:\n" ) ;
    for ( i = 0 ; i <= 9 ; i++ )
        printf ( "%d\t", arr[i] ) ;
    heapsort ( arr, 10 ) ;
    printf ( "\nAfter Sorting:\n" ) ;
    for ( i = 0 ; i <= 9 ; i++ )
        printf ( "%d\t", arr[i] ) ;

    getch( ) ;
}

/* creates heap from the tree*/
void makeheap ( int x[ ], int n )
{
    int i, val, s, f ;
```

```
    for ( i = 1 ; i < n ; i++ )
    {
        val = x[i] ;
        s = i ;
        f = ( s - 1 ) / 2 ;
        while ( s > 0 && x[f] < val )
        {
            x[s] = x[f] ;
            s = f ;
            f = ( s - 1 ) / 2 ;
        }
        x[s] = val ;
    }
}

/* sorts heap */
void heapsort ( int x[ ], int n )
{
    int i, s, f, ivalue ;
    for ( i = n - 1 ; i > 0 ; i-- )
    {
        ivalue = x[i] ;
        x[i] = x[0] ;
        f = 0 ;

        if ( i == 1 )
            s = -1 ;
        else
            s = 1 ;

        if ( i > 2 && x[2] > x[1] )
            s = 2 ;

        while ( s >= 0 && ivalue < x[s] )
        {
            x[f] = x[s] ;
            f = s ;
            s = 2 * f + 1 ;
```

```
            if ( s + 1 <= i - 1 && x[s] < x[s + 1] )
                s++ ;
            if ( s > i - 1 )
                s = -1 ;
        }
        x[f] = ivalue ;
    }
}
```

Output:

Heap Sort.
Before Sorting:
90   57   25   13   11   9   17   1   2   3
After Sorting:
1   2   3   9   11   13   17   25   57   90

Here, from **main( )** we have called two functions—**makeheap( )** and **heapsort( )**. As the name suggests, **makeheap( )** function is used to create the heap from the tree that can be built from the array **arr**. It receives two parameters—the base address of the array and the number of elements present in the array. Here, data of each element is compared with its child's data and parent and the child data is swapped if required. The function **heapsort( )** is called by passing two arguments—the base address of the array and the number of elements present in the heap. This function sorts the heap by eliminating the root elements one by one and moving them to the end of the array.

Merge Sort

Merging means combining two sorted lists into one sorted list. For this the elements from both the sorted lists are compared. The smaller of both the elements is then stored in the third array. The sorting is complete when all the elements from both the lists are placed in the third list (Refer Figure 9-13).

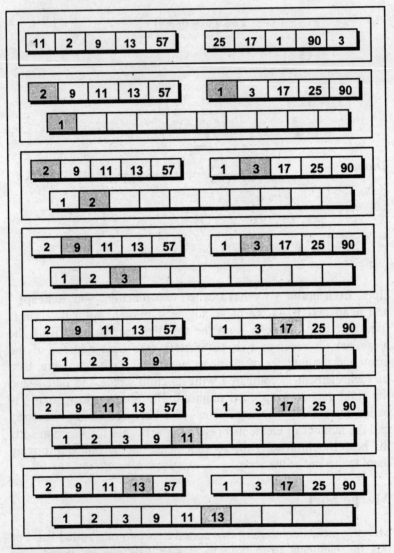

Figure 9-13. *Merge sort.*

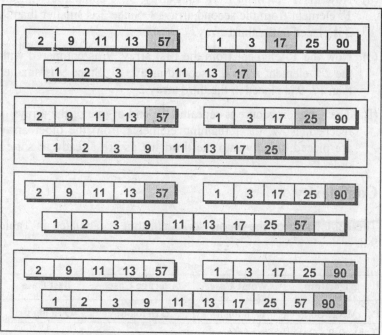

Figure 9-13. *(Contd.) Merge sort.*

Suppose arrays **a** and **b** contain 5 elements each. Then merge sort algorithm works as follows:

(a) The arrays **a** and **b** are sorted using any algorithm.

(b) The 0th element from the first array, 2, is compared with the 0th element of second array 1. Since 1 is smaller than 2, 1 is placed in the third array.

(c) Now the 0th element from the first array, 2, is compared with 1st element from the second array, 3. Since 2 is smaller than 3, 2 is placed in the third array.

(d) Now the **1ˢᵗ** element from first array, 9, is compared with the **1ˢᵗ** element from the second array, 3. Since 3 is smaller than 9, 3 is placed in the third array.

(e) Now the **1ˢᵗ** element from the first array, 9, is compared with the **2ⁿᵈ** element from the second array, 17. Since 9 is smaller than 17, 9 is placed in the third array.

(f) The same procedure is repeated till end of one of the arrays is reached. Now, the remaining elements from the other array are placed directly into the third list as are already in sorted order.

Complexity

The complexity of the merge sort algorithm is tabulated in Table 9-8.

Algorithm	Worst Case	Average Case	Best Case
Merge Sort	O (n log n)	O (n log n)	O (n log n)

Table 9-8. *Complexity of merge sort.*

The following program implements the merge sort algorithm:

```
#include <stdio.h>
#include <conio.h>

void main( )
{
    int a[5] = { 11, 2, 9, 13, 57 } ;
    int b[5] = { 25, 17, 1, 90, 3 } ;
    int c[10] ;
    int i, j, k, temp ;

    clrscr( ) ;
```

```
printf ( "Merge sort.\n" ) ;

printf ( "\nFirst array:\n" ) ;
for ( i = 0 ; i <= 4 ; i++ )
    printf ( "%d\t", a[i] ) ;

printf ( "\n\nSecond array:\n" ) ;
for ( i = 0 ; i <= 4 ; i++ )
    printf ( "%d\t", b[i] ) ;

for ( i = 0 ; i <= 3 ; i++ )
{
    for ( j = i + 1 ; j <= 4 ; j++ )
    {
        if ( a[i] > a[j] )
        {
            temp = a[i] ;
            a[i] = a[j] ;
            a[j] = temp ;
        }
        if ( b[i] > b[j] )
        {
            temp = b[i] ;
            b[i] = b[j] ;
            b[j] = temp ;
        }
    }
}

for ( i = j = k = 0 ; i <= 9 ; )
{
    if ( a[j] <=  b[k] )
        c[i++] = a[j++] ;
    else
        c[i++] = b[k++] ;

    if ( j == 5 || k == 5 )
```

```
            break ;
    }

    for ( ; j <= 4 ; )
        c[i++] = a[j++] ;

    for ( ; k <= 4 ; )
        c[i++] = b[k++] ;

    printf ( "\n\nArray after sorting:\n") ;
    for ( i = 0 ; i <= 9 ; i++ )
        printf ( "%d\t", c[i] ) ;

    getch( ) ;
}
```

Output:

Merge sort.

First array:
11   2   9   13   57

Second array:
25   17   1   90   3

Array after sorting:
1   2   3   9   11   13   17   25   57   90

Here, to begin with the arrays **a** and **b** are sorted. Then in a **for** loop one by one each element of **a** and **b** are merged in another array **c**. In the initialization part of **for** loop three variables **i**, **j** and **k** are initialized to **0**, these are indexes of the array **c**, **a** and **b** respectively. Inside the **for** loop a condition is checked whether the element of array **a** is less than that of the array **b**. If so then, the element of array **a** is stored in array **c**, otherwise the element of array **b** is stored in array **c**. If the element of array **a** is stored then the index **j** is incremented, otherwise the index **k** is incremented. While doing so if either of the array **a** or **b** is exhausted then the **for** loop is terminated. Outside the **for** loop all the elements of the other array (**a** or **b**) are stored in the array **c**, as they are already in sorted order.

External Sorting

External sorting is applied to the huge amount of data that cannot be accommodated in the memory all at a time. So data from the disk is loaded into memory part by part and. Each part that is loaded is sorted and the sorted data is stored into some intermediate file. Finally all the sorted parts present in different intermediate files are merged into one single file.

Initially the original file (file number 1) is partitioned into two files (file number 2 and 3). Then one item is read from each file (file number 2 and 3) and the two items are written in sorted order in a new file (file number 4). Once again one items is read from each partitioned files (file number 2 and 3) and these two records are written in sorted order in another new file (file number 5). Thus alternate pair of sorted items are stored in the file number 4 and 5. This procedure is repeated till the partitioned files (file number 2 and 3) come to an end.

Now following procedure is repeated twice:

(g) Read one item from file number 4 and 5 and write them in sorted order in file number 2.

(h) Read one item from file number 4 and 5 and write them in sorted order in file number 3.

Note that instead of creating two new files, the partitioned files (2 and 3) are being reused.

After this the following procedure is repeated 4 times:

(a) Read one item from file number 2 and 3 and write them in sorted order in file number 4.

(b) Read one item from file number 2 and 3 and write them in sorted order in file number 5.

In this way alternately items are moved from a pair of partitioned files to the pair of new files and from pair of new files to a pair of partitioned files. This procedure is repeated till the time we do not end up writing entire data in a single file. When this happens all the items in this file would be in sorted order.

The following program implements the external sort algorithm.

```
#include <stdio.h>
#include <conio.h>
#include <stdlib.h>

void shownums ( char * ) ;
void split ( char * ) ;
void sort ( char * ) ;

void main( )
{
    char str[67] ;

    clrscr( ) ;

    printf ( "Enter file name: " ) ;
    scanf ( "%s", str ) ;

    printf ( "Numbers before sorting:\n" ) ;
    shownums ( str ) ;

    split ( str ) ;
    sort ( str ) ;

    printf ( "\nNumbers after sorting:\n" ) ;
```

```
        shownums ( str ) ;

        getch( ) ;
}

/* Displays the contents of file */
void shownums ( char *p )
{
        FILE *fp ;
        int i ;

        fp = fopen ( p, "rb" ) ;
        if ( fp == NULL )
        {
                printf ( "Unable to open file." ) ;
                getch( ) ;
                exit ( 0 ) ;
        }

        while ( fread ( &i, sizeof ( int ), 1, fp ) != 0 )
                printf ( "%d \t", i ) ;

        fclose ( fp ) ;
}

/* Splits the original file into two files */
void split ( char *p )
{
        FILE *fs, *ft ;
        long int l, count ;
        int i ;

        fs = fopen ( p, "rb" ) ;
        if ( fs == NULL )
        {
                printf ( "Unable to open file." ) ;
                getch( ) ;
                exit ( 0 ) ;
```

```
}

ft = fopen ( "temp1.dat", "wb" ) ;
if ( ft == NULL )
{
    fclose ( fs ) ;
    printf ( "Unable to open file." ) ;
    getch( ) ;
    exit ( 1 ) ;
}

fseek ( fs, 0L, SEEK_END ) ;
l = ftell ( fs ) ;
fseek ( fs, 0L, SEEK_SET ) ;

l = l / ( sizeof ( int ) * 2 ) ;

for ( count = 1 ; count <= l ; count++ )
{
    fread ( &i, sizeof ( int ), 1, fs ) ;
    fwrite ( &i, sizeof ( int ), 1, ft ) ;
}

fclose ( ft ) ;

ft = fopen ( "temp2.dat", "wb" ) ;
if ( ft == NULL )
{
    fclose ( fs ) ;
    printf ( "Unable to open file." ) ;
    getch( ) ;
    exit ( 2 ) ;
}

while (   fread ( &i, sizeof ( int ), 1, fs ) != 0 )
    fwrite ( &i, sizeof ( int ), 1, ft ) ;

fcloseall ( ) ;
```

```
}

/* Sorts the file */
void sort ( char *p )
{
    FILE *fp[4] ;
    char *fnames[ ] =
                    {
                            "temp1.dat",
                            "temp2.dat",
                            "final1.dat",
                            "final2.dat"
                    } ;

    int i, j = 1, i1, i2, flag1, flag2, p1, p2 ;
    long int l ;

    while ( 1 )
    {
        for ( i = 0 ; i <= 1 ; i++ )
        {
            fp[i] = fopen ( fnames[i], "rb+" ) ;
            if ( fp[i] == NULL )
            {
                fcloseall( ) ;
                printf ( "Unable to open file." ) ;
                getch( ) ;
                exit ( i ) ;
            }

            fseek ( fp[i], 0L, SEEK_END ) ;
            l = ftell ( fp[i] ) ;
            if ( l == 0 )
                goto out ;
            fseek ( fp[i], 0L, SEEK_SET ) ;
        }

        for ( i = 2 ; i <= 3 ; i++ )
```

```
    {
        fp[i] = fopen ( fnames[i], "wb" ) ;
        if ( fp[i] == NULL )
        {
            fcloseall( ) ;
            printf ( "Unable to open file." ) ;
            getch( ) ;
            exit ( i ) ;
        }
    }

    i = 2 ;
    i1 = i2 = 0 ;
    flag1 = flag2 = 1 ;

    while ( 1 )
    {
        if ( flag1 )
        {
            if ( fread ( &p1, sizeof ( int ), 1, fp[0] ) == 0 )
            {
                /* If first file ends then the whole content of
                    second file is written in the respective target file */
                while ( fread ( &p2, sizeof ( int ), 1, fp[1] ) !=
                    0 )
                    fwrite ( &p2, sizeof ( int ), 1, fp[i] ) ;
                break ;
            }
        }

        if ( flag2 )
        {
            if ( fread ( &p2, sizeof ( int ), 1, fp[1] ) == 0 )
            {
                /* If second file ends then the whole content
                    of first file is written in the respective target  file */
                fwrite ( &p1, sizeof ( int ), 1, fp[i] ) ;
```

```
            while ( fread ( &p1, sizeof ( int ), 1, fp[0] ) != 
                0 )
                fwrite ( &p1, sizeof ( int ), 1, fp[i] ) ;
            break ;
        }
    }

    if ( p1 < p2 )
    {
        flag2 = 0 ;
        flag1 = 1 ;
        fwrite ( &p1, sizeof ( int ), 1, fp[i] ) ;
        i1++ ;
    }
    else
    {
        flag1 = 0 ;
        flag2 = 1 ;
        fwrite ( &p2, sizeof ( int ), 1, fp[i] ) ;
        i2++ ;
    }

    if ( i1 == j )
    {
        flag1 = flag2 = 1 ;
        fwrite ( &p2, sizeof ( int ), 1, fp[i] ) ;
        for ( i2++ ; i2 < j ; i2++ )
        {
            if ( fread ( &p2, sizeof ( int ), 1, fp[1] ) != 0 )
                fwrite ( &p2, sizeof ( int ), 1, fp[i] ) ;
        }
        i1 = i2 = 0 ;
        i == 2 ? ( i = 3 ) : ( i = 2 ) ;
    }

    if ( i2 == j )
    {
        flag1 = flag2 = 1 ;
```

```
                fwrite ( &p1, sizeof ( int ), 1, fp[i] ) ;
                for ( i1++ ; i1 < j ; i1++ )
                {
                        if ( fread ( &p1, sizeof ( int ), 1, fp[0] ) != 0 )
                                fwrite ( &p1, sizeof ( int ), 1, fp[i] ) ;
                }
                i1 = i2 = 0 ;
                i == 2 ? ( i = 3 ) : ( i = 2 ) ;
        }
    }

    fcloseall( ) ;
    remove ( fnames[0] ) ;
    remove ( fnames[1] ) ;
    rename ( fnames[2], fnames[0] ) ;
    rename ( fnames[3], fnames[1] ) ;
    j *= 2 ;
}

out :

    fcloseall( ) ;
    remove ( p ) ;
    rename ( fnames[0], p ) ;
    remove ( fnames[1] ) ;
}
```

Output:

```
Enter file name: record.dat
Numbers before sorting:
611    749    12     159    860    360    667    313    520    44
851    702    697    971    347    31     216    904    615    188
852    504    53     133    193    866    358    694    224    250
354    473    226    475    111    604    80     957    709    551
575    838    490    696    815    200    136    914    308    811
426    859    844
Numbers after sorting:
```

12	31	44	53	80	111	133	136	159	188
193	200	216	224	226	250	308	313	347	354
358	360	426	473	475	490	504	520	551	575
604	611	615	667	694	696	697	702	709	749
811	815	838	844	851	852	859	860	866	904
914	957	971							

Here, the function **split( )** is used to divide the original file into two partitioned files. The original file contains several numbers. This file can be programmatically created through a program "writerec.c" present on the accompanying CD. On execution of this program it asks the name of the file to be created and the number of items (numbers) to be written to it. It then generates these many numbers randomly and writes them into the specified filename. To be able to experience external sorting, do create a large number of items.

Next the function **sort( )** is called which sorts the two partitioned files and stores the result in the original file. The function **shownums( )** is straight forward. It simply reads each item from the file and displays it on the screen.

The function **split( )** receives only one parameter which is the name of the file that is to be split. This function creates two files **temp1.dat** and **temp2.dat**. If the source file contains 100 items, **temp1.dat** and **temp2.dat** would contain 50 items each after splitting.

The function **sort( )** receives only one parameter—the file name that is to be sorted. It opens the two partitioned files **temp1.dat** and **temp2.dat** and creates two new files **final1.dat** and **final2.dat** as intermediate files. In this function few variables are defined, out of which **p1** and **p2** are used to store the items into files, **i1** and **i2** are the counters that are used to store number of items written to the intermediate files. Two flag variables **flag1** and **flag2** are also maintained that are used to determine the file in which the item is to be written.

Exercise

[A] State whether the following statements are True or False:

(a) Sorting is the method of arranging a list of elements in a particular order.

(b) Linear search is more efficient than the binary search.

(c) In merge sort two unsorted arrays are merged.

(d) External sorting means the data that is to be sorted is stored in an external storage medium.

[B] Answer the following:

(a) What is the difference between an internal sorting and external sorting?

(b) Write a program that determines the first occurrence of a given sub-array within it.

(c) Suppose an array contains **n** elements. Given a number **x** that may occur several times in the array. Find
   – the number of occurrences of **x** in the array
   – the position of first occurrence of **x** in the array.

(d) Write a program that implements insertion sort algorithm for a linked list of integers.

(e) Write a program that sorts the elements of a two-dimensional array
   – row wise
   – column wise

CHAPTER
TEN

Graphs
Spread your tentacles

Networking! Be it any walk of life, that's the keyword today. Better your network, farther you would reach, and farther you spread your tentacles, better would be your network. And the crux of building and managing a network is hidden in a subject as innocuous as data structures in a topics called Graphs.

The only non-linear data structure that we have seen so far is tree. A tree in fact is a special type of graph. Graphs are data structures which have wide-ranging applications in real life like, Analysis of electrical circuits, Finding shortest routes, Statistical analysis, etc. To be able to understand and use the graph data structure one must first get familiar with the definitions and terms used in association with graphs. These are discussed below.

Definitions and Terminology

A graph consists of two sets—a set of edges say **v** and a set of edges, say **e**. The set of vertices is non-empty and the set of edges contains pairs of vertices. A Graph can be of two types—Undirected graph and Directed graph.

In an undirected graph the order of pair of vertices is unimportant. Hence the pairs **(v1, v2)** and **(v2, v1)** represent the same edge.

As against this, in a directed graph the order of vertices representing an edge is important. This pair is represented as **<v1, v2>**, where **v1** is the tail and **v2** the head of the edge. Thus **<v2, v1>** and **<v1, v2>** represent two different edges. A directed graph is also called Digraph. In Figure 10-1 the graph **G1** is an undirected graph whereas graph **G2** is a directed graph.

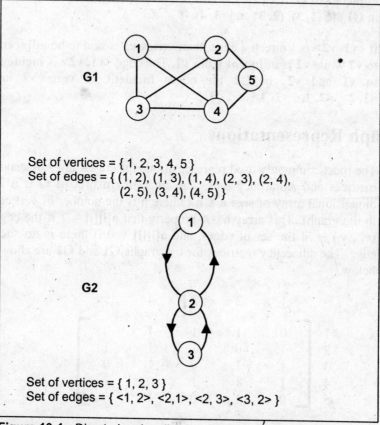

G1

Set of vertices = { 1, 2, 3, 4, 5 }
Set of edges = { (1, 2), (1, 3), (1, 4), (2, 3), (2, 4),
                 (2, 5), (3, 4), (4, 5) }

G2

Set of vertices = { 1, 2, 3 }
Set of edges = { <1, 2>, <2,1>, <2, 3>, <3, 2> }

Figure 10-1. *Directed and undirected graphs.*

Note that the edges of a directed graph are drawn with an arrow from the tail to the head.

Adjacent Vertices & Incident Edges

In an undirected graph if **(v1, v2)** is an edge in the set of edges, then the vertices **v1** and **v2** are said to be adjacent and that the edge **(v1, v2)** is **incident on** vertices **v1** and **v2**. The vertex 2 in **G1** is

adjacent to vertices 1, 3, 4 and 5. The edges **incident on** vertex 3 in **G1** are (1, 3), (2, 3) and (3, 4).

If <v1, v2> is a directed edge, then vertex **v1** is said to be **adjacent to v2** while **v2** is **adjacent from v1**. The edge <v1, v2> is **incident to v1** and **v2**. In **G2** the edges **incident to** vertex 2 are <1, 2>, <2, 1>, <2, 3> and <3, 2>.

Graph Representations

The most commonly used representations for graphs are Adjacency matrices and Adjacency lists. The adjacency matrix of **G** is a 2-dimensional array of size **n x n** (where n is the number of vertices in the graph). This array has a property that **a[i][j] = 1** if the edge (v_i, v_j) is in the set of edges, and **a[i][j] = 0** if there is no such edge. The adjacency matrices for the graphs **G1** and **G2** are shown below.

$$
\begin{array}{c c c c c c}
 & 1 & 2 & 3 & 4 & 5 \\
1 & \begin{bmatrix} 0 & 1 & 1 & 1 & 0 \\
2 & 1 & 0 & 1 & 1 & 1 \\
3 & 1 & 1 & 0 & 1 & 0 \\
4 & 1 & 1 & 1 & 0 & 1 \\
5 & 0 & 1 & 0 & 1 & 0 \end{bmatrix}
\end{array}
$$

$$
\begin{array}{c c c c}
 & 1 & 2 & 3 \\
1 & \begin{bmatrix} 0 & 1 & 0 \\
2 & 1 & 0 & 1 \\
3 & 0 & 1 & 0 \end{bmatrix}
\end{array}
$$

As can be seen from above, the adjacency matrix for an undirected graph is symmetric. The adjacency matrix for a directed graph need not be symmetric. The space needed to represent a graph using its adjacency matrix is n^2 locations. About half this space can be saved in the case of undirected graphs by storing only the upper or lower triangle of the matrix.

Adjacency Lists

In this representation the **n** rows of the adjacency matrix are represented as **n** linked lists. There is one list for each vertex in the graph. The nodes in list **i** represent the vertices that are adjacent from vertex **i**. Each list has a head node. The head nodes are sequential providing easy random access to the adjacency list for any particular vertex. The adjacency lists for graphs **G1** and **G2** are shown below.

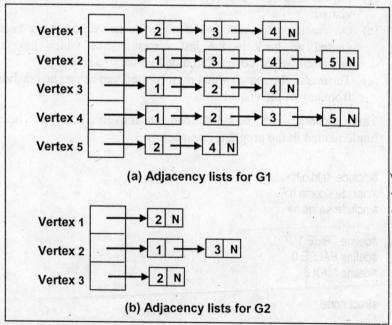

(a) Adjacency lists for G1

(b) Adjacency lists for G2

Figure 10-2. *Adjacency lists.*

Given the root node of a binary tree, one of the most common operations performed is visiting every node of the tree in some order. Similarly, given a vertex in a directed or undirected graph we may wish to visit all vertices in the graph that are reachable from this vertex. This can be done in two ways—using the Depth First Search and the Breadth First Search algorithm.

Depth First Search

The algorithm for Depth first search of an undirected graph is as follows:

(a) Visit a vertex, say **v**. Mark this vertex as visited.
(b) Select an unvisited vertex **w** adjacent to **v**.
(c) Repeat steps (a) and (b) till all adjacent vertices of **w** are visited.
(d) On reaching a vertex whose all adjacent vertices have been visited go back to the last vertex visited which has an unvisited vertex adjacent to it and go back to step (a).
(e) Terminate the search when no unvisited vertex can be reached from any of the visited ones.

This procedure is best-described recursively and has been implemented in the program given below.

```
#include <stdio.h>
#include <conio.h>
#include <alloc.h>

#define TRUE 1
#define FALSE 0
#define MAX 8

struct node
{
    int data ;
    struct node *next ;
```

```
} ;

int visited[MAX] ;

void dfs ( int, struct node ** ) ;
struct node * getnode_write ( int ) ;
void del ( struct node * ) ;

void main( )
{
    struct node *arr[MAX] ;
    struct node *v1, *v2, *v3, *v4 ;
    int i ;

    clrscr( ) ;

    v1 = getnode_write ( 2 ) ;
    arr[0] = v1 ;
    v1 -> next = v2 = getnode_write ( 8 ) ;
    v2 -> next = NULL ;

    v1 = getnode_write ( 1 ) ;
    arr[1] = v1 ;
    v1 -> next = v2 = getnode_write ( 3 ) ;
    v2 -> next = v3 = getnode_write ( 8 ) ;
    v3 -> next = NULL ;

    v1 = getnode_write ( 2 ) ;
    arr[2] = v1 ;
    v1 -> next = v2 = getnode_write ( 4 ) ;
    v2 -> next = v3 = getnode_write ( 8 ) ;
    v3 -> next = NULL ;

    v1 = getnode_write ( 3 ) ;
    arr[3] = v1 ;
    v1 -> next = v2 = getnode_write ( 7 ) ;
    v2 -> next = NULL ;
```

```
        v1 = getnode_write ( 6 ) ;
        arr[4] = v1 ;
        v1 -> next = v2 = getnode_write ( 7 ) ;
        v2 -> next = NULL ;

        v1 = getnode_write ( 5 ) ;
        arr[5] = v1 ;
        v1 -> next = NULL ;

        v1 = getnode_write ( 4 ) ;
        arr[6] = v1 ;
        v1 -> next = v2 = getnode_write ( 5 ) ;
        v2 -> next = v3 = getnode_write ( 8 ) ;
        v3 -> next = NULL ;

        v1 = getnode_write ( 1 ) ;
        arr[7] = v1 ;
        v1 -> next = v2 = getnode_write ( 2 ) ;
        v2 -> next = v3 = getnode_write ( 3 ) ;
        v3 -> next = v4 = getnode_write ( 7 ) ;
        v4 -> next = NULL ;

        dfs ( 1, arr ) ;
        for ( i = 0 ; i < MAX ; i++ )
            del ( arr[i] ) ;

        getch( ) ;
}

void dfs ( int v, struct node **p )
{
        struct node *q ;
        visited[v - 1] = TRUE ;
        printf ( "%d\t", v ) ;

        q = * ( p + v - 1 ) ;

        while ( q != NULL )
```

```
        {
            if ( visited[q -> data - 1] == FALSE )
                dfs ( q -> data, p ) ;
            else
                q = q -> next ;
        }
}

struct node * getnode_write ( int val )
{
    struct node *newnode ;
    newnode = ( struct node * ) malloc ( sizeof ( struct node ) ) ;
    newnode -> data = val ;
    return newnode ;
}

void del ( struct node *n )
{
    struct node *temp ;
    while ( n != NULL )
    {
        temp = n -> next ;
        free ( n ) ;
        n = temp ;
    }
}
```

Output:

1   2   3   4   7   5   6   8

In **main( )** the function **getnode_write( )** is called several times to create the lists. After creation of each list the address of the first node in the list is stored in an element of array **arr**, which is array of pointers.

When all the lists stand created the function **dfs( )** is called that visits each vertex and marks it as visited by storing a value in an array **visited** which is defined globally. To de-allocate the memory that is dynamically created a **for** loop is executed by passing the elements of the array **arr**.

The graph **G** in Figure 10-3 (a) is represented by its adjacency lists shown in Figure 10-3 (b). If a depth first search is initiated from vertex v_1, then the vertices of **G** are visited in the order: v_1, v_2, v_3, v_4, v_7, v_5, v_6, v_8.

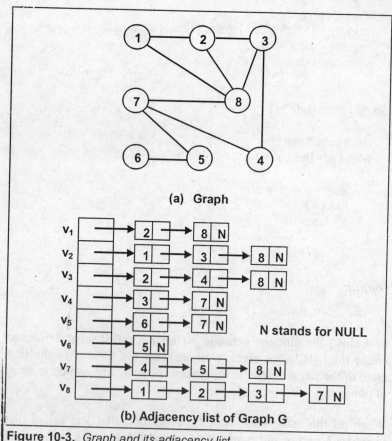

(a) Graph

(b) Adjacency list of Graph G

N stands for NULL

Figure 10-3. *Graph and its adjacency list.*

Breadth First Search

Let us now understand the Breadth First Search algorithm. In this algorithm we need to start at some vertex v and marks it as visited. Then visit all unvisited vertices adjacent to v. Then visit the unvisited vertices adjacent to these vertices and this process is continued. A breadth first search beginning at vertex v_1 of Figure 10-3 would first visit v_1 and then v_2 and v_3. Next vertices v_4, v_5, v_6 and v_7 will be visited and finally v_8. The following program implements this algorithm.

```c
#include <stdio.h>
#include <conio.h>
#include <alloc.h>

#define TRUE 1
#define FALSE 0
#define MAX 8

struct node
{
    int data ;
    struct node *next ;
} ;

int visited[MAX] ;
int q[8] ;
int front, rear ;

void bfs ( int, struct node ** ) ;
struct node * getnode_write ( int ) ;
void addqueue ( int ) ;
int deletequeue( ) ;
int isempty( ) ;
void del ( struct node * ) ;

void main( )
```

```
{
    struct node *arr[MAX] ;
    struct node *v1, *v2, *v3, *v4 ;
    int i ;

    clrscr( ) ;

    v1 = getnode_write ( 2 ) ;
    arr[0] = v1 ;
    v1 -> next = v2 = getnode_write ( 3 ) ;
    v2 -> next = NULL ;

    v1 = getnode_write ( 1 ) ;
    arr[1] = v1 ;
    v1 -> next = v2 = getnode_write ( 4 ) ;
    v2 -> next = v3 = getnode_write ( 5 ) ;
    v3 -> next = NULL ;

    v1 = getnode_write ( 1 ) ;
    arr[2] = v1 ;
    v1 -> next = v2 = getnode_write ( 6 ) ;
    v2 -> next = v3 = getnode_write ( 7 ) ;
    v3 -> next = NULL ;

    v1 = getnode_write ( 2 ) ;
    arr[3] = v1 ;
    v1 -> next = v2 = getnode_write ( 8 ) ;
    v2 -> next = NULL ;

    v1 = getnode_write ( 2 ) ;
    arr[4] = v1 ;
    v1 -> next = v2 = getnode_write ( 8 ) ;
    v2 -> next = NULL ;

    v1 = getnode_write ( 3 ) ;
    arr[5] = v1 ;
    v1 -> next = v2 = getnode_write ( 8 ) ;
    v2 -> next = NULL ;
```

```
        v1 = getnode_write ( 3 ) ;
        arr[6] = v1 ;
        v1 -> next = v2 = getnode_write ( 8 ) ;
        v2 -> next = NULL ;

        v1 = getnode_write ( 4 ) ;
        arr[7] = v1 ;
        v1 -> next = v2 = getnode_write ( 5 ) ;
        v2 -> next = v3 = getnode_write ( 6 ) ;
        v3 -> next = v4 = getnode_write ( 7 ) ;
        v4 -> next = NULL ;

        front = rear = -1 ;
        bfs ( 1, arr ) ;

        for ( i = 0 ; i < MAX ; i++ )
            del ( arr[i] ) ;

        getch( ) ;
}

void bfs ( int v, struct node **p )
{
        struct node *u ;

        visited[v - 1] = TRUE ;
        printf ( "%d\t", v ) ;
        addqueue ( v ) ;

        while ( isempty( ) == FALSE )
        {
            v = deletequeue( ) ;
            u = * ( p + v - 1 ) ;

            while ( u != NULL )
            {
                if ( visited [u -> data - 1] == FALSE )
```

```
            {
                addqueue ( u -> data ) ;
                visited [u -> data - 1] = TRUE ;
                printf ( "%d\t", u -> data ) ;
            }
            u = u -> next ;
        }
    }
}

struct node * getnode_write ( int val )
{
    struct node *newnode ;
    newnode = ( struct node * ) malloc ( sizeof ( struct node ) ) ;
    newnode -> data = val ;
    return newnode ;
}

void addqueue ( int vertex )
{
    if ( rear == MAX - 1 )
    {
        printf ( "\nQueue Overflow." ) ;
        exit(.) ;
    }

    rear++ ;
    q[rear] = vertex ;

    if ( front == -1 )
        front = 0 ;
}

int deletequeue( )
{
    int data ;

    if ( front == -1 )
```

```
    {
        printf ( "\nQueue Underflow." ) ;
        exit( ) ;
    }

    data = q[front] ;

    if ( front == rear )
        front = rear = -1 ;
    else
        front++ ;

    return data ;
}

int isempty( )
{
    if ( front == -1 )
        return TRUE ;
    return FALSE ;
}

void del ( struct node *n )
{
    struct node *temp ;

    while ( n != NULL )
    {
        temp = n -> next ;
        free ( n ) ;
        n = temp ;
    }
}
```

Output:

1   2   3   4   5   6   7   8

The working of functions **getnode_write( )** & **del( )** and arrays **arr[ ]** & **visited[ ]** is exactly same as in the previous program.

The function **bfs( )** visits each vertex and marks it visited. The functions **isempty( )**, **addqueue( )** and **deletequeue( )** are called while maintaining the queue of vertices.

Spanning tree

A spanning tree of a graph is an undirected tree consisting of only those edges that are necessary to connect all the vertices in the original graph. A spanning tree has a property that for any pair of vertices there exists only one path between them, and the insertion of any edge to a spanning tree form a unique cycle.

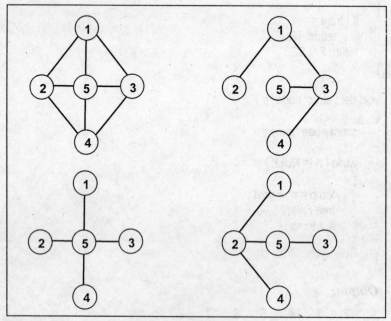

Figure 10-4. *Graph and its spanning trees.*

The particular spanning tree for a graph depends on the criteria used for generating it. The spanning tree resulting from a call to depth first tree is known as depth first spanning tree. Similarly, a spanning tree resulting from a call to breadth first tree is known as a breadth first spanning tree.

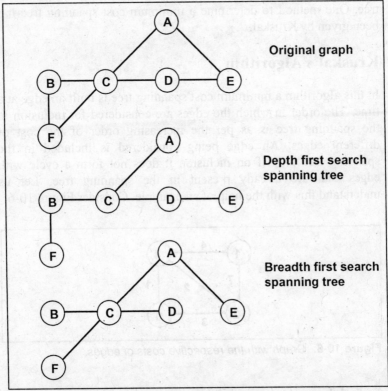

Figure 10-5. *Graph and depth / breadth first search spanning tree.*

The spanning tree is useful in

(a) analysis of electrical circuits
(b) shortest route problems

The cost of a spanning tree is the sum of costs of the edges in that tree. One method to determine a minimum cost spanning tree has been given by Kruskal.

Kruskal's Algorithm

In this algorithm a minimum cost spanning tree is built an edge at a time. The order in which the edges are considered for inclusion in the spanning tree is as per the increasing order of the cost of different edges. An edge being considered is included in the spanning tree only if on inclusion it does not form a cycle with edges that are already present in the spanning tree. Let us understand this with the help of an example. Consider Figure 10-6.

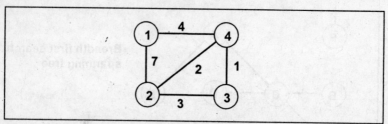

Figure 10-6. *Graph with the respective costs of edges.*

To find the minimum cost of spanning tree the edges are inserted to tree in increasing order of their costs. Figure 10-7 shows insertion or rejection of each edge. The meanings of symbols I, R, C, etc. used in the figure are as follows:

E - Edge
C - Cost
A - Action
T - Tree
I - Inclusion
R - Rejection

E	C	A	T
			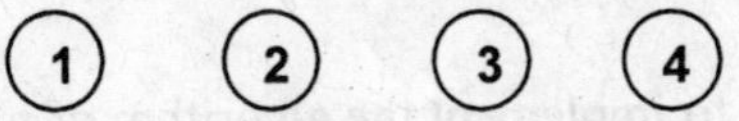
4-3	1	I	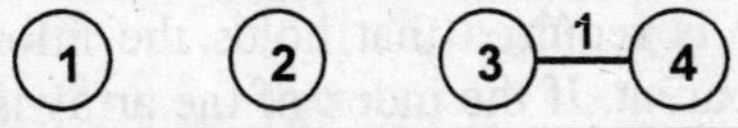
4-2	2	I	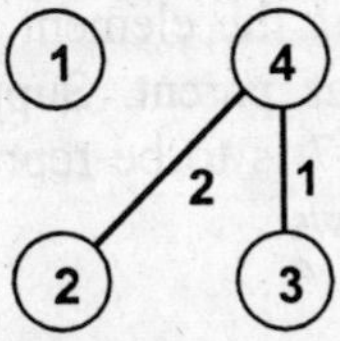
3-2		R	
4-1	4	I	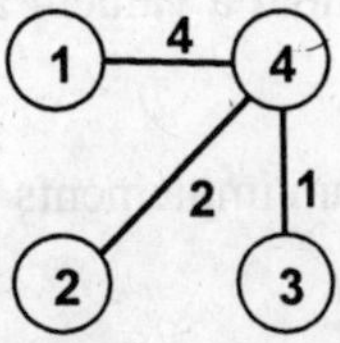

Figure 10-7. *Creating minimum cost spanning tree.*

To begin with edge 4-3 is inserted as it has the lowest cost 1. Then the edge 4-2 is inserted which has a cost 2. The next edge in the order of cost is 3-2, but it is rejected as it forms a cyclic path between the existing vertices. Then the edge 4-1 is inserted and it is accepted as it forms a non-cyclic path.

The minimum cost of spanning tree is given by the sum of costs of the existing edges, i.e. the edges that are inserted while building the spanning tree of minimum cost. In our case it is found to be 7 as it the sum of all the edges that are inserted. This can be verified by adding numbers that are given in column C (Cost) of Figure 10-7.

We know that to find minimum cost spanning tree the vertices are separated. Then each edge is inserted that joins the two vertices. As a result, a relation of parent-child is established between the two vertices.

In order to implement the algorithm of minimum cost spanning tree an array is required that holds the information about the vertices and its parent. If the index of the array is considered as vertex then its parent is given by the element present at that index. The root vertex holds itself as parent. Suppose the spanning tree that is shown in Figure 10-7 is to be represented by array then the array elements are as follows:

4, 4, 4, 4

Here all the indices hold a value 4 as it is the parent of the vertices 1, 2, 3, 4.

The following program implements the Kruskal's algorithm.

```
#include <stdio.h>
#include <conio.h>
#include <alloc.h>

struct lledge
{
    int v1, v2 ;
    float cost ;
    struct lledge *next ;
};
```

```
int stree[5] ;
int count[5] ;
int mincost ;

struct lledge * kminstree ( struct lledge *, int ) ;
int getrval ( int ) ;
void combine ( int, int ) ;
void del ( struct lledge * ) ;

void main( )
{
    struct lledge *temp, *root ;
    int i ;

    clrscr( ) ;

    root = ( struct lledge * ) malloc ( sizeof ( struct lledge ) ) ;

    root -> v1 = 4 ;
    root -> v2 = 3 ;
    root -> cost = 1 ;
    temp = root -> next = ( struct lledge * ) malloc ( sizeof ( struct lledge ) ) ;

    temp -> v1 = 4 ;
    temp -> v2 = 2 ;
    temp -> cost = 2 ;
    temp -> next = ( struct lledge * ) malloc ( sizeof ( struct lledge ) ) ;

    temp = temp -> next ;
    temp -> v1 = 3 ;
    temp -> v2 = 2 ;
    temp -> cost = 3 ;
    temp -> next = ( struct lledge * ) malloc ( sizeof ( struct lledge ) ) ;

    temp = temp -> next ;
    temp -> v1 = 4 ;
    temp -> v2 = 1 ;
    temp -> cost = 4 ;
```

```
    temp -> next = NULL ;

    root = kminstree ( root, 5 ) ;

    for ( i = 1 ; i <= 4 ; i++ )
        printf ( "\nstree[%d] -> %d", i, stree[i] ) ;
    printf ( "\nThe minimum cost of spanning tree is %d", mincost ) ;
    del ( root ) ;

    getch( ) ;
}
struct lledge * kminstree ( struct lledge *root, int n )
{
    struct lledge *temp = NULL ;
    struct lledge *p, *q ;
    int noofedges = 0 ;
    int i, p1, p2 ;

    for ( i = 0 ; i < n ; i++ )
        stree[i] = i ;
    for ( i = 0 ; i < n ; i++ )
        count[i] = 0 ;

    while ( ( ( noofedges < ( n - 1 ) ) && ( root != NULL ) )
    {
        p = root ;

        root = root -> next ;

        p1 = getrval ( p -> v1 ) ;
        p2 = getrval ( p -> v2 ) ;

        if ( p1 != p2 )
        {
            combine ( p -> v1, p -> v2 ) ;
            noofedges++ ;
            mincost += p -> cost ;
            if ( temp == NULL )
```

```
                {
                    temp = p ;
                    q = temp ;
                }
                else
                {
                    q -> next = p ;
                    q = q -> next ;
                }
                q -> next = NULL ;
            }
        }
        return temp ;
}

int getrval ( int i )
{
    int j, k, temp ;
    k = i ;
    while ( stree[k] != k )
        k = stree[k] ;
    j = i ;
    while ( j != k )
    {
        temp = stree[j] ;
        stree[j] = k ;
        j = temp ;
    }
    return k ;
}

void combine ( int i, int j )
{
    if ( count[i] < count[j] )
        stree[i] = j ;
    else
    {
        stree[j] = i ;
```

```
        if ( count[i] == count[j] )
            count[j]++ ;
    }
}

void del ( struct lledge *root )
{
    struct lledge *temp ;

    while ( root != NULL )
    {
        temp = root -> next ;
        free ( root ) ;
        root = temp ;
    }
}
```

Output:

```
stree[1] -> 4
stree[2] -> 4
stree[3] -> 4
stree[4] -> 4
The minimum cost of spanning tree is 7
```

In the program a linked list of edges is created in increasing ordei of cost. The structure also holds the two vertices that are to be joined by the edge. Then the function **kminstree( )** is called that forms the minimum cost spanning tree. This function in turn calls the function **getrval( )** and **combine( )**. The function **getrval( )** returns the parent of a particular vertex. The function **combine( )** inserts the edges and establishes the relation between the vertices.

The global variable **mincost** is a counter that counts the total minimum cost of the spanning tree. The array **stree[ ]** holds the information about the vertex and its parent. An array **count[ ]** is maintained that holds a flag and indicates whether the vertex is included in the tree or not.

After creating the tree, the values of the array and minimum cost of the tree is printed out. Then the dynamically allocated memory is de-allocated by calling a function **del( )**.

Shortest Path Algorithm

A minimal spanning tree gives no indication about the shortest path between two nodes. Rather only the overall cost is minimized. In real life we are required to find shortest path between the two cities. For example, an airliner would be interested in finding most economical route between any two cities in a given network of cities. The algorithm to find such a path was first proposed by E.W.Dijkstra.

Dijkstra's Algorithm

This algorithm can be best understood with the help of an example. Consider the digraph shown in Figure 10-8.

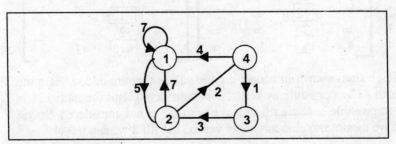

Figure 10-8. *Digraph.*

The adjacency matrix that shows the cost of edges of this digraph is as follows. Also, the matrix on the right-hand side indicates the path between the two vertices.

$$
\begin{array}{cccc}
1 & 2 & 3 & 4
\end{array}
$$

$$
\begin{bmatrix}
7 & 5 & \infty & \infty \\
7 & \infty & \infty & 2 \\
\infty & 3 & \infty & \infty \\
4 & \infty & 1 & \infty
\end{bmatrix}
\begin{bmatrix}
11 & 12 & \_ & \_ \\
21 & \_ & \_ & 24 \\
\_ & 32 & \_ & \_ \\
41 & \_ & 43 & \_
\end{bmatrix}
$$

Some of the values of adjacency matrix are infinity, which indicates that there is no direct path between the vertices. The blank sign in right-hand side matrix indicates that till now the path is not determined.

To calculate the minimum cost of any edge and determine the path between two vertices, one by one each vertex **v** is taken into consideration. Then the path from **v** is calculated. If the cost is found to be smaller than the previous cost then it is replaced with the new cost. Consider the vertex 1 in the given example. The adjacency matrix now holds the values as follows.

$$
\begin{array}{cccc}
1 & 2 & 3 & 4
\end{array}
$$

$$
\begin{bmatrix}
7 & 5 & \infty & \infty \\
7 & \boxed{12} & \infty & 2 \\
\infty & 3 & \infty & \infty \\
4 & \boxed{9} & 1 & \infty
\end{bmatrix}
\begin{bmatrix}
11 & 12 & \_ & \_ \\
21 & \boxed{212} & \_ & 24 \\
\_ & 32 & \_ & \_ \\
41 & \boxed{412} & 43 & \_
\end{bmatrix}
$$

The values shown in square are the values that are added. Here the path 412 is possible as vertex 1 is considered. But the path 124 is not possible because till now the vertex 2 is not considered. So via 2 we cannot travel to any other vertex, but till 2 we can travel.

Next the vertex 2 is considered. After this the following adjacency matrix is obtained.

	1	2	3	4
1	7	5	∞	[7]
2	7	12	∞	2
3	[10]	3	∞	[5]
4	4	9	1	[11]

	1	2	3	4
1	11	12	_	[124]
2	21	212	_	24
3	[321]	32	_	[324]
4	41	412	43	[4124]

Now the vertex 3 is considered. As a result the following adjacency matrix is obtained.

	1	2	3	4
1	7	5	∞	7
2	7	12	∞	2
3	10	3	∞	5
4	4	[4]	1	[6]

	1	2	3	4
1	11	12	_	124
2	21	212	_	24
3	321	32	_	324
4	41	[432]	43	[4324]

Note that after addition of the vertex 3, the paths between the vertices 4-2 and 4-4 are changed because these are the shortest as compared to earlier ones.

Finally, the vertex 4 is considered, which results into the adjacency matrix that holds the shortest path between any two vertices.

	1	2	3	4
1	7	5	[8]	7
2	[6]	[6]	[3]	2
3	[9]	3	[6]	5
4	4	4	1	6

	1	2	3	4
1	11	12	[1243]	124
2	[241]	[2432]	[243]	24
3	[3241]	32	[3243]	324
4	41	432	43	4324

The following program shows how to find the shortest the path between any two vertices.

```
#include <stdio.h>
#include <conio.h>
```

```
#define INF 9999

void main( )
{
    int arr[4][4] ;
    int cost[4][4] = {
                        7, 5, 0, 0,
                        7, 0, 0, 2,
                        0, 3, 0, 0,
                        4, 0, 1, 0
                    } ;
    int i, j, k, n = 4 ;

    clrscr( ) ;

    for ( i = 0 ; i < n ; i++ )
    {
        for ( j = 0; j < n ; j++ )
        {
            if ( cost[i][j] == 0 )
                arr[i][j] = INF ;
            else
                arr[i][j] = cost[i][j] ;
        }
    }

    printf ( "Adjacency matrix of cost of edges:\n" ) ;
    for ( i = 0 ; i < n ; i++ )
    {
        for ( j = 0; j < n ; j++ )
            printf ( "%d\t", arr[i][j] ) ;
        printf ( "\n" ) ;
    }

    for ( k = 0 ; k < n ; k++ )
    {
        for ( i = 0 ; i < n ; i++ )
        {
```

```
            for ( j = 0 ; j < n ; j++ )
            {
                if ( arr[i][j] > arr[i][k] + arr[k][j] )
                    arr[i][j] = arr[i][k] + arr[k][j];
            }
        }
    }

    printf ( "\nAdjacency matrix of lowest cost between the vertices:\n" ) ;
    for ( i = 0 ; i < n ; i++ )
    {
        for ( j = 0; j < n ; j++ )
            printf ( "%d\t", arr[i][j] ) ;
        printf ( "\n" ) ;
    }

    getch( ) ;
}
```

Output:

```
Adjacency matrix of cost of edges:
7    5    9999  9999
7    9999  9999  2
9999  3 -  9999  9999
4    9999  1    9999

Adjacency matrix of lowest cost between the vertices:
7    5    8    7
6    6    3    2
9    3    6    5
4    4    1    6
```

In the program an array **cost[ ]** is defined which is adjacency matrix of the cost of edges. In the array some values are 0 indicating that there is no direct path between the two vertices. One more array **arr[ ]** is defined which to begin with holds the value that the array **cost[ ]** holds. The only difference is instead of 0 it holds a value 9999, which is defined as **INF** (infinity). Then through nested **for** loops the lowest value is assigned to each element of the array **arr[ ]** if the value already present is found to be greater.

Exercise

[A] State whether the following statements are true or false:

(a) If **v1** and **v2** are two vertices of a directed graph **G**, then the edges **<v1, v2>** and **<v2, v1>** represent the same edge.

(b) For a graph there can exist only those many spanning trees as the number of vertices.

(c) To find minimum cost spanning tree edges are inserted in increasing order of their cost.

[B] Answer the following:

(a) What is the difference between the depth first tree and breadth first tree.

(b) Find all possible spanning trees for the graph that is shown in Figure 10-6.

(c) Write a program that finds
  – the number of vertices in a graph.
  – the number of adjacent vertices for a given vertex.

Index